The Social and Cognitive Impacts of e-Commerce on Modern Organizations

Mehdi Khosrow-Pour
Information Resources Management Association, USA

IGP
IDEA GROUP PUBLISHING
Hershey • London • Melbourne • Singapore

Acquisitions Editor: Mehdi Khosrow-Pour
Senior Managing Editor: Jan Travers
Managing Editor: Amanda Appicello
Development Editor: Michele Rossi
Copy Editor: Ingrid Widitz
Typesetter: Sara Reed
Cover Design: Lisa Tosheff
Printed at: Integrated Book Technology

Published in the United States of America by
Idea Group Publishing (an imprint of Idea Group Inc.)
701 E. Chocolate Avenue
Hershey PA 17033
Tel: 717-533-8845
Fax: 717-533-8661
E-mail: cust@idea-group.com
Web site: http://www.idea-group.com

and in the United Kingdom by
Idea Group Publishing (an imprint of Idea Group Inc.)
3 Henrietta Street
Covent Garden
London WC2E 8LU
Tel: 44 20 7240 0856
Fax: 44 20 7379 3313
Web site: http://www.eurospan.co.uk

Library of Congress Cataloging-in-Publication Data

The social and cognitive impacts of e-commerce on modern organizations /
Mehdi Khosrow-Pour, editor.
p. cm.
Includes bibliographical references and index.
ISBN 1-59140-249-2 (hardcover) -- ISBN 1-59140-274-3 (softcover) --
ISBN 1-59140-250-6 (ebook)
1. Electronic commerce. 2. Consumer behavior. I. Khosrowpour, Mehdi, 1951-
HF5548.32.S63 2004
658.8'7--dc22

2003025942

British Cataloguing in Publication Data
A Cataloguing in Publication record for this book is available from the British Library.

The views expressed in this book are those of the authors, but not necessarily of the publisher.

The Social and Cognitive Impacts of e-Commerce on Modern Organizations

Table of Contents

Preface

Organizations invest considerable time and money in developing and maintaining an electronic presence on the Internet. Large financial resources go toward the costs of technology, website design and software. However, successful e-commerce endeavors must look beyond the technology to ensure profitability. *The Social and Cognitive Impacts of e-Commerce on Modern Organizations* addresses the important questions: What motivates consumers to shop online? What determines which products they shop for? How can technology aid customers in decision-making? The chapters in this important new book examine the motivations of online shoppers and provide theoretical and practical examples of how organizations can maximize their electronic commerce endeavors by paying close attention to consumer habits and motives. These chapters, written by experts from around the world, address the most relevant and timely issues in the application and utilization of electronic commerce. Some of the topics covered include: e-government, unsolicited email, Internet alliances, consumer motives and technology trust. From the government of Scotland to small businesses and everything in between, the topics covered span organizations of many types and sizes.

Chapter 1, entitled, "Online Shopping for Positive and Negative Reinforcement Products" by Patricia Sorce, Victor Perotti and Stanley Widrick, Rochester Institute of Technology (USA), describes the emotional factors that influence online shopping. The authors apply operant conditioning theory to the question of which products and services consumers will shop for and buy online. The results of this exploratory study lay the groundwork for future research by introducing negative and positive reinforcement as a predictor of Internet shopping behavior.

Chapter 2, entitled, "Online Shopping Experience – A Conceptualization and Preliminary Results" by Maggie Guo, Texas A&M University (USA), focuses on consumer behavior in online retailing environments, attempts to give a review of current research on online consumer behavior and suggests a research agenda for the future. The chapter offers a model of the online shopping experience that examines the cognitive and affective aspects of the shopping behavior.

Chapter 3, entitled, "An Expanded E-commerce Process Model Serving E-commerce Entrepreneurs" by David Paper, Eric Pedersen, Utah State University (USA), describes the process that small business owners use to make decisions about electronic commerce ventures. This important chapter expands on the authors' earlier works and presents a model that describes the e-commerce process of small to medium sized enterprises.

Chapter 4, entitled, "Internet Shopping Model And Customer Perceptions – A Study Of UK Supermarkets" by Xianzhong Mark Xu, Martyn Roberts, University of Portsmouth (United Kingdom), examines electronic grocery shopping, a subset of B2C e-commerce. This chapter examines the Internet shopping models utilized by UK supermarkets and investigates Internet shoppers' attitudes and behaviors towards these models.

Chapter 5, entitled, "A Psychographic Approach to Segmenting the Electronic Shopper" by Leo R. Vijayasarathy, Colorado State University (USA), utilizes a psychological paradigm to examine Internet shoppers. This chapter examines different types of shoppers (home, community and apathetic) and evaluates their use of e-commerce. In addition to examining different types of shoppers the study concludes that traditional demographics such as age, gender, and so forth do not affect shopping preferences.

Chapter 6, entitled, "A Negotiation Agent System in E-Commerce" by Chuan-Feng Chiu and Timothy K. Shih, Tamkang University (Taiwan), describes an agent system used to aid buyers in decision-making. The proposed system assists the user in handling complex processes simultaneously and decreases the amount of time needed to compute processes. The authors then examine how this system can improve the Internet shopping experiences of consumers and businesses.

Chapter 7, entitled, "Business Interactions in A Virtual Organisation – Visualising Inter-Organisational Systems Complexity" by Karin Axelsson, Linköping University (Sweden), focuses on the complexity of inter-organisational systems (IOS) and proposes a model to analyze business interaction, the Business Action Theory (BAT) phase model. The paper describes how the proposed model can explain and create visual models of interorganizational business interactions such as business networks and virtual organizations.

Chapter 8, entitled, "Issues and Perceptions Of Unsolicited Commercial Electronic Mail" by Jack T. Marchewka, Chang Liu and Charles G. Petersen, Northern Illinois University (USA), discusses the problems associated with the enormous amount of unsolicited email sent and received. The chapter focuses on the costs to personal and organizational productivity, the threats of computer viruses and worms, the privacy concerns, the use of email filters, and other various attempts to control unsolicited email. A brief discussion of the call for legislative action to control and limit the flow of unsolicited email is included.

Chapter 9, entitled, "Impact of E-Learning during SARS Outbreak in Hong Kong" by Eric Wong, The Hong Kong Polytechnic University (Hong Kong), examines the use of electronic learning as a contingency measure during the SARS outbreak in 2003. The chapter identifies some of the practical difficulties involved in evaluating the academic performance of two groups of engineering students taking an introductory course - one group enrolled in e-learning and the other through the traditional classroom approach.

Chapter 10, entitled, "E-CRM Analytics and Data Integration" by Hamid R. Nemati, Christopher D. Barko and Ashfaaq Moosa, The University of North Carolina (USA), examines the value of integrating offline and online customer relationship management efforts. The results presented in this chapter suggest that organizations can gain significant competitive advantage through the use of E-CRM.

Chapter 11, entitled, "E-Government Scottish Style: Recent Developments and Some Emerging Issues" by Feng Li, University of Newcastle upon Tyne (United Kingdom), discusses e-government efforts in Scotland. This chapter looks at the discrepancy between e-government theory and practice in Scotland and examines some of the reasons for the gap. The authors look at the attitudes and practices that inhibit successful e-government efforts and offer suggestions for future efforts.

Chapter 12, entitled, "The Impact of the Role of the Government of Egypt on Electronic Commerce Development and Growth" by Sherif Kamel, American University in Cairo (Egypt), and Ahmed Ghoneim and Sherine Ghoneim, Cairo University (Egypt), examines the role of the Egyptian government in introducing, diffusing and institutionalizing electronic commerce. Specifically, this chapter describes the role of the government in regulating e-commerce in Egypt.

Chapter 13, entitled "Linking Technological Compatibility and Operational Capacity Constraints to Communication Technology Adoption" by Elliot Bendoly, Emory University and Fred Kaefer, Loyola University Chicago (USA), investigates the relationship between the willingness of business partners to use various communication technologies and a firm's operational capacity to accommodate the product/service demands of these potential partners as it relates to electronic data interchange (EDI). The chapter offers some practical advice for managers considering maximizing their EDI investment.

Chapter 14, entitled, "Pushing Elusive Alliances into the Light- Discovering the Value of Informal Networks on the Internet" by Rian van der Merwe and Leyland Pitt, Curtin University of Technology (Australia), uses the Social Network Theory as a framework to identify what the authors describe as "elusive alliances". These alliances are informal links and social networks on the Internet that can be valuable because of the social capital embedded in them. The authors discuss ways to capitalize on these networks.

Chapter 15, entitled, "Technology Trust in Internet-Based Interorganizational Electronic Commerce" by Pauline Ratnasingam, Central Missouri State University and Paul Pavlou, University of Southern California (USA), proposes a theoretical model to examine the effect technology trust has on business-to-business electronic commerce. The authors examine the perceived benefits from technology trust and evaluate its effect on organizational success.

Assuring successful e-commerce endeavors demands that organizations pay careful attention not only to establishing a web presence, but also to evaluating the motives and apprehensions of their potential customers. The chapters in the book address some of the key issues for businesses, governments and educational institutions to consider as they implement and refine their e-commerce initiatives. From evaluating consumer technology use to investigating how agent technology can be utilized to assist customers, the chapters in this book provide a timely look at the most current issues in electronic commerce. Academics, students, researchers, and managers will benefit from the practical examples and theoretical guidance offered in this book. As always, your valuable comments and feedback will be greatly appreciated.

Mehdi Khosrow-Pour
Editor
November 11, 2003

Chapter I

Online Shopping for Positive and Negative Reinforcement Products

Patricia Sorce, Rochester Institute of Technology, USA

Victor Perotti, Rochester Institute of Technology, USA

Stanley Widrick, Rochester Institute of Technology, USA

ABSTRACT

The present research applies operant conditioning theory to the question of what products and services consumers will shop for and buy online. Operant conditioning theory explains differences between products that are used to alleviate uncomfortable experiences (negative reinforcement) and those providing enjoyable experiences (positive reinforcement). The preliminary results described in this study confirmed the importance of operant conditioning as a factor in the behavior of online shoppers. For example, when asked to provide an open-ended list of products that they had shopped for, our respondents mentioned products that produce positive reinforcement 476 times versus only four mentions for those that create negative reinforcement. Furthermore, for a list of seventeen common product categories, the results showed that respondents were not only less likely to shop for negative reinforcement products but also even less likely to purchase negative products online than positive products. The results of this exploratory study lay the groundwork for future research by introducing negative and positive reinforcement as a predictor of Internet shopping behavior.

INTRODUCTION

With the failure of many online commercial sites, business managers are re-evaluating their approaches to e-Commerce. In the last few years, some research has been able to clarify the behavior of online shoppers. Much of this research focuses on understanding the shoppers themselves. However, several important management questions about products remain: What types of products will consumers seek or buy on the Internet? Why do consumers choose these products over other products? Are there different categories of products consumers will shop for but not purchase online? The authors propose using operant conditioning theory to answer these questions. The present research begins with a description of the existing literature relevant to Internet shopping behavior. After the literature review, operant conditioning theory and its application to understanding buyer behavior is discussed. Lastly, three hypotheses are presented that test whether the use of operant conditioning theory contributes to a more complete understanding of the online shopping process.

Shopping Behavior on the Internet

Much of the research in the last five years has focused on three general questions: Who will buy online, why do they choose this channel, and what do they buy? Regarding who will buy online, Bellman, Lohse and Johnson (1999) investigated several predictors for whether an individual will buy online. They found that the most important determinant of buying on the web was previous behavior such as using the Internet to search for product information (i.e., pre-purchase search). Bellman et al. concluded that several demographic variables such as income, education, and age have a modest impact on the decision of whether to buy online. More recent research has revealed that there are gender effects regarding attitudes towards shopping online. For example, Van Slyke, Comunale and Belanger (2002) found that men expressed greater intention to purchase on the Internet than women. They also found higher purchase intentions for those with more computer and Internet experience. In another study of shopping attitudes, Alreck (2002) found that womens' attitudes towards Internet shopping were less favorable than mens' attitudes but that women have more favorable attitudes towards other channels such as catalog and store shopping.

Other research has pointed to the importance of consumer risk perception in predicting Internet purchase behavior. For example, Vellido, Lisboa and Meehan (2000) found that online purchase behavior was best predicted by consumer risk perception of shopping on the Internet. In addition, Bhatnagar, Misra and Rao (2000) developed a two-part definition of perceived risk to examine its impact on Internet shopping behavior. Their two types of risk were product category risk and financial risk. High product category risk represented conditions when the product was technologically complex, satisfied ego needs of the purchaser, was high priced, or was sold based on its feel or touch. High financial risk was defined by fears about the safety of consumers' financial information online. Their results indicated that increases in both types of risk generally decreased the likelihood of online purchase behavior.

Why do people use the Internet to shop? Motives for shopping in traditional channels have long been a research focus of consumer and retailing research. Babin, Darden and Griffen (1994) identified two dominant shopping motives: shopping for fun (hedonic) and shopping with a goal in mind (utilitarian). Using a qualitative analysis, Wolfinbarger and Gilly (2001) demonstrated that these two motives are also typical of online shoppers. Goal-oriented shoppers valued four attributes of online shopping – convenience, informativeness, selection and the ability to control the shopping experience. The experiential shoppers reported browsing the Internet for fun through auctions, visits to hobby-related sites, and to bargain hunt. Internet shopping for fun takes advantage of the Internet as a vast repository of information. As the Internet matures, its importance as a source for product information is a major benefit of online shopping (Evans & Wurster, 1999). Though information-rich, the Internet does not seem to be used as a substitute for other sources of information. For example, Ramaswami, Strader and Brett (2000) reported that online shoppers of financial products used both online channels and personal channels (e.g., a broker) in their information search activities. Further, in a study of new car buyers, Ratchford, Telukdar and Lee (2001) found that heavy users of Internet sources were also heavy users of printed sources of information such as car ratings books and dealer brochures.

The perceived convenience of use of the Internet for searching and buying products has been well documented. The surveys (1994-1998) conducted by the Graphics, Visualization and Usability group at Georgia Tech conclude that the web delivers convenience and time savings for the online shopper. Bhatnagar, Misra and Rao (2000) found that customers' perceived convenience of shopping on the Internet had a positive impact on purchase behavior. However, Ramaswami, Strader and Brett (2000) found that for those that use online information sources for buying financial products, time availability was not associated with the propensity to conduct an online search for these products or to purchase these products. That is, those that were pressured for time did not use online shopping more than those who were less pressured for time. This result was supported by research conducted by Alreck and Settle (2002), who found a difference between consumer perception and behavior towards Internet shopping and time saving behavior. In terms of perception, consumers view both catalog and Internet shopping as time-saving as compared to other buying modes. However, when asked if they use Internet shopping to save time, consumers reported using it infrequently when compared to other shopping practices that save time such as going to the closest store or shopping during slow times.

While the characteristics of the shopper are important in predicting online buyer behavior, Internet shopping is also impacted by the type of product. As noted above, Bhatnagar, Misra and Rao (2000) found that high-risk products such as those that are technologically complex or high priced were less likely to be purchased online. Vijayswathy (2002) found that Internet shopping intentions were related to the tangibility of the product. High cost intangible items such as auto financing had a higher intention to purchase rating than high cost tangible products such as household appliances. Rosen and Howard (2000) hypothesize that homogeneous goods such as books and music are more suited to online sales than differentiated products that require a physical inspection.

The impact of the product category on shopping and buying using the Internet is the focus of the present study. A product typology based on operant conditioning theory that has been found to affect traditional shopping behavior is presented below.

Operant Conditioning Theory and Buying Behavior

Operant conditioning research has been discussed by marketers and published under terms such as behavior modification, reinforcement research, and conditioning theory (Nord & Peter, 1980; Peter & Nord, 1982; Rothschild & Gaidis, 1981). Positive reinforcement is the situation where an operant behavior increases in frequency with the subsequent presentation of positive stimuli. For example, the behavior of a child saying 'thank you' increases with the parent's presentation of a snack or treat only subsequent to the child uttering the words. Negative reinforcement is the situation where the operant behavior increases in frequency with the subsequent

Figure 1: The process of positive and negative reinforcement from operant conditioning theory

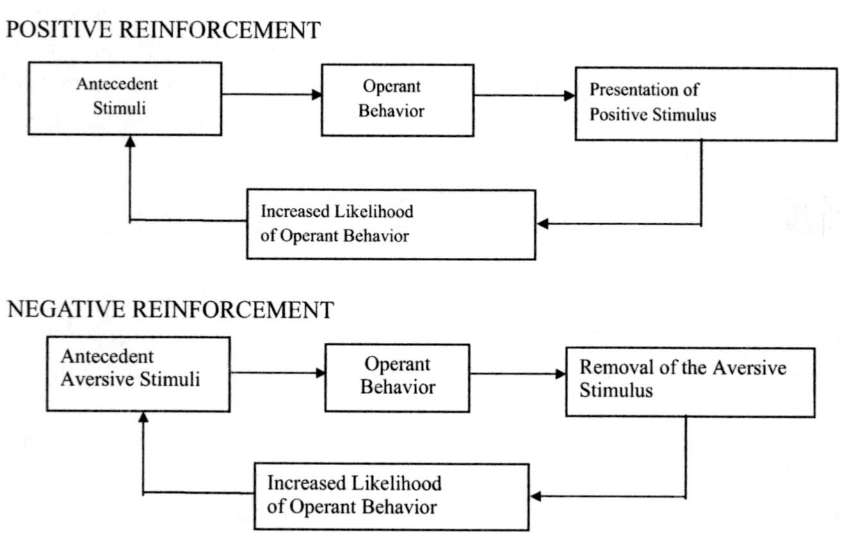

removal of an aversive stimulus. For example, the behavior of taking aspirin at the onset of a headache increases if it has removed the headache in the past. With both types of reinforcement, the probability of the operant behavior increases in future similar circumstances.

It is important to note that there is still confusion in the literature as to the definition of negative reinforcement. For example, one researcher has written, "... if a customer has a bad experience (receives negative reinforcement), the chance of her returning as a repeat purchases decreases. . .". In fact, this is an example of **punishment,** not negative reinforcement. Figure 1 provides graphical depiction of the process for positive and negative reinforcement.

It is useful to recognize that with positive reinforcement, the person is trying to maximize or at least satisfy his or her utility. With negative reinforcement, the person is trying to minimize his or her disutility. A rapid and long-term removal of the aversive stimulus that is causing the disutility will result in strong negative reinforcement.

Research into negative reinforcement has found several important behavior patterns (Blair & Shimp, 1992; Widrick & Fram, 1983). In the presence of an aversive stimulus, escape behaviors are normal for negative reinforcement consumption. For example, with the infestation of household pests (an aversive situation), there will be short time intervals between need awareness and consumption. In contrast, for products that result in positive reinforcement, product search behavior may result in more leisurely brand decisions. Widrick and Hibbs (1985) provided empirical support for this position where consumers reported a longer search process (more time spent shopping and greater distance traveled) for products that provided positive reinforcement (henceforth called positive products) than for those that provided negative reinforcement (henceforth called negative products). In their longer search, consumers also considered more brands of positive than negative products. Moreover, under conditions of negative reinforcement, avoidance of the aversive stimulus may generalize to shopping for the product. In a test of this hypothesis, Widrick and Fram (1983) found that people generally enjoy the process of shopping for positive products and services (e.g., sports equipment) but do not like to shop for products that provide negative reinforcement (e.g., auto repairs).

The research reviewed above indicated that for positive products, people like to shop for the products, spend more time in pre-purchase search activities and consider more brands. For negative products, people don't like to shop for them, spend less time in pre-purchase search and consider fewer brands. The research question addressed by this study is whether this pattern holds for shopping on the Internet.

Internet Shopping for Negative and Positive Reinforcement Products

Sorce, Perotti and Widrick (2002) tested the proposition that Internet shopping behavior is different for positive versus negative products. They reasoned that, for positive products, the Internet provides a rich information source that enhances the shopping experience, and people would be more likely to shop for them on the Internet rather than for negative products. However, this richness benefit could be offset by the time-savings benefit for negative products. If the Internet provides efficiency that reduces the time to shop for a product, then the Internet may be used more for negative than positive products. They tested the propensity to shop for, but not necessarily purchase, seventeen products online. They found that respondents were more likely to shop for positive products (e.g., sporting goods) online in a 3:1 ratio versus negative products (e.g., vacuum cleaners). They postulated that this was due to the escape behavior for some situations where negative reinforcement products are sought. In these cases, some consumers leave shopping to the very last minute when they cannot afford to wait for the mail delivery of the product to solve the problem. This explanation was supported by the finding that one negative product that had relatively high reported shopping behavior – virus protection software – was able to be delivered immediately via online download. This product had the highest reported online shopping behavior of all negative products tested.

The present research was designed to extend and test the understanding of Internet shopping behavior for negative and positive products by examining the propensity of consumers to *buy* online. Two new hypotheses will be tested (H2 and H3). As a basis for comparison, H1, which was confirmed in Sorce et al. (2002), will also be restated.

H1: Fewer negative products will be shopped for online than positive products.

The second hypothesis will test whether the results of pre-purchase search will also extend to the actual buying of goods and services online. Thus, the trend for purchasing products should be similar to the trend for shopping for products.

H2: Fewer negative products will be purchased online than positive products.

The third hypothesis will test whether the gap between searching for a product and actually purchasing that product will be greater for negative products than positive products.

H3: Given that a person did shop online for a product, a smaller percentage will buy negative products than positive products online.

Table 1: A-priori classification of 17 products by price and typical reinforcement

	Positive Reinforcement	***Negative Reinforcement***
High Price (> $35)	massage services jewelry travel services sporting goods	tires dishwasher security systems vacuum cleaner insurance virus detection software
Low Price (< $35)	CD/music garden tools toys wine	vitamins insect repellant pain relief medication

RESEARCH METHOD

Sample

A four-page questionnaire about online shopping habits was distributed to the sampled population of staff members at a large private northeastern university. Staff were selected using the Staff Council mailing list, which was grouped into six blocks. One-half of the voting blocks were selected (n=683) to receive the questionnaire via interoffice mail. The response rate for the staff was 29% (198 questionnaires were returned).

The questionnaire included several demographic variables: gender, age and years on the Internet. Almost three-quarters (73.9%) of the respondents were women; 14% were 29 years of age or younger, 58% were age 30-49, and 28% were age 50 or older. The average number of years using the Internet was slightly over five years.

Questionnaire Design

For the present study, three sections from the questionnaire were used. Respondents were first asked if they had shopped online for any goods or services. Shopping was explicitly defined as "using the Internet to research, browse for, or compare the prices of products and/or services, but not necessarily purchase the item". They were then asked to list examples of items they shopped for.

To support statistical testing, respondents were then given a list of 17 products, and for each were asked to indicate whether they had ever used the Internet to shop for or buy this item. The 17 products and services were selected to balance high price and low price as well as positive reinforcement and negative reinforcement. Table 1 shows the 17 products as they were classified by the researchers before the study.

RESULTS

Of the 198 people surveyed, almost all (90.5%) indicated that they used the Internet to shop for one or more products or services. When asked to identify what

Table 2: Open-ended responses of products respondents shopped for online

Product	**Number of Mentions (n=198 respondents)**
Books/music/movies	86
Clothing	73
Travel	67
Computer Related Hardware	32
Cars	33
Furniture & household	43
Electronics	16
Toys	30
Sporting goods	20
Hobby	10
Jewelry	12
Other positive products	54
Negative products	4
Total	480

they had purchased on the Internet, nearly every product mentioned using unaided recall was a product that provided primarily positive reinforcement. On average, each respondent reported 2.42 items. A content analysis of the open-ended item revealed that only four of the 480 products mentioned were classified as negative products (one mention each of: vitamins, cleaning equipment or products, pepper spray, security systems). The top products mentioned are presented in Table 2.

Hypothesis 1 stated that people would have a lower probability of Internet shopping for products that provide negative reinforcement than they will for products that provide positive reinforcement. A statistical test of these differences is presented below in Table 4. Table 3 provides a summary of the percentage of respondents who reported using the Internet to shop for and purchase these eight positive and nine negative products.

Relating to the first hypothesis, Table 3 shows that the use of the Internet to shop for positive products ranged from 69% for travel services to a low of 3.5% for massage services. In contrast, the negative products were much lower, ranging from a high of 17% for virus detection software to 2% for insect repellant. A similar pattern is seen when we examine the percentages of those who purchase online. Positively reinforcing product purchasing ranged from 44% for travel service to 0% for massage services. Negatively reinforcing product purchasing ranged from a high of 8.6% for virus detection software to 0% for dishwashers and vacuum cleaners. The final column in Table 3 contains the ratio of those people who shopped for each product who went on to purchase it online (% purchased/percent shopped

Table 3: Percentage of respondents who shop for and/or purchased each product online (n=198)

Product Category	*Percentage who have shopped for product online*	*Percentage who have purchased product online*	*Purchase/shopped for ratio*
Positive Products			
Travel Services	69.2%	43.9%	.63
CD/Music	53.0%	34.8%	.66
Toys	45.5%	30.3%	.67
Sporting Goods	41.1%	20.8%	.51
Jewelry	23.2%	9.1%	.39
Wine	16.2%	4.0%	.25
Garden Tools	11.1%	2.5%	.23
Massage Services	3.5%	0.0%	0
Negative Products			
Virus Detection Software	17.3%	8.6%	.49
Vitamins	15.7%	7.1%	.45
Insurance	12.7%	1.0%	.08
Tires	8.6%	2.0%	.23
Dishwasher	5.6%	0.0%	0
Vacuum Cleaners	5.6%	0.0%	0
Pain Relief Medicine	5.1%	1.0%	.19
Security System	2.0%	1.0%	.50
Insect Repellant	2.0%	0.5%	.25

for). For example, 63% of those who used the Internet to shop for travel services also purchased travel services online. The highest ratios were for travel services, cd/music and toys, all positive products.

Table 3 provides considerable evidence that customers are more likely to use the Internet to shop for and purchase positive products than for negative products. In order to statistically test this, six new variables were examined for each respondent. The six variables were:

- Positive shopped for number = # of positive products shopped for
- Negative shopped for number = # of negative products shopped for
- Positive purchased number = # of positive products purchased
- Negative purchased number = # of negative products purchased
- Positive Ratio = Positive purchased number/Positive shopped for number
- Negative Ratio = Negative purchased number/Negative shopped for number

Table 4: Average number of positive and negative products that survey respondents indicated shopping for online or purchasing online

	Positive Products (out of eight)	*Negative Products (out of nine)*	*Paired t-test*	*Degrees of Freedom*	*Significance*
Average Shopped for Number (%)	2.645 (33.1%)	0.731 (8.1%)	17.54	196	.000
Average Purchased Number (%)	1.469 (18.4%)	0.209 (2.3%)	14.06	195	.000
Purchased/ Shopped for Ration (%)	54.0%	31.8%	4.49	75	.000

These variables are summarized in Table 4 and permit formal testing of our hypotheses. A matched pairs t-test was computed on the average of the total number of positive and negative products each person reported shopping for. People reported shopping online significantly more for positive products (mean =2.645) than for negative products (mean =0.731) (t = 16.56, df=196, p< 0.000). For purchasing the product online, respondents reported buying online significantly more for positive products (mean = 1.469) than for negative products (mean proportion = .209) (t = 13.9, df =196=, p< 0.000).

Hypothesis 3 states that given that a person did shop for a product online, a smaller percentage will buy negative products than positive products. As presented above, about one out of three (33%) of our respondents reported shopping online for positive products while only one out of 10 (8.1%) reported shopping online for negative products. The ratio of respondents who reported shopping for positive products who also reported purchasing the positive product online was significantly larger (mean = .555) than for negative products (mean = .286) (t = 4.49, df = 75, p< 0.000).

In summary, our results indicated that for positive products, about one-third of respondents have searched the Internet for information and about half of those went on to make an Internet purchase. In contrast, for negative products, about one out of ten of our respondents have searched the Internet for information and about one-third of these went on to make an Internet purchase.

DISCUSSION

Implications and Conclusions

Consumers shopping online demonstrate the multifaceted and complex behavior that has been well documented for traditional shopping. Certainly, there are many factors that impact both the process and the frequency of online shopping. In fact, earlier research in this area has shown that technical expertise, online shopping familiarity, shopping intention (hedonic or utilitarian), time spent online, risk-perception, income, age, gender, education, and product tangibility all influence the behavior of Internet shoppers.

The present research expands our understanding of Internet shopping by introducing operant conditioning theory as an explanation of what products and services consumers will search for and buy online. The results of this study indicated that people were less likely to shop online for products and services that provide primarily negative reinforcement. We measured this in two ways: one open-ended question and one set of closed-ended questions. In the open-ended question, less than 1% of the products and services generated were for negatively reinforced products. When provided with a list of products, respondents indicated shopping online for positive products over negative products in almost a four-to-one ratio (2.65 to .73). This pattern of results is consistent with the findings of a series of World Wide Web User Surveys (1994-1998) conducted by the Graphics, Visualization and Usability (GVU) group at Georgia Tech. Specifically, in their 10th WWW Survey (GVU Survey, 1998), only 1.8% of responses were for primarily negative products when users were asked about which products they searched for with the intent to purchase.

Further, the present study demonstrated that even consumers that did shop online for negative products actually completed a transaction online less frequently than those shopping for positive products. Thus, if they used the Internet at all, negative product consumers primarily used the Internet as a source for information rather than as a means to make the transaction.

The results presented here have implications for both practitioners and scholars of Electronic Commerce. Web retailers are more likely to sell positive products than negative ones since our respondents both liked to shop for and did shop online for more positively reinforced products than negatively reinforced ones. Of course, some products can have multiple interpretations, and marketers of these ambiguous products would be well advised to emphasize the positive reinforcing aspects of their products. Perhaps some shoppers will be moved from the apathy of a negative product shopper to the activity of a positive product shopper.

In addition, the pattern of results may clarify the notion of convenience in Internet shopping. One commonly held belief is that the Internet is primarily used for efficiency and time-savings in shopping. Operant conditioning theory further suggests that this efficiency would be especially useful in avoiding the aversive experience of shopping for products that have negative reinforcement. However, our results suggest that this is not true. If shoppers were primarily using the convenience of the Internet to shorten the shopping experience for negative products, one would expect to see more reports of online shopping for negative products than for positive ones. However, the opposite was found. Sorce, Perotti and Widrick (2002) speculate that people postpone shopping for the negative reinforcing products until the onset of the aversive stimulus. The present study adds more support to this position by showing that shoppers for negative products make use of the Internet more as a source of information than as a storefront to perform transactions. For web sites that also have a real-world presence ("Bricks and Mortar stores"), providing extensive information about the negative products might be a good way to drive new business to the off-line shop. However, for pure eTailers, the cost of providing this information may well outweigh the benefit from presenting it.

For marketing scholars, the research presented here demonstrates the usefulness of understanding online shopping behavior in the context of the specific type of product the consumer is buying. One implication is that the construct of shopping convenience may need to be further refined. For example, for negative products, the convenience of the Internet as an information source may be significantly more important to consumers than its purchasing convenience. A second implication is that models that focus primarily on the shoppers themselves should also take into account aspects of the product. It seems likely that a compound model that combines both buyer characteristics and product attributes would be most successful in predicting online buyer behavior. Such a model presents a good opportunity for additional research.

Limitations

The study was intended as a preliminary exploration of the operant conditioning theory as an explanation for online buying behavior. As such, it suffers from several limitations. For one, the convenience group of staff members provided a sample that could be skewed in some way. A second and more important limitation is the subjectivity in positive and negative reinforcement. Whereas some people consider gardening to be a necessary, but tedious task, others see gardening as an enjoyable hobby. In this study, the authors pre-classified the products into the negative and positive categories, but it is likely that some subjects would classify them differently. A more controlled experiment that seeks to better control the subjectivity of the operant conditioning theory is planned for future research. Finally, additional research is needed to clarify how operant conditioning interacts with other known predictors of Internet shopping behavior. A good opportunity for future research would be to measure and control all of the variables that have been shown to influence online shopping.

REFERENCES

Alreck, P. (2002). Gender effects on internet, catalogue and store shopping. *Journal of Database Marketing*, 9(2), 150-162.

Alreck, P., & Settle, R.B. (2002, September). The hurried consumer: Time-saving perceptions of and catalogue shopping. *Journal of Database Marketing,* 10(1), 25-35.

Bellman, S., Lohse, G., & Johnson, E. (1999). Predictors of online buying behavior. *Communications of the ACM*, *42*(12), 32-38.

Bhatnagar, A., Misra, S., & Rao, H.R. (2000). On risk, convenience and Internet shopping behavior. *Communications of the ACM*, *43*(11), 98-105.

Blair, M.E., & Shimp, T.A. (1992). Consequences of an unpleasant experience with music: A second-order negative conditioning perspective. *Journal of Advertising*, March, 35-.

Evans, P., & Wurster, T. (1999). *Blown to bits: How the new economics of information transforms strategy.* Harvard Business School Press.

GVU. (1998). GVU's 10th WWW User Survey. Online at: http://www.gvu.gatech.edu/user_surveys/survey-1998-10/.

Nord, W.R., & Peter, J.P. (1980). A behavior modification perspective on marketing. *Journal of Marketing*, (Spring), 36-47.

Peter, J.P., & W. R. Nord, W.R. (1982). A clarification and extension of operant conditioning principles in marketing. *Journal of Marketing*, *46*(Summer), 102-107.

Ramaswami, S., Strader, T., & Brett, K. (2000-01, Winter). Determinants of online channel use for purchasing financial products. *International Journal of Electronic Commerce*, *5*(2), 95-118.

Ratchford, B., Telukdar, D., & Lee, M.-S. (2001, Spring). A model of consumer choice of the Internet as an information source. *International Journal of Electronic Commerce*, *5*(3), 7-22.

Rothschild, M.L., & Gaidis, W.C. (1981). Behavioral learning theory: Its relevance to marketing and promotions. *Journal of Marketing*, *45*(Spring), 70-78.

Sorce, P., Perotti, V., & Widrick, S. (2002). Predicting Internet shopping behavior as a function of negative and positive reinforcement. *Proceedings of the American Marketing Association's 2002 Winter Educator's Conference*, February.

Van Slyke, C.C., & Belanger, F. (2002, August). Gender differences in perceptions of web-based shopping. *Communications of the ACM*, *45*(8), 82-86.

Vellido, A., Paulo J. G. Lisboa & Meehan, K. (2000, Summer). Quantitative characterization and prediction of online purchasing behavior: A latent variable approach. *International Journal of Electronic Commerce,* *4*(4), 83-104.

Vijayasarathy, L. (2002). Product characteristics and internet shopping intentions. *Internet Research*, 12(5), 411-426.

Widrick, S.M., & Fram, E.H. (1983, Spring). Identifying negative products: Do customers like to purchase your products. *The Journal of Consumer Marketing*, *1*(2), 59-66.

Widrick, S.M., & Hibbs, J. (1985). Negative reinforcement theory: Speed of purchase when buying a negative product. *Southeast American Institute for Decision Science*, (February), 228-230.

Wolfinbarger, M., & Gilly, M. (2001). Shopping for freedom, control and fun. *California Management Review,* 43(2), 34-55.

Previously published in the Journal of Electronic Commerce in Organizations, 1(1), 42-54, Jan/Mar, 2003.

Chapter II

Online Shopping Experience: A Conceptualization and Preliminary Results

Yi Maggie Guo, Texas A&M University, USA

ABSTRACT

In this chapter, a model of online shopping experience is proposed to unify previous works of online consumer experience. Online shopping experience (OSE) is the interaction between shoppers and commercial web sites. It consists of physical, cognitive, and affective activities, and in-progress responses. Factors influencing shopping experience include individual characteristics of shoppers, characteristics of stores and commercial web sites, characteristics of products and shopping task, and other contextual factors. The outcomes of shopping experience have been studied in many ways. Based on this model, series of research questions can be asked to examine relationships between components of shopping experience and influencing factors, and between shopping experience and shopping outcomes. Preliminary results of a study are reported to illustrate the usefulness of the concept of online shopping experience.

INTRODUCTION

In modern society, it is obvious that the Internet has impacted the way we shop. This chapter focuses on consumer behavior in online retailing environments, attempts to give a review of current research on online consumer behavior and suggests a research agenda for the future. It first proposes a model of the Online Shopping Experience (OSE), and then reports preliminary results of an empirical study using the concept of OSE. The model is different from other models in that it explicitly studies the cognitive and affective aspects of consumer behavior in online environments. The preliminary results support the applicability of the model in studying online consumer behavior. Further research will enhance our understanding of social and cognitive effects of Electronic Commerce on people, and yield fruitful findings to aid in the design of better online shopping environments, which has the capability to invoke better shopping experiences from both shoppers' and retailers' perspective.

There have been numerous studies in marketing and information systems that examined online shopping. This chapter takes a multi-disciplinary approach. A unified framework is proposed based on a review of past and current research on online consumer behavior. The framework is centered on the concept of Shopping Experience (SE), which is defined as the episodes of interaction between customers and commercial establishments. Applied to online environments, Online Shopping Experience (OSE) is the interaction between customers and commercial web sites. Similar to SE, the following attributes describe OSE: duration, breadth, depth, and intensity. We emphasize the dynamic and situated nature of *shopping*. Thus, OSE consists of a range of activities, including physical, cognitive, and affective activities, and in-progress responses. Also, OSE is situated among influential factors, such as characteristics of the store/site, the shopper, and the product or task involved. It produces outcomes as well. Once a shopping experience ends, the outcome becomes part of consumers' knowledge and past experience, which will impact the next shopping experience. Flow, an engrossing and enjoyable experience, is an optimal shopping experience. This conceptualization of Online Shopping Experience addresses the dynamic and situated nature of shopping by using both processes (activities) and states (in-process responses). The model incorporates and unifies major theories used by researchers to investigate online consumer behavior.

After presenting the concept of Online Shopping Experience, we lay out a research agenda to examine its nature and attributes, the factors influencing the experience, and the shopping outcomes. Since OSE is a newly defined concept, studies conducted so far are exploratory in nature, as an effort to verify the concept and to further refine its definition and structure. The chapter contributes to our existing knowledge by (1) mapping and relating scattered studies in different fields under a unified framework and (2) providing a starting point for further investigation efforts. Research in this stream is a unique effort to understanding online consumer behavior through a microscopic, exploratory approach, by looking into the internal states and processes during interactions between a shopper and web sites. Results from the studies will extend our knowledge of consumer behavior and human-computer interaction by including the Internet as a distinctive medium. The newly gained understanding will provide a basis for future research on site usability and technological advances. It will also supply guidelines for site design and shed light on optimal web retailer strategy.

The purpose here is threefold. First, a general outline of past and current research on online consumer behavior is presented as the basis of the proposed model. Second, a research agenda with propositions is developed and methodological issues are also discussed. Third, preliminary results from a study are presented to illustrate the usefulness of the concept of Online Shopping Experience.

UNDERSTAND YOUR CUSTOMERS ONLINE

Understanding customers, their needs and behavior, is always the core and a necessity to sustain success in selling, whether the product is goods or services. This understanding enables a seller to help its clients fulfill their needs in a pleasant manner. In return, the seller fulfils its own goals, generating revenue and profit, and hopefully, a seller can continue doing so. In online retailing environments this requirement still holds, but with new challenges. Online shopping environments are made up of the Internet (the underlying communicational support) and the web (the hypertextual and hypermedia presentation medium); they are different from brick-and-mortar stores. An online environment is a virtual environment. When compared to the five senses in a physical store, online environments present products and information with limited sensory stimuli; so far only visual and audio are readily available. Furthermore, the whole process of shopping online lacks social intervention. No salespersons, cashiers, or any other customers exist in the direct physical setting of the customer. On the other hand, it possesses potentially unlimited "reach" and accessibility, in terms of the volume of information available and transience of geographic locations, which is unimaginable for a physical store. Therefore, it is critical to understand the impact of this new medium on consumer shopping behavior. We ask questions like: Do they behave differently in comparison to a conventional environment? If so, how different? Do their needs change? What role does the new medium play in affecting their decision-making and attitude forming?

Because the Internet is a different medium and a distinct distribution channel with its own right (e.g., Butler & Peppard, 1998; Hoffman & Novak, 1996; Schlosser, 2003), it is natural to study its impact on consumer behavior (Barwise, Elberse& Hammond, 2002). The questions above are the most fundamental issues for several reasons. First, contrary to the earlier prediction of drastic increases in online spending and change of buying habits, overall electronic commerce is merely satisfactory. Despite the anticipated incentive and customer value of utilizing online technology, customer acceptance of the Internet as a major and routine shopping place is still not "revolutionary" (Barwise et al., 2002). Studying online consumer behavior may help us understand why. Secondly, although online shopping is not as commonplace as once thought, it still holds potential to increase at a greater speed in the next few years (Barwise et al.). Studying online consumer behavior will help us better realize this potential.

There has been a great amount of research in both the information systems and marketing fields regarding this phenomenon, taking different approaches, applying various theories, and following a range of methodologies. In order to put them into perspective, we propose a concept of Shopping Experience (SE), defined as episodes of interaction of a customer with retailing establishments. It is a general definition and can be applied in different contexts. Thus, Online Shopping Experience (OSE) is defined as episodes of interaction of a customer with commercial web sites. We do not dictate the one-to-one customer/store (site) relationship in shopping experience. That means shopping experience can be between a customer and several stores/sites. For example, one whole afternoon spent in the mall looking around constitutes one entire experience, although visiting individual stores may be different chapters within the episode. In online environments, the separation of trips to different sites becomes tricky since it is so easy for a surfer to go from one site to another by a click of mouse. Customers even open several windows simultaneously and browse the sites alternatively. However, to keep it simple at the beginning, the empirical studies conducted so far are restricted to one web site. Future research will expand to scenarios of multiple sites.

Shopping Experience is situated among influential factors, such as store/site, shopper, product/task and so on. Shopping Experience also produces outcomes. Once a shopping experience ends, the outcome acts as knowledge and past experience in customers, which will impact the next shopping experience. The outcomes also impact stores and products, although not as directly as on the shoppers. This model is suited for retailing in both conventional and online environments. Since marketing is one of the most natural and important contributing fields to this inquiry, we draw more on marketing literature discussing physical stores to describe the major components of the model. However, our focus is Online Shopping Experience.

ONLINE SHOPPING EXPERIENCE

The world of experience is produced by the man who experiences it.
-- Neisser (1967, p. 3)

Our conceptualization of Online Shopping Experience addresses the dynamic and situated nature of shopping by including both activities (processes) and in-process responses (states). According to Underhill (1999), the very nature of shopping experience is determined by "Where shoppers go, what they see, and how they respond" (p. 44). OSE consists of the following components.

Physical Activities

These are the physical behaviors of a shopper. In a conventional setting, a shopper walks, reads, sees, touches, smells, listens, tastes (if possible), tries on, talks, buys, and leaves. If we have a camera following a customer, at the end, we can reconstruct his/her path in the store. If we accumulate the videotapes and compare them, we will have a better idea of our customers' traverse pattern and discover the problematic designs of a store (Underhill, 1999). In our model for online environments, people *navigate*, *orientate*, *browse*, *consult helpers*, *view products*, *make a purchase*, and *manage their accounts*. Those activities are straightforward. By observing shoppers' online movements, we can also find faulty designs of a web site. For example, we use the number of clicks that a visitor goes through as a measure of how easy it is to find the information needed in a site.

Cognitive Activities

While physical activities are visible and readily observed, cognitive and affective activities are more subtle and harder to trace. However, they bear equal importance to understanding consumers, if not more. Cognitive activities are the mental processes and states a shopper undergoes during a shopping visit. They include recognizing the perceived stimuli, relating them together, and with past knowledge, comprehending and integrating the new information, deciding what to do with it, and planning the next step. Meanwhile, emotions intervene with and are affected by these cognitive processes. Existing marketing literature provides abundant studies in this regard and this is a basis for our model. The traditional, generic model of consumer problem solving is a linear, staged model with six steps. After *recognizing the problem* (a need), consumers *search for information* both internally and externally. Then a *purchase* (or no purchase) *decision* is made once *alternatives* have been formed and evaluated. The actual *purchase* and *post-purchase evaluation* follows. In our model, problem recognition is assumed at this point and post-purchase evaluation is out of scope. Thus, product-related cognitive activities are: *product information comprehension*, *product evaluation*, *product comparison*, and *decision-making*. In addition to product-related stimuli, shoppers are surrounded by other environmental cues and affected by them (Eroglu, Machleit& Davis, 2001). Therefore, cognitive activities also include *environmental cue perception* and *environmental cue evaluation*.

Affective Activities

This is the emotional attribution component of Shopping Experience. Not only do consumers carry out both experiential and goal-oriented shopping tasks (Mowen, 1988), but many consumption activities produce both hedonic and utilitarian outcomes (Babin, Darden& Griffin, 1994). Emotions interact with the cognitive system in response to external stimuli (Cohen & Areni, 1991). We extend the notion of affectivity to be an ongoing activity during shopping, not just one of the outcomes.

That is, shoppers are evaluating and attributing their emotions continuously (maybe subconsciously) throughout the course of shopping.

Researchers have studied the emotional states in the context of the impact of environmental cues on a person in that environment. Environmental psychologists (e.g., Mehrabian & Russell, 1974) drew the Stimulus-Organism-Response (SOR) paradigm to study how environment (Stimulus) influences people's internal states (Organism) and their behavior (Response). The mediating internal states are the emotional responses and are classified into three dimensions: pleasure, arousal, and dominance (PAD). *Pleasure-displeasure* is the positive or negative state of emotion, the degree to which the person feels good, joyful, happy, or satisfied in the situation; *arousal-nonarousal* refers to excitement level, the degree to which a person feels excited, stimulated, alert, or active in the situation; and *dominance-submissiveness* refers to the extent to which the individual feels in control of, or free to act in, the situation. Dominance is the inverse of the judged potency of the environment. These feeling states can be assessed from verbal reports using the semantic differential method. Although there are arguments that other emotional measures provide richer assessment of the emotional responses (Machleit & Eroglu, 2000), PAD is one of the most frequently used in marketing studies regarding retail store design (e.g., Donovan & Rossiter, 1982; Havlena & Holbrook, 1986).

In-Process Responses

Since Shopping Experience is an ongoing interaction between the store/site and its shoppers, it is beneficial to recognize in-process responses during shopping in order to comprehend the diversity patterns in unfolding shopping experiences (Chebat & Dube, 2000). Besides the emotional responses, two in-process responses of importance are *perceived usefulness (PU)* and *perceived ease of use (PEOU)*. Both of them are from the well-developed Technology Acceptance Model (TAM). TAM uses these two sets of behavioral beliefs to predict system usage. Perceived ease of use is the user's perception of the amount of effort needed to use the system and perceived usefulness is the user's perception of the degree to which using the system will improve his/her job performance (Davis, 1989). In the context of online shopping, people constantly make assessment on the usefulness and ease of use of a web site. Based on the assessment and emotions, they form *behavioral intentions*. Based on the intentions, shoppers may display either approach or avoidance behavior as the result. The *approach–avoidance behavior* manifests into a variety of actions, including physical approach or avoidance, willingness to explore or not to, willingness to affiliate or not to, performance, and/or other verbal and nonverbal communications (Donovan & Rossiter, 1982; Mehrabian & Russell, 1974). Although perceived usefulness and perceived ease of use have been studied in the context of online shopping behavior (e.g., Koufaris, 2002), none of the studies conceptualized these beliefs and intentions as changing process variables.

Descriptive Attributes

For the sake of completeness, several descriptive attributes are included. They are duration (length of a shopping visit), breadth (number of product categories looked at), depth (number of products in a product category looked at), and intensity (length of time spent on each product). Those attributes are informative, but we concentrate more on the internal processes and states.

Optimal Shopping Experience — Flow

Shopping can be entertaining too. People feel intrinsically satisfied with control and involvement (Jones, 1999). This state is very similar to flow, which is "the crucial component of enjoyment" (Csikszentmihalyi, 1975, p. 11). It is a "peculiar dynamic state—the holistic sensation that people feel when they act with total involvement" (p. 36) and an "ordered, negentropic state of consciousness" (Csikszentmihalyi,

Table 1: General characteristics of flow experience

1	Precondition	"A balance between the challenges perceived and the skills a person brings to it" (Csikszentmihalyi, 1988, p.30) "A challenging activity that requires skills" (Csikszentmihalyi, 1990, p. 49)	Challenge and skill
2	Precondition	"The activity must have relatively clear goals." (Csikszentmihalyi, 1988, p. 32)	A clear goal
3	Precondition	"Provide rather quick and unambiguous feedback" (Csikszentmihalyi, 1988, p. 32)	Feedback
4	Dimension	"A centering of attention on a limited stimulus field" (Csikszentmihalyi, 1975, p. 40) "Concetration on the track at hand" (Csikszentmihalyi, 1990, p. 58)	Concentration
5	Dimension	"The merging of activity and awareness" (Csikszentmihalyi, 1990, p.53) "People become so involved in what they are doing that the activity becomes spontaneous, almost automatic; they stop being aware of themselves as separate from the actions they are performing." (p. 53)	Mergence
6	Dimension	"There is the sense that the outcomes of the activity are, in principle, under the person's own control" (Csikszentmihalyi, 1988, p. 33) "Lacking the sense of worry about losing control" (Csikszentmihalyi, 1990, p.59) "The sense of exercising control in difficulty situations" (Csikszentmihalyi, 1990, p. 61)	Sense of control

Table 1: (cont.) General characteristics of flow experience

7	Dimension	"Distorted sense of time" (Csikszentmihalyi, 1988) "The transformation of time," "Time no longer seems to pass the way it ordinarily does" (Csikszentmihalyi, 1990, p. 66)	Time distortion
8	Dimension	"Lose temporarily the awareness of self" (Csikszentmihalyi, 1988) "There is not enough attention left over to allow a person to consider either the past or the future, or any other temporarily irrelevent stimuli" (Csikszentmihalyi, 1990, p. 61) "The loss of the sense of a self separate from the world around it is sometimes accompanied by a feeling of union with the environment" (Csikszentmihalyi, 1990, p. 63)	Loss of self-consciousness
9	Result	"The key element of an optimal experience is that it is an end in itself" (Csikszentmihalyi, 1990, p. 67)	Autotelic experience

1988, p. 34). In this state, actions transit seamlessly from one to another, displaying an inner logic. The person involved experiences a smooth transition, total control of his/her actions, and no distraction.

For flow to occur, the task should have a clear goal and a quick, unambiguous feedback mechanism. Also, the perceived challenges the activity presents and skills the person possesses should match (balance of challenges and skills) so that the activity will neither *bore* the person (too easy) nor make her/him *anxious* (too

Table 2: Online shopping experience components

Processes	
Physical Activities	Navigating, orientating, browsing, viewing product, consulting helper, purchasing, managing account
Cognitive activities	Product information comprehension, product information evaluation, product comparison, purchase decision making, environmental cue perception, environmental cue evaluation
Affective activities	Negative/positive emotion attribution
In-process responses	Perceived usefulness, perceived ease of use, approach/avoidance behavior (behavioral intention)
Flow	Interactivity, focused attention, enjoyment, time distortion, telepresence

hard). Both challenges and skills have to pass a certain threshold for flow to happen; otherwise the person shows *apathy* towards the activity (Csikszentmihalyi & Csikszentmihalyi, 1988). The dimensions of flow experiences include focused concentration, "merging of activity and awareness", perceived control, time distortion, and loss of self-consciousness (that is, "a transcendence of self"). As the result, "consciousness is in harmony and the self—invisible during the flow episode—emerges strengthened" and "the negentropic quality of the flow experience makes it autotelic, or intrinsically rewarding" (Csikszentmihalyi, 1988, pp. 32-33). Please refer to Table 1 for a summary of flow characteristics.

There are concepts of flow (or autotelic) personality and flow activity, which refer to a personality that has the ability to experience flow easily and an activity that makes it easy for people to achieve flow, respectively. Both will influence the occurrence of flow. Furthermore, flow is a dynamic, evolving force. It is hard to be in flow for a substantially long period of time since the perceived challenges and skills are changing over time. In most cases, a person with ever-increasing skills will feel bored eventually unless the activity becomes more challenging at the same time.

Directly applying flow in online shopping behavior was pioneered by Hoffman and Novak (1996). First, flow in a hypermedia computer mediated environment (CME) is defined as a state that is a seamless sequence of responses facilitated by machine interactivity, which is inherent to the web. The way they classify the dimensions of flow in web navigation is slightly different from the original structure by Csikszentmihalyi. The requirement of a clear goal is assumed here. Besides other experiential dimensions, telepresence is added to reflect the dislocation effect of

Figure 1: A general model of online shopping experience

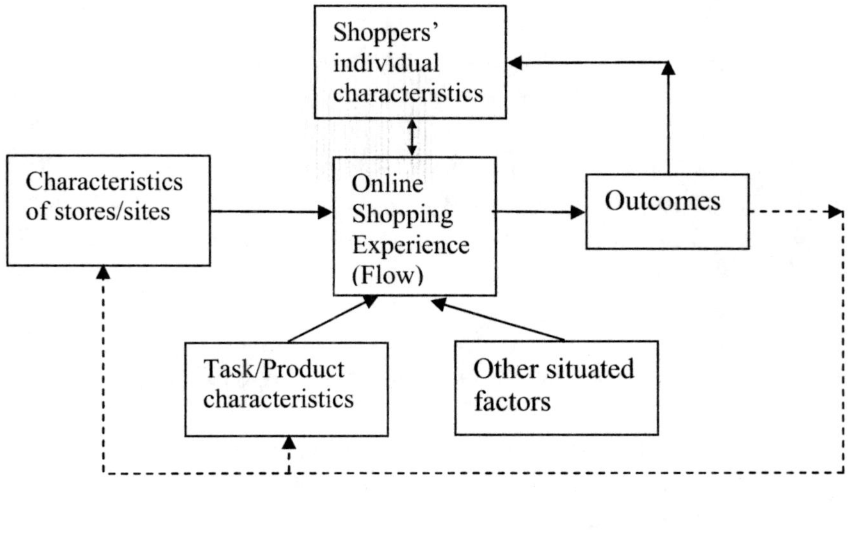

web surfing. Furthermore, consumers show better learning and more exploratory and participatory behaviors as consequences of flow.

Flow is posited as an optimal shopping experience in our model. Our ultimate goal is to be able to design online shopping environments that are capable of maximizing the flow feeling in as many shoppers as possible. The components of Online Shopping Experience are summarized in Table 2.

A GENERAL MODEL OF ONLINE SHOPPING EXPERIENCE — PUT EXPERIENCE AT THE CENTER

In this section, a general model of Online Shopping Experience (Figure 1) is introduced. In this model, Shopping Experience is placed at the center as the main focus. Influential factors are individual differences, store/site characteristics, and task and product characteristics, among others. This arrangement reflects our effort to follow the vision of experiential economy and marketing (Pine & Gilmore, 1998; Schmitt, 1999, 2003; Schmitt, Rogers & Vrotsos, 2004). Experiential marketing (Schmitt, 1999) calls for a change of traditional marketing approach by focusing on customer experience management, which is the process of strategically managing a customer's entire experience with a product or a company. It was shown that customers' experience with ads, stores, and web sites has an impact on attitudes and purchase intentions (Schmitt, 2003).

Individual Characteristics of Shoppers

Shoppers are the driving force in unfolding episodes of shopping. On the other hand, shoppers get direct feedback, expand their knowledge, and change their beliefs and attitude, instantly and continuously. That's why a two-headed arrow is used to denote the relations between shoppers and a shopping experience.

Individual differences in a variety of aspects have been empirically proven to influence consumer perception and behavior. Thus, those characteristics are believed to play an important role in shopping experiences because shoppers are the major actor in shopping episodes. Characteristics that have been studied are demographics (Li, Kuo& Russell, 1999), general shopping orientation (Stone, 1954; Vijayasarathy, 2003) and motivation (Childers, Carr, Peck& Carson, 2001), general attitude toward the medium in question, environmental (including online environment) deposition (Grossbart, Hampton, Ramonhan& Lipidus, 1990; Grossbart, Mittelstasredt, Curtis& Rogers, 1975) and other personal traits, prior knowledge of the product and store, past experience, and so on.

Two characteristics calling for special attention are skills and flow personality. First, skills are associated with perceived ease of use and perceived control. Balance of skills and challenges is the precondition for the occurrence of flow. Online shopping involves using a computer and the Internet; thus, it is only natural to relate computer skills or computer self-efficacy (more specific, Internet self-efficacy) to the use of online stores or services (Kaufaris, 2002; O'Cass & Fenech, 2003). Besides the Internet skills, there are other skills involved, such as knowledge of products and sites. For flow personality, personal traits, such as novelty (Novak, Hoffman, & Yung, 2000) and cognitive spontaneity (Ghani, 1995), have been used as measures of individual flow personality.

Characteristics of Stores/Sites

Some aspects are the same in both physical and virtual stores, such as market position, stores/sites types, and product assortment and variety. Regarding Shopping Experience (both conventional and online), design aspect plays an important and unique role in invoking emotions. We will focus on this factor below.

Stores are containers of an array of sensory stimuli. So, store features can be described in terms of sensory variables too. Basic classification is to group them according to people's five senses. Marketing researchers also included other attributes besides the pure sensory stimuli. Two popular categorizations of environmental cues have been suggested by Baker (1986) and Bitner (1992). Baker (1986) classifies the cues into Social Factors (people in the store, i.e., customers and salespeople), Design Factors (visual cues such as layout, color, cleanliness), and Ambient Factors (non-visual cues, such as smells, sounds, and lighting). With some similarities, Bitner (1992) breaks those variables into Ambient cues (cues that affect the five senses), Layout and Functionality (the way in which store furniture, machinery, and equipment are arranged as well as their ability to facility consumers to attain their goals), and Signs, Symbols, and Artifacts (all explicit and implicit signals that serve as communicators to the customers).

In a framework to study online consumer behavior (Eruglu et al., 2001), the environmental cues of online stores are categorized into high task-relevant and low task-relevant cues. The framework suggests a systematic investigation of those cues' effects on internal states (affect and cognitions), and eventually on the shopping outcome—approach/avoidance response. It is an example of the approach that studies the impacts of individual design elements, more or less continuing the tradition of retail atmospherics. A couple of studies (e.g., Liang & Lai, 2000, 2002; Lohse & Spiller, 1999) relate individual features to certain consumer behaviors. Some studies examined one variable a time. In one study, information load, expressed as complexity and novelty, is associated with online exploratory and shopping behavior in a field experiment using ten of the most popular commercial web sites (Huang, 2000). Another paper suggests examining navigational cues for their impact on shoppers' attitude and behavior (Dailey, 2003).

Another approach is to treat the web site design as a wholesome construct with underlying factors. This is the approach taken by studies on site quality (Aladwani & Palvia, 2002; Barnes & Vigden, 2002; Loiacono, Watson& Goodhue, 2002) and site usability (Nielsen, 2000; Palmer, 2002). Some measures are objective, and some are user perceptions. For example, WebQual (Barnes & Vigden, 2002) measures design quality by three dimensions: usability, information quality, and interaction quality. This approach has several advantages over the first one. First, it is hard or impossible to compare sites by comparing numerous individual design elements directly. Secondly, the design, as a whole, affects shoppers, although particular cues might be prominent. Thirdly, site design changes and technology advances over time, so it would be hard to compare research results over time if we tie our research too closely to design elements.

Task and Product Characteristics

The task and product involved represent an important aspect of shopping and have long been thought to impact consumer behavior in both offline and online channels. Two broad categories of activities in which consumers engage during shopping are experiential and goal-directed. The distinctions are summarized in Novak, Hoffman, and Duhachek (2003). Goal-directed and experiential activities are different in terms of motivation (extrinsic versus intrinsic), benefits (utilitarian versus hedonic), orientation (instrumental versus ritualized), involvement (situational versus enduring), search mode (directed, pre-purchase versus non-directed, browsing, ongoing), choice (goal-directed versus navigational), and results (planned purchases, re-purchasing versus compulsive shopping, impulse buys). Goal-directed activities are thought to be more cognitive and "work"-oriented, while experiential activities are to be more affective and fun. This is true in online environments as well. Furthermore, people shop online for different reasons: freedom, control, and fun (Wolfinbarger & Gilly, 2001).

A couple of studies examined effects of shopping task regarding the flow experience in online environments. Flow has been found to occur in both goal-oriented and experiential activities (Novak et al., 2003). In another experimental study, the effects of web navigation design (static web pages versus dynamic web pages) and user motivation (information seeking versus entertainment seeking) on experiencing flow are put under investigation (Wan & Nan, 2001). It was posited that the match situations (static web site with information seeking motives, dynamic web site with entertainment seeking motives) would facilitate positive emotions and experience, resulting in high evaluation and high behavioral intention. Although the interaction between the two factors (web feature and user motivation) was significant, the congruency effect was not symmetric.

In addition to task, the product at hand plays an important role in shopping experience too. It is common sense that we spend more time and energy to purchase a car than milk; it is commonly thought that a car is a high involvement product while milk is a routine, low involvement product. The products we are seeking influence the way we approach the shopping and purchasing activity. A study of Internet shopping found that product types, based on cost and tangibility, had a direct effect on intentions to shop using the Internet (Vijayasarathy, 2003).

It is impossible to exhaust the list of factors influencing Shopping Experience, but we have listed most important ones here. Some other factors that have been looked at are social and cultural issues (Laroche, Saad, Kim& Browne, 2000) and time constraints (Titus & Everett, 1995).

Shopping Outcomes

The outcomes of Shopping Experience are of special importance to retailers. Our ultimate goal in studying SE is to achieve desired results via creating a better experience. Outcomes of a shopping trip are multi-faceted. The most direct measures are actual purchase and spending (Donovan, Rossiter, Marcoolyn& Nesdale, 1994), for objectivity and straightforwardness. Customer subjective responses are also used to evaluate a shopping experience, in both online and traditional environments. Such measures include customer (user) satisfaction (Devaraj, Fan& Kohli, 2002; McKinney, Yoon& Zahedi, 2002; Palmer, 2002; Szymanski & Hise, 2000), attitude/mode change (Eruglu, Ellen & Machleit, 1991; Spies, Hesse & Loesch, 1997; Yoo, Park & Maclnnis, 1998), intention of return/use (Baker, Parasuraman, Grewal & Voss, 2002; Koufaris, 2002; Palmer, 2002), image forming (Baker, Grewal & Parasuraman, 1994; Markin & Lillis, 1976) and so on. Other outcomes studied by the marketing and IS fields (in the context of EC) are need fulfillment and expectation confirmation (Bhattacherjee, 2001; McKinney et al., 2002). These outcomes are thought to drive customer satisfaction and are suitable for cases where actual buying is not the goal.

Once a shopping experience ends, the outcome acts as knowledge and past experience in customers, which will impact the next shopping experience. The relationships between other factors and shopping experience are straightforward. Noteworthy is that the collective shopping outcome will eventually impact stores and products in that retail managers and product manufacturers try to improve their stores and products based on these outcomes. Since it is hard to say whether one particular shopping experience will affect a store design or a product, these relationships are denoted by a dashed line.

UNIFYING RELATED THEORIES

There has been a great amount of research in both the information systems and marketing fields studying online consumer behavior, taking different approaches, applying various theories, and following a range of methodologies. We posit that the Online Shopping Experience (OSE) is the unifying concept to put all the research into perspective. We will examine the relations of this concept with three major theories.

OSE and Flow Theory

How does flow theory relate to our model of Online Shopping Experience? The flow state is a special case of shopping experiences wherein people feel gratification and enjoyment. It has been found that people experience flow in various web activities (Chen, Wigand & Nilan, 1998, 1999). Flow can be measured in duration and intensity (Smith & Sivakumar, 2003). Also, flow theory suggests additional attributes of Shopping Experience other than emotional responses expressed as PAD, such as time distortion and dislocation. Although it is not normal in a regular physical shop to feel flow, some retailers and service providers are striving to create such feeling, like theme parks and theme stores/restaurants (Pine & Gilmore, 1998). While flow theory does not necessarily entail certain physical and cognitive activities, since people feel flow in a variety of activities, it does result in more exploratory and participating behavior.

The relationship of our model and the flow theory can also be seen in several other aspects. First, according to flow theory, the balance of the actor's skills and the challenges confronting him/her is a critical precondition for flow to occur. Skills and challenges are conceptualized in a shopper's individual characteristics and the retailing establishment characteristics, respectively, in our model. Secondly, the need for a quick, clear feedback mechanism relates to store and site features. Thirdly, the requirement of equilibrium between skills and challenges is a perfect example of the situational aspect of flow. It is determined by the task at hand. OSE is modeled as a situated phenomenon as well. Furthermore, the dynamics between skills and challenges is embodied in the user's perception of control, which can be thought of as one of the in-process responses of OSE. Lastly, in regard to consequence, the consequences of a flow shopping experience include the intention to return and actual revisits, since people want to repeat the same good feelings. Those consequences are also shopping outcomes in our model.

OSE and Technology Acceptance Model

Based on the Theory of Reasoned Action and the Theory of Planned Behavior (TPB, Ajzen, 1991), the Technology Acceptance Model (TAM) is a specific adaptation

Figure 2: Technology acceptance model (Venkatask & Davis, 1996)

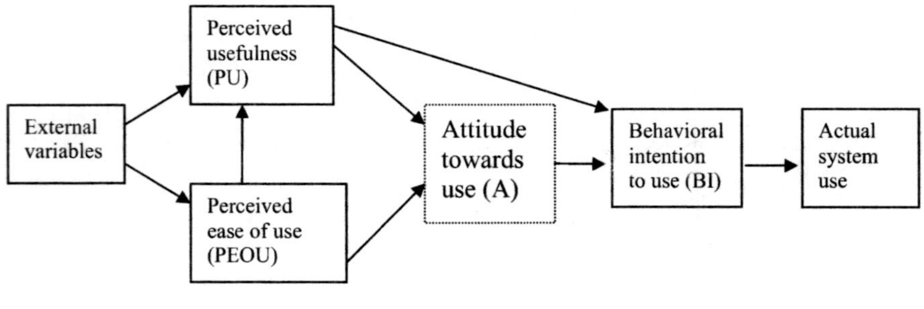

of those social psychology theories predicting specific behavior to understand user adoption behavior of Information Technology. They state that behavioral achievement depends jointly on motivation (intention) and ability (behavioral control). Attitude toward the behavior, subjective norms, and perceived control all influence intentions and each other.

When applied to IT adoption, TAM uses two sets of specific behavioral beliefs, perceived usefulness (PU) and perceived ease of use (PEOU), to predict system usage. Perceived usefulness is an outcome expectancy, while perceived ease of use is a process expectancy (Venkatech, 1999). Intentions to use have been found to be a good predictor of the actual system usage and can be used as a dependent variable (Venkatesh & Davis, 1996). Thus, behavioral intention is the function of the user's beliefs about ease of use and usefulness. Furthermore, PU is influenced by PEOU, in that the easier a technology is to use, the more useful it seems to be, holding other conditions constant. With time or increased experience, the effect of ease of use on behavioral intention becomes indirect via PU. The effects of external variables (e.g., system quality or user characteristics) on intentions are mediated by these two key beliefs. Figure 2 shows the relationships among these constructs.

TAM has been widely applied and empirically supported; there are studies trying to explain the individual adoption behavior of online retailing using TAM as well. In a web survey, TAM is found to be a valid theoretical framework (O'Cass & Fenech, 2003). In another study of online customers, a variable of compatibility from innovation diffusion theory was added and was hypothesized to affect perceived usefulness and attitude toward using. Data analysis found support for the TAM core elements as well as for compatibility (Chen, Gilllenson & Sherrell, 2002).

After comparing the flow theory and TAM, it is not difficult to find similarities and relations between their constructs. The precondition of matching challenges and skills for flow to occur is echoed in user perception of ease of use in TAM. Perception of control in flow is exactly the same as perceived behavioral control in the theory of planned behavior and in extended models of TAM. Moreover, these variables are more situational than depositional in that task and individual characteristics play roles in them. Although flow theory emphasizes intrinsic rewards as one of the benefits autotelic experience brings, it does recognize external rewards (Csikszentmihalyi, 1988). Those benefits are reflected as, at least in part, perceived usefulness in TAM. The result of flow is that people want to repeat the experience, which has the counterpart in TAM as adoption behavior.

As a matter of fact, researchers have been using both TAM and flow to explain why people are "addicted" to Web surfing (Agarwal & Karahanna, 2000). An external, situated variable called cognitive absorption, based on flow theory, along with self-efficacy, was argued to influence perceived usefulness and perceived ease of use. In a study of flow in computer mediated communication (Trevin & Webster, 1992), individual differences in terms of computer skills were thought to influence flow in human computer interaction and perceived challenge (according to flow

Figure 3: An S-O-R framework of retailing environments

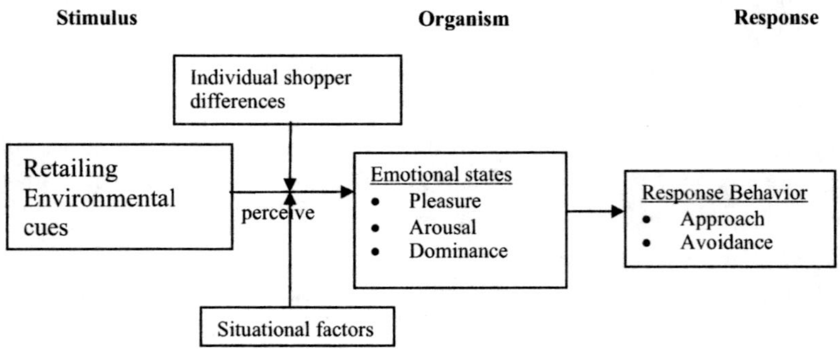

theory), which was treated as perceived ease of use from TAM in the research model. Koufaris (2002) furthered this approach to test the effects of variables from both theories on customers' intention to return and unplanned buying after their first visit to a virtual store, under the rationale that an online customer is both a shopper and a computer user. Shopping enjoyment and perceived usefulness of the site were found to predict the intention to return.

If we compare our model of Online Shopping Experience (Figure 1) and TAM (Figure 2), we can see the matches between them. First, various external variables in TAM can be grouped into the influential factors of our model. Secondly, the behavioral intention and actual usage can be thought of as outcomes in our model. Thirdly, although most TAM studies only examine cross-section data, a few longitudinal studies found the moderating effect of experience, which is the feedback loops in our model. Finally, perceived usefulness and perceived ease of use are the results of cognitive activities. TAM does not describe the details of user behavior during interacting with the technology. In this sense, TAM treats the interaction as a black box. That's why some of the studies try to combine flow with TAM so that the dynamic aspect can be probed. Although it is fruitful, we assert that this approach is not enough and OSE is a more systematic way to discern patterns of the ongoing interaction.

OSE and Retail Atmospherics

Atmospherics is "the conscious designing of space to create certain effects in buyers"; more specifically, "it is the effort to design buying environments to product specific emotional effects in the buyer that enhance his purchase probability" (Kolter, 1974, p. 50). It is mainly based on a Stimulus-Organism-Response (SOR) framework. This model states that an environment (e.g., a store) is a Stimulus, containing various cues perceived by customers. It influences a person's internal emotional states (Organism), which result in approach or avoidance response/behavior (Responses)

(Mehrabian & Russell, 1974; Donovan & Rossiter, 1982). This framework has been taken into marketing and retailing research in a fairly straightforward manner to design customers' behavior via environmental cues. Please see Figure 3, which is an adaptation of the SOR framework in the retailing environment.

The SOR framework fits into our general model of OSE well. The retailing environmental cues are a subset of retailing establishment characteristics. Moderator variables, such as individual shopper differences and situational factors, have counterparts in our model too. The emotional responses and the relations with environmental cues, which have been extensively investigated, are a very good supplementation to flow theory and TAM via incorporating the emotional aspect into OSE. It also can be used to quantify flow in terms of PAD. The behavioral responses (approach versus avoidance) are conceptualized as in-progress responses to reflect the on-going nature of shopping. Extended responses (such as spending and revisit) fall into outcomes in our model.

RESEARCH QUESTIONS AND METHODOLOGICAL ISSUES

In this section, the use of this general model and methodological issue are briefly discussed. Typically, a useful framework can guide further research by summarizing and integrating past research, suggesting potential constructs and variables, and/or generating propositions and formulating testable hypotheses. The five propositions listed below are just examples of possible research questions generated from the general model.

Proposition 1. The characteristics of a retailing establishment (store type, store features, design quality, and so on) will affect OSE and its components.

Proposition 2. The characteristics of a shopper in terms of personal traits, shopping knowledge and orientation, and gender will affect his/her OSE and its components.

Proposition 3. The characteristics of the task at hand will affect OSE and its components.

Proposition 4. Other situational factors (cultural and social environmental factors) may affect OSE and its components.

Proposition 5. OSE will affect shopping outcomes (spending, satisfaction, return intention, image, and so on).

Although we focus on Online Shopping Experience, we can see from these propositions that the definition and model of Shopping Experience is not limited to any type of medium. It provides a consistent approach to study shopping behavior in different channels and makes comparisons clear and straightforward. For example, we can study facilitating factors for flow in online shopping in particular, and we can also replace OSE with any other kind of shopping experience.

Since the phenomenon we are studying is a situated, conditioned, dynamic, individual experience (Chen et al., 1999), qualitative and quantitative methods are requested. Finneran and Zhang (2002) observed that data collection methods in studying flow in human-computer interaction are dominantly the self-reported survey and retrospective questionnaires after controlled experiments, and pointed out that "surveying non-situated, generalized factors does not account for the dynamism of each factor and how its fluctuation influence flow". They suggested protocol analysis of concurrent verbalization or retrospective writing as one of the tools to collect rich contextual data.

Another useful method is the Experience Sampling Method (ESM). It was developed originally in 1976 using electronic pagers to prompt respondents to report on their thoughts and feelings (Csikszentmihalyi & Csikszentmihalyi, 1988). Since then, it has been used extensively in flow studies, and versions of the Experience Sampling Form (ESF) have been created. Chen et al. (1998) adapted this method using a computer application to collect data when computer users were surfing the Internet. However, the major challenge of those methods is to design the task and study procedure so that the interfering effect is reduced to a minimum.

Besides those self-reported data, client-side tracking is necessary to provide enough detailed, objective data. In an ideal situation, visitors' mouse movements are captured; web pages visited are recorded for later analysis. Data collected can be used either on their own or in conjunction with other kinds of data. The analysis and coding of this rich data set is challenging, but surely rewarding.

Table 3: Subject information

Subject No.	***Gender***	***Major***	***Level***	***Attitude toward shopping online***	***Familiarity with the site***
1	Male	MIS	Graduate	Like	No
2	Male	MIS	Senior	Like	No
3	Female	MIS	Graduate	Like	No
4	Male	Math	Graduate	Does not like	No
5	Female	MIS	Graduate	Like	Yes
6	Female	MIS	Senior	Like	No
7	Male	MIS	Senior	Like	No

PRELIMINARY STUDY AND RESULTS

Since Online Shopping Experience is a newly defined concept, studies conducted so far are exploratory in nature as an effort to verify the concept and to further refine its definition and structure, if needed. In this section we report on a study using protocol analysis to probe internal processes and states of online shoppers.

When the purpose is to explore people's experiences and problem solving procedures, one useful qualitative research technique is protocol analysis, which is also known as cognitive response, thought verbalization, and think-aloud. Essentially, this technique involves subjects verbalizing their thoughts, either concurrently or retrospectively. The data collecting technique of concurrent verbalization asks participants to verbalize their thoughts during the activity. The benefit of using this method is its introspective nature, and that it gives the responses right away. The report produced is "the most sensitive index for perceptual process" (Ericsson & Simon, 1984, p. 32). It provides rich data and allows a closer look at the unfolding course. It also reduces the effect of memory loss and the chance of introducing subject bias due to later rationalization and justification. This method has been successfully used both in information systems (e.g., Kim, Hahn & Hahn, 2000; Sen, Vinze, & Liou, 1994) and marketing (e.g., Li, Daugherty & Biocca, 2001).

Study Design and Procedure

In the study, a protocol analysis approach with concurrent verbalization was used to closely observe consumer behavior and explore the components of Online Shopping Experience. Subjects were asked to carry out a purchasing task of personal items (a birthday gift for a best friend, a piece of furniture, some sportswear for self) on a particular web site. One of the constraints was the budget, which was set at $150. Subjects could take as much time as needed. A total of seven students participated, who were upper level undergraduate and graduate students of a MIS course at a major university. The subject information is summarized in Table 3.

The task was designed to be relevant and real to the subjects. We tried hard to stimulate as much consideration and interaction as possible by asking them to purchase multiple items under the budget. This was to overcome some of the disadvantages of using students as subjects, who were coming for extra credit points and were eager to leave. Although there is a widely held disapproval of using students as a convenient sample, we believe students make a fairly good representation of online shoppers for our purposes. Studies have shown that the majority of online shoppers are young, with high education and good computer skills. The subjects in our study were an "expert panel" in that they were heavy computer and Internet users and experienced in shopping online. Hence, using a student sample was suitable for our objective to verify the concept and reveal more attributes. It is similar to the initial stage of a construct development using experts and a focus group.

The subjects were asked to verbalize their thoughts when interacting with the site. A demonstration of verbalization and a training session were given to familiarize

Table 4: Coding rules

		Rules	code
	Physical activities		***PA***
1	Navigating	If the segment shows phrases that depict the notion of navigation, label the segment as PA-NG. Some example phrases include "go to … department", "back to …"	PA-NG
2	Orientating	If the segment shows phrases that depict the notion of orientation, label the segment as PA-OR. Some example phrases include "where am I?", "how can I go to …"	PA-OR
3	Browsing	If the segment shows phrases that the customer is browsing through products, label the segment as PA-BW.	PA-BW
4	Viewing products	If the segment shows phrases that customer is viewing the product, label the segment as PA-VP. For example, customer reads the product description or view image.	PA-VP
5	Consulting helper	If the segment shows phrases that suggest customer is using a shopping aid, such as keyword search, label the segment as PA-CH.	PA-CH
6	Purchasing	If the segment shows phrase that suggests customer is conducting purchase, label the segment as PA-PC. Purchasing in online environment involving adding to shopping bag and, shipping, and payment.	PA-PC
7	Account management	If the segment shows phrase that suggests customer is conducting account management activities, such as creating an account or filling out registration forms, label the segment as PA-AM.	PA-AM
	Cognitive activities		***CA***
8	Product Information comprehending	If the segment shows phrases that depict the notion of comprehension of information on the web page, label the segment as CA-PIC. Some example phrases include "so, it is a toy."	CA-PIC

table continued on next page

them with the technique before they carried out the real task. The majority of them finished about in thirty minutes. Software was used to capture both subjects' voices and movements on the computer. Upon completion of the task, subjects filled out a short demographic questionnaire. The verbalizations were transcribed and their mouse movements were recorded into text for further analysis.

Data Analysis and Results

Both the subjects' verbalization and mouse movements have been transcribed and segmented into protocols. Based on our structure of Online Shopping Experience, twenty-three coding rules in five categories were derived to code these pro-

Table 4 (cont.): Coding rules

9	Product Information evaluating	If the segment shows phrases that depict the notion of evaluation of information on the web page, label the segment as CA-PIE. Some example phrases include "this one will look nice in my room" Or "a nice description."	CA-PIE
10	Product comparing	If the segment shows phrases that depict the notion of comparison of information on the web page, label the segment as CA-PComp. Some example phrases include "this one is cheaper than another one."	CA-PComp
11	Decision making	If the segment shows phrases that depict the buying (or not buying) decision-making, label the segment as CA-DM. Some example phrases include "I think I am going to buy …"	CA-DM
12	Environmental cue perceiving /comprehending	If the segment shows phrases that depict the perception of web site design, label the segment as CA-ECP. Some example phrases include "small font" and "red background."	CA-ECP
13	Environmental cue evaluating	If the segment shows phrases that depict the evaluation of web site design, label the segment as CA-ECE. Some example phrases include "nice design", "hard to read", and so on.	CA-ECE
	Affective activities		
14	Emotion attributing – positive	If the segment shows phrases that depict a positive emotion attribution, label the segment as AA-EAP. Some example phrases include "I like the site."	AA-EAP
15	Emotion attributing – negative	If the segment shows phrases that depict a negative emotion attribution, label the segment as AA-EAN. Some example phrases include "it is boring."	AA-EAN
	In-process responses		***IR***
16	Perceived usefulness	If the segment shows phrases that depict an assessment of usefulness of the web site and online shopping, label the segment as IR-PU. Some example phrases include "it is more convenient."	IR-PU

table continued on next page

tocols. The list of coding rules can be found in Table 4. A total of 1,195 protocols were coded. For example, if the protocol reads, "I don't like the site", it is coded as AA-EAN, which is Affective Activity—Emotional Attribution Negatively. If the protocol reads, "this bookcase would look nice in my room", it is coded as CA-PIE, which is Cognitive Activity—Product Information Evaluation.

The coding results are summarized in Tables 5 and 6. First, we can see all the categories that are presented in our data. Furthermore, people underwent many cognitive and physical activities. They also made comments on how they felt, such

Table 4 (cont.): Coding rules

17	Perceived ease of use (control)	If the segment shows phrases that depict an assessment of ease of use, label the segment as IR-PEOU. Some example phrases include "it is straightforward" and "it is confusing."	IR-PEOU
18	Behavioral intention	If the segment shows phrase that depict an intention of approaching or avoiding, label the segment as IR-BI. Some example phrases include "I want to leave." And "let me check out more."	IR-BI
	Flow experience		***FE***
19	Interactivity	If the segment shows the phrases that depict a notion of web site interactivity/responsiveness, label the segments as FE-I. Some example phrases include "it was slow."	FE-I
20	Time distortion	If the segment shows phrases that depict a notion of time distortion, label the segment as FE-TD. Some example phrases include "time flies by" and "I didn't notice it took so long."	FE-TD
21	Telepresence	If the segment shows phrases that depict a notion of telepresence, label the segment as FE-Tele. Some example phrases include "like I were in the store."	FE-Tele
22	Focused attention	If the segment shows phrases that depict a notion of attention focusing, label the segment as FE-FA. Some example phrases include "didn't notice other things surrounding me."	FE-FA
23	Intrinsic enjoyment	If the segment shows phrases that depict a notion of intrinsic enjoyment, label the segment as FE-IE. Some example phrases include "shopping is fun."	FE-IE

as how easy the site was to use and how useful the web site was, as in-progress responses. Affective activities were relatively fewer. It may be because people rarely attribute their emotions in a basically neutral situation, unless the experience was extreme, especially a negative one. A breakdown of negative and positive emotional attribution shows that more negative feelings were captured.

In the flow category, all the comments were on Interactivity. We suppose this is the aspect that influences shoppers' experience of flow the most. In addition, other dimensions of flow do not lend themselves to verbalization. The results suggest that we should study flow using other methods in later studies. However, we still believe that shoppers who are in flow and who are not in flow behave differently. Studies can be designed to compare and contrast behavioral patterns (in terms of physical activities, cognitive activities, affective activities, and in-progress responses) under these two situations.

Our panel study has shown that Online Shopping Experience is a useful concept to study this situated, pre-conditioned, dynamic, personal experience. It consists of both internal states and processes. Limitations include using a convenient

Table 5: Summary of protocols by categories

Subject	*1*	*2*	*3*	*4*	*5*	*6*	*7*	*Total*
Physical activities	46	41	70	63	49	56	49	373
Cognitive activities	56	87	117	96	129	90	60	635
Affective activities	2	11	5	4	4	4	0	30
In-progress responses	11	30	29	10	17	12	8	117
Flow	4	7	8	8	1	9	3	40
Sum	**119**	**176**	**229**	**181**	**200**	**170**	**120**	**1195**

Table 6: Protocols broken down by rules

Subject	*1*	*2*	*3*	*4*	*5*	*6*	*7*	*Total*
PA-NG	9	7	25	8	6	24	10	89
PA-OR	1	6	9	10	3	4	1	34
PA-BW	4	2	8	11	7	9	8	49
PA-VP	5	6	8	3	9	4	4	39
PA-CH	2	0	0	7	1	0	4	14
PA-PC	21	15	17	16	11	11	18	109
PA-AM	4	5	3	8	12	3	4	39
CA-PIC	10	10	11	15	33	11	13	103
CA-PIE	6	11	15	19	31	10	9	101
CA-Pcomp	0	0	2	0	1	0	0	3
CA-DM	4	6	12	3	5	4	6	40
CA-ECP	28	38	48	40	43	41	25	263
CA-ECE	8	22	29	19	16	24	7	125
AA-EAP	0	5	1	0	1	3	0	10
AA-EAN	2	6	4	4	3	1	0	20
IR-PU	0	6	5	1	2	1	2	17
IR-PEOU	5	11	5	1	1	3	2	28
IR-BI	6	13	19	8	14	8	4	62
FE-I	4	7	8	8	1	9	3	40
FE-TD	0	0	0	0	0	0	0	0
FE-Tele	0	0	0	0	0	0	0	0
FE-FA	0	0	0	0	0	0	0	0
FE-IE	0	0	0	0	0	0	0	0
Sum	**119**	**176**	**229**	**181**	**200**	**170**	**120**	**1195**

sample and small sample size. If possible, we would conduct a similar study with a stratified sample. That is, we will include students from different majors who are also proficient in computer and Internet usage. Furthermore, we will do the same to include shoppers with various online shopping histories and different skills in terms of computer usage. We will be able to find patterns among different groups by doing that.

Also, the verbalization technique has been criticized for the interference it causes to subjects' train of thought, and thus may be superficial. However, it is a good starting point to break the black box of online consumer experience. Lastly, it is always a challenge to design a good task that is real and engaging, and to ensure internal validity and enhance external validity. In future studies, we will strive for a better-designed task.

More data analysis can be done. First we may want to look into the sequential patterns of the activities. Do online shoppers still follow the problem-solving steps? What are the impacts of the conveniences of hypertext links for ads and recommendations? Will that lead to a discovery of more wanted products or simply distract shoppers from the task at hand? And also, the linkage of particular web site features with certain activities and states would prove to be interesting. For example, what often triggers negative emotional attribution?

CONCLUSION AND FUTURE RESEARCH

In this article we propose a concept of Online Shopping Experience and a general model of shopping experience to understand online consumer behavior. First of all, this model is a broad depiction of consumer behavior research. From the analysis in the previous sections, we can see the proposed concept of OSE and the general model tie different theories together well. These theories (namely, flow theory, the Technology Acceptance Model, and Retail Atmospherics) have overlaps and are complementary to each other. This is the first time we integrate them together into a general framework. The model can be used to generate research questions, in addition to putting studies into perspective. Secondly, with an emphasis on consumer experience, we start to embrace the so-called experiential economy. Our conceptualization of Online Shopping Experience explicitly includes components of cognition and affectivity, treating shoppers as both rational decision-makers and emotional animals. It is also a unique approach to opening the black box of online consumer experience by recognizing the dynamic, on-going, and situational nature of shopping by incorporating in-progress responses, and making it possible and easy to discern any micro-processes within stages of shopping.

However, since Online Shopping Experience is a newly defined concept, a programmatic approach is necessary to study it. Exploratory studies are undertaken to verify the initial structure of the concept using both qualitative and quantitative methods. The study reported in this chapter took a microscopic view using concurrent verbalization to observe consumers when they were interacting with web sites. The results have shown that OSE is a useful structure to study online consumer behavior. It is comprehensive and fine enough to capture the details and changes of the subjective experiences of consumers.

Several studies are needed in the future to further our understanding of online shopping experience. First, a study of the same with a stratified sample will be conducted to see any contrasting patterns among groups with different backgrounds in computer and Internet usage. Secondly, it would be interesting to compare and contrast patterns in terms of components of online shopping experience between flow experiences and non-flow experiences. We can design two situations: one is easy for shoppers to be in flow and one is not. Participants' verbalizations and navigation patterns are then compared to see if any differences exist. Third, controlled experiments will be used to systematically test effects of selected factors on people's shopping experience and experiencing of flow when shopping online. For example, a study has been planned to examine the impacts of site familiarity, task, and product factors on flow experience. The Experience Sampling Method will be used to capture "on the spot" data of shoppers' in-progress responses. After we gain more understanding, other factors can be included. To keep things simple, empirical studies conducted so far are restricted to one web site. Future research will expand to situations with multiple sites.

We believe that the studies will provide a deeper understanding into facilitating factors of optimal online shopping experience, and eventually we will be able to create this optimal experience by design, in response to the goal to "maximize flow involvement in as many people as possible" (Csikszentmihalyi, 1975, p. 203). This chapter is just a starting point of a journey of engrossing investigations and discoveries.

REFERENCES

Agarwal, R., & Karahanna, E. (2000). Time flies when you're having fun: Cognitive absorption and beliefs about Information Technology usage. *MIS Quarterly, 24*, 665-694.

Ajzen, I. (1991). The theory of planned behavior. *Organizational Behavior and Human Decision Processes, 50*, 179-211.

Aladwani, A.M., & Palvia, P.C. (2002). Developing and validating an instrument for measuring user-perceived web quality. *Information & Management, 39*, 467-476.

Babin, B.J., Darden, W.R., & Griffin, M. (1994). Work and/or fun: Measuring hedonic and utilitarian shopping value. *Journal of Consumer Research, 20*, 644-656.

Baker, J. (1986). The role of the environment in marketing services: The consumer perspective. In J. Czepeil, C. Comgramm & J. Shanaban (Eds.), *The services challenge: Integrating for competitive advantage* (pp. 79-84). Chicago, IL: American Marketing Association.

Baker, J., Grewal, D., & Parasuraman, A. (1994). The influence of store environment on quality inference and store image. *Journal of the Academy of Marketing Science, 22*, 328-339.

Baker, J., Parasuraman, A., Grewal, D., & Voss, G.B. (2002). The influence of multiple store environment cues on perceived merchandise value and patronage intentions. *Journal of Marketing, 66,* 120-141.

Barnes, S.J., & Vigden, R.T. (2002). An integrative approach to the assessment of e-commerce quality. *Journal of Electronic Commerce Research, 3*, 114-127.

Barwise, P., Elberse, A., & Hammond, K. (2002). Marketing and the Internet. In B. Weitz & R. Wensley (Eds.), *Handbook of marketing* (pp. 527-557). London: Sage Publications.

Bhattacherjee, A. (2001). An empirical analysis of the antecedents of electronic commerce service continuance. *Decision Support Systems, 32*, 201-214.

Bitner, M.J. (1992). Servicespaces: The impact of physical surroundings on customers and employees. *Journal of Marketing, 56*, 57-71.

Butler, P., & Peppard, J. (1998). Consumer purchasing on the Internet: Processes and prospects. *European Management Journal, 16,* 600-610.

Chebat, J.-C.C., & Dubé, L. (2000). Evolution and challenges facing retail atmospherics: The apprentice sorcerer is dying. *Journal of Business Research, 49,* 89-90.

Chen, H., Wigand, R.T., & Nilan, M. (1998). Optimal flow experience in web navigation. *Proceedings of Information Resources Management Association International Conference,* Boston, MA, USA, (pp. 633-636).

Chen, H., Wigand, R.T., & Nilan, M.S. (1999). Optimal experience of web activities. *Computers in Human Behavior, 15*, 585-608.

Chen, L.-d., Gillenson, M.L., & Sherrell, D.L. (2002). Enticing online consumers: An extended technology acceptance perspective. *Information & Management, 39,* 705-719.

Childers, T.L., Carr, C.L., Peck, J., & Carson, S. (2001). Hedonic and utilitarian motivations for online retail shopping behavior. *Journal of Retailing, 77,* 511-535.

Cohen, J.B., & Areni, C.S. (1991). Affect and consumer behavior. In T. S. Robertson & H.H. Kassarjian (Eds.), *Handbook of consumer behavior* (pp. 188-240). Englewood Cliffs, NJ: Prentice-Hall.

Csikszentmihalyi, M. (1975). *Beyond boredom and anxiety: Experiencing flow in work and play*. San Francisco: Jossey-Bass Publishers.

Csikszentmihalyi, M. (1988). The flow experience and its significance for human psychology. In M. Csikszentmihalyi & I.S. Csikszentmihalyi (Eds.), *Optimal experience: Psychological studies of flow in consciousness* (pp. 15-35). Cambridge, MA: Cambridge University Press.

Csikszentmihalyi, M. (1990). *Flow: The psychology of optimal experience*. New York: Harper & Row Publishers.

Csikszentmihalyi, M., & Csikszentmihalyi, I. (1988). Introduction to part IV. In M. Csikszentmihalyi & I.S. Csikszentmihalyi (Eds.), *Optimal experience: Psychological studies of flow in consciousness* (pp. 251-265). Cambridge, MA: Cambridge University Press.

Dailey, L. (2003). Navigational web atmospherics: Explaining the influence of restrictive navigation cues. *Journal of Business Research*. Retrieved July 15, 2003 online: http://www.sciencedirect.com/science/article/B6V7S-4619P3K-5/2/8bfdd608dda6dd40398dfcf069f11076.

Davis, F.D. (1989). Perceived usefulness, perceived ease of use, and user acceptance of Information Technology. *MIS Quarterly, 13*, 319-340.

Devaraj, S., Fan, M., & Kohli, R. (2002). Antecedents of B2C channel satisfaction and preference: Validation e-commerce metrics. *Information Systems Research, 13*, 316-333.

Donovan, R.J., & Rossiter, J.R. (1982). Store atmosphere - An environmental psychology approach. *Journal of Retailing, 58*, 34-57.

Donovan, R.J., Rossiter, J.R., Marcoolyn, G., & Nesdale, A. (1994). Store atmosphere and purchasing behavior. *Journal of Retailing, 70*, 283-294.

Ericsson, K.A., & Simon, H.A. (1984). *Protocol analysis: Verbal reports as data*. Cambridge, MA: The MIT Press.

Eroglu, S.A., Ellen, P.S., & Machleit, K.A. (1991). Environmental cues in retailing: Suggestions for a research agenda. *Proceedings of the 1991 Symposium on Patronage Behavior and Retail Strategy*, Louisiana State University, USA, (pp. 51-60).

Eroglu, S.A., Machleit, K.A.M., & Davis, L.M. (2001). Atmospheric qualities of online retailing: a conceptual model and implications. *Journal of Business Research, 54*, 177-184.

Finneran, C., & Zhang, P. (2002, August). The challenges of studying flow within a computer-mediated environment. *Proceedings of the 8th America Conference of Information Systems, Dallas,* 1047-1054.

Ghani, J.A. (1995). Flow in human-computer interactions: Test of a model. In J.M. Carey (Ed.), *Human factors in information systems: Emerging theoretical bases* (pp. 291-309). Norwood, NJ: Ablex Publishing Corporation.

Grossbart, S.L., Hampton, R., Ramonhan, B., & Lipidus, R.S. (1990). Environmental dispositions and customer response to store atmospherics. *Journal of Business Research, 21*, 225-241.

Grossbart, S.L., Mittelstaedt, R.A., Curtis, W.W., & Rogers, R.D. (1975). Environmental sensitivity and shopping behavior. *Journal of Business Research, 3,* 281-294.

Havlena, W.J., & Holbrook, M.B. (1986). The varieties of consumption experience: Comparing two typologies of emotion in consumer behavior. *Journal of Consumer Research, 13*, 394-404.

Hoffman, D.L., & Novak, T.P. (1996). Marketing in hypermedia computer-mediated environments: Conceptual foundations. *Journal of Marketing, 60*, 50-68.

Huang, M.H. (2000). Information load: Its relationship to online exploratory and shopping behavior. *International Journal of Information Management, 20*, 337-347.

Jones, M.A. (1999). Entertaining shopping experiences: An exploratory investigation. *Journal of Retailing and Consumer Services, 6,* 129-139.

Kim, J., Hahn, J., & Hahn, H. (2000). How do we understand a system with (so) many diagrams? Cognitive integration process in diagrammatic reasoning. *Information Systems Research, 11*, 284-303.

Kolter, P. (1974). Atmospherics as a marketing tool. *Journal of Retailing, 49,* 48-64.

Koufaris, M. (2002). Applying the technology acceptance model and flow theory to online consumer behavior. *Information Systems Research, 13,* 205-233.

Laroche, M., Saad, G., Kim, C., & Browne, E. (2000). A cross-cultural study of in-store information search strategies for a Christmas gift. *Journal of Business Research, 49*, 113-126.

Li, H., Daugherty, T., & Biocca, F. (2001). Characteristics of virtual experience in electronic commerce: A protocol analysis. *Journal of Interactive Marketing, 13*, 13-30.

Li, H., Kuo, C., & Russell, M.G. (1999). The impact of perceived channel utilities, shopping orientations, and demographics on the consumer's online buying behavior. *Journal of Computer-Mediated Communication, 5*. Retrieved March 7, 2003, online: http://www.ascusc.org/jcmc/vol5/issue2/hairong.html.

Liang, T.-P., & Lai, H.-J. (2000, January). Electronic store design and consumer choice: An empirical study. *Proceedings of the 33rd Hawaii International Conference on System Sciences, USA, 6,* 6042-6051.

Liang, T.-P., & Lai, H.-J. (2002). Effect of store design on consumer purchases: An empirical study of on-line bookstores. *Information & Management, 39*, 431-444.

Lohse, G.L., & Spiller, P. (1999). Internet retail store design: How the user interface influences traffic and sales. *Journal of Computer-Mediated Communication, 5*. Retrieved March 7, 2003, from http://www.ascusc.org/jcmc/vol5/issue2/lohse.htm.

Loiacono, E.T., Watson, R.T., & Goodhue, D.L. (2002, Winter). WebQual: A measure of web site quality. *Proceedings of the American Marketing Association: Winter Marketing Educators' Conference,* Austin, Texas, (pp. 432-438).

Machleit, K.A., & Eroglu, S.A. (2000). Describing and measuring emotional response to shopping experience. *Journal of Business Research, 49*, 101-111.

Markin, R.J., & Lillis, C.M. (1976). Social-psychological significance of store space. *Journal of Retailing, 52*, 43-54.

McKinney, V., Yoon, K., & Zahedi, F. (2002). The measurement of web-customer satisfaction: An expectation and disconfirmation approach. *Information Systems Research, 13*, 296-315.

Mehrabian, A., & Russell, J.A. (1974). *An approach to environmental psychology*. Cambridge, MA: MIT Press.

Mowen, J.C. (1988). Beyond consumer decision-making. *The Journal of Consumer Marketing, 5*, 15-25.

Neisser, U. (1967). *Cognitive psychology.* Englewood Cliffs, NJ: Prentice-Hall, Inc.

Nielsen, J. (2000). *Design web usability*. Indianapolis, IN: New Riders Publishing.

Novak, T.P., Hoffman, D.L., & Duhachek, A. (2003). The influence of goal-directed and experiential activities on online flow experiences. *Journal of Consumer Psychology, 13*, 3-16.

Novak, T.P., Hoffman, D.L., & Yung, Y.-F. (2000). Measuring the flow construct in online environment: A structural modeling approach. *Marketing Science, 19*, 22-44.

O'Cass, A., & Fenech, T. (2003). Web retailing adoption: Exploring the nature of Internet users' web retailing behavior. *Journal of Retailing and Consumer Services, 10,* 81-94.

Palmer, J. (2002). Web site usability, design, and performance metrics. *Information Systems Research, 13*, 151-167.

Palmer, J.W., & Griffith, D.A. (1998). An emerging model of web site design for marketing. *Communications of the ACM, 41*, 44-51.

Pine II, B.J., & Gilmore, J.H. (1998). Welcome to the experience economy. *Harvard Business Review, 76*, 97-105.

Schlosser, A.E. (2003). Computers as situational cues: Implications for consumers' product cognitions and attitudes. *Journal of Consumer Psychology, 13,* 103-112.

Schmitt, B.H. (1999). *Experiential marketing: How to get customers to sense, feel, think, act, and relate to your company and brands.* New York: The Free Press.

Schmitt, B.H. (2003). *Customer experience management: A revolutionary approach to connecting with your customers*. Hoboken, NJ: John Wiley & Sons.

Schmitt, B.H., Rogers, D.L., & Vrotsos, K. (2004). *There's no business that's not show business: Marketing in an experience culture.* Upper Saddle River, NJ: Financial Times Prentice Hall.

Sen, A., Vinze, A., & Liou, S.F.T. (1994). Role of control in the model formulation process. *Information Systems Research, 5*, 219-248.

Smith, D.N., & Sivakumar, K. (2003). Flow and Internet shopping behavior: A conceptual model and research propositions. *Journal of Business Research.*

Retrieved July 15, 2003 online: http://www.sciencedirect.com/science/article/B6V7S-460WN18-3/2/d7ab33a58dabb33e4f8152f5117ec3a1.

Spies, K., Hesse, F., & Loesch, K. (1997). Store atmosphere, mode and purchasing behavior. *International Journal of Research in Marketing*, *14*, 1-17.

Stone, G.P. (1954). City shoppers and urban identification: Observations on the social psychology of city life. *American Journal of Sociology, 60*, 36-45.

Szymanski, D.M., & Hise, R.T. (2000). E-satisfaction: An initial examination. *Journal of Retailing*, *76*, 309-322.

Titus, P.A., & Everett, P.B. (1995). The consumer retail search process: A conceptual model and research agenda. *Journal of the Academy of Marketing Science, 23*, 106-119.

Trevino, L.K., & Webster, J. (1992). Flow in computer-mediated communication: Electronic mail and voice mail evaluation and impacts. *Communication Research, 19*, 539-573.

Underhill, P. (1999). *Why we buy: The science of shopping*. New York: Simon & Schuster.

Venkatesh, V. (1999). Creation of favorable user perceptions: Exploring the role of intrinsic motivation. *MIS Quarterly, 23*, 239-260.

Venkatesh, V., & Davis, F.D. (1996). A model of the antecedents of perceived ease of use: Development and test. *Decision Science, 27*, 451-481.

Vijayasarathy, L.R. (2003). Shopping orientations, product types and Internet shopping intentions. *Electronic Markets, 13,* 67-79.

Wan, F., & Nan, N. (2001, September). *Web users' optimal on-line experience: An examination of the effects of web navigation design and web user motive.* Presented at Experiential 3-D E-commerce Conference, East Lansing, Michigan, USA.

Wolfinbarger, M., & Gilly, M.C. (2001). Shopping online for freedom, control, and fun. *California Management Review, Berkeley, 43*, 34-55.

Yoo, C., Park, J., & Maclnnis, D.J. (1998). Effects of store characteristics and instore emotional experiences on store attitude. *Journal of Business Research, 42*, 253-263.

Chapter III

An Expanded E-Commerce Process Model Serving E-Commerce Entrepreneurs

David Paper, Utah State University, USA

Eric Pedersen, Dixie State College, USA

ABSTRACT

In a previous study, we explored successful e-commerce small to medium-sized enterprises (SMEs) to formulate an e-commerce (electronic commerce) process model. We adopted a qualitative research method to obtain a rich description of the e-commerce process. We then interviewed 15 entrepreneurs from established SME operations. From deep analysis of this data, we were able to devise an emergent model. This study extends the original model by conducting subsequent interviews with the 15 SME entrepreneurs. Our goal was to better understand the model by exploring omitted, missing, or incomplete elements. Hence, subsequent interviews asked respondents to identify key elements of the model that may have been omitted, and if so, where do they fit in the model? Deep analysis of the subsequent data allowed us to expand the original model.

INTRODUCTION

The phenomenal growth of the Internet since the mid-1990s has fostered an explosion of electronic business on the web, known as e-commerce (Nataraj & Lee, 2002; Motiwalla & Khan, 2003). The Internet has grown from a few thousand people in 1993 to over 150 million in 1999, and is expected to grow to over a billion by 2004 (Bingi et al., 2000). Forecasts have estimated that the total value of worldwide e-commerce will exceed $400 billion by the year 2002 (IDC, 2000). Kalakota and Whinston (1997) define e-commerce as "the buying and selling of information, products, and services via computer networks" (p.3), the computer networks primarily being the Internet. The Cabinet Office (1999) expand this definition to include the use of Internet technologies (email and intranets) to exchange or share information either within the firm itself or with external stakeholders. However, hundreds of Internet companies have gone out of business in the past few years, causing tens of thousands of lost jobs and billions of squandered dollars in investment capital (Nataraj & Lee, 2002; Perotti et al., 2003). Of the failures, over half were e-commerce, and one-third were content providers. The failure of dot-coms is a staggering 75% in the first two years (Nataraj & Lee, 2002). Many of these failures were small and medium-sized enterprises (SMEs) (Bertsch et al., 2002; Daniel et al., 2002; Marquess, 2001). One of the most commonly cited reasons for failure has been lack of a workable strategic business model to guide e-commerce efforts (Glass, 2001; Marquess, 2001; Nataraj & Lee, 2002).

The original study (Paper et al., 2003) introduced an e-commerce process model for SMEs. In this study, we extend the model by returning to the respondents and asking them to identify key missing elements and how these elements might fit. We used the same qualitative methodology to obtain a more complete and rich description of the e-commerce process. Rich (or thick) description refers to thorough descriptions or details of a phenomenon that create verisimilitude and produce in the reader feelings that he or she has experienced the events described (Creswell, 1998; Denzin, 1989; Erlandson et al, 1993; Lincoln & Guba, 1985; Merriam, 1988). The interview pool consisted of the same 15 e-commerce SME entrepreneurs. From deep analysis of the new data set, we were able to extend the previous model.

This chapter includes related literature, the chosen research methodology, the research process we adopted for the original study and this study, the data analysis, the findings, and our conclusions.

RELATED LITERATURE

Strategic process research has a rich history dating back to the early 1960s (Anthony, 1965; Ansoff, 1965; Chandler, 1962). These seminal works laid the foundations for what we know today as strategic management. The focus of these early works was almost entirely on the internal aspects of the strategic process. Porter (1980a) shifted the established paradigm to an external focus with the introduction of his competitive forces model. Porter's model focused on how to strategically deal with the firm's competitive (external) forces. Porter (1980b) was also credited with introducing the value chain as a key strategic management issue. The value chain paradigm suggests that competitive advantage can be reached if an organization adopts a strategic orientation on its constituency along the value (customer-supply) chain. That is, the strategic thrust should be on manufacturing products or developing services in alignment with suppliers to satisfy customer expectations.

Resource-Based View

The resource-based view of strategy is the most introspective and is centered on the firm itself (Porter, 1991). It argues that the origins of competitive advantage are valuable resources (or core competencies) that the firm possesses. These resources tend to be intangible assets such as skills, relationships, and reputation and are seen as relatively immobile. Porter suggests that the implicit focus of this literature is on the underpinnings of successful diversification. Prahalad and Hamel (1990) suggest that successful firms are successful because they have unique resources and they nurture these resources to be successful. Porter argues that this process is circular reasoning.

Resources are not valuable unless they allow firms to perform activities that create advantages in particular markets (Porter, 1991). The competitive value of resources can be enhanced or eliminated by changes in technology, competitive behavior or buyer needs (Porter, 1996). The immobility of resources is then as much of a risk as it is an advantage because other firms in competition either have the same resources or can obtain them. Porter argues that competitive advantage is based on the specific activities an organization performs. That is, organizations really distinguish themselves by the unique manner in which their system of processes operates.

IT Foundations

Anthony's model (1965) provided the foundation for identifying conventional information systems. The model was first applied in the information management field by Zani (1970). During the 1970s and 80s, many other conceptual frameworks were developed for information systems. Gorry and Scott Morton (1971) and Keen and Scott (1978) focused on systems designed especially for managerial decision makers. King (1983a, 1983b) and Rockart (1979) concentrated on information systems planning topics. Nolan (1973, 1979) and Nolan and Gibson (1974) focused on IBM planners and the development lifecycle of large systems. Rockart and Treacy (1981, 1982) specialized in systems targeted for top managers.

IT Paradigm Shifts

The principal role of information systems in the past was that of operational and management support (Rackoff et al., 1985). This notion began to change with the publication of two seminal works (Cash & Konsynski, 1985; Rockart, 1979) that emphasized the potential use of information technology to affect the competitive position of the firm. Another paradigm shift occurred in 1988 when Henderson and Sifonis introduced the idea that strategic IS planning and strategic business planning share many commonalities. This seminal paper began the debate on the impact of IS technologies on the competitive capability of the firm. The debate centers around whether IS planning should or should not be an integral part of the strategic planning process.

Given the tremendous information technology investments currently budgeted by Fortune 500 companies, it seems natural that IS planning be a critical aspect of any strategic planning initiative (Gurbaxani et al., 2000). A related stream of research is assessing the relationship between IS investments and firm performance. Sicar et al. (2000) found that IS and corporate investments have a strong positive relationship with sales, assets, and equity, but not with net income. Gurbaxani et al. (2000) conducted a firm-level analysis of IS budgets. They found production theory could be applied to information services to yield useful insights from both a theoretical and managerial perspective. Chircu and Kauffman (2000) extend the limits-to-value model of Davern and Kauffman to explore market and process-level factors that impact value flows to firms for their IT investments. Their research enabled them to develop an IT valuation framework to assist organizations in making their investments in e-commerce pay off.

Productivity Paradox

Brynjolfsson (1993) explored the relationship between IT and productivity. Brynjolfsson was interested in finding why a productivity paradox exists related to IT investments. That is, why does investment in IT not necessarily lead to increases in productivity? Managers are increasingly questioning their huge IT investments when productivity gains are not apparent.

Brynjolfsson argues that the causes of the productivity paradox must be understood before we can learn how to remove the obstacles to higher productivity growth. One of the author's most compelling arguments is that IT investments may not be quantifiable because of the intangibles, such as better responsiveness to customers and increased coordination with suppliers. Brynjolfsson and Hitt (1998) argue that the focus should be on how to make IT more effective rather than the purely economic productivity paradox. They posit that computerization does not automatically increase productivity, but is an essential component of organizational changes that do increase productivity. Business and organizational processes must be reengineered in coordination with IT investments to increase the probability of performance increases.

Hitt and Brynjolfsson (1996) separate the issue of IT value into three dimensions: 1) the effect of IT on productivity, 2) the effect of IT on business profitability, and 3) the effect of IT on consumer surplus. The authors believe that this multidimensional approach is more realistic because, depending on one's vantage point, one, two, or all three dimensions may be important or one dimension may be more important than another. Although this stream of research is becoming more prominent, the relationship between IT investments and firm performance is still very complex and requires more research (Brynjolfsson, 1993; Brynjolfsson & Hitt, 1998; Hitt & Byrnjolfsson).

Internet and E-Commerce Adoption

During the late 1990s, the Internet came into prominence. The Internet is a special medium because it has important properties that facilitate commerce (Subirana & Carvajal, 2000). Subirana and Carvajal delineate several important properties. First, the Internet can be used 24 hours a day, 7 days a week by anyone from practically anywhere. Second, the Internet allows for a variety of interactive communications, namely email (asynchronous one-to-one communication), chat (synchronous many-to-many communication), news groups (asynchronous many-to-many communication), and even voice and video. Third, the Internet can be used to provide services combined from various providers because it allows for hyperlinks (hot links). An emerging trend is the aggregation and dis-aggregation of information-based product components (Bakos, 1998). Finally and most importantly, the Internet is very inexpensive for both the user and the service provider. The entry barriers from a technical standpoint are very low (Dewan et al., 2000). To start an Internet site, one can rent space on an Internet service provider for a small monthly fee. Since the Internet is based on open standards, one can configure an open source server at no additional costs except for technical expertise.

Also in the late 1990s, research on the success and failure of adoption of e-commerce began to appear. Businesses adopt new technologies to remain competitive (Morone, 1993) or to refresh strategy (Crossan et al., 1999). Specifically, reasons to adopt IT include expanding market reach, decreasing costs, enhancing company image, expediting information exchange with customers, providing faster response to customers, and creating new business opportunities (Chan & Mills, 2002). However, some organizations seem to manage technology successfully, while others struggle (Woiceshyn, 2000). Woiceshyn argues that the ability to learn as an organization directly influences successful adoption.

Corbitt (1997) suggests two themes that indicate success or failure of e-commerce adoption—uncertainty and equivocality. Uncertainty refers to the absence of information and equivocality refers to the existence of multiple, conflicting interpretations about a given organizational situation (Kydd, 1989). Uncertainty resolution depends on the extent of knowledge and information about the e-commerce process in question (Corbitt, 2000). Without understanding the process, managers and/or users cannot effectively conduct e-commerce. Equivocality resolution depends upon proper social interactions (i.e., discussion and debate) so that intuition, judgment, and beliefs can contribute to the enactment of a shared interpretation (Kydd, 1989).

Chan and Swatmann (1999) note that management involvement is imperative for the success of e-commerce implementation. While Roberts (1995) suggests that top management is the most influential group affecting implementation success, Chan and Swatmann (1999) suggest that process (line) managers with direct supervisory accountability and implementation responsibility are the most crucial element in ensuring success. Although it is not clear which management level is most crucial to e-commerce implementation success, it is clear that managers at all levels play an important role in the process.

The Technology Acceptance Model (TAM) (Davis, 1989; Davis et al., 1989; Igbaria et al., 1995; Seddon, 1997) has been employed in e-commerce research (Gefen & Straub, 2000). The TAM is widely used to study IT adoption and it assumes that the intention to use IT is affected by user attitude. Diffusion of Innovation Theory (Rogers, 1983; 1995) and the Theory of Planned Behavior (TPB) (Azjen, 1985) have also been used for identifying adoption variables specific to e-commerce (Tan & Teo, 2000).

Dewan et al. (2000) argue that e-commerce technologies have significantly reduced sellers' costs of collecting buyer preference information and managing multiple prices. Online sellers can now offer custom products at discriminatory prices. Further, e-commerce technologies offer significant advantages to early adopters who gain market share and profits at the expense of the conventional seller. Srinivasan et al. (2002) posit that differences in e-commerce adoption among firms can be attributed to a sense-and-respond capability (the authors term this concept as technological opportunism) of firms with respect to new technologies. Antecedent actions that promote adoption include focusing on the future, top management advocacy of new technologies in general, and moving toward an adhocracy culture from a hierarchy culture.

E-Commerce Adoption by SMEs

E-commerce is a cluster of separate innovations (Prescott & Conger, 1995; Van Slyke, 1997; White et al., 1998). With the almost ubiquitous availability of the Internet and low entry costs, smaller organizations can choose which of these innovations they make use of and in what sequence (Hamill & Gregory, 1997; Webb & Sayer, 1998; Dutta & Evrard, 1999; Poon & Swatman, 1999). The core activities of the organization help determine the types of innovations that should be adopted. For example, recruitment and advertisement will require innovations that foster external communications such as aesthetic 'static' web pages with easy access to pertinent organizational emails. In contrast, taking orders and receiving payments require more sophisticated innovations that foster back-end retrieval, database connectivity (inserting, updating, deleting, and querying capabilities), and 'dynamic' web pages that allow navigation based on interactions with users.

A limited number of studies have sought to measure the level of e-commerce adoption (White et al., 1998) or other IT adoption in SMEs (Smith, 1999). Weiss

(2000) and Ruth (2000) suggested that smaller organizations are less likely to adopt e-commerce than larger ones. The reasons most cited were lack of resources, expertise, and experience with technology. Cragg and King (1993) discovered that the strongest inhibitors to adoption for small firms were lack of IS knowledge, lack of managerial time, poor support, and limited financial resources. Ruth surveyed e-commerce activity of small companies in New Jersey and found that they were hesitant about adopting e-commerce because they were unsure of what it would take to be successful in such a venue. Locke (2000) found that 41% of New Zealand SME owners surveyed about e-commerce were still unsure about what the concept meant. In New Zealand, this is a significant finding because 99.4% of all businesses are SMEs (fewer than 100 employees) and a staggering 85% of all businesses have five employees or less (Cameron et al., 1997). An Australian study (Van Beveren, 2002) and a Malaysian study (Foong, 1999) also found that smaller organizations tend to adopt less readily than large ones.

Ein-Dor and Segev (1978) suggest that computerization is less likely to succeed in SMEs because they lack the resources of larger organizations. However, the recent and dramatic drop in hardware prices, the low entry barriers of the Internet, and the availability of user-friendly small business applications is allowing more SMEs to successful compete on the Internet (Foong, 1999).

Daniel et al. (2002) posited that adoption of e-commerce by SMEs proceeds in a set of sequential stages and that the stage of adoption depends on a set of contextual variables both at an industry and organizational level. Their positions were supported by their empirical study. Similar to adoption, it was found that small firms gain experience and knowledge in a sequence of steps or stages (Frank, 1988; Dosi, 1988; Reid & Smith, 2000). Achievement of the first stage of a project allows the organization to gain experience that can then be used to move on to the next stage of development. The process of going from one stage to the next enables the organization to gain even further experience and knowledge. Stage models are common in technology-based fields of new ventures (Drazin & Kazanijian, 1990; 1993).

E-Commerce Process

The reason why firms of any kind succeed or fail is inextricably tied to strategy (Porter, 1991). "Strategy encompasses all the major activities undertaken in the strategy process and should focus practitioners and scholars alike on what's important", that is, what drives the amount and nature of corporate success (Oliver, 2001, p. 7). An effective strategy is a careful plan or method for achieving an end. Without strategy there is no rationale for how one will achieve one's purposes (Betts, 2000). Since strategy is so important, it should be systematically derived (Van Reusen, 1996). Strategy is interdisciplinary in nature and its reach is throughout the organization (Oliver, 2001).

However, we found no research discussing the process of e-commerce in a strategic and holistic sense. This may be because e-commerce is a new field. Henderson and Sifonis (1988) present a model of the IS planning process. Although not directly related to the e-commerce process, both should share many of the same elements or themes. Their model illustrates the links between vision, strategy, goals, CSFs, strategic data models, IS products and services, and a cyclical link from these to competitive issues back to strategy. Absent from the model are web-related issues (but the Internet wasn't fully developed in 1988) and risk assessment. E-commerce research lacks a dynamic theory of strategy as exists in the management literature (Porter, 1991). Logically, businesses involved in e-commerce could follow existing strategic business models, but these models do not consider the unique potential of the web.

The Corbitt (2000) model focuses on the e-commerce process strategy. This model is limited to e-commerce management, the e-commerce group and directors, consultants, and the environmental influences. The Corbitt model does not consider critical IT issues such as technical delivery, ongoing innovation, and risks associated with new IT. The Laperche (2001) model focuses exclusively on the type of factors involved in e-commerce and the chain of creation and circulation of information. The Fahey et al. (2001) model focuses on the business processes, assets, strategy, rivals (competition), and customer solutions. Both the Laperche and Fahey et al. models focus on important aspects of the e-commerce strategic process but are not comprehensive. Bridge and Peel (1999) focus on the strategic behavior of SMEs. They explore the association between strategic planning, computer use, and types of business applications. However, their study is a one-time cross-sectional piece that only looks at whether there is a relationship between strategy and computer use. They do not discuss the strategic process of SMEs specifically. We found no literature that explores the strategic process or the e-commerce of SMEs.

Clearly, the existing literature on e-commerce strategy evolved from the business strategy and IT adoption literatures. The e-commerce strategic process has many similarities to traditional business strategy. However, we believe that the technical aspects of e-commerce provide unique challenges to establishing an effective SME strategic e-commerce process model. We therefore embarked on an exploratory study of e-commerce SMEs to derive a preliminary model of the strategic process components and their interrelationships. We returned to this study to refine and extend the model.

RESEARCH METHODOLOGY

Patton notes that qualitative methods support learning what people think and feel and are most suitable when the focus of the research is on the *process* (how) and *interactions* rather than the *outcomes* of a particular event or phenomenon. To get a balanced perspective of the human experience, we need to describe the experience of individuals as they encounter specific situations (Barritt, 1986). "Phenomenon are experiences; thus phenomenology means the study of experience" (Barritt et al.,

1985, 4, p. 19). The phenomenologist's task is to fully understand the experience from the perspective of the subject, rather than correlate it with a cause or other phenomenon (Dukes, 1984) in order to gain an *emic* perspective (Creswell, 1998). An *emic* perspective is a holistic picture (a synthesis of all aspects learned about the group and showing its complexity in a natural setting) of the social group that incorporates the views of the members in the group (Creswell, 1998).

Phenomenology should thereby give us insight into how people perceive and understand business components, the dynamic process, and the process flow of e-commerce. Since we originally wanted to explore *if successful e-commerce SMEs use a guiding strategic process model, and if they do, ask them to articulate the model components and their interrelationships*, we chose interpretative phenomenology because it offers a way to discover meaning from a group of individuals concerning a complex phenomenon (Creswell, 1998; Patton, 1990). Our revisit of the model continues to embrace the tradition of phenomenology by using the exact data collection, analysis, and synthesis process used in the first study.

Phenomenology emphasizes describing and understanding (Borch & Arthur, 1995). It adopts a *social constructivist* position that believes that the world is socially constructed (Ambrosini & Bowman, 2001; Creswell, 1998). That is, people construct their world and they can experience it as something more than a human construction. This implies that meaning cannot be 'objective' in the positivist sense because it is subjectively constructed by people (Ambrosini & Bowman; Creswell, 1998; Patton, 1990).

Phenomenology is driven by the intention to clarify and really understand the original phenomena (Schipper, 1999). As phenomenological researchers, we explore the phenomena as it is originally experienced by the people and organizations under study (Schipper, 1999). The actors' (people involved in the phenomena) definition of the situation is what is sought (Ambrosini & Bowman, 2001). This definition is constructed in and out of interaction between human beings and their world, and developed and transmitted within an essentially social context (Crotty, 1998).

Interpretive research methods have not been used widely in IS research (Orlikowski & Baroudi, 1991). However, in 1999 a special issue in MIS Quarterly laid the foundation for future interpretive field studies in IS. The unstated goal of this special issue series was to "expand the acceptance of intensive research in the information systems field and to help us all get *beyond method*" (Markus & Lee, 1999, p. 35).

The goal of interpretive research is to develop a deep understanding of the phenomenon under study (Gibbons, 1987; Orlikowski & Baroudi, 1991);that is, to answer questions about the nature of the phenomena with the purpose of describing and understanding the phenomena from the participant's point of view (Leedy, 1997). We chose phenomenology because it "fit" with our style of collecting and analyzing data.

RESEARCH PROCESS

The phenomenon we return to is the e-commerce process used by successful SME entrepreneurs. Specifically, we wish to extend the authors' original e-commerce process model (in Paper et al., 2003). The revisit analysis included fifteen follow-up interviews with the same participants approximately two years after the original set of interviews. During interview sessions, we presented the original model and asked respondents to articulate omitted, missing, or incomplete elements of the model.

Clarifying Researcher Bias

Consistent with the original study (and the edicts of phenomenology), we made an overt attempt to clarify (or bracket) bias wherever possible. The first author [DP] has extensive experience in both industry and academia and therefore has a broad and informed perspective of the business world. The second author [EP] has extensive experience in academia and consulting (with e-commerce SMEs). He also has an informed perspective of the SME world. EP's e-commerce consulting experience with the 15 organizations allowed us to gain entry.

To bracket (suspend) researcher bias that might be introduced by having EP conduct interviews with organizations with whom he has consulted, DP conducted the interviews. DP had no history or prior contact (except for the original interviews) with the respondents prior to the outset of this study. Bracketing is fundamental for setting aside all prejudgments in a phenomenological study (Creswell, 1998). We enlisted a qualified person to act as a peer reviewer. His duty was to provide an external and non-biased check of the research as requested by Ely et al. (1991), Erlandson et al. (1993), Glesne and Peshkin (1992), Lincoln and Guba (1985), and Merriam (1988). His input was ideal because he was not involved in any phase of the data collection and analysis. He is qualified because he has extensive reviewing and academic experience.

Data Collection

Interactions with the 15 SMEs began five years ago. EP has been heavily involved in commercially viable e-commerce initiatives for the past five years. After many interactions with customers and entrepreneurs, he began to suspect that e-commerce success is not an accident. His e-commerce businesses survived the dot.com fiasco in the late 1990s and are surviving the current recession. EP was interested in finding out why his e-commerce businesses succeeded while many others failed. Therefore, he teamed with DP to investigate the SME e-commerce process. EP has also consulted with many e-commerce SMEs, and he saw an opportunity to gather rich data. In early 2001, he approached the 15 SMEs with the idea of participating in this study. They all agreed to participate. We believe this to be a result of the trust he has built over the past five years with these SMEs.

While many phenomenological studies involve participants at a single site, Creswell (1998) reminds us that the key factor for participant selection is that all participants have experienced the phenomenon under investigation. The participants selected for this study all had extensive experience in the process of SME e-commerce. The researchers provided verbal informed consent, informing participants of their level of voluntary participation, confidentiality of specific corporate secrets, and the ability to withdraw from the study at any time.

DP conducted both sets of interviews (the original interviews and the return interviews for this study) since he had no prior e-commerce consulting experience and had never met any of the respondents. DP audiotaped each interview session, which lasted approximately one hour. Consistent with Yin (1994), audiotapes were transcribed within 48 hours to reduce data loss. Consistent with Creswell (1998), a set of open-ended questions was brought to the original interview sessions, but respondents were encouraged to talk about their interests, ideas, and feelings about e-commerce. A set of refined questions and the e-commerce model that emerged from the first study were brought to this study. This time, the questions centered on encouraging respondents to identify flaws and/or omissions inherent in the model.

The first set of interviews took approximately four months and began in early 2001. The return (follow-up) set of interviews took approximately three months and began in late 2002.

Data Analysis

We followed the process advocated by Creswell (1998) for both the original data set and the current one. We created and organized the data so that both researchers had the same transcripts in the same form. We then read through the text and made marginal notes to form initial codes. During the iterations, EP and DP highlighted text to expose statements of meaning and then grouped statements into meaning units or themes. Consistent with Moustakas (1994), we found statements of meaning about how individuals were experiencing the topic and gave each statement equal worth (called horizontalization of the data).

Coding Process

For the original data set, EP and DP independently conducted three coding iterations of the data. Each coding entailed a complete review of the transcripts to identify emergent themes. After each review, EP and DP would discuss the themes and reach agreement. Each theme was given a special code (of two characters) agreed upon by EP and DP to simplify the coding process. Ely et al. (1991) stress the need for an external "audit" of the research process as a method for providing credibility. Therefore, after the third and final iteration, an outside person was asked to peer-review the choice of themes. He was given a clean set of transcripts (in original form prior to the first coding iteration, with no marginal notes or coding) to reduce the chance of introducing bias into the peer review process. He made an initial read of the transcripts and verified that the themes DP and EP developed were logically derived. He also evaluated the three-step iteration process to judge if DP and EP logically reduced the data. In the final analysis, he decided that the final set of 10 themes logically emerged from the original data set and that the iteration process was properly conceived and executed. For the return study, we followed the same process of transcription, but the coding was based on the themes that emerged from the original study. Of course, there were variations from the original model that came about from analysis of the second set of data.

From the original data set, a total of 14 agreed upon themes emerged from the first coding of data—fundamental skills (FS), knowledge (KN), opportunity identification (OI), market research (MR), business research (BR), competitive assessment (CA), market assessment (MA), strategy development (SD), technical delivery (TD), web review (WR), risk assessment (RA), initial launch-implementation (IL), new innovation (NI), and on-going innovation (OG).

After the second coding, we reduced the number of themes to 11—FS and KN were merged into fundamental skills & knowledge (FK). EP and DP agreed that these two themes were consistently grouped together in the text. MR and BR were merged into MR. DP originally separated the two themes but agreed with EP that the focus of the text was on the marketing aspect. CA and MA were merged into CA. DP separated these two themes but agreed with EP that MA was really part of MR.

After the third and final coding, we reduced the number of themes to ten. EP and DP agreed that the text made it clear that NI and OG were really the same theme. After reading the text for the third time, it was obvious that new innovations are really ongoing, so we merged NI and OG into OG. Table 1 illustrates the themes that emerged from each coding. EP and DP debated theme reductions after comparing notes.

Table 1: Coding process for meaning units (themes)

Themes	***1st Iteration***	***2nd Iteration***	***3rd Iteration***
1	FS	FK	FK
2	KN		
3	OI	OI	OI
4	MR	MR	MR
5	BR		
6	CA	CA	CA
7	MA		
8	SD	SD	SD
9	TD	TD	TD
10	WR	WR	WR
11	RA	RA	RA
12	IL	IL	IL
13	NI	NI	
14	OG	OG	OG

Building the Original Model—Phase One

To enhance the credibility of the original study, we revisited each of the 15 informants. We had two purposes in mind. First, we wanted to conduct member checks (Ely et al., 1991; Erlandson et al., 1993; Glesne & Peshkin, 1992; Lincoln & Guba, 1985; Merriam, 1988; Miles & Huberman, 1994) to solicit the informants' views of the credibility of our findings and interpretations. Lincoln and Guba consider member checks to be "the most critical technique for establishing credibility" (p. 314) through the use of triangulation. Consistent with Yin (1994), we reviewed company documentation, records, and policies to further establish credibility through triangulation. Creswell (1998) includes peer review as one of the means to establish credibility through triangulation. Hence, we involved KM as a peer reviewer. Second, we wanted to show the informants how we arrived at the final 10 themes. We explained the analysis process and used Table 1 as a graphical guide. All 15 informants agreed that the 10 themes were imperative for success. They also agreed that the ten themes were the best representation of the components of the e-commerce process for SMEs.

We then asked informants to place the themes in an order that made sense with the way they conduct e-commerce. All informants agreed that fundamental skills & knowledge (FK), opportunity identification (OI), and market research (MR) should be the first three components in the process. Eleven informants placed competitive assessment (CA) and strategy development (SD) as the next two themes. The remaining four reversed the order, placing strategy development before competitive assessment. We then revisited the remaining four informants to discuss the ordering. We found that they were used to lumping competitive assessment with strategy development and misinterpreted the competitive assessment theme. After the discussion, the four agreed that competitive assessment should naturally precede strategy development. All 15 informants agreed that technical delivery (TD), web review (WR), and risk assessment (RA) should follow strategy development, in that order. Ten informants placed initial launch-implementation (IL) and on-going innovation (OG) as the remaining themes. The remaining five reversed this order. We then revisited these remaining informants to garner why they made this choice. In each case, they perceived on-going innovation as a precursor to launching an initiative. We explained to them that what was meant by this theme was post-implementation innovation, not creativity or innovative thinking prior to launch. Once they understood the definition of the theme, we obtained unanimity in the ordering.

We revisited all informants with the fully ordered theoretical model (Figure 1) to elicit their opinions. They were unanimous in expressing excitement toward the model. That is, they agreed with the themes and ordering and thought it to be a profound and useful model for anyone involved in the e-commerce process. From the three coding iterations to arrive at the themes, member checking, and a final visit with the complete model, we believe that we reached an *emic* perspective; an understanding from *their* eyes. From the data-analysis process, we identified emerg-

Figure 1: Original e-commerce model

ing themes that provide insightful understanding of how e-commerce entrepreneurs experience the successful process of e-commerce.

Refining the Model — Phase Two

The return study enabled us to refine the model (Figure 2). First, we were able to add a new category—finance development. Second, we changed the ordering in the process of risk assessment. Third, we added comments and questions answered for each category. All of these refinements emerged from the return transcripts in the same manner as the original model emerged. The richer descriptions offered by returning for another round of interviews established a more complete model of successful SME electronic commerce processes.

FINDINGS

Initially, we set out to explore *if successful e-commerce SMEs use a guiding strategic process model, and if they do, to ask them to articulate the model components and their interrelationships*. From careful analysis of the original data set, the model in Figure 1 emerged. We then returned to the original respondents for a second round of interviews with the purpose of refining the model. Our goal was to adjust

Figure 2: Revised e-commerce model

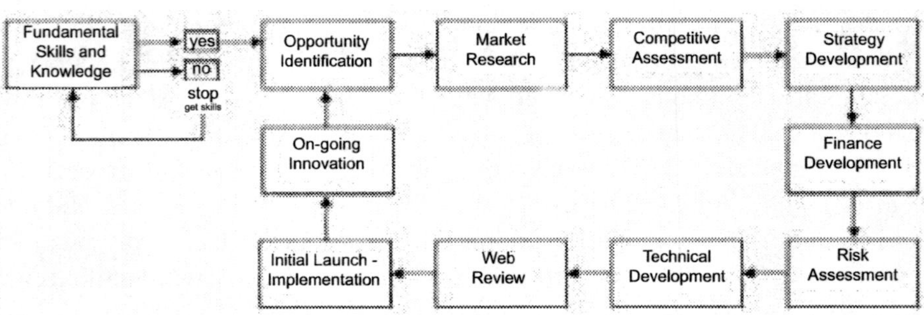

the model for possible key omissions. We believed that once the respondents had a chance to review the original model, they would identify errors or omissions, given sufficient time between the interview cycles. This section articulates the components of the model with refinements added in each resulting from the return analysis.

Fundamental Skills and Knowledge

The model begins with this component. Both sets of interviews revealed that an e-commerce entrepreneur must possess a basic understanding of Internet use and Internet connectivity in order to maximize success. Without a basic knowledge of how to use the Internet and how the Internet infrastructure works, the entrepreneur places him- or herself at a distinct disadvantage. Phrases in the transcripts such as "without the fundamentals of the Web, we would be out of business," "basic [Internet] skills allow us to conduct business more smoothly," "I didn't know anything about the technical aspects of the Web, that's what I pay others for. But I at least understand how it works and how a customer can navigate," and, "if I didn't understand the basics, I wouldn't be able to help our designers improve customer navigation," helped us develop this theme.

The ***STOP*** in Figures 1 and 2 provide a message to not move onto the second component without first understanding the Internet. Phrases such as "My past failings on the Web were because we didn't understand the technology. We thought that we could just move a business to the Web. Boy were we wrong," "I recommend to anyone starting an Internet business to stop and think about the differences of Web business before looking at opportunities," and "Stop and think. Do you understand Web technology ... if not, you're probably going to fail before you start," led us to add the **STOP** to the model.

Opportunity Identification

The purpose for the e-commerce initiative reported by each informant varied. For instance, some informants wanted to sell products, while others wanted to generate revenues through advertising dollars. Some wanted to provide services and some wanted to provide online customer support or patient information. Identifying and clarifying the business opportunity was unanimously agreed to be the first step of the process (if the skills and knowledge of the web are present) and was supported by the data. "Once you have an idea or opportunity you want to explore, you must do some preliminary research about the idea," " ... ideas are great, but you need to focus on what are the best opportunities for being competitive on the Web," " ... we knew what we wanted to do but we had to make sure that the opportunity would work electronically," and " ... before we went ahead, we asked ourselves: Is the opportunity real? Does it match our strategic business plan? Do we have the resources? Can we make a profit?" Another comment was, "is the opportunity real?"

Market Research

Market research follows opportunity identification and is more comprehensive and specific in nature. As one informant described it:

Market research requires one to dig deeply into the details of the idea/opportunity theme and answers questions such as:
What specifically will I offer (product, services, etc.)?
Who are the target consumers (include demographic profiles, age, sex, income, etc.)?
What is the market size and where do I fit into the market?
What value will I offer to customers?
What exactly does the customer want and at what price?
Are there potential customers I know and trust to test my specific proposals on?
What business model and strategy will be used?
What competitive advantages do I have?
What advantages do my competitors have?
How will the company generate revenues?

Other respondents suggested that " ... market research shows that you understand the market you are trying to enter and demonstrates an ability to enter the market" and " ... market research is to be able to explain how to enter the market, secure a niche, maintain a market share and achieve the stated financial projections."

Competitive Assessment

A competitive assessment is really an awareness of who the competitors are in the marketplace. "When we conduct a competitive assessment, we explain the strengths and weaknesses in relation to our competitors in our [market] niche." "Competitive assessment can only be conducted after the [market] research ... it is like a SWOT analysis with our competitors." "The competitive assessment helps us form a plan to deal with our competitive weaknesses and hopefully take advantage of competitors' weaknesses."

Competitive assessments are simply " ... a systematic way of evaluating and scoring a web site". The information you get from a competitive evaluation can help you determine where competitors are strong and where they are weak, what you need to do to be competitive in the marketplace and areas you need to strengthen, improve, or highlight as a strength.

Strategy Development

Strategy involves using one's advantages and minimizing one's weaknesses. " ... strategy is key to Web startup and implementation and governs our course of action." "Strategy should permeate any e-commerce initiative because without it, you have no roadmap to guide efforts." "Strategy must be systematic and based upon your competitive assessment." "Competitive assessment and strategy should be tightly coupled."

An overriding theme that emerged was that the development and implementation of an SME e-commerce strategy was the key to success. That is, an entrepreneur should come to understand that success in the e-commerce environment is driven by strategy. The notion that competitive assessment and strategy must be tightly coupled to ensure a systematic development and implementation of strategy also emerged.

Finance Development

The omission of finance development in the original model was clearly an oversight. Upon review, every SME interviewee discussed revenues, costs, and financial management issues. Many of the SME entrepreneurs discussed methods of financing their electronic commerce initiatives in terms of debt-free, equity only for start-up, and debt financing as part of the mixture of capital development in their organization. All interviewees agreed that adding the category was critical to a successful electronic commerce process.

Some of the comments included, "one to three year budget projections are a must," "sweat equity is very important and also very easy to secure in an e-commerce business," and "limited or minimum capital is a good beginning."

Risk Assessment (and Reduction)

The change in position of Risk Assessment in the model was an overwhelming concern during the return interview cycle. Some participants suggested that one should address risk elements throughout the process and that it would be difficult placing it in a specific place in the process. Others suggested risk assessment should be placed near finance development and somewhere close to strategy development. All interviewees, in the end, agreed that placing risk assessment immediately following finance development in the process was appropriate.

Risk is exposure to possible loss or injury (Phillips, 1997). From the transcripts we found that most of the successful e-commerce initiatives that are still in business approached risk from a conservative, long-term approach to identifying, minimizing, and managing risk. "Risk is even more of an issue with our company because we don't have deep pockets. We tend to be conservative." "We can't afford too much risk because we are relatively small in terms of budget flexibility." "We have to be conservative with money because we have few shareholders, a lot of competition, and tight operating margins."

Risk reduction permeated the text. Here are the comments from one informant:

The greatest risks are most often the technical and human risks. Can the technology do what we want it to do? Do we have technically skilled people who can write code or put together systems to accomplish business goals? Much of what is developed for an electronic commerce company involves human intellectual capital and computer and information technology or equipment.

One overriding risk reduction strategy is the use of sweat equity. " ... give people ownership by providing stock based upon a pre-agreed performance level. As owners, they have a stake in the outcome." "Have a contract with the new owners so they won't so easily leave. As owners, they have a say in what goes on." "Sweat equity can be used for initial startup, opportunity, market, and risk assessments." " ... sweat equity can be used to develop and design the initial technology solution or capability, the web site, initial sales and marketing, etc." "By following a well-prepared and conceptualized startup plan; much of the initial company startup activities can be 'free' to the company by using sweat equity concepts."

Partnering can also reduce risk. "You can partner with an organization that already has the equipment, networking infrastructure or facilities. This can drastically reduce equipment and facilities risks and overall startup dollars needed."

The text revealed that equipment is a bargain. "Never try to save money on equipment. Equipment is very cheap when compared to personnel." "Build growth capability into the initial equipment purchases." "Don't be cheap on the basics such as servers, routers, computers, network lines, and software."

Hiring good people is also important. "If you select good people initially, you limit the number of stockholders to those individuals who are part of the startup and committed to corporate success because they are also owners." "Hire good people and avoid debt as much as possible." "Refuse to be tempted by highly leveraged capital, in spite of what might be taught in MBA classes."

Using open source technology is good strategy. "There is no cost to acquire open source technologies. We can use these savings in other critical areas. Of course there are people costs associated with open source solutions, but there is no evidence that these costs are any higher than those of proprietary solutions." "We've found that open source is much cheaper and more effective in the long run." "We love open source, but if your company has limited technical capabilities, proprietary solutions may be the way to go."

Technical Delivery

Technical delivery encompassed the artistic, technical, and business elements related to web site design. "We need artists because the technology alone won't attract customers to our site." "I hire technical people to code and maintain the Web server. I hire people with graphics and artist experience to help the aesthetics of our site. We want to appeal to our customers in a media that has a lot of competing sites." "Very few people can handle technical and artistic assignments, so I have at least one of each on a project delivery team." " ... yes, we use the term technical delivery because designing a site isn't enough. Delivery means that it is designed and ready to be reviewed."

We learned from the transcripts that the more an e-commerce entrepreneur understands about the artistic, technical, and business implementations, the better the resulting web site design. We also learned that excellent web site design should be a combined effort between web programmers, artists, and business developers.

Web Review

"Once delivered, the Web site must be reviewed by an independent body that acts as the user or customer. We used to review our own sites, but that was disastrous." "We independently review our site. This has helped us considerably to reduce the risk of failure." "We don't consider delivery complete until we have a third party review our site for design issues especially. It's hard for them to review the site with our strategy in mind because they don't know our business." "Review early and often." "Reviewing is an important step to keeping the process systematic." "We have found that our independently reviewed sites have done better than our old ones [that were not reviewed] because our customers keep coming back."

Web review appears to be a critical step after the site is designed and ready for delivery. Review allows an objective party to look over what you've done and make positive suggestions for improvement. It is clear that review can also help reduce business risk because an unprofessional site is not a good way to attract and keep customers happy.

Initial Launch and Implementation

In the text, we found many elements concerning a comprehensive startup plan and the implementation of such a plan. We coded these elements within the theme of initial launch and implementation of the e-commerce site. We interpreted from the text that these elements, socially constructed from the informants, improve the chances of success when launching an e-commerce site. The elements were low to zero start-up risk (LZSR), projected financial statements (PRFS), securing capital with minimal risk (SCMR), no debt financing (NODF), significant sweat equity of team members at or before launch or start-up (SETM), business structure that includes stock for key personnel (BSKP), equity financing that matched exit strategies over time (EFMS), personal risk assessments of team members (PRAT), selection of key team members (SKTM), and securing key team members commitment (SKTC).

Informants generally agreed that LZSR, SCMR, NODF, SETM, BSKP, EFMS, and SKTM were critical to a successful launch. "A wise and disciplined startup team is critical to make sure the e-commerce process is a success." "Without a good team, the project will fail. To make the team happy, we gave them ownership through stocks and other types of profit sharing." "Teams are key, but cheap capital without too much debt is essential." "Too much debt will kill a start up, but we also count on a good team of people to pull us through the tough times." "The most important issues related to startup are securing a good team, operating with low debt, and giving your people ownership so that their sweat means something to them." "We sweat the big things, but our teams must sweat with us. We secure our people with stocks and profit sharing. Low debt is also important even with low rates." "I have failed before because I got into debt troubles so this is number one. A close second is our people's sweat. Give them a reason to work hard through owning a piece. Financing must match the overall business plan and strategy." "Strategy must be capitalized properly to the business. People ownership is next."

Although PRFS, PRAT, and SKTC were less pervasive in the text than the other seven elements, some of the informants found them important. "Financial statements should project potential earnings even in a start up venture." "Sometimes projected financial statements are just as important as strategy and team development." "We secure teams by conducting personal risk assessments. We need to have some way to evaluate the best team members." "Ownership increases team member commitment to the cause." "Get ownership first, but evaluation is also key to maintaining good teams." Table 2 illustrates the elements of each theme in relation to informants' transcripts. The blank cells show elements not in the text of an informant's transcript, while the dot (•) shows that the text mentioned the element in some form.

On-Going Innovation

The text provided evidence that e-commerce initiatives must continue to innovate, change, and adapt in order to remain competitive. "Continuous innovation has kept us competitive. It seems that we have no choice in the current environment." "Innovate, innovate, innovate are the three things you must do to survive in the e-commerce world." "We find ourselves reengineering our processes so frequently that we never seem to stop changing and tweaking. We have found this to be our edge." "Change is part of the e-commerce world regardless of the industry. We hire people that are willing to keep learning and thrive in an ever-changing environment." "Adapt and change. That's what we expect out of our people and team projects." "I can't remember what it's like to be in a slowly changing environment. I don't know anyone in our business that remains in our business without being able to adapt and change with the technology and market." "Out with the old, in with the new."

We opined from our analysis that successful e-commerce initiatives must continue to improve and re-engineer with an attitude of constant innovation to adapt in an ever-changing world of technology and electronic business.

CONCLUSION

Our original goal was to explore if successful e-commerce SMEs use a guiding strategic process model, and if they do, what the model components and their interrelationships are. Strictly adhering to the methodological edicts of phenomenology,

Table 2: Elements in the IL theme.

Elements	1	2	3	4	5	6	7	8	9	10	11	12	13	14	15
LZSR	•	•	•	•		•	•		•	•	•	•	•	•	•
PRFS	•				•					•			•		
SCMR		•	•		•	•	•	•	•	•		•		•	
NODF	•		•		•	•	•	•	•	•	•		•	•	
SETM	•	•	•		•	•	•		•	•	•		•	•	•
BSKP		•	•	•	•		•	•	•	•	•		•	•	•
EFMS		•		•		•	•		•	•		•	•		•
PRAT	•							•					•		
SKTM	•	•	•	•	•	•	•	•	•	•	•	•	•	•	•
SKTC	•			•						•			•		•

we were able to socially construct a preliminary model of the SME e-commerce process. We were also able to articulate the order of the e-commerce process and some of the important interrelationships between the components. The goal of the return study was to revisit the original model to test for omissions or errors. The results of the return study indicated that the model was valid for the most part, but needed a few adjustments to be more realistic.

Each of the respondents in the return study agreed that the model was improved from its initial development. The follow-up interviews provided a clearer outline of the positioning of the categories and specific elements and the addition of a new one. One participant suggested the model improved from about 85-90% complete in the initial study to more than 95% complete because as a result of the return study.

REFERENCES

Ajzen, I. (1985). From intentions to actions: A theory of planned behavior. In J. Kuhl & J. Beckmann (Eds.), *Action control: From cognition to behavior* (pp. 11-39). Springer-Verlag.

Ambrosini, V., & Bowman, C. (2001). Tacit knowledge: Some suggestions for operationalization. *Journal of Management Studies, 38*(6), 811-829.

Ansoff, H.I. (1965). *Corporate strategy: Techniques for analyzing industries and competitors*. New York: McGraw-Hill.

Anthony, R.N. (1965). *Planning and control systems: A framework for analysis*. Boston, MA: Harvard University Press.

Bakos, J.Y. (1998). The emerging role of electronic marketplaces on the Internet. *Communications of the ACM, 41*(8), 35-42.

Barritt, L.S. (1986). Human science and the human image. *Phenomenology + Pedagogy, 4*(3), 14-21

Barritt, L., Beekman, T., Bleeker, H., & Mulderij, K. (1985). *Researching education practice*. Grand Forks, ND: University of North Dakota Press.

Bertsch, T., Busbin, J., & Wright, N. (2002). Gaining competitive advantage in e-tailing through marketing management and value-added uses of technology. *Competitiveness Research, 12*(2), 49-56.

Betts, R.K. (2000). Is strategy an illusion? *International Security, 25*(2), 5-51.

Bingi, P., Mir, A., & Khamalah, J. (2000). The challenges facing global e-commerce. *Information Systems Management, 17*(4), 26-34.

Borch, O.J., & Arthur, M.B. (1995). Strategic networks among small firms: Implications for strategy research methodology. *Journal of Management Studies, 32*(4), 419-439.

Bridge, J., & Peel, M.J. (1999). A study of computer usage and strategic planning in the SME sector. *International Small Business Journal, 14*(4), 82-87.

Brynjolfsson, E. (1993). The productivity paradox of Information Technology. *Communications of the ACM, 36*(12), 67-77.

Brynjolfsson, E., & Hitt, L.M. (1998). Beyond the productivity paradox. *Communications of the ACM, 41*(8), 49-55.

Cabinet Office, The. (1999). *e-commerce@its.best.uk.* The Performance and Innovation Unit, UK.

Cameron, A., Massey, C., & Tweed, D. (1997). New Zealand small business: A review. *Chartered Accountants Journal of New Zealand, 4*, 4-12.

Cash, J.I., Jr., & Konsynski, B.R. (1985). IS redraws competitive boundaries.*HarvardBusiness Review*, *63*(2), 134-142.

Chan, C., & Swatman, P.M.C. (1999). B2B E-commerce implementation: The case of BHP Steel. *Conference Paper*, RMIT University, Melbourne.

Chan, Y.P., & Mills, A.M. (2002). Motivators and inhibitors of e-commerce technology adoption: Online stock trading by small brokerage firms in New Zealand. *Journal of Information Technology Cases and Applications*, *4*(3), 38-56.

Chandler, A.D. (1962). *Strategy and structure: Chapters in the history of the industrial enterprise*. Cambridge, MA: MIT Press.

Chircu, A.M., & Kauffman, R.J. (2000). Limits to value in electronic commerce-related IT Investments. *Journal of Management Information Systems*, *17*(2), 59-80.

Corbitt, B.J. (1997). Implementing policy for homeless kids in schools: Reassessing the micro and macro levels in the policy debate in Australia. *Journal of Education Policy*, *12*(3), 165-176.

Corbitt, B.J. (2000). Developing intraorganizational electronic commerce strategy: An ethnographic study. *Journal of Information Technology*, *15*(2), 119-130.

Cragg, P., and King, M. (1993). Small-firm computing: Motivators and inhibitors. *MIS Quarterly*, *17*(1), 47-60.

Creswell, J.W. (1998). *Qualitative inquiry and research design*. Thousand Oaks, CA: Sage.

Crossan, M.M., Lane, H.W., & White, R.E. (1999). An organizational learning framework: From intuition to institution. *Academy of Management Review, 24*(3), 522-537.

Crotty, M. (1998). *A narrative approach to organization studies*. London: Sage.

Daniels, E., Wilson, H., & Myers, A. (2002). Adoption of e-commerce by SMEs in the UK. *International Small Business Journal*, *20*(3), 253-270.

Davis, F.D. (1989). Perceived usefulness, perceived ease of use, and user acceptance of Information Technology. *MIS Quarterly*, *13*(3), 319-340.

Davis, F.D., Bagozzi, R.P., and Warshaw, P.R. (1989). User acceptance of computer technology: A comparison of two theoretical models. *Management Science*, *35*(8), 982-1003.

Denzin, N.K. (1989). *Interpretive interactionism*. Newbury Park, CA: Sage.

Dewan, R., Jing, B., & Seidmann, A. (2000). Adoption of Internet-based product customization and pricing strategies. *Journal of Management Information Systems*, *17*(2), 9-28.

Dosi, G. (1988). Sources, procedures and microeconomic effects of innovation. *Journal of Economic Literature*, *26*(3), 1120-1171.

Drazin, R., & Kazanijian, R.K. (1990). Research note and communications. A re-analysis of Miller and Friesen's life cycle data. *Strategic Management Journal*, 11(4), 319-325.

Drazin, R., & Kazanijian, R.K. (1993). Applying the DEL technique to the analysis of cross classification data: A test of CEO succession and top management TeamResearch note and communications. A re-analysis of Miller and Friesen's life cycle data. *Strategic Management Journal*, *11*(4), 319-325.

Dukes, S. (1984). Phenomenological methodology in the human sciences. *Journal of Religion and Health*, *23*(3), 197-203.

Dutta, S., & Evrard, P. (1999). Information Technology and organisation within European small enterprises. *European Management Journal*, *17*(3), 239-251.

Ein-Dor, P., & Segev, F. (1978). Organizational context and the success of management information systems. *Management Science*, *24*(10), 1067-1077.

Ely, M., Anzul, M., Friedman, T., Garner, D., & Steinmetz, A.C. (1991). *Doing qualitative research: Circles within circles*. New York: Falmer.

Erlandson, D.A., Harris, E.L., Skipper, B.L., & Allen, S.D. (1993). *Doing naturalistic inquiry: A guide to methods*. Newbury Park, CA: Sage.

Fahey, L., Srivastava, R., Sharon, J.S., & Smith, D.E. (2001). Linking e-business and operating processes: The role of knowledge management. *IBM Systems Journal*, *40*(4), 889-907.

Foong, S. (1999). Effect of end-user personal and system attributes on computer-based information system success in Malaysian SMEs. *Journal of Small Business Management*, *37*(3), 81-87.

Frank, M.Z. (1988). An intertemporal model of industrial exit. *Quarterly Journal of Economics*, *103*(2), 333-344.

Gibbons, M.T. (1987). Introduction: The politics of interpretation. In M.T. Gibbons (Ed.), *Interpreting politics*. New York: New York University Press.

Glass, R.L. (2001). What can we learn from the dot-com debacle? *The DATA BASE for Advances in Information Systems*, *32*(2), 8-10.

Glesne, C., & Peshkin, A. (1992). *Becoming qualitative researchers: An introduction*. White Plains, NY: Longman.

Gorry, A., & Scott Morton, M. (1971). A framework for management information systems. *Sloan Management Review*, *13*(1), 55-70.

Gurbaxani, V., Melville, N., & Kraemer, K. (2000). The production of information services: A firm-level analysis of information systems budgets. *Information Systems Research*, *11*(2), 159-176.

Hamill, J., & Gregory, K. (1997). Internet marketing in the internationalisation of UK SMEs. *Journal of Marketing Management*, *13*(1-3), 9-28.

Henderson, J.C., & Sifonis, J.G. (1988). The value of strategic IS planning: Understanding consistency, validity, and IS markets. *MIS Quarterly*, *12*(2),

186-200.

Hitt, L.M., & Brynjolfsson, E. (1996). Productivity, business profitability, and consumer surplus: Three different measures of Information Technology Value. *MIS Quarterly*, *20*(2), 121-142.

IDC. (2000). E-commerce market forecasts. Online: *www.nua.ie/surveys.*

Igbaria, M., Guimareas, T., & Davis, G.B. (1995). Testing the determinants of microcomputer usage via a structural equation model. *Journal of Management Information Systems*, *11*(4), 87-114.

Kalakota, R., & Whinston, A. (1997). *Electronic commerce: A manager's guide.* Reading, MA: Addison-Wesley.

Keen, P., & Scott Morton, M. (1978). *Decision support systems: An organizational perspective.* Reading, MA: Addison-Wesley.

King, W. (1983a). Achieving the potential of decision support systems. *Journal of Business Strategy*, *3*(3), 84-91.

King, W. (1983b). Strategic planning for MIS. *MIS Quarterly*, *2*(1), 27-37.

Kydd, C.T. (1989). Understanding the information content in MIS management too. *MIS Quarterly*, *13*(3), 277-381.

Laperche, B. (2001). The hidden face of electronic commerce between enterprises. *Information & Communications Technology Law*, *10*(3), 273-283.

Leedy, P.D. (1997). *Practical research planning and design* (6th ed.). Prentice-Hall.

Lincoln, Y.S., & Guba, E.G. (1985). *Naturalistic inquiry*. Beverly Hills, CA: Sage.

Locke, S. (2000). SMEs remain relatively resilient-for now. *NZ Business*, (July), 20-22.

Markus, M.L., & Lee, A.S. (1999). Special issue on intensive research in information systems: Using qualitative, interpretive, and case methods to study Information Technology—Forward. *MIS Quarterly*, *23*(1), 35-38.

Marquess, K. (2001). Crash and learn. *ABA Journal*, *87*(2), 42-47.

Merriam, S. (1988). *Case study research in education: A qualitative approach*. San Francisco, CA: Jossey-Bass.

Miles, M.B., & Huberman, A.M. (1994). *Qualitative data analysis: a Sourcebook of new methods,* 2nd ed.. Thousand Oaks, CA: Sage.

Mintzberg, H. (1991). The effective organization: Forces and forms. *Sloan Management Review*, *32*(2), 54-67.

Mintzberg, H., & Lampel, J. (1999). Reflecting on the strategy process. *Sloan Management Review*, *40*(3), 2-30.

Morone, J.G. (1993). Technology and competitive advantage – The role of general management. *Research-Technology Management*, *2*, 16-25.

Motiwall, L.F., & Khan, M.R. (2003. Financial impact of e-business initiatives in the retail industry. *Journal of Electronic Commerce in Organizations*, *1*(1), 55-73.

Moustakas, C. (1994). *Phenomenological research methods*. Thousand Oaks, CA: Sage.

Nataraj, S., & Lee, J. (2002). Dot-com companies: Are they all hype? *SAM Advanced Management Journal*, *67*(3), 10-14.

Nolan, R. (1973). Plight of the EDP manager. *Harvard Business Review*, *51*(3), 143-152.

Nolan, R. (1979). Managing the crises in data management. *Harvard Business Review*,*57*(2), 115-126.

Nolan, R., & Gibson, C. (1974). Managing the four stages of EDP growth. *Harvard Business Review*, *52*(1), 76-88.

Oliver, R.W. (2001). Real-time strategy: What is strategy anyway? *The Journal of Business Strategy*, *22*(6), 7-10.

Orlikowski, W. J., & Baroudi, J. J. (1991). Studying Information Technology in organizations: Research approaches and assumptions. *Information Systems Research*, *2*(1), 1-28.

Paper, D., Pedersen, E., & Mulbery, K. (2003). An e-commerce process model: Perspectives from E-commerce entrepreneurs. *Journal of Electronic Commerce in Organizations*, *1*(3), 28-49.

Patton, M.Q. (1990). *Qualitative evaluation and research methods* (2nd ed.). Newbury Park, CA: Sage.

Perotti, V., Sorce, P., & Widrick, S. (2003). An exploratory study of operant conditioning theory as a predictor of online product selection. *Journal of Electronic Commerce in Organizations*, *1*(1), 42-54.

Phillips, J.T. (1997). Do electronic objects create business risk? *Records Management Quarterly*, *31*(1), 37-41.

Poon, S., & Swatman, P.M.C. (1999). An exploratory study of small business Internet commerce issues. *Information and Management*, *35*(1), 9-18.

Porter, M.E. (1980a). *Competitive strategy: Techniques for analyzing industries and competitors*. New York: Free Press.

Porter, M.E. (1980b). *Competitive strategy: Creating and sustaining competitive advantage*. New York: Free Press.

Porter, M.E. (1991). Towards a dynamic theory of strategy. *Strategic Management Journal*, *12,* 95-117.

Porter, M.E. (1991). What is strategy? *Harvard Business Review*, *74*(6), 61-79.

Prahalad, C.K, & Hamel, G. (1990). The core competence of the corporation. *Harvard Business Review*, *68*(3), 79-92.

Prescott, M., & Conger, S. (1995). Information Technology innovations: A classification by IT locus of impact research approach. *The Database for Advances in Information Systems*, *26*(2-3), 20-41.

Rackoff, N., Wiseman, C., & Ullrich, W.A. (1985). Information systems for competitive advantage: Implementation of a planning process. *MIS Quarterly*, *9*(4), 285-294.

Reid, G.C., & Smith, J.A. (2000). What makes a new business start up successful? *Small Business Economics*, *14*(3), 165-182.

Roberts, B. (1995). *Report for BT supply management EDI implementation review*.

Rockart, J. (1979). Chief executives define their own data needs. *Harvard Business Review*, *57*(2), 81-92.

Rockart, J., & Treacy, M. (1981). *Executive information systems.* Center for Information Systems Research, CISR Working Paper Number 65, Massachusetts Institute of Technology, Cambridge, Massachusetts.

Rockart, J., & Treacy, M. (1982). The CEO goes on-line. *Harvard Business Review*, *60*(1), 82-88.

Rogers, E.M. (1983). *Diffusion of innovations* (3rd ed.). New York: The Free Press.

Rogers, E.M. (1995). *Diffusion of innovations* (4th ed.). New York: The Free Press.

Ruth, J-P.S. (2000). So far small biz is only dabbling in e-commerce. *Business News New Jersey*, *13*(23), 24.

Schipper, F. (1999). Phenomenology and the reflective practitioner. *Management Learning*, *30*(4), 473-485.

Seddon, P.B. (1997). A respecification and extension of the DeLone and McLean model of IS success. *Information System Research*, *8*(3), 240-253.

Sircar, S., Turnbow, J.L., & Bordoloi, B. (2000). A framework assessing the relationship between Information Technology investments and firm performance. *Journal of Management Information System*, *16*(4), 69-97.

Smith, J.A. (1999). The behaviour and performance of young micro firms: Evidence from businesses in Scotland. *Small Business Economics*, *13*(3), 185-200.

Srinivasan, R., Lilien, G.L., & Rangaswamy, A. (2002). Technological opportunism and radical technology adoption: An application to e-business. *Journal of Marketing*, *66*, 47-60.

Straub, D.W., Keil, M., & Brenner, W. (1997). Testing the technology acceptance model across cultures: A three county study. *Information and Management*, *33*, 1-11.

Subirana, B., & Carvajal, P. (2000). Transaction streams: Theory and examples related to confidence in Internet-based electronic commerce. *Journal of Information Technology*, *15*(1), 3-6.

Tan, M., & Teo, T.S.H. (2000). Factors influencing the adoption of Internet banking. *Journal of Association for Information Systems*, 1(5), 1-42.

Van Beveren, J., & Thomson, H. (2002). The use of electronic commerce by SMEs in Victoria, Australia. *Journal of Small Business Management*, *40*(3), 250-253.

Van Reusen, A.K. (1996). The self advocacy strategy for education and transition planning. *Intervention in School and Clinic*, *32*(1), 49-55.

Van Slyke, C. (1997). The diffusion of technology cluster innovation: The case of the Internet. Paper presented to *Americas Conference on Information Systems*, Indianapolis, 15-17 August, URL (consulted March 2002).

Webb, B., & Sayer, R. (1998). Benchmarking small companies on the Internet. *Long Range Planning*, *31*(6), 815-827.

Weiss, M. (2000). Manufacturers not making full use of tech. *Atlanta Business Chronicle*, *22*(54), 20.

White, M.D., Abels, E.G., & Gordon-Murnane, L. (1998). What constitutes adoption on the web: A methodological problem in assessing adoption of the World Wide Web for electronic commerce. *Journal of the American Society for Information Science*, *35*, 217-266.

Woiceshyn, J. (2000). Technology adoption: Organizational learning in oil firms. *Organization Studies*, *21*(6), 1095-1118.

Yin, R.K. (1994). *Case study research: Design and methods*. Thousand Oaks, CA: Sage.

Zani, W. (1970). Blueprint for MIS. *Harvard Business Review*, *48*(6), 95-100.

Previously published in the Journal of Electronic Commerce in Organizations, 1(3), 28-47, July/Sept, 2003.

Chapter IV

Internet Shopping Model and Customer Perceptions: A Study of UK Supermarkets

Xianzhong Mark Xu, University of Portsmouth, UK

Martyn Roberts, University of Portsmouth, UK

ABSTRACT

A major growth area in electronic commerce (EC) is organisations that directly interact with their customers (Business to Consumer EC). The supermarket sector is at the forefront of this development. However, it has been widely reported that e-retailing for grocery shopping, for example, Webvan, particularly in the U.S., has not been successful. Little empirical evidence is documented to reveal whether customers shopping patterns have significantly changed toward Internet shopping. By using a case study approach and a questionnaire survey, this study reports the Internet shopping models adopted by the major UK supermarkets, and examines consumer shopping behaviour and their attitudes toward the Internet for grocery shopping.

INTRODUCTION

The grocery retail industry has traditionally had a rather complex trading and logistic structure and manual processes. E-Commerce has provided a great opportunity for substantial cost saving and shortening or eradication of supply chains (Ng et al.,

1998). Early application of using trading networks in the grocery retail industry was based on electronic data interchange (EDI). EDI automated basic business transactions, resulting in faster and less error prone transactions (Norris et al., 2000). For example, goods spend less time in depots and arrive fresher at supermarkets (Seth & Randal, 1999). It has been seen that most supermarkets in the U.S. and the UK embraced the Internet and now offer their customers the facility to shop online, together with delivery services (Kinsella, 2000). Pure play Internet grocery retailers have emerged, yet reported failures in many cases (Ring & Tigert, 2001). In the UK, online grocery shopping with major supermarkets has become prevalent and appears successful; for example, Tesco, the UK's largest grocery retailer, claimed that it already made profit from its online sales in 2001. Tesco's success has been widely cited in most recent research (Reinhard, 2001; Ring & Tigert, 2001; Tanskanen et al., 2002). UK supermarkets are looking to entice shoppers into buying more than the basics and are exploring new ideas and innovations to make grocery shopping more interesting.

The benefits of using the Internet by merchants have been widely discussed, that is, improved inventory control, customization of offering, quick delivery to customers and online advertising (Spar & Bussgang, 1996; Poon, 2000). With regard to online grocery shopping, it is speculated that online shopping offers supermarkets not only the opportunity to gain new customers, but also to improve customer loyalty and customer services. However, little empirical evidence is documented to reveal how the logistic model used to support the online channel is justified from the company managers' point of view.

The aim of this study is to develop further understanding of Internet shopping in the supermarket sector by examining:

1) How do supermarkets as merchants offer online shopping services with a focus on the picking-up model?
2) How do customers perceive the Internet shopping channel compared to the conventional supermarket shopping?

LITERATURE REVIEW

A few recent studies on e-retailing and online grocery shopping, which are based primarily in the U.S., have been reported. These studies are briefly reviewed in order to help refine the focus of our investigation, and to form a base for follow-up discussion and comparison.

Ring and Tigert (2001) assert that the online grocery industry has not achieved success. In particular, pure play Internet grocery retailers can hardly survive compared to traditional "brick and mortar" food retailers. This is mainly due to substantial operating costs that make the pure Internet grocery retailers less competitive, and lack of a profitable business model and customer base. They argue that Internet grocers dramatically overestimated the size of the market for grocery shopping from home. Although their argument is substantiated with evidence drawn from Internet Grocer Webvan and Peapod's failures, it cannot be considered without examining other types of online grocery shopping, for example, the Internet shopping channel launched by existing supermarkets. In another study, Starr (2003) took a step further to examine the cost and revenues that led to demise of the Internet Grocer Webvan. His study revealed that Webvan's failure centred on its large investment in building the modern distribution centers (DC), and its under-utilization of warehouse capacity, mismanagement of the supply chain, and also the high cost of switching customers to Internet shopping. However, Petco.com (PETsMART.com) and drugstore.com are cited as examples of successfully accommodating online selling and shipping issues. The former uses existing in-store facilities to handle picking-up and delivery, showing an example of blending Internet and in-store capabilities; the latter provides a successful example of taking orders via the Internet and allowing customers to pick-up in the retail store. These studies suggest that the pick-up and delivery approach seems critical to formulate the business model of Internet grocery shopping.

Another stream of studies concentrates on online consumers' behaviours, perceptions and benefits of grocery shopping. Jarvenpaa and Todd (1997) studied U.S. consumer reactions to Internet shopping, and found that consumers do not entirely appreciate the new way of shopping as speculated. For example, consumers are impressed by the breadth of stores on the web but disappointed with the depth and prices of merchants' offerings; consumers feel Internet shopping is generally enjoyable, but at the same time frustrating; goal-directed shopping is proved difficult although consumers perceive the potential for time savings. Consumers have negative responses to customer services on the WWW. Jarvenpaa and Todd's (1997) study sheds lights on consumer reactions to online shopping in general, but not specifically to online grocery shopping. However, much of their findings have been confirmed by recent studies. Alreck and Settle (2002_a) surveyed 1800 U.S. consumers on the role of time perception of shopping, and found that both Internet shopping and catalogue shopping are perceived to be more time saving than other forms of shopping—for example, television shopping. However, respondents use Internet and catalogue shopping very infrequently compared with other practices.

Morganosky and Cude (2002) conducted a longitudinal study of online food shopping in ten U.S. markets, and report that a majority of respondents in all three of the studies cited convenience as the most important motivational driver for using the online grocery shopping service. Saving time has also been perceived as important. The reasons for no longer using online shopping include moving out of the area, new competition moving into the area, online system too slow, delivery personnel and cost of the services. Surprisingly, security is not reported as a concern by U.S. consumers. This appears to be different from UK consumers' views, as reported by Dennis et al. (2002) from a survey-based study, that online shoppers are concerned with the security and payment aspects of buying goods online. However, in a U.S.-based study, Udo (2001) did report that privacy and security are the main impediments to Internet shopping. In descending order of importance, he reveals U.S. consumers' concerns are: privacy, security and trust, impersonation and forged identify, child protection, electronic mail safety and censorship.

Another impediment to Internet shopping, particularly for UK consumers, is access to the Internet. This is uncovered by Saran (2002), who conducted a quarterly survey of 1,006 UK consumers from a variety of social and economic backgrounds on utilisation of the Internet for shopping. The study shows that 43% of correspondents did not have access to the Internet at home, while 50% did not own a person computer.

The profile of online grocery shoppers is also portrayed in various studies. Morganosky and Cude (2002) describe that compared to the general population, online shoppers were better educated, had relatively higher incomes, and tended to be somewhat younger. In terms of gender of online shoppers, Morganosky and Cude (2002) suggest that they were predominantly female. However, based on a questionnaire survey of 300 U.S. men and women consumers, Alreck and Settle (2002_b) report that the male and female attitudes toward Internet shopping are roughly the same. Women tend to regard shopping as a fairly social and pleasurable activity, whereas men have a general aversion to shopping. Women have a more positive image of store shopping and catalogue shopping than men.

In summary, the literature review suggests the following speculation: the Internet shopping model appears critical to the success of e-retailing for grocery shopping; consumers' profiles, the motivation and concerns of online grocery shopping have not been generally agreed upon. This triggers the need to further examine the Internet business models and customers' views of shopping groceries on the Internet.

METHODOLOGY

A case study approach is used to explore the supermarket online shopping model. The two largest UK supermarkets Sainsbury and Tesco, are chosen, because the two companies use different picking-up models, which significantly distinguish the two types of online grocery shopping. The study is based primarily on secondary data sources, largely from the two companies' web sites, company internal reports and consultants' reports.

Studying the consumer's perception on traditional and online supermarket shopping is based on a questionnaire survey that is conducted primarily in three cities in the South of England. The questionnaire was distributed electronically (via email) to 210 contacts of the authors. The criteria for selecting the sample is that the person contacted owns a PC and/or had ready access to the Internet. 160 valid responses were received, which represents a 76 percent response rate. The questionnaire was initially piloted on 10 persons to ensure clarity and reliability.

Table 1: Demographic profile of respondents

Age Range	***Frequency***	***%***	***Male***	***%***	***Female***	***%***	***Average weekly spending in grocery shopping (£)***
Under 25	83	51%	58	36.3%	25	15.6%	23.19
26-35	48	30%	29	18.1%	19	11.9%	39.47
36-45	14	9%	11	6.9%	3	1.9%	63.92
46-55	9	6%	5	3.1%	4	2.5%	63.33
Over 56	6	4%	4	2.5%	2	1.3%	41.66
Total	160	100%	107	67%	53	33%	

The results from the pilot study are excluded from the analysis. The demographic profile of the respondents is given in Table 1.

The authors acknowledge that the sample seems biased towards a younger age and male dominated group. However, as De Kare-Silver (2000) indicates, these people are usually confident in the use of new technologies. The dominance of males in the sample (67 percent) is consistent with the argument that one of the key challenges of World Wide Web—based shopping is the male-dominated user base, although primary household shoppers are predominantly female (Jarvenpaa & Todd, 1997; Morganosky & Cude, 2002). Care was taken to include females in the sample since they are a specific target group for Internet shopping by the grocery retailers. For example, Tesco has invested 12 million pounds over three years in a web site aimed at the more mature women with a family who might be tempted to do their shopping at home (FT_a, 2000).

Table 2: Access to the Internet

Access to the Internet	***Frequency***	***% Percentage N = 160***
Home	50	31.3
College	39	24.4
Work	30	18.8
Internet Cafes	17	10.6
Library	12	7.5
Other	8	5.0
Total	156	97.5

The sample's weekly spending on grocery shopping confirms the age range of the respondents, that is, the relatively young and perhaps without families group spends less than 20 pounds, and the more elderly age groups tend to spend more. 97.5 percent of the sample had access to the Internet, as shown in Table 2. One-third of the respondents access the Internet from home. The other two popular access routines to the Internet are from the workplace and university/colleges.

The findings are reported in the next two sections.

SUPERMARKETS' BUSINESS MODEL FOR INTERNET SHOPPING

The main grocery supermarkets in the UK are Tesco, Sainsbury, Asda, Somerfield, Waitrose, Iceland, Safeway, and Morrison. Most of the supermarket companies have invested in electronic shopping. However, the difference remains in whether they select goods directly from the shelves of local outlets (in-store picking up) or whether they set up dedicated "Picking Centres (DC)" in addition to the existing stores. The two models are depicted in Figure 1.

Tesco: In-Store Picking Up Model

The In-Store Picking Up model is adopted by Tesco supermarket. Tesco is the largest grocery retailer in the UK, with 255 superstores, 220 supermarkets and 48 neighborhood stores. It is the first in the UK to provide Internet shopping services—Tesco.com—to its home shopper in 1996. Tesco's Internet Shopping is

Figure 1: Supermarket Internet shopping model

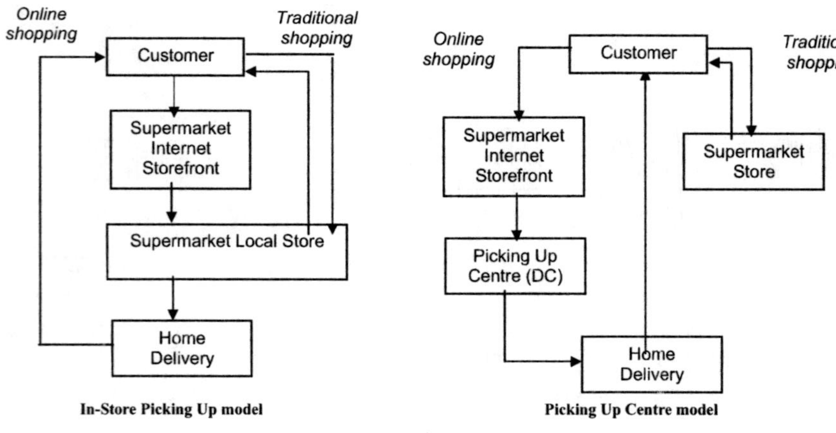

represented by Tesco Home Shopper, which is a computer program that allows customers to choose and order almost any product in stock at a local Tesco store from the Internet and to have their orders delivered to their home. Customers have access to about 20,000 different stocked items and can place their orders at any time of day or night. Tesco provides the software the customer will need on CD-ROM. This includes a database of products and prices, which the customer can browse offline to make up the order. Customers can update product and price lists by downloading a small file stored on the Tesco Home Shopper Customer Support web site. The orders are then sent via the Internet to the local branch for picking up and home delivery. The items are picked off the shelves by Personal Shoppers. The personal shoppers use a specially-equipped shopping cart with a display unit, which gives them the best routes through the store and a list of the items to be picked as they go down each aisle. Items are scanned as they're dropped into each customer's tray. Once the shopping cart is filled, the trays are loaded directly into the delivery vans that are ready and waiting behind each store. Any items that have been substituted are carefully placed on the top of each order so they can be reviewed and accepted or rejected when the order is delivered. Orders are delivered in a time slot chosen by the customers between 8.30 a.m. and 9.30 p.m. The delivery charge for each order is five pounds.

The purpose of adopting an in-store based model is for customers to have a shopping experience that is consistent with that of physically shopping at a local Tesco store, and also to increase inventory turnover and operational efficiency. The advantages of using its existing store base have been justified by the managers of Tesco.com (Seybold, 2002):

- Customers prefer to purchase online from the store in which they would normally shop in person, thus receiving the same price for each item online as the price in the store nearest their home.
- Track consumers' shopping patterns; identify each customer's favourite products to avoid being out of stock of needed items.
- Permit regional pricing variations to be maintained in order to react to competitors' price changes.
- Can pick any products from the whole store range (about 20,000-25,000 product lines) without restricting the number of lines available from a distribution center.
- No need to build new picking centers, thus avoiding heavy investment in infrastructure.
- Roll out the service faster than the picking up center model.

Ring and Tigert (2001) comment on Tesco's in-store model by stating that Tesco's net margins are about five times higher than those in the U.S., and the concentration of UK population and industry makes it more economic for Tesco to promote the services using national media than the U.S. chains that are mainly regional. Compared to Webvan, Reinhardt (2001) argues that Tesco.com benefits from the reputation of the parent company.

Sainsbury: Picking-Up Centre (DC) Model

Sainsbury uses a Picking Up center model. The strategy is to build dedicated picking centres (like the U.S. DC for Internet Grocers) with a primary aim to serve large urban areas or potential new customers. Sainsbury has struggled with growth and profits due to fierce competition in supermarkets. In response, it has refurbished and extended stores nationwide, has developed new information systems to improve Business-to-Business transactions (Global Netexchange) and has developed an electronic shopping service—Sainsbury To You (www.sainsburystoyou.co.uk)–as Sainsbury's Internet shopping channel. Sainsbury has opened a 120,000 sq. ft. picking centre at Park Royal, northwest London, with a stock capacity of 15,000 products and the capacity to deliver them to any home within the London Orbital Motorway (i.e., M25). This is Europe's largest and most technologically advanced grocery picking center. Sainsbury's To You covers over 50% of UK households through opening another medium to large-sized picking center in Manchester. Customers places their grocery order via the Internet, payment is by credit card and the orders are pulled off every two hours. Orders are downloaded and automatically routed to the closest picking up center according to postcode. Sainsbury also uses computer-controlled order picking techniques to enhance the picking accuracy in an effort to improve customer satisfaction. Products are selected off the shelves by specially trained Orderline Shoppers. The picking center acts much like any other Sainsbury's retail stores, in that it orders its stock (15,000 product lines) from one of the group's conventional distribution warehouse. Sainsbury outsources transportation for product delivery, and the cost of each delivery is five pounds.

The picking center model is also adopted by Wal-Mart controlled Asda supermarket giant. A range of 6000 items of food and non-food products are available via Asda's "Asda@home" site. The Internet shopping services are available in five metropolitan clusters around Lancashire, west Yorkshire, the Midlands, the SouthEast and Glasgow. Customers can place their orders via the Internet, phone or fax and groceries will be delivered the next day within a two hour time slot agreed upon with the customer. There is a 3.50 pounds per delivery charge, but delivery is free for orders over 99 pounds, which is more competitive than Tesco's and Sainsbury's.

The picking up centre model has been justified by Sainsbury's marketing director that offering Internet shopping through picking centres does not have to disrupt existing stores. The company can service a wider area, spread costs over that area, target potential new customers, and reduce the cost of picking the product. Other advantages include completely focusing on the home shoppers. Dedicated picking systems and staff that are uninterrupted by the store operation will greatly reduce handling errors. This achieves scale of economy due to the capacity to handle a much greater number of Internet shopping orders than stores, and also drives costs down through automation and improved accuracy of processing customer orders.

The main benefits of using picking centers are emphasized by Asda's e-commerce director that the picking-up centre would ensure that the online channel is not conflicting with their core customers in the main stores and also ensuring good availability and product quality, as well as an efficient delivery service.

It is worthy of noting that the picking-up center adopted by Sainsbury and Asda supermarkets looks the same as the U.S. distribution center used by Webvan, but they are not the same concept in terms of Internet shopping model. Webvan is a pure play web-based grocery retailer, whereas Sainsbury and Asda are "click and mortar" models, that is, existing supermarkets with Internet shopping channels. This "click and mortar" model enables greater advantages than pure e-grocery retailer in brand reputation, customer bases, and consumer trust.

Intercept Model and Cluster Model

An alternative picking-up model—"Intercept Model"—has not been seen in the UK supermarket sector, but is reported in use in Belgium and the U.S. (Ring & Tigert, 2001). This is a delivery system that does not directly deliver groceries to the customers' home, but to several "pick-up" points for consumers to collect their orders. It is reported that GIB (Belgium) delivers online ordered groceries to 18 "pick-up" points in the greater Brussels market from GIB warehouse, and the trucks stay "on station" from 4 p.m. to 9 p.m. for customers to pick up from on their way home. Shoplink in Boston uses a similar model to GIB to deliver orders to the parking lots of customers' business buildings at the end of the day. Tanskanen et al. (2002) argue that unattended reception of goods could reduce home delivery costs, and thus suggest a "Clusters Model" similar to the "Intercept Model". This is to build a refrigerated reception box at the customer's location, or shared reception box clusters for unattended delivery. The clusters can even be located in an office building parking lot for people to load their groceries into their car when leaving for home. The two models are depicted in Figure 2.

In summary, both picking-up models can benefit from using advanced information technology to improve online picking-up/delivery effectiveness and efficiency. However, the in-store picking-up model appears to be pursuing a strategy of maintaining customer retention and customer loyalty, since it targets customers in the existing market, whilst the picking-up center model appears to be pursuing a strategy of market expansion, since it targets a group of new customers through minimising the disruption to the existing stores. The in-store picking model may have a high level of cannibalization of their brick and mortar store sales, whilst the picking-up centre certainly needs a high investment in infrastructure. It is suggested (Tanskanen et al., 2002) that in early phases, picking from an existing store is clearly the least expensive alternative. When sales volume grows, picking from a dedicated center becomes less expensive. This will happen when e-grocery sales volumes reach between 2 million euro and 5 million euro per annum. The cost of

Figure 2: Intercept model and cluster model

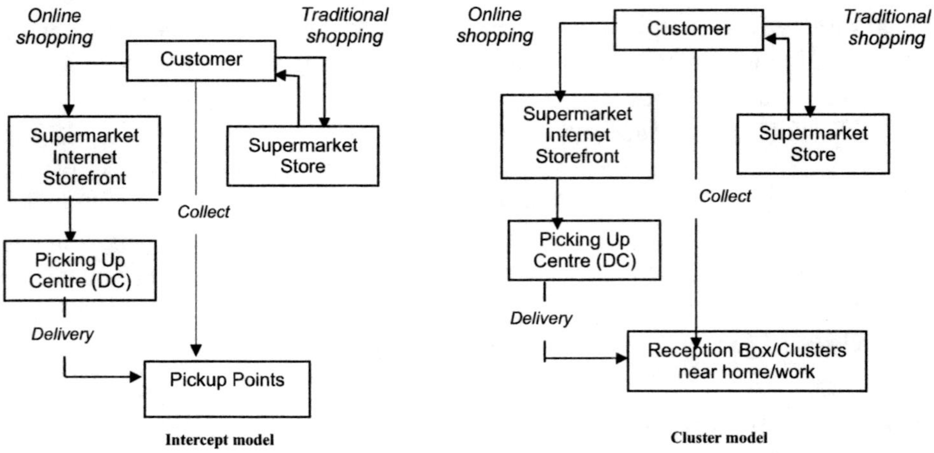

picking at this volume becomes less than 17 percent of the total value of the goods. When sales exceed 10 million euro, the cost of order assembly at a pick center is about 10 percent of the total sales value.

CUSTOMERS' PERCEPTIONS ON GROCERY SHOPPING

Perceptions On Conventional Supermarket Shopping

This study firstly examined what factors are important in affecting customers' preference for a particular supermarket. The results are presented in Table 3.

Table 3: Factors affecting consumers shopping preference

Factors	***Responses***	***Percent (%) N = 160***
Prices	135	84
Quality	95	59
Convenience	80	50
Accessibility	38	24
Service Provided	25	16
Choice & Range of Products	20	13

The data indicates that price is the most important factor in determining which stores customers to go. This is followed by products/services quality and convenience. This confirms Jeff Bezos's (founder of Amazon) remarks that "a retailer needs to be excellent in all the areas that customers are interested in—like prices, selection, easy of use (convenience) and services, if it is to be successful" (FT_b, 2000).

Reasons in Favour of Conventional Shopping

About 40 percent of the responses are in favour of conventional shopping. Twenty percent describe that they enjoy going to supermarkets because they want to find bargains; product price seems sensitive for grocery shopping. Fifteen percent indicate that they like to choose food through the variety and new products that are available. De Kare-Silver (2000), based on Kalchas's research, suggests that products which traditionally need to be touched, tasted or smelled are prima facie less likely to sell well online. However, products and services without those characteristics will have electronic appeal. This is in line with Ring and Tigert's (2001) argument that for many shoppers, seeing, touching, and smelling are important in shopping for fresh foods. Ten percent of the responses are related to social aspect of shopping, that is, shopping with family members, meeting friends, etc.

Reasons for Disliking Conventional Shopping

Sixty-six percent (107 persons) of the sample responded that they did not enjoy shopping in supermarkets. As shown in Table 4, most of the respondents believe supermarket shopping is rather time-consuming and tiring; a necessity which can be described as a chore. Some respondents made comments that support Doyle's (1998) argument that conventional shopping is often a chore, frustrating and un-enjoyable.

Perceptions on Online Supermarket Shopping

Jarvenpaa and Todd (1997) report that there is a mixed view about Internet shopping; that is, some people who are positive about Internet shopping are also

Table 4: Reasons for disliking shopping in supermarkets

Reasons	***Responses***	***Percentage (%)*** ***N = 160***
Time-Consuming	42	26.3
Tiring	33	20.6
Necessity	20	12.5
Too Many People	8	5.0
Shopping Alone	4	2.5
Total	107	66.9

negative. They suggest that individuals hold mixed views of shopping on the Internet and tested whether their views are not necessarily related to general demographic characteristics. Our study reveals that there is no one single overwhelming reason for or against Internet shopping for groceries. Respondents perceived the potential benefits of Internet shopping but also expressed concerns of stepping toward Internet shopping.

Reasons Against Internet Shopping

The survey shows that 16 percent of the respondents (26 persons) have bought products or services from the Internet; among those, only 7.5 percent (12 persons) have shopped from a supermarket Internet site, although 39 percent (62 persons) have visited supermarket Internet sites. It appears that current usage of the Internet for grocery shopping is among a small group of users. This is in line with Tanskanen et al.'s (2002) argument that in Europe, there have been very few dot.com e-groceries, and none of them have seriously challenged conventional supermarket chains. Brick and mortar retailer chains have dominated the development of electronic grocery shopping in Europe. Even in the U.S., online grocery shopping is still in its infancy, with only 10 percent of online shoppers reporting that they purchased grocery items online (Food Marketing Institute, 2000; quoted by Morganosky & Cude, 2002).

According to the 12 (7.5%) respondents who made a purchase from a supermarket Internet site, Tesco is the most preferred Internet site for grocery shopping. Because of this very small sample size, it is impossible to establish whether the Tesco Internet shopping model is perceived better than other models. As revealed early in this study, consumers mainly look for quality products with cheap prices from traditional supermarkets, but seek convenience, time saving and a better deal from Internet shopping (will be discussed later). It can be speculated that consumers are not interested in the difference between the 'In-store picking up' model and the 'Picking-up centre' model. In other words, their shopping behaviour and attitudes may not directly relate to the supermarkets' Internet shopping model, but relate to what benefits resulted from that particular model. The reasons against Internet shopping are outlined in Table 5.

Security concern is the most important reason given by respondents for not buying groceries online. This supports Dennis et al.'s (2002) assertion that UK shoppers are concerned about security and payment aspects of buying online. Despite the fact that investment and trials in technological infrastructure are moving fast and security is one area where advances are being made (De Kare-Silver, 2000), consumers appear to lack confidence in Internet security. As widely expected, they are particularly concerned with privacy (personal information), secured transactions and payment processing on the Internet, and repudiation, that is, denial of order or payment being made or received.

Table 5: Reasons against Internet shopping

Reasons	***Responses***	***Percent (%) N = 160***
Security concern	84	52.5
Cannot Judge Quality	28	17.5
Delivery Charges	25	15.6
Lack of Social Contact	23	14.4
Better Prices in Stores	14	8.8
No Interest	6	3.8
Lack of Knowledge	4	2.5
Internet Charges	3	1.9

Not being able to display a variety of products is another disadvantage expressed by respondents. Although most of the supermarket sites include a huge variety of products available for Internet shopping, it seems that the feeling that the consumers have in a supermarket store surrounded by thousands of packages and products is not the same as the one that they have in front of their computer desktop. For example, consumers can make impulse purchases by walking the aisles, and select items that were not on the pre-planned shopping list (Ring & Tigert, 2001). This survey reveals that 17.5 percent of the respondents indicate that product quality cannot be judged on the Internet. This is particularly true when using the Internet for grocery shopping. Jarvenpaa and Todd (1997) examined consumers' perception on products on the Internet, and reported that product variety is viewed positively for the web as a whole but not for individual merchants because of a lack of product depth. However, the responses generated in our study do not support Komenar's (1997) argument that with grocery shopping, many transactions are repeating purchases and the brand name alone is often sufficient to provide re-assurance of quality in order for consumers to do their shopping with confidence. It can be agreed with Sterne (1999) that many of the new home shopping methods are not suitable for selling all products. For many products, such as groceries, the goods have to be delivered specially, not left on the doorstep, which makes home delivery more expensive.

It is interesting to note that delivery charges and better prices in stores are the reasons that prevent potential customers from using online shopping. This can be explained by Ring and Tigert's (2001) early study that low price is always the first or second most important determinant of store choice in grocery shopping. Our data confirms Jarvenpaa and Todd's (1997) finding that 20 percent of respondents said they expected to see lower prices on the web. They were also concerned about additional charges and were surprised not to find better deals. The finding is in line with the assertion that some consumers are price-sensitive and do not value the increased convenience provided by the WWW (Rigdon, 1995).

Table 6: Reasons for Internet shopping

Reasons	***Responses***	***Percent (%)*** ***N = 160***
Convenience	34	21.3
Time Saving	21	13.1
Better Prices	15	9.4
More Variety	6	3.8
Total	76	47.5

It is confirmed that lack of social contact is a major limitation for Internet grocery shopping and e-commerce in general. Our early discussion suggests that conventional supermarket shopping offers opportunities for gaining social experiences.

Reasons for Internet Shopping

With only 7.5 percent of the respondents having actually shopped from the supermarket Internet sites, it is a little unexpected that 47.5 percent of the responses are in favor of changing from traditional grocery shopping to Internet shopping. The underlying reason appears to be that Internet shopping would help them avoid some of the negative aspects of conventional shopping. Table 6 shows the details:

The data indicate that convenience and time saving (21.3 percent and 13.1 percent) are the main reasons that make the respondents think positively of using the Internet for home grocery shopping as opposed to visiting the supermarket/superstore. In addition, respondents comment that the great advantage of Internet shopping is to assist busy working persons/families. This confirms De Kare-Silver's (2000) argument that Internet shopping might offer advantages to the demanding modern consumer, who is often described as overworked, stressed and time-poor, and who will probably respond positively to the virtual store that can deliver satisfactorily. Finding good deals (9.4 percent responses) from the supermarket virtual store is another incentive for whose who are price sensitive; however, neither Tesco nor Sainsbury attempts to make online products cheaper than products in the brick and mortar stores.

In addition, 19 respondents comment that home delivery brings great convenience for people who dislike grocery shopping. This particularly reflects a group of people as suggested by Komenar (1997) who do not have to travel to stores to pick up goods, despite subscription and delivery costs. This finding supports Jarvenpaa and Todd's (1997) argument that effort reduction and convenience are the most salient reasons to shop on the World Wide Web.

As Doyle (1998) observed, virtual stores are open 24 hours a day, seven days a week and they are particular suitable for busy consumers who have the opportunity to spend more time on more rewarding pursuits. Also, those who dislike grocery shopping will have the option to buy products from a distance without going to supermarkets.

CONCLUSION

This study has revealed various business models adopted by the UK major supermarkets and a mixed view of consumers toward Internet shopping for groceries. A significant number of people will stick to conventional supermarkets for grocery shopping because of the nature of social contacts and the need to touch and feel products. However, there are a great number of consumers who see Internet shopping as beneficial, and their attitude would change toward Internet shopping, although current purchasing from the Internet is surprisingly low. The main driving forces of grocery shopping online are convenience and time savings, but consumers are sensitive on product price, delivery charge and Internet access costs, which could become great obstacles for luring more customers into Internet shopping. The deepest concern on Internet shopping is security. Consumers were wary of giving out their credit card details and expressed lack of confidence in the supermarkets' ability to keep their personal details confidential. Difficulty in judging quality and freshness of products and losing social contacts and experiences are also affecting factors preventing people from switching to Internet shopping.

Internet shopping seems well established and available to a large and growing section of the population, but the supermarkets have only scratched the surface. The implication of this study is that supermarkets' e-commerce strategy needs to be reshaped in light of better understanding of customers' attitudes and perceptions in both traditional and Internet shopping. It can be suggested that the current e-commerce strategy adopted by the supermarkets could retain a small group of consumers who seek convenience and time savings from Internet shopping and home delivery. In order to gain more Internet shoppers, in a short or intermediate term, supermarkets should focus on increasing product variety and improving visualisation of multiple quality dimensions, and providing better offers through reducing product price and removing delivery charges. There are a large number of potential Internet shoppers who are price sensitive and their expectation is that Internet shopping should offer a better deal. Internet shopping could allow lower prices owning to lower costs for merchants, lower costs per customer contact, and lower maintenance costs. In particular, in choosing which picking-up model to use for the virtual store, one should consider not only the efficiency of operations, but also value added to the customers. In the long range, the success will depend on the development of advanced Internet security protocols—for example, secured transaction and payment processing, consumer confidence, as well as improved e-commerce legal environment and IT infrastructure for easy Internet shopping, for example, legislation on privacy protection, repudiation, and free Internet access.

The results generated from this survey need to be interpreted with caution, mainly due to limited access to the merchants' data and the limited sample selected in the south of England. Particularly, only 7.5 percent of respondents actually made purchases from the supermarkets' Internet sites; this makes rigorously examining the relationship between consumer shopping behaviour/perception and supermarket Internet shopping model/strategy impossible. Further studies can be conducted in this direction based on experienced Internet shoppers. Despite the limitations, this study is one of the first focusing on consumer perceptions on both traditional and Internet shopping in the supermarkets sector in the UK. Most of the results confirm the findings reported from U.S. based studies, which suggest that consumers in general hold similar views toward Internet shopping regardless of industry and individual characteristic differences.

REFERENCES

Alreck, P.L., & Settle, R.B. (2002a, September). The hurried consumer: Time-saving perceptions of Internet and catalogue shopping. *The Journal of Database Marketing, (UK), 10*(1), 25-35.

Alreck, P.L., & Settle, R.B. (2002b). Gender effects on Internet, catalogue and store shopping. *The Journal of Database Marketing, (UK), 9*(2), January, 150-162.

De Kare-Silver, M. (2000). *e-Shock 2000*. London: Macmillan.

Dennis, C., Harris, L., & Sandhu, B. (2002). From bricks to clicks: Understanding the e-consumer. *Qualitative Market Research: An International Journal, (UK), 5*(4), 281-290.

Doyle, D.P. (1998). *Adding value to marketing – The role of marketing in today's profit-driven organization*. London: Kogan Page.

Food Marketing Institute. (2000). The e-tail experience: What grocery shoppers think about online shopping. Washington, DC: FMI.

$FT_{a.}$ (2000). Tesco to Invest $18 millions in women's website. *Financial Times*, 20 June.

$FT_{b.}$ (2000). Obsessed with customer service and experience. *Financial Times*, 02 February.

Jarvenpaa, S.L., & Todd, P.A. (1997). Consumer reactions to electronic shopping on the World Wide Web. *International Journal of Electronic Commerce, 1*(2), Winter, 59-88.

Kinsella, R. (2000). Profits in store for e-supermarkets. *Financial Management*, October, 4.

Komenar, M. (1997). *Electronic marketing*. Chichester, UK: Wiley.

Morganosky, M.A., & Cude, B.F. (2002). Consumer demand for online food retailing: Is it really a supply side issue? *International Journal of Retail & Distribution Management, (UK), 30*(10), 451-458.

Ng, H., Pan, Y.J., & Wilson, T.D. (1998). Business use of the World Wide Web: A report on further investigations. *International Journal of Information Management, 18*(5), 291-314.

Norris, M., West, S., & Gaughan, K. (2000). *eBusiness essentials*. Chichester: Wiley.

Poon, S. (2000). Business environment and Internet commerce benefit – A small business perspective. *European Journal of Information Systems, 9*, 72-81.

Reinhardt, A. (2001). Tesco bets small – and wins big (Tesco's online shopping venture). *Business Week*, (USA), (October), 14-19.

Rigdon, J.E. (1995). Blame retailers for web's slow start as a mall. *Wall Street Journal*, August 16, B1-B6.

Ring, L.F., & Tigert, D.F. (2001) Viewpoint: The decline and fall of Internet grocery retailers. *International Journal of Retail & Distribution Management, (UK), 29*(6), 264-271.

Saran, C. (2002). Consumers are not inspired by the Internet. *Computer Weekly*, (UK), February, 16.

Seth, A., & Randall, G. (1999). *The grocers*. London: Kogan Page.

Seybold, P. (2002). Shopping online at Tesco. Online source: Business Line, Financial Daily from the Hindu Group Publications. Available online: *http://www.blonnet.com/catalyst/2002/03/07/stories.*

Spar, D., & Bussgang, J.J. (1996). The net rules. *Harvard Business Review*, (May/June), 125-133.

Starr, M.K. (2003). Application of POM to e-business: B2C e-shopping. *International Journal of Operations & Management, (UK), 23*(1),105-124.

Sterne, J. (1999). *World Wide Web marketing*. Wiley.

Strader, T.J., & Shaw, M.J. (1997). Characteristics of electronic markets. *Decision Support Systems, 21,* 185-198.

Tanskanen, K., Yrjöla, H., & Holmström, F. (2002). The way to profitable Internet grocery retailing – Six lessons learned. *International Journal of Retail & Distribution Management, (UK), 30*(4), 169-178.

Udo, G.J. (2001). Privacy and security concerns as major barriers for e-commerce: A survey study. *Information Management and Computer Security, (UK), 9*(4), 165-174.

Previously published in the Journal of Electronic Commerce in Organizations, 1(2), 32-43, Apr/June, 2003.

Chapter V

A Psychographic Approach to Segmenting the Electronic Shopper

Leo R. Vijayasarathy, Colorado State University, USA

ABSTRACT

Shopping Orientations are psychographic measures that have been used to discern consumers' preferences for shopping media. In this study, shopping orientations and their relationship with consumers' actual use and intention to use online shopping are examined. Data for the study were collected through a survey that was mailed to a stratified sample of 800 consumers. Usable responses were received from 281 survey participants, who were classified into three shopping segments—home, community, and apathetic—based on their shopping orientations. The three shopping segments were found to differ on online shopping measures. Specifically, the home shopping segment was found to be positively associated with online shopping in contrast to the community and apathetic shopping segments. Further analysis revealed that there were no significant associations between shopping segments and commonly used demographic variables including gender, age, income, and education. Implications of these findings are discussed, along with suggestions for future research.

INTRODUCTION

A popular approach to studying the phenomenon of online shopping has been the adoption of intention-based theories, including the theory of reasoned action (Fishbein & Ajzen, 1975), theory of planned behavior (Ajzen, 1985, 1989), and the technology acceptance model (Davis, 1989; Davis et al., 1989). These theories model an individual's intent to engage in a behavior as a function of his/her salient beliefs and attitudes towards the behavior of interest. Studies that have applied and tested these theories (e.g., Bhattacherjee, 2000; Chen et al., 2002; Gefen & Straub, 2000; Limayem et al., 2000) can offer valuable guidelines to online retailers to help them focus on those aspects of online shopping that are important to customers (e.g., ease of use) and/or make improvements in areas which are found to be lacking (e.g., security). However, for purposes of market segmentation, it is essential to explore the external variables, whose influence on intentions and behavior is theorized by Fishbein and Ajzen (1975) to be fully mediated by beliefs and attitudes.

These external variables could include demographic, personality, and psychographic characteristics that can help Internet marketers to segment their market for customized advertisement, promotion, service, and retention campaigns. Demographic indicators such as age, gender, income, and ethnicity may have, especially during the Internet's nascent stage, been accurate indicators of who shops online. But with the global diffusion of the web and the steady narrowing of the digital divide, demographics may no longer be reliable predictors of online shopping.

Therefore, in this study we explore the relationship between another segmentation factor, namely shopping orientations, and intentions to use online shopping. As a psychographic measure, shopping orientations are intended to capture the motivations of shoppers and/or the desired experiences and goals they seek when completing their shopping activities (Stone, 1954). For example, an in-home shopper may be motivated by convenience, while a personalizing shopper may value the interaction experience with a known sales clerk.

While demographic indicators such as age, gender, marital status, and income have been traditionally used in the study of consumer behavior and market segmentation, shopping orientations have also emerged as reliable discriminators for classifying different types of shoppers based on their approach to shopping activities (Gehrt & Carter, 1992; Lumpkin & Burnett, 1991-92). Researchers have tapped into shopper orientations to study patronage behavior among elderly consumers, catalog shoppers, out-shoppers and mall shoppers (Bloch et al., 1994; Evans et al., 1996; Gehrt & Shim, 1998; Korgaonkar, 1984; Lumpkin, 1985; Lumpkin et al., 1986; Shim & Mahoney, 1992). By extending this psychographic construct to online shopping, our study aims to contribute to the knowledge and understanding of consumer response to electronic modes of shopping.

It is becoming increasingly clear that in order to survive, and more importantly, to succeed, online merchants should embrace and actively pursue fundamental principles of good retailing that apply to any medium. One of these principles is knowledge about existing and potential customers and their preferences and behaviors. Shopping orientations have been shown to be reliable predictors of customer patronage behavior in other retail formats such as catalog and mall shopping. Therefore, it is expected that the study of shopping orientations can also help electronic retailers identify and understand those consumers who prefer to shop online and the reasons why. Further, shopping orientation could be used to segment customers and formulate different strategies based on each segment's relative propensity to adopt and use online shopping.

REVIEW OF SHOPPING ORIENTATIONS LITERATURE

Stone (1954) proposed the idea that shoppers can be classified based on their approach to shopping activities. He identified four types of shoppers—economic, personalizing, ethical, and apathetic. An economic shopper would attempt to maximize her returns by carefully evaluating price, quality, and value. This type of shopper can be expected to spend considerable amount of time collecting information about the available alternatives before making a purchase decision. The personalizing shopper would be inclined to build close relationship with the store personnel and tend to make purchases close to home. For shoppers who fall under this category, shopping at stores where they can interact with salespeople and clerks on a personal level is important. If a shopper makes it a point to shop at stores in his immediate neighborhood with the objective of keeping the monies within the community, he can be labeled an ethical shopper. In order to preserve and build his community, this shopper would feel obligated to patronize local stores. Finally, an apathetic shopper disdains shopping, and would try and find ways to minimize the effort involved in completing a shopping activity.

In addition to the four orientations discussed above, researchers have suggested other classifications for shoppers. For example, Bellenger and Korgaonkar (1980) identified a recreational shopper as someone who views shopping as a social activity. Typically, this type of shopper would use shopping as an opportunity to meet with friends, and combine shopping with other social activities such as dining out. Similarly, other researchers have proposed classifying shoppers based on preferences for in-home shopping and mall shopping (Darden & Reynolds, 1971; Hawes & Lumpkin, 1984; Lumpkin et al., 1986), shopping proneness (Arora, 1985), fashion consciousness and leadership (Gutman & Mills, 1982; Tatzel, 1982), shopping involvement and seriousness (Shim & Kotsiopulos, 1993), shopping confidence and decisiveness (Moye & Kincade, 2003), and the importance placed on convenience (Lumpkin & Hunt, 1989).

Shopping orientations have been used primarily in marketing, retailing, and advertising research to segment or classify consumers (Hawkins et al., 1989), understand the motivations behind shopping behavior and habits (Tauber, 1972), identify preferences for different types of information and entertainment media (Moschis, 1976; Lumpkin & Darden, 1982), analyze the usage rates of specific product categories (Darden & Reynolds, 1971), discern why consumers differ on the extent to which they spread their purchases across multiple retail stores (Mägi, 2003) ascertain pertinent store attributes (Darden & Ashton, 1974-75; Oates et al., 1996), and explain consumers' patronage of a specific store or type of retail outlet (Korgaonkar, 1981, 1984). As the last research stream is the most relevant to the current study, we next discuss some of the findings related to shopping orientations and consumers' choice of specific modes of shopping.

Korgaonkar (1981) collected data through personal interviews from 486 adult shoppers and tested hypothesized relationships between shopping orientations and preference for shopping at catalog showrooms. He concluded that patrons of catalog showrooms were more likely to have an economic rather than recreational or in-home shopping orientation. In a later study, Korgaonkar (1984) examined the relationship between shopping orientations and seven different types of non-store retailers including catalogers, direct mail solicitors, and door-to-door salespersons. A cluster analysis of the shopping orientations data gathered through interviews of 146 consumers identified four groups. Of these, the convenience and price-conscious (i.e., economic shopper) groups, in comparison to the brand-conscious group, were found to be more inclined to patronize non-store retailers.

Similar results were also reported by Gehrt and Carter (1992), who explored the orientations associated with catalog shopping with data collected from 297 North American (Canadian) respondents through mall-intercept interviews. Interestingly, Gehrt et al. (1992) conducted a study similar to that of Gehrt and Carter (1992), but with data collected from European subjects, and found that the same shopping orientations of convenience and recreation were also significant predictors of French consumers' intentions to use catalog shopping.

The above studies have demonstrated that unlike the relationships between demographics (i.e., age, income, education, and occupation) and non-store patronage intentions, which have been inconsistent and contradictory across studies (Berkowitz et al., 1979; Darian, 1987; Gillett, 1970; Lumpkin & Hawes, 1985; Peters & Ford, 1972; Reynolds, 1974), the associations between the latter and shopping orientations are more stable. Gehrt and Carter (1992) contend that the demographic-based studies have produced contradictory results primarily because these studies tended to focus on building profiles of the non-store/catalog shopper with the implicit assumption that only individuals and families who place a higher valuation on time (based on Stigler's (1961) economics of information theory) would be inclined to patronize non-store retailers. They suggest that the inclusion of shopping orientations would help build a more accurate profile of the non-store shopper.

While some of the shopping orientation studies have targeted the general consumer, others have focused on specific consumer segments such as Asians (Eun-Ju et al., 2002; Ho et al., 1997; Ownbey & Horridge, 1997; Siu et al. 2001), Hispanics and Anglos (Lill et al., 1981; Valencia, 1983), the elderly (Lumpkin, 1985), rural shoppers (Lumpkin et al., 1986), browsers (Jarobe & McDaniel, 1987), direct marketing consumers (Lumpkin & Hawes, 1985), and in-home electronic shoppers (Bickle & Shim, 1993; Shim & Mahoney, 1991). Even though they pertain to electronic shopping in the pre-Internet era, the latter two studies are relevant to this current research and their results are discussed below.

Both Bickle and Shim (1993) and Shim and Mahoney (1991) studied consumer acceptance and use of videotex, a term used to describe electronic communication devices and services that provided access to email, news, and shopping (Goldstucker et al., 1986; Moschis et al., 1985). Bickle and Shim (1993) analyzed data from a subset of 600 respondents to a survey mailed to a random sample of 1000 subscribers to a U.S. based videotex service. The subset, which included 138 electronic shoppers, was categorized into heavy and non-heavy purchasers and tested for differences by shopping orientations. As expected, the results indicated that the heavy purchasers were more in-home shopping oriented than the non-heavy purchasers. However, the additional finding that non-heavy purchasers were more price-conscious appears to be contradictory to the earlier findings that economically-oriented shoppers liked non-store retail alternatives (Korgaonkar, 1981, 1984). But, given the state of electronic shopping in the early 1990s, the result is not surprising. Shopping through videotex would not have appealed to the economically-oriented given the relative newness of the service, the high cost of the enabling technologies, the additional expense of subscribing to the service, the dependence on proprietary networks, and the exclusive/limited choice of vendors.

Shim and Mahoney's (1991) findings from data collected through a survey of 132 videotex subscribers who were also electronic shoppers echo the results of Bickle and Shim (1993). They found that price conscious shoppers (whom they labeled conservative/worried shoppers) were the least satisfied with electronic shopping. In contrast, the comparative/user-friendly shoppers and recreative/innovative shoppers were more enthusiastic towards electronic shopping.

More recently, researchers have extended the shopping orientations construct to the examination of electronic shopping on the Internet. Analyzing data collected from an online survey of 999 U.S. Internet users, Li et al. (1999) conclude that web buyers were more convenience and less experientially-oriented than non-web buyers. However, they did not find any significant difference between the two groups on recreational and economic orientations.

In a quasi-experimental study involving 201 student subjects, Vijayasarathy and Jones (2000) found that in-home shopping and mall shopping orientations were significant discriminators between low- and high-intentions to shop online. Another study (Vijayasarathy, 2003) that collected data from a sample of 767 adult consumers showed that in-home and economic orientations had a positive effect, and local shopping orientation (which encompassed ethical and personalizing orientations) had a negative effect on intentions to use online shopping. Further, the above study also found that products classified by cost and tangibility did not have any moderating effects on the relationship between shopping orientations and online shopping intentions. On a normative level, Paden and Stell (2000) contend that the customization of web design and content based on a person's shopping orientation would be crucial for attracting and retaining customers.

RESEARCH QUESTIONS

This study aims to extend the application of shopping orientations to the context of online shopping by seeking answers to the following two research questions:

Do consumers' actual use of the Internet for shopping and their intentions to engage in this behavior differ by orthogonally distinct shopping segments that are derived from shopping orientations?

Are there any significant associations between the shopping segments and demographic variables?

To seek answers to these research questions, six shopping orientations are considered in this study. These include home, mall, economic, recreational, personalizing, and ethical shopping orientations. Home shopping orientation is an indication of a shopper's preference to shop from home in order to save time, minimize travel to shopping centers, or overcome the limitations of product variety, availability, and price at local stores. A consumer who prefers to shop from home is likely to have had experience with in-home shopping modes such as mail-order catalogues and television shopping. The similarity or transferability of the home-shopping experience to online shopping can favorably motivate online purchase intention (Balabanis & Vassileiou, 1999). In contrast, mall-oriented shoppers consider these shopping centers to be the best places to shop. They prefer to shop at physical stores and like the variety of stores that malls tend to offer (Bloch et al., 1994). Based on their preference for shopping at brick-and-mortar stores, this type of shopper may be less inclined to shop using the Internet.

As discussed earlier, a shopper with an economic orientation is a deliberate shopper who considers multiple alternatives on relevant criteria such as price and quality before committing to a purchase. This person actively attempts to find ways that will generate the best value for his/her investment in the purchase of a product or service. As a retail channel, the Internet offers a number of benefits that may appeal to an economically-oriented shopper. It can provide an abundance of product related information that can help a shopper make detailed comparisons among competing alternatives. Further, the availability of shopping agents such as mySimon.Com, which collate and present price and features information from multiple vendors for a given product, can save time and make the task of comparison shopping more efficient. In addition to comparison shopping, cost savings generated by disintermediation, virtual store-fronts, and digital delivery may be passed on to consumers in the form of lower prices on products and services. For an economic shopper, the assistance with evaluating alternatives and the potential for maximizing value makes the Internet an attractive shopping medium.

A recreational shopper tends to combine shopping with social activities. This type of shopper may use shopping as an occasion to meet with friends and/or an opportunity to dine out. While the adjective recreational can be used to qualify any activity, pastime, or hobby that is mentally or physically refreshing, in this study, recreational is intended to describe social activities in the physical world. This distinction is necessary since virtual activities such as online browsing, chatting and messaging could very well be recreational. Since online shopping in its present form is typically not geared for socializing, the recreational shopper can be expected to have low intention to shop using the Internet. Personalizing and ethical shoppers are also expected to be less enthusiastic about online shopping. The impersonal nature of most online transactions may turn-off personalizing shoppers, who would prefer to interact with a "live" salesperson or clerk with whom they have built a relationship. Similarly, the prospect of shopping for products and services from vendors who may not have any ties to the local community may be unacceptable for ethical shoppers.

In summary, consumers with home and economic shopping orientations can be expected to be more likely to engage in online shopping than those who exhibit mall, recreational, personalizing, and/or ethical shopping orientations.

METHOD

Data Collection Procedures

Data for this study were collected as part of a larger mail survey of consumer perceptions about Internet shopping. Participants in the study were adults residing in an upper mid-western city with a population of about 80,000. A database of residential properties information from the city's assessment department was used to select the target subjects for the study. Of the 19,600 residential properties (single family, duplexes, and condominiums) listed in the database, a proportional random sampling was done to identify 3,000 potential respondents. First, using the assessed values of the homes as surrogates for actual household incomes, the 19,600 properties were stratified into eight categories. Then, to arrive at the target sample of 3,000 respondents, a proportional number of households were randomly selected from each of the eight stratified levels. These proportions approximately reflected the percentages of U.S. households by income levels published by the U.S. Census Bureau (www.census.gov/prod/99pubs/p60-206.pdf). Further, the 3,000 respondents selected were evenly split between males and females. Finally, of the

3000 respondents, only 800 (selected by the same proportional random sampling technique) were targeted for collecting the data relevant for this study. The other 2,200 respondents were sent a different survey instrument that was intended for studying other aspects of Internet shopping that are not discussed in this paper.

A four-page questionnaire was used as the research instrument. It was first pre-tested in an iterative manner among a convenience sample of colleagues, students, and other consumers drawn from the general public (Moore & Benbasat, 1991). The 52 respondents in this test sample were asked to provide comments on the relevance and wording of the questionnaire items, length of the survey, and time taken to complete it. Based on the feedback received, some of the questionnaire items were dropped. Further, the questionnaire layout was modified, and the wording of some of the questions was changed to improve clarity.

Thirteen items derived from prior literature (Bellenger & Korgaonkar, 1980; Darden & Ashton, 1974-75; Darden & Reynolds, 1971; Hawes & Lumpkin, 1984; Lumpkin, 1985) were used to determine shopping orientations. Respondents were asked to indicate on a seven-point scale the extent to which they agreed or disagreed with statements intended to assess their preference for certain shopping behaviors. Intention to use the Internet for shopping (in general, not with respect to any specific retailer or product type) was measured with three items adapted from Taylor and Todd (1995). The first two items used a seven-point scale anchored by 1 (strongly disagree) and 7 (strongly agree), while the last item was anchored by 1 (very improbable) and 7 (very probable). The instrument also included measures for assessing the level of Internet usage and other relevant demographic indicators. A listing of the items used to measure the research variables is provided in Table 4 and the Appendix.

As a pilot test to gauge response rate, an initial mailing was sent to 100 of the chosen sample of 800 respondents. The survey package consisted of a cover letter, questionnaire, and pre-paid return envelope. A drawing to win one of 10 $25 gift certificates, redeemable at any area restaurant or retail store, was offered as an incentive to respond to the survey. As a reminder, a follow-up post-card was sent to all of the respondents a week after the initial mailing. Thirty completed questionnaires were returned for a response rate of 30 percent, which was higher than the 10 to 20 percent range that is typical for consumer surveys (Biner & Kidd, 1994; Haggett & Mitchell, 1994; Gendall et al., 1995).

Following the pilot test, the remaining 700 subjects were sent the questionnaire package. The initial mailing was followed-up with a post-card encouraging participation in the study. A total of 260 responses were received for a response rate of 37.1 percent. Of these, nine questionnaires were returned blank or incomplete. The predominant reasons cited for these incomplete questionnaires were the lack of a personal computer at home and/or an Internet connection, and insufficient knowledge or experience using the Internet for shopping purposes. Combining the remaining 251 questionnaires with the 30 from the pilot study yielded a total of 281 usable cases for an overall response rate of 35.1 percent, which was well

Table 1: T-test results for non-response bias

COMPARISON CRITERIA	RESPONDENTS (N=184)	NON-RESPONDENTS (N=616)	T-VALUE	D.F.	2-TAILED SIG.
ASSESSED VALUE OF HOMES	$157,485	$167,680	-1.39	798	.164

above the range reported for consumer mail surveys (Biner & Kidd, 1994; Haggett & Mitchell, 1994; Gendall et al., 1995).

To test for possible non-response bias, a t-test was conducted using the assessed value of the respondents' homes. The result showed no significant difference between the respondents and non-respondents (Table 1). Only 184 of the 281 valid responses included identification information such as the name of the respondent to be able to match them with their respective properties in the mailing database. Therefore, the means for the two comparison groups (respondents and non-respondents), and consequently the t-test result, may not be accurate. Subject to this unavoidable limitation, the non-response bias analysis indicates that the respondents' household incomes are not significantly different than those of the non-respondents. Further, the difference in response rates between females (38.8%) and males (30.8%) was small, ensuring that the data collected were representative of both genders.

Respondent Profile

Among the respondents, there were 155 (55 percent) females and 123 (44 percent) males; 201 (72 percent) principal shoppers and 74 (26 percent) who weren't, 232 (83 percent) who were married and 48 (17 percent) who were single, divorced, separated, or widowed; and 171 (61 percent) with a bachelor's or higher degree and 110 (39 percent) with less than a four-year degree. The average number of people in the respondents' households was 3.05 (median = 3). A majority of the respondents (64 percent) were in the 35 to 54 age category, while approximately half of the them (47 percent) indicated a household income of $75,000 or greater. More detailed information about the age, income and educational attainment of the respondents is provided in Table 2. This table, which also provides comparisons with U.S. demographics, indicates that besides gender distribution, our respondent group is not representative of the population. In general, our sample over-represents married middle-aged individuals who have higher educational attainment and higher household income. Our results, therefore, may not be generalizable to all segments of the population.

Most of the respondents (88 percent) had used the Internet, and 53 percent of them had been using it for two years or more. The average Internet usage time among respondents was 5.6 hours (median = 3.0 hours) per week. A sizable number (65 percent) of the respondents indicated that they had shopped on the Internet for

Table 2: Frequency distributions for demographics: Respondents vs. United States population

a) Gender

GENDER	RESPONDENTS (COUNT)	RESPONDENTS (%)	U.S. POPULATION (%)[2]
FEMALE	155	55.8	52.3
MALE	123	44.2	47.7
NOT REPORTED	3		
TOTAL	281	100.0	100.0

b) Age

AGE	RESPONDENTS (COUNT)	RESPONDENTS (%)	U.S. POPULATION (%)
18-243	5	1.8	9.4
25-34	33	11.8	19.9
35-44	90	32.3	22.5
45-54	91	32.6	18.7
55-64	34	12.2	12.1
65-74	18	6.4	9.1
75 AND OLDER	8	2.9	8.3
NOT REPORTED	2		
TOTAL	281	100.0	100.0

c) Household income

INCOME	RESPONDENTS (COUNT)	RESPONDENTS (%)	INCOME (U.S. CENSUS CATEGORIES)[4]	U.S. POPULATION (%)
LESS THAN $30,000	9	3.6	LESS THAN $25,000	29.3
$30,000 TO $44,999	30	12.0	$25,000 TO $34,999	12.5
$45,000 TO $59,999	44	17.7	$35,000 TO $49,999	15.5
$60,000 TO $74,999	35	14.1	$50,000 TO $74,999	18.9
$75,000 TO $99,999	55	22.1	$75,000 TO $99,999	10.4
$100,000 OR MORE	76	30.5	$100,000 OR MORE	13.4
NOT REPORTED	32			
TOTAL	281	100.0	TOTAL	100.0

continued on next page

Table 2: Frequency distributions for demographics: Respondents versus United States population (continued)

d) Education

HIGHEST LEVEL OF EDUCATION	RESPONDENTS (COUNT)	RESPONDENTS (%)	U.S. POPULATION (%)[5]
NOT A HIGH SCHOOL GRADUATE[6]			15.8
HIGH SCHOOL	29	10.3	33.1
TECHNICAL DEGREE/ 1-3 YEARS OF COLLEGE[7]	81	28.8	25.4
BACHELOR'S DEGREE	107	38.1	17.0
GRADUATE DEGREE	64	22.8	8.6
TOTAL	281	100.0	100.0

e) Marital status

MARITAL STATUS	RESPONDENTS (COUNT)	RESPONDENTS (%)	U.S. POPULATION (%)[8]
SINGLE[9]	26	9.3	23.9
MARRIED	232	82.9	59.5
DIVORCED	12	4.3	9.8
SEPARATED[10]	1	0.4	
WIDOWED	9	3.2	6.8
NOT REPORTED	1		
TOTAL	281	100.0	100.0

[1] *U.S. population demographics obtained from the* Statistical Abstract of the United States: 2001, *published by the U.S. Department of Commerce, Economics and Statistics Administration, U.S. Census Bureau.*

[2] *The distribution for the U.S. population is for persons 25 years old and over.*

[3] *For the U.S. population, the percentage reported is for the age range 20 to 24.*

[4] *Some of the income categories used in our survey are different from the ones used by the U.S. Census.*

[5] *The distribution for the U.S. population is for persons 25 years old and over.*

[6] *Our survey did not include a category for "Not a high school graduate".*

[7] *We assumed that the "Some college, but no degree" and "Associate's degree" categories used by the U.S. census were equivalent to the "Technical degree" and "1-3 years of college" categories used in our survey.*

[8] *The distribution for the U.S. population is for persons 18 years old and over.*

[9] *For the U.S. population, the percentage reported is for the "Never Married" category.*

[10] *The U.S. Census did not have a "Separated" category.*

an average of 14 (median = 4) times in the past 12 months and spent an average of $610 (median = $100) on online purchases over the same time period. The most frequently cited items (at least by 10 percent of the respondents) shopped for on the Internet included travel (35 percent), apparel, clothing, or shoes (29 percent), books (28 percent), toys/games (20 percent), consumer electronics (17 percent), computer software (16 percent), music/video (16 percent), computer hardware (15 percent), sporting goods (14 percent), automobiles (13 percent), movie/concert tickets (12 percent), online brokerage (11 percent), and online banking (10 percent). Table 3 presents a more comprehensive breakdown of the respondents' experience with the Internet.

Two hundred and forty-four respondents (87 percent) reported having a personal computer at home, and 14 (5 percent) indicated that they owned a WebTV. Of the 257 respondents (92 percent) who had access to the Internet, 85 percent had access from their home, and 66 percent were able to connect to the Internet from work. For a majority (80 percent) of the respondents, dial-up modem was the common Internet connection option, while 5 percent reported having DSL and a handful (2 percent) indicated using a cable modem.

Table 3: Frequency distributions for respondents' experience with the Internet

a) Internet use

USED THE INTERNET	RESPONDENTS (COUNT)	RESPONDENTS (%)
YES	246	88.2
NO	33	11.8
NOT REPORTED	2	
TOTAL	281	100.0

b) Length of Internet use

LENGTH OF INTERNET USE	RESPONDENTS (COUNT)	RESPONDENTS (%)
LESS THAN 6 MONTHS	16	6.6
6 MONTHS – 1 YEAR	28	11.5
1 TO 2 YEARS	49	20.2
2 TO 4 YEARS	77	31.7
OVER 4 YEARS	73	30.0
NOT REPORTED	38	
TOTAL	281	100.0

continued on next page

Table 3 (cont.): Frequency distributions for respondents' experience with the Internet

c) Prior experience with Internet shopping

SHOPPED USING THE INTERNET	RESPONDENTS (COUNT)	RESPONDENTS (%)
YES	182	65.5
NO	96	34.5
NOT REPORTED	3	
TOTAL	281	100.0

Based on the above information, it appears that the majority of the respondents were welleducated, married, and middle-aged, and enjoyed a higher than average household income. Further, most of the respondents had a fair amount of Internet and online shopping experience.

Data Analyses and Results

We followed similar data analysis procedures as those conducted by Gehrt and Shim (1998). First, factor analysis was performed on the 13 items used to gauge shopping orientations. Second, the factor scores were used in a series of cluster analyses to identify orthogonal shopping segments. Third, analysis of variance (ANOVA) was employed to detect differences in both the actual use of online shopping (as reported by the respondents) as well as intentions to use it in the future by the shopping segments. And finally, chi-square analyses were used to determine if there were significant differences between demographic variables and the identified shopping segments. Next, each of the above analyses is discussed in detail.

Factor Analysis

The Bartlett test of sphericity was significant (Chi-Square: 1034.09; Significance: 000) and the KMO measure of sampling adequacy (Index: 0.71) was satisfactory, indicating the appropriateness of performing factor analysis (Norusis, 1985). Principal component analysis with varimax rotation was used to identify the underlying factors among the thirteen items. A four-factor solution that cumulatively explained 65.17 percent of the variance with eigenvalues greater than 1 emerged from the analysis. The item loadings for two factors representing home and economic shopping orientations were as expected. However, the items measuring mall and social shopping orientations loaded on a single factor and were labeled mall socializing orientation. Further, the items measuring ethical and personalizing orientations also loaded on a common factor, and were given the label of local shopping orientation. Cronbach's alpha (Cronbach, 1970) for the home, economic, mall socializing, and local shopping

Table 4: Results of principal components analysis

SCALE ITEMS	*FACTORS*			
	HOME	**ECONOMIC**	**MALL SOCIALIZING**	**LOCAL**
I like to shop from home (for example, using mail-order catalogues, the TV or the Internet).	**0.846**	-0.102	-0.078	-0.070
I shop from home because I cannot find what I want in local stores.	**0.692**	0.157	0.098	-0.049
Shopping from home is more convenient than going to the store.	**0.869**	-0.016	-0.105	-0.096
I make it a rule to shop at a number of stores before I buy.	-0.027	**0.821**	0.132	-0.042
I can save a lot of money by shopping around.	0.108	**0.808**	0.193	-0.074
I like to have a great deal of information before I buy.	-0.019	**0.795**	-0.003	0.270
I enjoy going to big shopping malls.	0.007	0.283	**0.754**	-0.264
Shopping malls are the best places to shop.	-0.088	0.267	**0.678**	-0.245
I like to go shopping with a friend.	0.098	-0.090	**0.699**	.357
I often combine shopping with lunch or dinner at a restaurant.	-0.002	-0.017	**0.704**	0.288
Shopping gives me a chance to get out and do something.	-0.085	0.096	**0.723**	0.059
I like to shop where people know me.	-0.074	0.134	0.020	**0.785**
I owe it to my community to shop at local stores.	-0.134	-0.027	0.083	**0.772**
EIGENVALUE	2.625	2.182	2.011	1.654
% OF VARIANCE	20.194	16.784	15.471	12.721
CUMULATIVE %	20.194	36.978	52.449	65.170

orientation factors were 0.74, 0.77, 0.77, and 0.68 respectively. The rotated factor matrix and other pertinent results of the analysis are presented in Table 4.

Convergent and discriminant validities were assessed using the multitrait-multimethod (MTMM) approach (Bagozzi & Phillips, 1982; Campbell & Fiske, 1959). All inter-item correlations for each shopping orientation were significant at the 0.01 level, suggesting strong convergent validities. To determine discriminant validities, the within-scale item correlations were compared with the across-scale item correlations. Campbell and Fiske (1959) recommend that to support discriminant validity, the within-scale correlations should be greater than the across-scale correlations for one-half of all possible comparisons. For home, economic, and

Table 5: Results of cluster analysis (3 cluster solution)

SHOPPING SEGMENT	*SHOPPING ORIENTATION*				*NO. OF RESPONDENTS*
	Home	Economic	Mall Socializing	Local	
Community Shopper	-0.346	0.193	0.694	**0.543**	106
Home Shopper	0.668	0.084	-0.673	0.104	103
Apathetic Shopper	-0.536	-0.485	-0.070	-1.138	60
F-Ratio	52.460	10.022	76.739	92.678	
Significance	.000	.000	.000	.000	

local shopping orientations, the within-scale correlations were greater than across-scale correlations for 100 percent of all potential comparisons. The percentage was slightly lower for mall socializing orientation (98 percent), but still well above the suggested threshold.

Cluster Analyses

We next performed cluster analyses to identify orthogonally distinct shopping segments. The preceding factor analysis had helped reduce the data set to four dimensions and also generated the scores for input to this analysis stage. K-means clustering, a non-hierarchical procedure that is recommended for the derivation of more stable cluster solutions (Hair et al., 1992) was used to determine the optimal number of shopping segments. First, we generated cluster solutions for two, three, and four groups, and then evaluated each solution on the distinctiveness of its groups. This was done by a) examining if the cluster scores for each of the four factors differed significantly across the k (2, 3 or 4) clusters using F tests, and b) performing pair-wise comparisons between the k clusters on a post-hoc basis using Scheffe's test (Gehrt & Shim, 1998).

Applying the above evaluation criteria, the two cluster solution was dropped, as only two of the four cluster scores differed significantly between the two clusters. Both the three and four cluster solutions passed the first test since the F-ratios that gauged the differences between the cluster scores across the three or four clusters were all significant. However, the three cluster solution emerged as the optimal solution, since 83.33 percent (10 out of 12) of its pair-wise comparisons were significantly different in contrast to the 66.66 percent (16 out of 24) significant pair-wise comparisons for the four cluster solution. Following Gehrt and Shim's (1998) example, we performed a split-sample analysis and found support for the three cluster solu-

Table 6a: ANOVA results by shopping segments

Online Shopping	Statistics	Shopping Segments			Source	df	Sum of Squares	Mean Square	F	Sig.
		Community Shopper	Home Shopper	Apathetic Shopper						
Actual Use	Mean	5.96	10.55	5.00	Between	2	1508.41	754.20	4.44	.013
	Std. Dev.	9.24	17.50	9.36	Within	255	43302.09	169.81		
Intention to Use	Mean	3.28	4.37	3.25	Between	2	76.90	38.45	14.46	.000
	Std. Dev.	1.60	1.73	1.52	Within	265	704.64	2.66		

tion across the two samples. This provided some assurance for the stability of the solution and served as a measure of cross-validation (Lastovicka, 1982).

An examination of the results of the three cluster solution presented in Table 5 shows that local shopping differs most across the three shopping segments (F-ratio: 92.68), followed by mall socializing shopping orientation (F-ratio: 52.46), home shopping orientation (F-ratio: 52.46), and economic shopping orientation (F-ratio: 10.02). Based on the cluster scores for the four shopping orientations, we labeled

Table 6b: Results of post-hoc Scheffé tests for pair-wise differences between shopping segments

Online Shopping	***Statistics***	***Pair-wise Comparisons***		
		Community Shopper vs.		Home Shopper vs.
		Home Shopper	Apathetic Shopper	Apathetic Shopper
Actual Use	Mean Difference	-4.59	0.96	5.55
	Sig.	.045	.906	.041
Intention to Use	Mean Difference	-1.09	0.04	1.12
	Sig.	.000	.990	.000

the three shopping segments as Community Shopper (a shopper who combines shopping with socializing and who prefers to shop at local malls where he/she knows the sales personnel), Home Shopper (a shopper who prefers to shop from home), and Apathetic Shopper (a shopper who is indifferent to shopping and/or to any particular medium of shopping).

Analysis of Variance (ANOVA)

A single item measured respondents' use of online shopping in the past 12 months, and three items were employed to assess their intention to use it in the future. For the latter measure, factor analysis showed that all items loaded on a single dimension, and the reliability co-efficient was 0.88 (Cronbach, 1970). We conducted ANOVAs to answer our first research question: Does the use of online shopping and intentions to use it in the future differ by shopping segments? The results presented in Table 6a provide affirmative answers that actual use and future intentions to shop online are different across the shopping segments. Further, the post-hoc pair-wise comparisons (Table 6b) reveal that the home shopping segment is significantly different from the community and apathetic shopping segments on both actual use and intentions to use online shopping.

Chi-Square Analyses

Since a psychographic measure of consumers on their shopping orientations may not be readily available to marketers, we conducted chi-square analyses to ascertain if there were any significant differences between commonly used demographic indicators including gender, age, income, and education and the shopping segments. These results, presented in Table 7, show that none of the chi-square statistics are significant, suggesting that shopping segments are not discernible from demographic indicators. The implications of these findings are discussed in the next section.

Table 7: Analyses of differences between shopping segments and demographic variables

Demographics		Shopping Segments			
		Community	Home	Apathetic	Totals
Gender					
Male	Count	43	50	26	119
	Row %	36.1	42.0	21.8	
	Col %	41.3	48.5	44.1	
Female	Count	61	53	33	147
	Row %	41.5	36.1	22.4	
	Col %	58.7	54.5	55.9	
Totals		104	103	59	266
Pearson Chi-Square – Value: 1.10, df: 2, Sig: .578					
Age					
18-34	Count	15	13	9	37
	Row %	40.5	35.1	24.3	
	Col %	14.3	12.7	15.0	
35-54	Count	62	71	43	176
	Row %	35.2	40.3	24.4	
	Col %	59.0	69.6	71.7	
> 54	Count	28	18	8	54
	Row %	51.9	33.3	14.8	
	Col %	26.7	17.6	13.3	
Totals		105	102	60	267
Pearson Chi-Square – Value: 5.32, df: 4, Sig: .256					
Income					
< $45,000	Count	16	13	9	38
	Row %	42.1	34.2	23.7	
	Col %	17.0	14.3	16.4	
$45,000 -$75,000	Count	34	30	13	77
	Row %	44.2	39.0	16.9	
	Col %	36.2	33.0	23.6	
	Count	44	48	33	125

continued on next page

Table 7 (cont.): Analyses of differences between shopping segments and demographic variables

	Row %	35.2	38.4	26.4	
	Col %	46.8	52.7	60.0	
Totals		94	91	55	240
Pearson Chi-Square – Value: 3.14, df: 4, Sig: .535					
Education					
High School	Count	13	7	6	26
	Row %	50.0	26.9	23.1	
	Col %	12.3	6.8	10.0	
Some Post Secondary	Count	39	26	14	79
	Row %	49.4	32.9	17.7	
	Col %	36.8	25.2	23.3	
Bachelor's	Count	31	44	27	102
	Row %	30.4	43.1	26.5	
	Col %	29.2	42.7	45.0	
Graduate	Count	23	26	13	62
	Row %	37.1	41.9	21.0	
	Col %	21.7	25.2	21.7	
Totals		106	103	60	269
Pearson Chi-Square – Value: 8.83, df: 6, Sig: .184					

DISCUSSION AND IMPLICATIONS

In the last two years, the pervasive myth that building Internet retail sites will automatically trigger customer patronage has been laid to rest (Malone, 2001; Thomas, 2002). The demise of thousands of online businesses that banked on slick web sites and multi-million dollar advertisement campaigns is a painful but educative reminder that for all the hype, the Internet is just another channel for communication, transaction, and distribution. Irrefutably, the digital channel offers some unique advantages over other media, including interactive communications, rapid comparison shopping, lower transaction costs, innovative arrangements for the sampling and consumption of digital products, and the elimination of time and spatial barriers. However, this new medium of commerce has its own drawbacks, such as reduced opportunities for sensory shopping, social shopping, face-to-face interactions with sales personnel, and the postponement of the consumption or enjoyment of tangible goods.

The inherent limitations of the Internet have been compounded by poorly designed online storefronts, limited product selection, poor customer service, tedious check-out procedures, botched orders, tardy deliveries, security lapses, and privacy invasions. Further, even though the popularity of broadband Internet connections are on the rise, the majority of the U.S. households use slower dial-up connections, which could detract from a satisfying online shopping experience. Given these problems, which are not atypical of innovations, it is becoming increasingly clear that online shopping may not hold the same attraction for all consumers, and its diffusion may follow the same bell-shaped curve as that of other innovations (Rogers, 1995) rather than the radical adoption rates that were optimistically forecasted in the late 1990s.

Therefore, a promising avenue of research would be the identification of consumer segments that would most likely form the core of the early majority or pragmatists. This group is crucial for the successful diffusion of innovations, because unlike the innovators and early adopters who tend to be technology enthusiasts, it is the pragmatists who adopt an innovation for its perceived benefits. The results of this study suggest that the home shopper segment could potentially comprise the early majority that can help build the momentum and critical mass for the successful diffusion of the online shopping innovation.

Both in terms of actual use of online shopping and intentions to use it in the future, the home shopper segment was found to be significantly different from the community and apathetic shopper segments. Home shopping orientation encompasses the dimensions of convenience, enjoyment, and/or necessity. Consumers may prefer in-home shopping modes on account of their convenience, or their recreational appeal, and/or the lack of local shopping alternatives. In this study, the single items that captured each of the three dimensions loaded on a single factor. While finer levels of analysis and interpretation with respect to the specific dimensions of home shopping orientation and their relationship to Internet shopping could be done by future studies, results of this study strongly suggest that consumers' home shopping orientation could be a reliable predicator of Internet shopping intentions.

Further, it can be inferred that patrons of direct/catalogue sales could be more easily persuaded to adopt online shopping. This consumer group has a preference for in-home shopping modes and has experience and a level of comfort with shopping using non-store alternatives (Bickle & Shim, 1993; Vijayasarathy & Jones, 2000; Vijayasarathy, 2003). Therefore, even though some among this group may be averse to technology or may not have the required equipment or resources to engage in electronic shopping, online retailers hoping to build their customer base should actively pursue this consumer segment.

In contrast to the home shopper, it appears that the community and apathetic shoppers use online shopping less and also have lower intentions to use it in the future. These results are not surprising, since the community shopper, as segmented by our data analyses, is one who prefers to shop locally in the community and enjoys the social aspects of shopping in a mall (Vijayasarathy & Jones, 2000; Vijayasarathy, 2003). Similarly, the apathetic shopper, as the name implies, would be indifferent to shopping and therefore, may exhibit little enthusiasm for it, irrespective of the medium.

The "pure play" online retailers, who only have a virtual presence, may be at a distinct disadvantage when it comes to attracting the community shopper. But others, who use online stores as a complement and/or supplement to their traditional brick-and-motor outlets, may be able to convince this shopper segment to take advantage of the multiple interfaces for communication, transaction, and distribution. For example, a supermarket chain with local ties to the community could encourage its customers to access coupons, and even place orders at its virtual store, which could then be picked up at a convenient time from one of its physical stores. Or, the local performance center could impress its patrons of the advantages of reserving their seats online by providing virtual seating charts, choice seats, and special discounts.

While the pursuit of apathetic shoppers may appear to be futile, it is quite possible that this shopper segment could be enticed to try the online medium, if shopping could be integrated into or made peripheral to other activities that may be of greater interest to this group. For example, merchants specializing in outdoor-equipment could potentially attract an apathetic shopper by offering a wealth of information such as camping and hiking tips, weather forecasts, and trail maps. Or a retailer of computer games may offer its customers the opportunity to try their products online and even play against other gaming enthusiasts. The Internet's capabilities for interactivity, multi-media experience, and customization is well-suited for attracting the apathetic shopper by designing storefronts that cater to their primary interests (e.g., entertainment, information gathering, virtual chatting, etc.), but also offer shopping as a non-intrusive secondary activity.

Unlike the associations between shopper segments (based on shopping orientations) and demographic indicators that were reported by Gehrt and Shim (1998), our results suggest no such relationships. At least, for the three shopper segments identified in our study, it appears that there are no differences among them by gender, age, income, and education. The implications of these findings are that online shopping is not limited to any specific demographic group, and therefore, the creation of profiles of the online shopper based on demographics may be misleading. Although obtaining psychographic measures may not be as easy as gathering demographic information about potential customers, these measures have been shown to be more reliable in assessing Internet shopping intentions. Shopping orientations can be assessed indirectly through surrogate indicators, such as patronage of mail-order catalogers, or directly, by including shopping orientation questions in professional market research surveys that seek demographic or other pertinent information from consumers in exchange for monetary or other in-kind incentives.

LIMITATIONS AND SUGGESTIONS FOR FUTURE RESEARCH

Limitations to this study are in the areas of sampling and non-response bias. The sample was drawn from a highly homogenous group residing in a single city, probably lacking the diversity that can be expected from a comparable sample chosen from across the entire country. A stratified sampling procedure was used to reflect the general population based on income levels. However, since household income data for the target sample was not available, a surrogate measure (assessed home value) was used. Even though the correlation between income levels reported by the respondents and assessed home values was significant at the 0.01 level (Spearman's Rho: 0.594), the substitute measure is not a perfect indicator of household income. Moreover, as shown in Table 2 and discussed in the Respondent Profile section, our sample is not representative of the general U.S. population. Therefore, our results may be more applicable to wealthier, middle-aged, married consumers with a higher level of education.

While the six shopping orientations included in this study were chosen specifically for their possible relevance to the online shopping environment, a number of other orientations such as price-oriented, time-oriented, psycho-socializing, and aesthetic, that have been advanced in prior literature, may also be equally pertinent. Future studies can examine the relevance of these other shopping orientations in the context of online shopping. Further, the components of home shopping orientation including necessity, convenience, and enjoyment can also be analyzed individually for their influence on consumer intentions to shop using the Internet.

In this study, a conscious decision was made to examine "intention to shop" rather than "intention to purchase". Shopping, which may include purchasing, also encompasses the acts of browsing, comparing, evaluating, and decision-making. Therefore, the study's conclusions about the relationships between shopping orientations and online shopping patronage have to be considered within the general context of shopping. Future research can examine the associations between shopping orientations and the specific acts that comprise shopping.

CONCLUSION

The success of Internet auctioneer eBay and the survival of electronic retailing giant Amazon.com have demonstrated that the online medium is a viable channel for both traditional as well as innovative business exchanges between retailers and their customers. Further, the e-commerce retail sales figures compiled and published by the U.S. Department of Commerce (www.census.gov/mrts/www/current.html) since the fourth quarter of 1999 suggests that there is a steady double-digit growth in e-commerce activity. Other factors such as the continuous growth in the number of Internet users and broadband subscribers, and the rapid pace of technological improvements and innovations also hold the promise for greater acceptance of the digital medium by consumers (Malone, 2001).

Of course, the rash of bankruptcies among Internet retailers and dramatic declines in stock values of Internet-related businesses in the past few years have brought the sobering realization that along with the opportunities, electronic retailers also face many challenges including the tasks of identifying, attracting, and retaining customers. Shopping orientations have been used in prior research to identify patronage intentions towards different retail formats including non-store alternatives such as catalog and television shopping. We have made a similar attempt, by employing shopping orientations to the study of online shopping.

Our results suggest that shopper segments—community, home, and apathetic—derived from shopping orientations differ on both actual use of online shopping and intentions to use it in the future. Specifically, the home shopper segment was found to have the strongest affinity for online shopping. Contrary to expectations, there were no significant associations between the shopping segments and demographic variables. Therefore, there is a need to profile the online shopper using more sophisticated psychographic measures such as shopping orientations, rather than relying solely on demographics.

REFERENCES

Ajzen, I. (1985). From intention to actions: A theory of planned behavior. In J. Kuhl & J. Beckmann (Eds.), *Action control: From cognition to behavior* (pp. 11-39). New York: Springer Verlag.

Ajzen, I. (1989). Attitude, structure, and behavior. In A.R. Pratkanis, S.J. Breckler & A.G. Greenwald (Eds.), *Attitude structure and function* (pp. 241-274). Hillsdale, NJ: Lawrence Erlbaum Associates.

Arora, R. (1985). Involvement: Its measurement for retail store research. *Journal of the Academy of Marketing Science*, *13*, 229-241.

Bagozzi, R.P., & Phillips, L.W. (1982). Representing and testing organizational theories: A holistic construal. *Administrative Science Quarterly*, *27*(3), 459-489.

Balabanis, G., & Vassileiou, S. (1999). Some attitudinal predictors of home-shopping through the Internet. *Journal of Marketing Management*, *15*, 361-85.

Bellenger, D.N., & Korgaonkar, P. (1980). Profiling the recreational shopper. *Journal of Retailing*, *56*(3), 77-92.

Berkowitz, E.N., Walton, J.R., & Walker, O.C., Jr. (1979). In home shoppers: The market for innovative distribution systems. *Journal of Retailing*, *55*(Summer), 15-33.

Bhattacherjee, A. (2000). Acceptance of e-commerce services: The case of electronic brokerages. *IEEE Transactions on Systems, Man, and Cybernetics*, *30*(4), 411-420.

Bickle, M.C., & Shim, S. (1993). Usage rate segmentation of the electronic shopper: Heavy versus non-heavy dollar volume purchasers. *International Review of Retail, Distribution & Consumer Research, 3*(1), 1-18.

Biner, P.M., & Kidd, H.J. (1994). The interactive effects of monetary incentive justification and questionnaire length on mail survey response. *Psychology & Marketing, 11*(5), 483-492.

Bloch, P.H., Ridgway, N.M., & Dawson, S.A. (1994). The shopping mall as consumer habitat. *Journal of Retailing, 70*(1), 23-42.

Campbell, D.T., & Fiske, D.W. (1959). Convergent and discriminant validation by the multitrait-multimethod matrix. *Psychological Bulletin, 56,* 81-105.

Chen, L., Gillenson, M.L., & Sherrell, D.L. (2002). Enticing online consumers: An extended technology acceptance perspective. *Information & Management, 39*(8), 705-719.

Cronbach, L.J. (1970). *Essentials of psychological testing.* New York: Harper and Row.

Darden, W.R., & Ashton, D. (1974-75). Psychographic profiles of patronage preference groups. *Journal of Retailing, 50*(4), 99-112.

Darden, W.R., & Reynolds, F.D. (1971). Shopping orientations and product usage rates. *Journal of Marketing Research, 8*(November), 505-508.

Darian, J.C. (1987). In-home shopping: Are there consumer segments? *Journal of Retailing,63*(Summer), 163-186.

Davis, F.D. (1989). Perceived usefulness, perceived ease of use, and user acceptance of information technology. *MIS Quarterly, 13*, 318-339.

Davis, F.D., Bagozzi, R.P., & Warshaw, P.R. (1989). User acceptance of computer technology: A comparison of two theoretical models. *Management Science, 35*(8), 982-1003.

Eun-Ju, L., Fairhurst, A., & Dillard, S. (2002). Usefulness of ethnicity in international consumer marketing. *Journal of International Consumer Marketing, 14*(4), 25-48.

Evans, K.R., Christiansen, T., & Gill, J.D. (1996). The impact of social influence and role expectations on shopping center patronage intentions. *Journal of the Academy of Marketing Science, 24*(3), 208-218.

Fishbein, M., & Ajzen, I. (1975). *Belief, attitude, intention, and behavior: An introduction to theory and research.* Reading, MA: Addison-Wesley.

Gefen, D., & Straub, D.W. (2000). The relative importance of perceived ease of use in IS adoption: A study of e-commerce adoption. *Journal of the Association for Information Systems, 1*(Article 8).

Gehrt, K.C., Alpander, G.G., & Lawson, D. (1992). A factor-analytic examination of catalog shopping orientations in France. *Journal of Euromarketing, 2*(2), 49-69.

Gehrt, K.C., & Carter, K. (1992). An exploratory assessment of catalogue shopping orientations. *Journal of Direct Marketing, 6*(1), 29-39.

Gehrt, K.C., & Shim, S. (1998). A shopping orientation segmentation of French consumers: Implications for catalogue marketing. *Journal of Interactive Marketing, 12*(4), 34-46.

Gendall, P., Hoek, J., & Esslemont, D. (1995). The effect of appeal, complexity, and tone in a mail survey covering letter. *Journal of Marketing Society, 37*(3), 251-258.

Gillett, P.L. (1970). A profile of urban in-home shoppers. *Journal of Marketing, 34*(July), 40-45.

Goldstucker, J.L., Moschis, G.P., & Stanley, T.J. (1986). Possible effects of electronic shopping on restructuring of distribution channels. *International Journal of Retailing, 1,* 20-32.

Gutman, J., & Mills, M.K. (1982). Fashion life style, self-concept, shopping orientation, and store patronage: An integrative analysis. *Journal of Retailing, 58*(2), 64-86.

Haggett, S., & Mitchell, V.W. (1994). Effects of industrial prenotification on response rate, speed, quality, bias, and cost. *Industrial Marketing Management, 23*(2), 101-110.

Hair, J.F., Jr., Anderson, R.E., Tatham, R.L., & Black, W.C. (1992). *Multivariate data analysis with readings* (3rd Ed.). New York: McMillan.

Hawes, J.M., & Lumpkin, J.R. (1984). Understanding the outshopper. *Journal of the Academy of Marketing Science, 12*(Fall), 200-218.

Hawkins, D.J., Best, R.J., & Coney, K.A. (1989). *Consumer behavior: Implications for marketing strategy* (4th Ed.). Homewood, IL: Irwin.

Ho, F.N., Ong, B.S., & Lee, S. (1997). A multicultural comparison of shopping patterns among Asian consumers. *Journal of Marketing Theory & Practice, 5*(1), 42-51.

Jarobe, G.R., & McDaniel, C.D. (1987). A profile of browsers in regional shopping malls. *Journal of the Academy of Marketing Science, 15*(1), 46-53.

Korgaonkar, P.K. (1981). Shopping orientations of catalog showroom patrons. *Journal of Retailing, 57*(1), 78-90.

Korgaonkar, P.K. (1984). Consumer shopping orientations, non-store retailers, and consumers' patronage intentions: A multivariate investigation. *Journal of the Academy of Marketing Science, 12*(1), 11-22.

Lastovicka, J.L. (1982). On the validation of lifestyle traits: A review and illustration. *Journal of Marketing Research, 19,*February, 126-138.

Li, H., Kuo, C., & Russell, M.G. (1999). The impact of perceived channel utilities, shopping orientations, and demographics on the consumer online buying behavior. *Journal of Computer-Mediated Communication, 5.* Online: http://www.ascusc.org/jcmc/vol5/issue2/hairong.html.

Lill, D.J., Peterson, R.T., & Wall, L.C. (1981). How small business can use consumer shopping types as a planning tool. *American Journal of Small Business, 6*(1), 36-47.

Limayem, M., Khalifa, M, & Frini, A. (2000). What makes consumers buy from Internet? A longitudinal study of online shopping. *IEEE Transactions on Systems, Man, and Cybernetics*, *30*(4), 421-432.

Lumpkin, J.R. (1985). Shopping orientations segmentations of the elderly consumer. *Journal of the Academy of Marketing Science*, *13,* Spring, 271-289.

Lumpkin, J.R., & Burnett, J.J. (1991-1992). Identifying determinants of store type choice of the mature consumer. *Journal of Applied Business Research*, *8*(1), 89-102.

Lumpkin, J.R., & Darden, W.R. (1982). Relating television preference viewing to shopping orientations, life styles, and demographics: The examination of perceptual and preference dimensions of television programming. *Journal of Advertising*, *11*(4), 56-67.

Lumpkin, J.R., & Hawes, J.M. (1985). Retailing without stores: An examination of catalog shoppers. *Journal of Business Research*, *13,* 139-151.

Lumpkin, J.R., Hawes, J.M., & Darden, W.R. (1986). Shopping patterns of the rural consumer: Exploring the relationship between shopping orientations and outshopping. *Journal of Business Research*, *41*(1), 63-81.

Lumpkin, J.R., & Hunt, J.B. (1989). Mobility as an influence on retail patronage behavior of the elderly: Testing conventional wisdom. *Journal of the Academy of Marketing Science*, *17,* 1-12.

Mägi, A.W. (2003). Share of wallet in retailing: The effects of customer satisfaction, loyalty cards and shopper characteristics. *Journal of Retailing*, *79,* 97-106.

Malone, T.W. (2001). The future of e-business. *Sloan Management Review*, *43*(1), 104.

Moore, G.C. (1991). Development of an instrument to measure the perceptions of adopting an Information Technology innovation. *Information Systems Research*, *2*(3), 192-222.

Moschis, G.P. (1976). Shopping orientations and consumer uses of information. *Journal of Retailing*, *52*(2), 61-70, 93.

Moschis, G.P., Goldstucker, J.L., & Stanley, T.J. (1985). At-home shopping: Will consumers let their computers do the walking? *Business Horizons*, *28*(2), 22-29.

Moye, L.N., & Kincade, D.H. (2003). Shopping orientation segments: Exploring differences in store patronage and attitudes toward retail store environments among female apparel consumers. *International Journal of Consumer Studies*, *27*(1), 58-71.

Norusis, M. (1985). *SPSSX advanced statistics guide*. New York: McGraw-Hill.

Oates, B., Shufeldt, L., & Vaught, B. (1996). A psychographic study of the elderly and retail store attributes. *Journal of Consumer Marketing*, *13*(6), 14-27.

Ownbey, S.F., & Horridge, P.E. (1997). Acculturation levels and shopping orientations of Asian-American consumers. *Psychology & Marketing*, *14*(1), 1-18.

Paden, N., & Stell, R. (2000). Using consumer shopping orientations to improve retail web site design. *Journal of Professional Services Marketing*, *20*(2), 73-85.

Peters, W.H., & Ford, N.M. (1972). A profile of urban in-home shoppers: The other half. *Journal of Marketing*, *36*(1), 62-64.

Reynolds, F.D. (1974). An analysis of catalog buying behavior. *Journal of Marketing*, *38*(3), 47-51.

Rogers, E.M. (1995). *The diffusion of innovations* (4th ed.). New York: Free Press.

Shim, S., & Kotsiopulos, A. (1993). A typology of apparel shopping orientation segments among female consumers. *Clothing and Textiles Research Journal*, *12*(1), 73-85.

Shim, S., & Mahoney, M.Y. (1991). Shopping orientation segmentation of in-home electronic shoppers. *International Review of Retail, Distribution & Consumer Research*, *1*(4), 437-453.

Shim, S., & Mahoney, M.Y. (1992). The elderly mail-order catalogue user of fashion products. *Journal of Direct Marketing*, *6*(1), 49-58.

Siu, N.Y.M., Wang, C.C.L., Chang, L.M.K., & Hui, A.S.Y. (2001). Adapting consumer style inventory to Chinese consumers: A confirmatory factor analysis approach. *Journal of International Consumer Marketing*, *13*(2), 29-47.

Stigler, G.J. (1961). The economics of information. *Journal of Political Economy*, *69,* 213-225.

Stone, G.P. (1954). City shoppers and urban identification: Observations on the social psychology of city life. *American Journal of Sociology*, *60,* 36-45.

Tatzel, M. (1982). Skill and motivation in clothes shopping: Fashion conscious, independent, anxious, and apathetic consumers. *Journal of Retailing*, *58*(4), 90-96.

Tauber, E.M. (1972). Why do people shop? *Journal of Marketing*, *36*(4), 46-59.

Taylor, S., & Todd, P.A. (1995). Understanding Information Technology usage: A test of competing models. *Information Systems Research*, *6*(2), 144-176.

Thomas, J.W. (2002). Skipping MR a major error. *Marketing News*, *36*(5), 50.

Valencia, H. (1982). *Shopping orientations among Hispanics and Anglos in the United States*. Unpublished doctoral dissertation, Georgia State University, Atlanta, GA.

Vijayasarathy, L.R. (2003). Shopping orientations, product types and Internet shopping intentions. *Electronic Markets*, *13*(1), 67-79.

Vijayasarathy, L.R., & Jones, J.M. (2000). Intentions to shop using Internet catalogues: Exploring the effects of product types, shopping orientations, and attitudes towards computers. *Electronic Markets: The International Journal of Electronic Commerce & Business Media*, *10* (1), 29-38.

APPENDIX

Scale Items for Intention to Use Online Shopping

Please indicate the extent to which you agree or disagree with the following statements. (anchored by 1 – Strongly disagree and 7 – Strongly agree)

- I use (intend to use) the Internet frequently to do my shopping. (Intent 1)
- I use (intend to use) the Internet whenever appropriate to do my shopping. (Intent 2)

Please indicate the probability that you will shop using the Internet in the near future. (anchored by 1 – Very improbable and 7 – Very probable) (Intent 3)

Internet Usage Questions

1. Have you used the Internet? ___ Yes ___ No
2. How long have you been using the Internet?
   ___ Less than 6 months ___ 6 months to 1 year ___ 1 to 2 years
   ___ 2 to 4 years ___ More than 4 years

3. On average, how many hours do you spend per week using the Internet?
   ___ Hours

4. In general, have you shopped for any products or services using the Internet?
   ___ Yes ___ No
5. Over the past 12 months, approximately how many times have you shopped for products or services using the Internet? ___
6. Over the past 12 months, approximately how much have you spent on purchases using the Internet? $ ___

Demographic Questions

1. What is the highest level of education you have completed?
   ___ High school ___ Technical degree ___ 1-3 years of college
   ___ Bachelor's degree ___ Graduate degree
2. Please indicate your marital status.
   ___ Single ___ Married ___ Divorced ___ Separated ___ Widowed
3. Which of the following age groups are you in?
   ___ Under 18 ___ 18-24 ___ 25-34 ___ 35-44
   ___ 45-54 ___ 55-64 ___ 65-74 ___ 75 and older

4. Please indicate your gender.
   ___Female___Male
5. Approximately, what is your total household income?
   __Less than 30,000 __$30,000 to 44,999 __$45,000 to 59,999
   __$60,000 to 74,999 __$75,000 to 99,999 __$100,000 or greater

Previously published in the Journal of Electronic Commerce in Organizations, 1(3), 48-72, July/Sept, 2003.

Chapter VI

A Negotiation Agent System in E-Commerce

Chuan-Feng Chiu,Tamkang University, Taiwan

Timothy K. Shih, Tamkang University, Taiwan

ABSTRACT

Due to the growth of Internet and computing power of PCs, activities in the real world have been changed with the help of computers. Internet commerce became an interesting research area along with the change of this new computing environment. In a traditional commerce environment, negotiation was an interest topic in the past. In the new Internet commerce environment, computer-supported negotiation becomes interesting in academics. In this chapter, a computer-supported negotiation agent system on the Internet to help buyers to make decisions is then proposed. We believe that a negotiation problem does not focus only on one issue, but rather on multiple issues. Therefore, our negotiation mechanism is based on a multi-attribute utility theory. And, the negotiation strategy focuses on the weighting adjustment on multiple issues. On the other hand, software agent is a useful technology in this new computing environment and the technology has several advantages to solve different computing problems. In a negotiation process the user cannot handle the complex process individually. Also, the process is a time consuming task. Thus, we use the advantage of agent technology as the major system developed approach. With the help of the technology the system can be more efficient in many Internet commerce applications.

INTRODUCTION

With the growth of the Internet, online transactions grow rapidly with services or goods sold on the Internet. Electronic commerce activities are increasing continuously. In the commerce activities of the real world, several merchants could apply the same product or service with different values of product attributes. In general, a buyer does not care about only one issue of a product or service. He/she would consider several issues and set different parameters within these issues and obtain the best choice. In this chapter, a negotiation mechanism and system is proposed as a negotiation mediator between one user and multiple sellers. The negotiation process is a multi-issue negotiation problem. Therefore, a mechanism based on multi-attribute utility theory is proposed and developed. On the other hand, negotiation is a time consuming task for users. Fortunately, agent technology has several advantages that include automatic intelligence, proactivity and reactivity, and so forth, and is suitable for designing a computer supported negotiation system. Therefore, an agent-based negotiation system is proposed.

Negotiation

Negotiation (Faratin, Sierra, Jennings & Buckle, 1999; Guttman & Maes, 1998a, 1998b; Wu & Soo, 1999; Sandholm & Lesser, 1997; Iizuka, Suzuki, Yamamoto & Ohuchi, 1999; Caglayan & Harrison, 1997; Kang & Lee, 1998; Hammer, Huang, Huang, Pluempitiwiriyawej, Lee, Li, Wang, Liu & Su, 2000; Russel & Norvig, 1995; Lomuscio, Wooldridge & Jennings, 2000) is a popular topic in the academic research on electronic commerce. Negotiation is a process in which all parties in the process want to obtain a better benefit with respect to their own preference. According to the number of the participants the negotiation type can be modeled as one-to-one negotiation, one-to-many negotiation, many-to-many negotiation, and many-to-one negotiation (Bui, Yen, Hu & Sankaran, 2001). One-to-one negotiation is a bargaining process between two parties. One-to-many negotiation is the auction process in which several buyers compete with each other to win the goal. Many-to-one negotiation is a reverse auction process that includes one buyer and several sellers. And, many-to-many negotiation is the process in which a broker mediates transactions for several buyers and sellers. According to the number of buyer and seller participants, the summarization of the negotiation types is showed in Table 1.

In Lomuscio, Wooldridge, and Jennings (2000), several research challenges and directions about the automatic negotiation research are proposed. They reveal the basic components of the negotiation process, which include negotiation protocol, negotiation domain and the agent utility function. A negotiation approach based on the multi-issues negotiation is proposed in Faratin, Sierra, Jennings and Buckle (1999). They defined each role's task in the process and how the interaction of these parties can enable them to reach their goals. Their approach is based on the negotiation rules to achieve the negotiation agreementA negotiation system based on the

Table 1: Types of negotiation

		Buyer Participants	
Seller Participants		One	Many
	One	Bargaining	Auction
	Many	reverse auction	mediators

multi-agent decision technology is proposed in Guttman and Maes (1998a,1998b). They use multi-attribute utility theory and distributed constraint satisfaction as the design discipline. Sandholm and Lesser considered the negotiation problem to be a distributed decision problem and proposed analysis of the distributed cooperative problem of self-interest agent in Sandholm and Lesser (1997). They also proposed the analysis approach and simulation result in the chapter. There exists another approach to solve the negotiation problem, which is game theory. A negotiation protocol based on the theory is proposed in Wu and Soo (1999). They used the third party to ensure the credible problem. They proposed operations in the game theory-based multi-agent negotiation protocol with incomplete knowledge. On the other hand, the negotiation issues are not limiting in one issue, but the processes may be various between several issues. In Sycara (1992), the first system was proposed that could solve the conflicts between multiple issues. Auction-based negotiation research is another negotiation protocol in the past. The topic came from the traditional economic theory. Several auction protocols have existed, including English Auction, Dutch Auction, first-price sealed-bid auction and Vickrey Auction (Bichler, 2000; Wurman, Walsh & Wellman, 1997; McAfee & McMillan, 1987). In 1998 an auction system was proposed that can manage simultaneous auctions and separate each interface of each concurrent auction (Wurman, Wellman & Walsh, 1998). In Sandholm and Huai (2000) they proposed the auction house design based on the mobile agent technology. In their system agents can move to the auction house dynamically.

Agent Technology

Intelligent software agent is a popular technology for solving problems. The software agent can be defined such that the agent is a computing component to performing some tasks according to the knowledge. The attributes that include autonomy, proactivity, and reactivity are the advantage of the software agent, and these are the attributes of the agent-based negotiation system also. An intelligent agent could be able to perceive the environment and make changes to satisfy the design policy of the agent, and the agent could exhibit behavior to satisfy the design goals. On the other hand, because of the growth of Internet agents that have mobile capability, agents could move to other places in the Internet.

Several researchers have discussed the agent technology in the past. In Kiniry and Zimmerman (1997), the authors presented the concept of the agent-based software architecture. The agent communication language and the agent architecture are two important issues. In order to achieve information and message sharing, the agent communication language is the basic mechanism. In order to build the agent computing environment, the agent architecture is another critical problem.

BASAR is a personalized agent system that keeps the web links based on the user bookmarks (Pham & Karmouch, 1998). The system is able to support information updating and reduce the number of links by deleting less frequently used items. In Nwana (1996), a web-based information browse agent is proposed. The system uses the KQML as the agent communication language and reduces networking load. And in order to reduce the complexity of browsing, it uses the structure meta-information mechanism.

With the advent of the Internet computing architecture, the mobility is the new ability of the agent. Hence the agent with the mobile capability has appeared and has become the new research topic. The mobile agent technology overview can be found in Kraus and Magedanz (1996), http://www.trl.ibm.com/aglets/, and http://www.objectspace.com/products/voyager/. Aglets (W3C, 1998) is a mobile agent platform based on the Java technology. The system uses Agent Transfer Protocol as the agent communication infrastructure and the architecture is able to support persistence, security, and agent collaboration. Voyager [30] and Concordia [31] are another two mobile agent systems that also support the agent communication and agent computing environment. The mobile agent platform, MAGNA, and its architecture are proposed in Krause and Magedanz (1996).

In order to design an agent-based negotiation system, we conclude with some issues in the following:

- A mechanism for agents to understand users' requirement: Negotiation would be complete in the same context. Different domains of context could not be negotiated as well.
- Agent platform for executing agents: The agent would be executed in the place that supports agent life cycle and communication.
- Ensure the security for negotiation and agents.
- Apply negotiation strategy to agents to reach agreement.
- A communication mechanism for agents to exchange information would be
- Agent ontology would be designed for communication: Common knowledge is an important infrastructure for agents to communicate with each other.

- Agent interface for users: An interface between users and agents would be designed to be easily exchanged and understood by humans.

The chapter is organized as follows. We describe the motivation and related research in Section 1. We propose the negotiation system model in Section 2. In Section 3 we propose the negotiation-making strategy based on the MAUT theorem. We explain the agent-based negotiation system in Section 4 and propose the negotiation markup language that is used by negotiation agents to exchange the negotiation proposal. Finally, we give a brief conclusion in Section 5.

THE NEGOTIATION MODEL

In the computer supported negotiation system, the negotiation computing model is the basic element, so the negotiation model is proposed in the section first. All parties in the negotiation process would use the negotiation model as the computing kernel. In the following sub-sections the basic negotiation components and computation strategy are described.

The Components of Negotiation

The parties in the negotiation process must achieve their own goals and each party has its private preference. On the other hand, we address the fact that all parties in the negotiation processes are not only interested in one attribute, but in several attributes. The negotiation parties would not make a decision with the price only, and all interesting attributes would influence the negotiation result. So the buyer would send a request proposal including all the interests he/she likes and then the sellers will send the counter-proposal with respect to the buyer's proposal. The buyer would offer the initial request about his/her demands first. The initial request must be translated to the quantitative representation, and then the quantitative request would be sent to several sellers and the request buyer's agent and the seller's agent will begin to negotiate with each other. In the process we stated the negotiation process as a combination of searching, matching and decision strategies. We state the basic functions in the negotiation process as follows:

Searching: The online products or services would be various so that the buyer cannot decide on the better ones for a short while. So in the negotiation process, we must provide the search function to help buyers to find the interests.

Matching: In the real world a product or service will have several combinations within it and with the different combinations the result will be various, so we must provide the matching mechanism to fit the needs precisely.

Decision strategy: The buyer will negotiate with the seller to make the best decision and maximize the buyer's gain. So the negotiation strategy is the most important function in the process. We use the multi-attribute utility theory to achieve the negotiation goal with respect to the buyers' and the sellers' needs.

Ontology: Because of the variety of the product's attributes, the knowledge about each product or service should be the same between the buyers and the sellers. The ontology will avoid the problem of ambiguity within the buyers' and the sellers' knowledge.

Communication: The negotiation between the buyers and the sellers can be treated as the conversation process. We must provide the mechanisms, including the conversation message format and the communication channel.

The Negotiation Support System

The negotiation processes in the real world include several criteria to negotiate. Each party would have its own preference about these criteria. The preference will be different according to the different domains; for example, the hotel reservation will have the attributes including the price, the air condition and the capacity of the room. So in this chapter we use multi-attribute utility theory to model the negotiation problem. First we define a negotiation system as follows:

A negotiation support system $NSS = \{b, S, R, C, U, T\}$

b is the buyer in the negotiation process.

S is a set of all the sellers in the process, $S = \{s_1, s_2, \ldots s_i\}$

R is a set of negotiation attributes, $R = \{r_1, r_2, \ldots, r_j\}$

C is a set of constraints of the buyer and the sellers; each party in the process has different constraints or preferences. The preference includes the maximum and the minimum range of each attribute.

U is set of different utility functions with respect to each buyer and seller.

T is a time period of the negotiation life cycle.

So the negotiation process can be modeled as follows:

$$\mathrm{b} \rightarrow S : R \times C_b \times U_b \rightarrow proposal$$
$$S \rightarrow b : R \times C_S \times U_S \rightarrow counter\text{ - }proposal$$

Each phase of the negotiation process includes the buyer sending he proposal to the sellers and the sellers sending the counter-proposal to the buyer. The process would be continued until the parties reach the agreement or the deadline of the negotiation.

The basic idea of the multi-attribute utility theory is a problem that the results come from two or more attributes. Based on the multi-attribute utility and the preference of each party, we can model the score of the negotiation decision in *Equation(1)*.

$$d(x) = \sum_{i=1}^{n} w_i u_i(x) \qquad (1)$$

$d(x)$ is the total value of the decision function of the party x.
w_i is the weight of the attribute i which comes from the preference of the party x.
$u_1(x)$ is the utility function of attribute i of the party x. The utility function is defined as the score of each attribute with respect to the attribute scale.

In order to update the decision score we consider the response from the opposite side to be an importance factor in adjusting the negotiation decision. Much literature considers the new negotiation decision that is based on the value from the opposite side and adjusts the utility score with respect to the response. But in the chapter we consider that the weight adjustment is another direction in the negotiation decision process. In the real commerce environment the value of the product attributes is fixed and would not change, but the response value of the negotiation process would influence the attribute weight and the negotiation decision. So we design the *Equation(2)* as the formula to revise the weight with respect to each response attribute and generate a new proposal or counter-proposal.

$$w_i = w_i + w_i \times \frac{pv_i - pv_i'}{\max rv - \min rv} \qquad (2)$$

pv is the proposal value of the buyer or the counter-proposal value of sellers. maxrv is the maximum range value of the attribute according to the preference. minrv is the minimum range value of the attribute according to the preference.
w_i is the weight value of the ith attribute.

Figure 1 is shown in the following as the logic view of the computation of each attribute. Ideally the pv value would be in the interval of the maxrv and minrv.

The pv value would be in the negotiation interval if the parties continue to negotiate. Otherwise the pv value would be the best case or under the tolerate value and then the pv value would be adjusted to the better one. The adjustment mechanism will be shown in the next section.

THE NEGOTIATION STRATEGY

The decision-making strategy is the main issue in the negotiation protocol. Therefore, first the message flow of the negotiation process is proposed in the following, and then a Decision Making Machine that is a practical approach for the negotiation protocol is proposed.

Figure 1: Computation range of attribute value

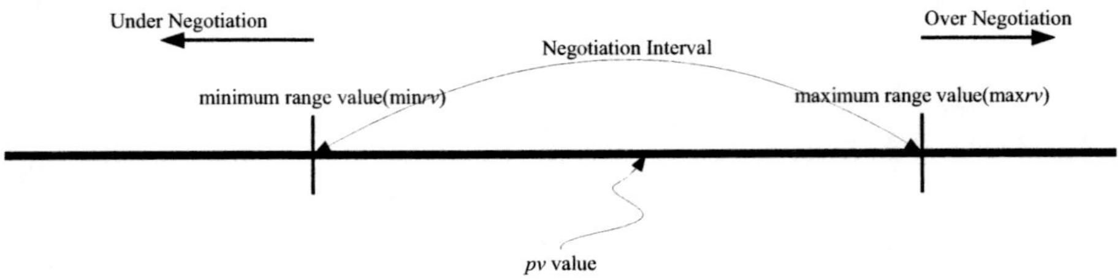

Message Flow of the Negotiation

In the negotiation process the second important module is the negotiation protocol. In Figure 2 the design of the negotiation protocol is proposed. The buyer would send the initial requests to the buyer's agent and the requests includes the buyer's need, the highest and lowest bound of the requested product or service, and the valid time of the negotiation process. The buyer's agent would receive the initial request and decompose the request into several individual sub-goals. For example, a travel trip would be decomposed into a flight reservation, hotel reservation, and the train tickets reservation. Then the sub-goals would be transformed into the quantitative value of each goal with respect to the goal's attributes. The searching agent and the matching would search and match these sub-goals to fit the buyer's needs. Then the suitable seller's agents would get the serial number that is the identification of the negotiation process. Then the buyer's agent would receive the proposal request from the seller's agent. On the other hand the buyer's agent would be cloned to serve the different goals' negotiation. Then the buyer's and the seller's agent would begin to negotiate with the goal. In the negotiation phase the buyer's agent and seller's agent would compute the utility value that was proposed by the previous section and generate the proposal and counter-proposal in each negotiation phase. And the computation flowchart is shown in the figure. Each buyer's agent and each seller's agent would repeat the negotiation phase until the end of the valid negotiation time or until the agreement appears. The agreement rules can be the one of the following:

- A seller's agent would accept the proposal completely; that is, the seller's agent can provide the product or service according to the proposal and meet with the proposal description.
- The distance of the vector of the buyer's and seller's goals' attributes is smaller than a threshold which is an experience value of the past negotiation process.
- The valid negotiation time is expired.

At last the original buyer agent would receive each cloned buyer agent's negotiation results. Then the Buyer Agent would integrate the results into complete results for the buyer.

The Decision-Making Machine

In order to model the decision of the negotiation process, the Decision-Making Machine is proposed to make a decision with respect to each side of seller and buyer preferences. The Decision-Making Machine is shown in Figure 3. In the Decision-Making Machine the assumption is that the maximum range value (max*rv*) and minimum range value (min*rv*) are indicated in the meaning of attribute domain, but not the value of attribute domain in general. Therefore, the min*rv* and max*rv* of buyers and sellers are always in conflict and the max*rv* and min*rv* of buyers is opposite to those of sellers. The machine is divided into two basic elements that include buyer side and seller side. In the following the decision-making process in the Decision-Making Machine is described in detail between buyer side and seller side.

Buyer Side

The *Initial State* is the starting point of the negotiation process and the state will be triggered by the counter-proposal from the seller. According to the attribute value in the counter-proposal, the machine would compare the proposal value (*pv*) with the minimum range value (min*rv*) and the maximum range value (max*rv*) within the preference.

Figure 2: Flow of the negotiation message

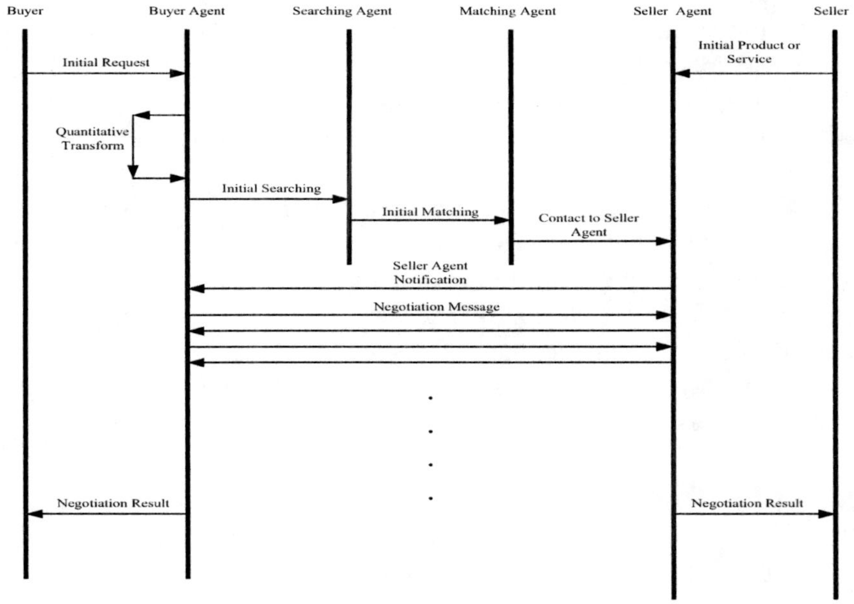

Figure 3: Decision-making machine

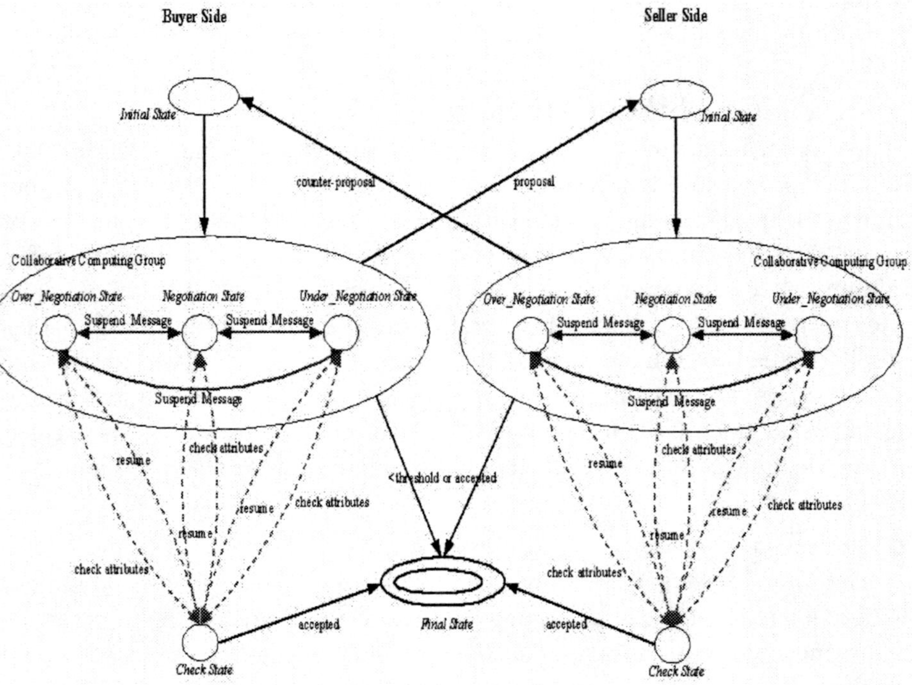

If the *pv* value is larger than max*rv* then the state would go to the *Over_Negotiation State*. In this state the machine would go to the Check State that would check other attributes' *pv* values. If the other *pv* values are all between the min*rv* and max*rv*, then the counter-proposal would be accepted and go to the *Final State*. Otherwise, the machine would keep the *pv* value in the max*rv* and compute new proposals with other attributes.

On the contrary, if the *pv* value is smaller than the min*rv* then the state would go to the *Under_Negotiation State* and adjust the *pv* value to min*rv*, that is, *pv* = min*rv*.

If *pv* value is between the min*rv* and max*rv*, then the state would go to the *Negotiation State* in which the buyer and the seller would negotiate with each other and generate the new proposal. In the other hand the optimal solution would be difficult to find. So in the *Negotiation State* if the distance between the proposal and counter-proposal is smaller than a threshold, then the negotiation would reach the agreement and go to the *Final State*. The *Final State* is the agreement of the negotiation process.

Seller Side

The *Initial State* is also the starting point of the negotiation process and the state will be triggered by the proposal from the buyer. According to the attribute value in the proposal, the machine would compare the proposal value (*pv*) with the minimum range value (min*rv*) and the maximum range value (max*rv*) within the seller preference.

If the *pv* value is larger than max*rv* then the state would go to the *Under_Negotiation State* and adjust the *pv* value to max*rv*, that is, *pv* = max*rv*.

On the contrary, if the *pv* value is smaller than the min*rv* then the state would go to the *Over_Negotiation State*. In this state the machine would go to the *Check State* that would check other attributes' *pv* values. If the other *pv* values are all between the min*rv* and max*rv*, then the proposal would be accepted and go to the *Final State*. Otherwise, the machine would keep the *pv* value in the min*rv* and compute new counter-proposals with other attributes.

If *pv* value is between the min*rv* and max*rv*, then the state would go to the *Negotiation State in* which the buyer and the seller would negotiate with each other and generate the new counter-proposal. In the other hand, because of the same reason of buyer side in the *Negotiation State*, if the distance between the proposal and counter-proposal is smaller than a threshold then the machine would get to the *Final State*.

In the figure the special round component is Collaborative Computing Group and the component would be responsible for computing the utility score with respect to every attribute. If one of the attribute's computing will go to the *Check State* then the attribute would broadcast the Suspend Message to every other attribute's computing agent and execute the checking process. If the state failed then the machine would go back to the Collaborative Computing Group and continue to compute the decision. Algorithm 1 is the procedure used to generate the utility score in the Decision-Making Machine.

SYSTEM ARCHITECTURE AND IMPLEMENTATION

In order to support the run-time environment for the negotiation agent, the negotiation agent system software architecture is proposed to meet the requirement. The basic software architecture design is shown in Figure 4. The architecture in-

Algorithm 1 : Generating Utility Score

for each attribute

for each scale

$$new\_value = \sum_{i=1}^{n} w_i u_i(x)$$

if new_value > utility_score

utility_score = new_value

return utility_score

cludes the agent generation component, agent manager component, ontology, agent databases, buyer's agents, and seller's agents. The agent generation would initialize an agent for the buyer. In the generating process the system would find the suitable seller agents and establishe the connection between the buyer's agent and these sellers' agents. And then the agents can negotiate with each other. When the agent is initialized, the agent manager would control the life cycle and the interaction between these agents. Since the agents would negotiate with common knowledge, the ontology would store the specification of the product or the service, and this would ensure the consistent knowledge between agents. The agent database would store the status of these agents in the system.

The Buyer Agent or Seller Agent software architecture is showed in Figure 5. The buyer agent or seller agent would include the preference and the constraint requirement as the basic initial parameters. The Decision-Making Component is responsible for making new proposal decisions or counter-proposal decisions with respect to the preference and constraints. The component would include the Decision-Making Machine. The Behavior Controller would control the agent behavior that includes the proposal generation or the message flow in the context of the agent in the negotiation process. The Negotiation History would hold the negotiation records including proposals and counter-proposals of each negotiation phrase. The last package is the communication package which is responsible for providing the communication mechanism to the buyer or seller agent and providing a flexible information exchange mechanism for the purpose. Although the KQML is used to be the agent communication language, the KQML only defines the communication

Figure 4: Negotiation agent system architecture

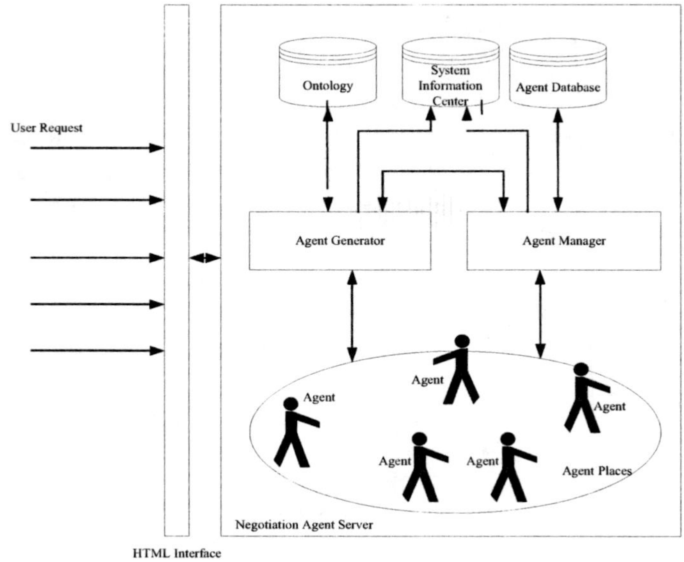

Figure 5: Buyer/seller agent software architecture

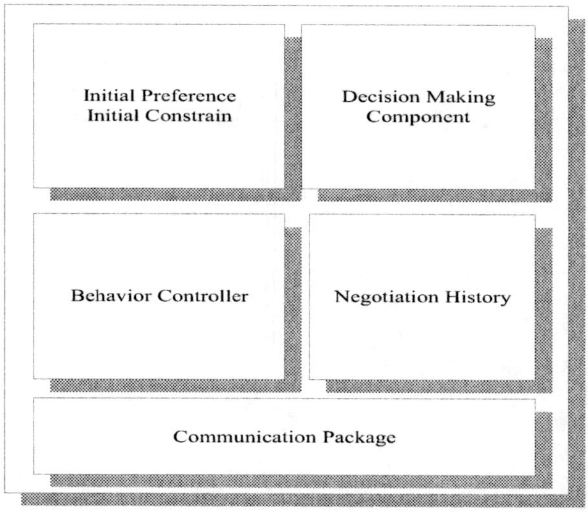

syntax and does not include information exchange content. Therefore, in the chapter the information exchange mechanism uses the XML as the basic message format protocol; that is, each proposal or counter-proposal would be encapsulated in the XML-based document. XML is a subset of SGML language and the mechanism is suitable for information exchange. Hence we create a new definition and manipulation language for the agent negotiation capabilities based on the XML technology in this chapter. So we design a new agent communication language, Agent Negotiation Markup Language(ANML), for the negotiation protocol. Figure 6 shows the DTD for the ANML language and Figure 7 shows an example of the negotiation message based on the ANML.

The proposal or counter-proposal message is composed of several parameters to negotiate, as revealed in the figure. The message includes sender identification, receiver identification, message identification number, message deliver time, negotiation valid time, signature, negotiation target and several attributes with respect to the target. The signature would ensure the message security in the negotiation process. Only the valid agent can view the proposal and reply to the proposal. The attributes would include the negotiation attributes' names and values in the proposal. These attributes would be the negotiation attributes in the negotiation system.

CONCLUSION

In this chapter we proposed an interactive negotiation agent system in Internet Commerce. The review of agent technology and the negotiation process is proposed in this chapter. The decision selection mechanism is proposed and based

Figure 6: The DTD of ANML

```
<!DOCTYPE NEGOTIATION_PROPOSAL [
<!ELEMENT NEGOTIATION_PROPOSAL PROPOSAL>
<!ELEMENT PROPOSAL (SENDER, RECEIVER, MSGNUMBER, DELIVER_TIME,
VALID_TIME, SIGNATURE, TARGET, ATTRIBUTES)>
<!ELEMENT SENDER (#PCDATA)>
<!ELEMENT RECEIVER (#PCDATA)>
<!ELEMENT MSGNUMBER (#PCDATA)>
<!ELEMENT DELIVER_TIME (#PCDATA)>
<!ELEMENT VALID_TIME (#PCDATA)>
<!ELEMENT SIGNATURE (#PCDATA)>
<!ELEMENT TARGET (#PCDATA)>
<!ELEMENT ATTRIBUTES (NAME)*)>
<!ELEMENT NAME (#PCDATA)>
<!ELEMENT PROPOSAL_VALUE (#PCDATA)>
<!ATTLIST NAME
PROPOSAL_VALUE CDATA #REQUIRED>
]>
```

Figure 7: An example of ANML

```
<PROPOSAL>
    <SENDER >1239405</ SENDER>
    <RECEIVER>1209764</RECEIVER>
    <MSGNUMBER >msg339983</MSGNUMBER>
    <DELIVER_TIME>2002/2/2 14:20:35</DELIVER_TIME>
    <VALID_TIME>2002/2/2 20:00:00</VALID_TIME>
    <SIGNATURE>hch6e3f9jjce0</ SIGNATURE>
    <TARGET>Mobile Phone PT110</TARGET>
    <ATTRIBUTES>
        <NAME PROPOSAL_VALUE="200">price</ NAME>
        <NAME PROPOSAL_VALUE="55">weight</ NAME>
        <NAME PROPOSAL_VALUE="red">color</ NAME >
        .
        .
        .
    </ATTRIBUTES>
</PROPOSAL>
```

on the multi-attribute utility theory to make decisions in the negotiation processes. The Decision-Making Machine is proposed to obtain the mechanism and to be the strategy-computing kernel in the chapter. Our main contribution is to provide the computer-mediated mechanism to help users to make decision easily. On the other hand, the negotiation is time-consuming work for humans, so the proposed system would solve such problems on the World Wide Web with the advantage of the agent technology. However, the users' privacy is an important issue of the web application too. To protect users' preference and users' agents is the most important task in the future Internet commerce environment. For this reason, designing a robust security mechanism to protect the user information and agents is the other issue in the agent-based negotiation system research.

REFERENCES

Bichler, M. (2000). A roadmap to auction-based negotiation protocols for electronic commerce. *Proceedings of the 33rd Annual Hawaii International Conference on System Sciences,* 1857-1866.

Bui, T., Yen, J., Hu, J., & Sankaran, S. (2001). A multi-attribute negotiation support system with market signaling for electronic markets. *Group Decision and Negotiation, 10,* 515-537.

Caglayan, A., & Harrison, C. (1997). Agent sourcebook: A complete guide to desktop, Internet, and intranet agents. Wiley Computer Publishing.

Dharap, C., & Freeman, M. (1996). Information agents for automated browsing. *Proceedings of the 1996 ACM CIKM Conference (CIKM'96),* Rockville, Maryland, USA (pp. 296-305).

Faratin, P., Sierra, C., Jennings, N.R., & Buckle, P. (1999). Designing r esponsive and deliberative automated negotiators. *Proceedings of AAAI Workshop on Negotiation: Settling Conflicts and Identifying Opportunities,* Orlando, FL.

Genesereth, M.R. (1994). Software agents. *Communication of the ACM, 37*(7), July, 48-54.

Guttman, R., & Maes, P. (1998a). Agent-mediated integrative negotiation for retail electronic commerce. *Proceedings of the Workshop on Agent Mediated Electronic Trading (AMET'98)*, Minneapolis, Minnesota, (May).

Guttman, R., & Maes, P. (1998b). Cooperative vs. competitive multi-agent negotiations in retail electronic commerce. *Proceedings of the Second International Workshop on Cooperative Information Agents (CIA'98),* Paris (July 3-8).

Hammer, J., Huang, C.B., Huang, Y.H, Pluempitiwiriyawej, C., Lee, M., Li, H., Wang, L., Liu, Y., & Su, S.Y.W. (2000). The IDEAL approach to Internet-based negotiation for e-business. *Proceedings of 16th International Conference on Data Engineering,* (pp. 666-667). Online: *http://www.merl.com/projects/concordia/http://www.objectspace.com/products/voyager/http://www.trl.ibm.com/aglets/.*

Iizuka, H., Suzuki, K., Yamamoto, M., and Ohuchi. (1999). Learning of words in negotiation between autonomous agents. *Proceeding of IEEE International Conference on Systems, Man, and Cybernetics (SMC '99), 2,* 598-603.

Kang, J.-K., & Lee, E.-S. (1998). A negotiation model in electronic commerce to reflect multiple transaction factors and learning. *Proceedings of 12th International Conference on Information Networking (ICOIN-12),* (pp. 275-278).

Kiniry, J., & Zimmerman, D. (1997). A hand-on look at Java mobile agents. *IEEE Internet Computing, 1*(4).

Krause, S., & Magedanz, T. (1996). Mobile service agents enabling intelligence on demand in telecommunications. *Proceedings of the 1996 IEEE Global Telecommunications Conference,* London, (pp. 78-84).

Lomuscio, A., Wooldridge, M., & Jennings, N.R. (2000). A classification scheme for negotiation in electronic commerce. In C. Sierra and F. Dignum (Eds.), *A European perspective on agent-mediated electronic commerce.* Springer Verlag.

McAfee, R., & McMillan, P.J. (1987). Auction and bidding. *Journal of Economic Literature, 25,* 699-738.

Nwana, H.S. (1996). Software agents: An overview. *Knowledge Engineering Review, 11*(3).

Pham, V.A., & Karmouch, A. (1998). Mobile software agents: An overview. *IEEE Communication Magzine,* (July).

Russell, S., & Norvig, P. (1995). *Artificial intelligence: A modern approach.* Prentice Hall.

Sandholm, T., & Huai, Q. (2000, March/April). Nomad: Mobile agent system for an Internet-based auction house. *IEEE Internet Computing, 4*(2), 80-86.

Sandholm, T., & Lesser, V. (1997). Coalitions among computationally bounded agents. *Artificial Intelligence, 94*(1), Special issue on Economic Principles of Multiagent Systems, 99-137

Sycara, K. (1992). The PERSUADER. In D. Shapiro (Ed.), *The encyclopedia of artificial intelligence.* John Wiley & Sons.

Thomas, C.G., & Fischer, G. (1997). Using agents to personalize the Web. *Proceedings of the 1997 ACM IUI Conference (IUI'97),* Orlando, Florida, USA (pp. 53-60).

W3C. (1998). *XML 1.0 specification.*

Wu, S.-H., & Soo, V.-W. (1999). Game theoretic reasoning in multi-agent coordination by negotiation with a trusted third party. *Proceedings of Autonomous Agent'99,* Seattle, Washington, USA.

Wurman, P.R., Walsh, W.E., & Wellman, M.P. (1997). Flexible double auctions for electronic commerce: Theory and implementation. *Decision Support Systems.*

Wurman, P.R., Wellman, M.P., & Walsh, W.E. (1998). The Michigan Internet AuctionBot: A configurable auction server for human and software agents.

Proceedings of the Second International Conference on Autonomous Agents, (pp. 301-308).

Previously published in the Journal of Electronic Commerce in Organizations, 1(1), 1-16, Jan/Mar, 2003.

Chapter VII

Business Interactions in a Virtual Organisation: Visualising Inter-Organisational Systems Complexity

Karin Axelsson, Linköping University, Sweden

ABSTRACT

This chapter focuses upon the complexity of inter-organisational systems (IOS)—on one hand enabling organisations to become successful actors conducting electronic commerce, and on the other hand being organisationally very complex and demanding to develop, implement, and use, since several organisations with differing objectives are involved. The chapter proposes a model to analyse business interaction, the business action theory (BAT) phase model. The aim of the chapter is to show how BAT can increase the understanding of business interaction conducted in complex inter-organisational contexts, such as business networks and virtual organisations. In order to achieve this purpose the BAT phase model is applied on a virtual organisation. The model visualises and gives structure to the business interaction within this network of organisations. Understanding of such business interaction is important when developing and implementing IOS, since (part of) the business interaction will be conducted through the IOS.

INTRODUCTION

Inter-organisational systems (IOS) are information and communication technology-based systems that transcend legal organisational boundaries (e.g., Konsynski,

1992; Kumar & van Dissel, 1996). This kind of system is no new phenomenon; the concept has been discussed since the 1960s and had a peak of interest in the 1980s (Cavaye & Cragg, 1995, p. 14). The last years' increased focus on business networks, co-operation across organisational boundaries, and virtual organisations has, though, put an even greater emphasise on IOS issues. In many of today's organisations co-operation and relationships with other organisations are vital, and Information Technology (IT) is an important enabler to such inter-organisational activities (Timmers, 1999; Senn, 2000). IT-supported business activities on an inter-organisational level are often characterised as electronic commerce. There are many definitions of electronic commerce: for example Timmers' (1999, p. 4) general definition, *"doing business electronically"* or Turban et al. (2000, p. 4), who define electronic commerce as *"an emerging concept that describes the process of buying and selling or exchanging of products, services, and information via computer networks including the Internet."* These definitions of electronic commerce do not exclude intra-organisational IT-supported activities. This chapter will, however, put its emphasis on inter-organisational issues, even though there is always a mutual dependency between intra- and inter-organisational activities.

New organisational forms, such as business networks and virtual organisations, imply that the complexity in inter-organisational relationships has increased in several dimensions. An organisation has relations to many other organisations, acting as both customers and suppliers. Each organisation is depending on several other organisations, is involved in inter-organisational development projects with other organisations, and acts as a part in many co-existing dyads, supply chains, networks, and alliances. These very complex inter-organisational contexts that have become many organisations' daily situation put increased demands on each organisation's ability to understand and relate to issues concerning business interaction. Thus, it is urgent to develop knowledge and models regarding business interaction analysis.

Initially, many textbooks and journal articles discussing electronic commerce viewed the phenomenon as an important way to handle the pressure put on modern organisations, without discussing difficulties of electronic commerce in particular detail (e.g., Tapscott et al., 1998; Turban et al., 2000). At the same time, IOS and electronic data interchange (EDI) literature has highlighted these difficulties for a long time (e.g., Cunningham & Tynan, 1993; Webster, 1993; Kumar & van Dissel, 1996). More than 10 years ago, Konsynski (1992, p. 45) already stressed the fact that IOS implies an increased complexity while involving several organisations in the development and use; for example, loss of control and influence, increased uncertainty, consensus problems, and standardisation problems. In recent electronic commerce literature, however, the conflict between possible benefits from electronic commerce and difficulties in developing IT and organisations successfully for this purpose has been more thoroughly acknowledged (e.g., Rayport & Jaworski, 2001; Chaffey, 2002; Turban, 2002). The dot com crash has resulted in many lessons to be learned (e.g., Lientz & Rea, 2001). There is also an increasing interest in these issues when discussing trust in inter-organisational relationships (Tomkins, 2001) and trust in electronic commerce (e.g., Keen et al., 2000; Kim & Prabhakar, 2000). Chan and Swatman (2002) also highlight the complexity of business-to-business electronic commerce and recognise what they perceive as a gap in the theory about the electronic commerce implementation process.

This chapter takes its point of departure in this complexity, when introducing a model for analysing business interaction between organisations conducting, in this case, electronic commerce. The business action theory (BAT) phase model (e.g., Goldkuhl, 1998; Axelsson et al., 2002) divides business interaction between a customer and a supplier into six phases, consisting of generic business actions. Business interaction is defined as business communication and exchange of value. Different kinds of exchange take place in these generic, interactive phases. Implementing and using IOS demand understanding of the business actions conducted by two or more organisations. The BAT phase model views a customer and a supplier from a symmetric perspective. This implies that even though the relationship between the customer and the supplier might be asymmetric regarding, for example, size, power, commitment, or dependence, the relationship will be analysed in a balanced, symmetric way. If we relate this to the IOS complexity introduced above, the BAT phase model is suitable to use in IOS development and implementation processes since these kinds of processes involve at least two organisations that need to be analysed. The motives for using the BAT phase model for this kind of analysis are first of all that the model gives structure to complex business transactions inherent in inter-organisational relationships thanks to its phase division. The model also assists us in understanding this complexity by breaking down interactions between buyers and sellers into understandable business actions (such as negotiating, ordering, promising, etc.). Yet another aim addressed by the model focuses on communicative aspects of these transactions, which is an important understanding in any systems development process.

The main purpose of this chapter is to show how BAT can increase the understanding of business interaction conducted in complex inter-organisational contexts, such as business networks and virtual organisations. In order to achieve this purpose the BAT phase model is applied on a virtual organisation (called Netshop), that is, several co-operating firms acting together as one organisation towards customers (Hedberg et al., 1997). This is done in order to show how the model visualises and gives structure to business interaction within a network of organisations. Understanding of such business interaction is important when developing and implementing IOS, since (part of) the business interaction will be conducted through the IOS. If IOS development and implementation are performed without enough understanding of existing business interactions there is an obvious risk that successful ways of action are abandoned and less functional routines are preserved. Understanding of existing business interaction is also useful when the IOS already is in use, since such understanding might serve as a basis for future improvements of both business processes and the IOS.

Thus, the chapter addresses issues important for practitioners in organisations that are about to enter an IOS-supported partnership as well as organisations already using an IOS. Knowledge about how business interaction can be analysed and understood is vital for both these groups. Additionally, the chapter proposes BAT as a theoretical model to conduct business interaction analysis, which makes researchers an important target group for the chapter as well.

The development and adoption of BAT has so far been focused on dyads, that is, on a pair of organisations acting as customer and supplier (e.g., Axelsson et al., 2000). The theory is, though, extended beyond dyadic analysis between two actors in this chapter. BAT is here used to illustrate business interaction between a customer and a virtual organisation consisting of several interacting business actors (i.e., different legal units). This wider scope is in accordance with Kurnia and Johnston (2000), who argue that empirical studies of IOS adoption so far have been concerned with individual organisations or pair-wise relationships. Instead, they propose an expanded unit of analysis to be able to capture the complexity and dynamics of interactions between organisations (ibid.). Cousins (2002) means that using the relationship between two organisations as the unit of analysis is incorrect, since there are numerous interfaces between two organisations in a single relationship. Instead, he emphasises that the analysis should cover many relations between different persons in the two organisations. The relationship should not be viewed as an entity, but as an intra- and inter-organisational process (ibid.). The BAT phase model may be seen as a process model of business interaction, where relationships between different individuals are being analysed within different business phases. In that sense several interfaces between the organisations are part of the business interaction analysis.

After this introduction, the complexity of IOS is further discussed in the second section, in order to give a foundation for the chapter. Then, the theoretical sources of BAT are presented in the third section, together with a description of the BAT phase model. In the fourth section, the BAT model is applied on a virtual organisation in order to give an empirical illustration of how business interaction analysis might be conducted. The findings are then discussed in the fifth section. Conclusions from the analysis are presented in the final section, followed by some remarks about future research.

THE IOS COMPLEXITY

Organisations have become closer connected to each other, both through establishing strategic partnerships and developing technical artefacts together (Håkansson & Snehota, 1995; Hedberg et al., 1997). This shift in focus from intra- to inter-organisational issues has been on-going for a long time. In order to be a competitive business actor, it is no longer enough only to make internal activities and processes more efficient. Organisations also have to interact with customers, suppliers, and other stakeholders in a successful way. Doing business builds to an increased extent upon deep and long-term relationships. Organisations tend to adjust their processes to each other and such mutual adjustments often imply inter-organisational development projects. Håkansson and Snehota (1989, p. 187) stated that *"no business is an island"* and this phrase has become even more evident as the IT revolution over the last ten years has generated enormous possibilities for IT-supported interaction between organisations. Tang et al. (2001, p. 50) also emphasise that effective use of IOS for electronic commerce requires organisations to co-ordinate and integrate the flow of information and materials within and across organisations.

Senn (2000, p. 25) distinguishes between five classes of IOS: electronic data interchange (EDI), electronic funds transfer (EFT), electronic forms, integrated messaging, and shared databases. He also characterises IOS as mainly concentrated on business-to-business interaction. The communication infrastructure of an IOS is predetermined and the organisations that share an IOS have defined and pre-established relationships (ibid.). Kumar and van Dissel (1996) stress that IOS exist in order to support and implement co-operation and strategic alliances between two or more organisations. They develop an interdependency-based typology for IOS, distinguishing between:

- Pooled information resource IOS (pooled interdependency)
- Value/supply chain IOS (sequential interdependency)
- Networked IOS (reciprocal interdependency)

These IOS types are ordered along the dimension of interdependency in inter-organisational relationships. Kumar and van Dissel (ibid.) use these three types of IOS to discuss the risks of conflict attached to each IOS type. By doing so, they provide important understanding of how different types of IOS must be handled in order to manage the associated risks in a feasible way. The IOS type most relevant to discuss in this chapter is the value/supply chain IOS resulting in sequential interdependency between a customer and a supplier, whose business process is partly or fully conducted through an IOS. This is done even though the metaphoric value/supply chain is not really applicable to the virtual organisation discussed later in the chapter. Kumar and van Dissel's discussion is, however, relevant to the IOS complexity affecting customers and suppliers in the empirical example. For an extensive literature review of the evolution of supply relationships (chains and networks) over time (see Kinder, 2003).

An example of a value/supply chain IOS is an EDI or Internet-based application used for transferring standardised business documents (such as orders, confirmations, and invoices) between the customer and the supplier. This kind of system could also be labelled an inter-organisational ERP system; see for example Ash and Burn (2003), who discuss the implementation and use of what they call "e-ERP systems". Viewed in a BAT perspective this means that communicative business actions are made through the IOS. As both Kumar and van Dissel (ibid.) and Webster (1993) claim, such systems and the standardisation work needed to develop them might lead to conflicts and power shifts between the business actors.

When focusing on value/supply chain IOS, there are some major risks of potential conflicts associated. Kumar and van Dissel (1996) mention investments done to establish the IOS that have little or no value in other business interactions, that is, software development and implementation. They also discuss information asymmetry, which deals with the risks of one business actor taking advantage of the other by using information inaccessible for the other actor. Another potential risk is that resources are transferred to the business partner as part of the relationship, which cannot be returned if the relationship is terminated; that is, information and know-how. Kumar and van Dissel (ibid.) also identify technical risks if the IOS is built on immature and untested technologies or standards. Yet another potential risk is sub-optimisation in the supply chain, if an IOS is developed to optimise the business actions between two business actors who take place in a larger value system (ibid.).

When reviewing IOS literature over the last ten years, it is obvious that many authors emphasise that IOS development should not be viewed as solely a technical solution to rationalise the external flow of documents (e.g., Streng & Sol, 1992; Swatman et al., 1994). To achieve possible advantages out of IOS, each actor has to change and develop its organisation, including both manual and computerised routines (Nygaard-Andersen & Bjørn-Andersen, 1994). Changing internal business processes is, though, not enough since inter-organisational interaction implies reciprocal influence between internal and external business processes (Davenport, 1993). This means that developing and implementing IOS should comprise both intra- and inter-organisational changes and these changes need to be conducted in coherence of each other. Konsynski (1992, p. 61) claims, for example, that *"The best leverage of the IOS opportunity lies in redesign, re-engineering, or re-rationalization of business processes, not just in one organization, but across many organizations."* A key issue here is that IOS development might lead to organisational development and strengthened relations between organisations.

IOS imply many possibilities to make organisations more effective, to improve quality of customer service, and to facilitate co-operation across organisational boundaries, just to mention a few issues. Nevertheless, there is a severe complexity in IOS development and implementation since two or more organisations are involved in the process. Developing and implementing intra-organisational systems implies that conflicting goals and expectations should be handled within one organisation, which might be a challenge in many cases (e.g., Axelsson & Avdic, 2001). In the case of IOS development and implementation, this challenge is multiplied since several organisations have to negotiate and agree upon common solutions and decisions. Thus, the fact that IOS adoptions span organisational boundaries adds complexity to the situation (Kurnia & Johnston, 2000).

The adoption of IOS and electronic commerce forces organisations to make decisions in a more complex way than before. Debreceny et al. (2002) highlight that there has to be a simultaneous focus on (1) integration of internal systems; (2) development of IOS; (3) adoption of new IT-enabled business models; and (4) wholesale restructuring of existing business models. This wide range of decision areas makes it obvious that it is important not to delimit IOS adoption to a shift of communication media and rationalisation of internal processes, as mentioned above. IOS is not only a technical artefact for information transfer between organisations. Inter-organisational interaction supported by IOS also implies commitments being offered and fulfillled. This is one of the main ideas in BAT, which will be discussed further in the next section. Several studies have, however, shown that neglecting social and relational dimensions of IOS is a common, but less successful, strategy for IOS development and utilisation (Kumar & van Dissel, 1996; Kumar et al., 1998). Instead, technology tends to be the actual focus of venture, often resulting in low usage rates, dissatisfaction, unachieved expectations, and general failure of IOS (Allen et al., 2000, p. 36). Chan and Swatman (2002) show that non-technical factors (i.e., management and business factors) are important for the success of the electronic commerce implementation process.

Differences between organisations might cause problems when developing and implementing IOS; thus, if treated in a sound way organisational differences may instead be possibilities for inter-organisational learning, change and improvements. Nevertheless, as Kumar and van Dissel (1996, p. 295) conclude, *"the promise of cooperation, if not nurtured, can easily degenerate into conflict."* This literature review thus shows that increasing the understanding of the IOS complexity is a vital research aim.

There are several authors highlighting the importance of understanding business interaction to conduct successful IOS development and implementation projects. Kumar and van Dissel (ibid., p. 296) stress the importance of metaphors such as common understanding, peace, and diplomacy for IOS to become strategic instruments of great promise. Allen et al. (2000, p. 36) state that handling the relational dimension of IOS in a successful way requires a well-defined foundation and rules common to all co-operating organisations. Formulating such rules implies cultural awareness and understanding of each other's business objectives in establishing an IOS. Analysing business interaction with the help of BAT is one way to gain common understanding of the involved organisations' business interaction and their underlying objectives.

The BAT phase model mainly addresses aspects of the IOS complexity related to visualisation and analysis of business actions, business communication, and exchange of value. The IOS complexity covers, however, many other aspects such as trust in relationships, social dimensions (e.g., inter-personal relationships between employees in the organisations, which long-term relationships often are built upon), and so on. These aspects are not explicitly addressed by the BAT phase model, even though the application of the model might generate results that could shed some light on these issues as well.

BUSINESS ACTION THEORY

The business action theory (BAT) conceptualises business interaction. Business interaction is defined as consisting of business communication and exchange of value. BAT divides business interaction into six generic phases encompassing generic, interactive business actions between supplier and customer; for example offer, express purchase interest, order, confirm order, deliver, and pay. Different types of exchange, material and immaterial, occur in these six phases.

The first version of BAT was presented by Goldkuhl (1996). The theory has then been further refined and grounded in both theory and practice, documented by, for example, Goldkuhl (1998), Melin and Goldkuhl (1999), Axelsson et al. (2000), Goldkuhl and Melin (2001), Lind and Goldkuhl (2001), Axelsson et al. (2002), and Axelsson (2003). The following presentation of BAT builds upon these earlier works.

Grounding BAT in Theory

A dyad consists of a supplier and a customer performing actions directed towards each other. These actions together form a business interaction. Dahlqvist (1998, p. 14) defines interaction as denoting a relation, or a process, between different actors. Interaction is seen as the process by which the co-ordination of activities and/or resources is managed (ibid.). Parts of this business interaction consist of exchange of information (i.e., business communication) and parts of it can be labelled as exchange of value, for example, exchange of products (goods/services) versus money. The business communication cannot be seen as solely information transfer. Instead, within the language action perspective, communication and language use are conceived as action. Speech act theory implies that *speaking is acting* (Austin, 1962; Searle, 1969). Speech act theory is an important theoretical source for BAT. Thus, the business communication consists of communicative acts that include both representation of the world talked about and certain "relationship creators". When performing a communicative act, an actor is not only presenting some facts of the world. The customer is *doing* something when communicating with the supplier; for example, commitments and expectations are raised when the customer makes an order and the supplier promises to deliver the goods. When business communication is supported by an IOS, these communicative actions are performed through the system. If we relate this to the complexity of IOS discussed in the previous section, this implies that BAT aims at establishing understanding of the business actions (and their purposes) necessary when developing and implementing an IOS. Unless the business actions are analysed thoroughly, there is a severe risk that the IOS development and implementation processes only focus on technical issues and, thus, result in failure of the IOS as mentioned by, for example, Allen et al. (2000).

A theory of business interaction like BAT benefits from a proper understanding of communication given by, for example, the speech act theory of Austin (1962), Searle (1969) and Habermas (1984). The main point in speech act theory that has been adopted in BAT can be characterised by Austin's (1962) critique of the "descriptive fallacy" in philosophy and science, that is, the misconception that language is used only for description of the world. We use language to describe the world, but we also do a lot of other things with language. We promise, request, command, declare, issue, appoint, excuse and thank, just to mention some typical speech acts.

Speech act theory is, though, not the only theoretical foundation of BAT. Besides understanding communication, it is important to rely on business relationship theories, for example the network perspective or industrial network approach (e.g., Håkansson & Snehota, 1995) and relationship marketing (e.g., Grönroos, 1994; Gummesson, 1999). From these kinds of theories, BAT gains its business context. Business relationship theories contribute to BAT by introducing important concepts like business dyad, network, relation, interaction, transaction, and so on.

BAT Phase Model

The ideas of BAT are manifested in the BAT phase model, which illustrates the business interaction between a supplier and a customer. The phases describe the generic acts that are performed when a supplier sells something and a customer purchases something. The graphical BAT model is presented in Figure 1, where the different phases are made explicit. BAT divides business interaction into six generic phases: (1) establishing business prerequisites phase; (2) exposure and contact search phase; (3) proposal phase; (4) contractual phase; (5) fulfillment phase; and (6) assessment phase.

The first phase is concerned with establishing prerequisites for performing business. On the supplier side the keyword is *ability*. The supplier must have ability (a capacity and know-how) to perform business, to make offers and contracts and to fulfill these contracts. This ability can exist within the supplier's own organisation, but it can also be mobilised by the supplier from other actors outside the organisation. The virtual organisation described later in the chapter can be seen as a special case of such ability mobilisation. The customer does not have the corresponding ability (or has certain reasons for not utilising such ability). In the operations of the customer there are *lacks and needs,* which may be satisfied by potential suppliers and their products (goods/services). This first phase represents the processes of establishing prerequisites for business interaction.

The second and third phases can together be viewed as a *business interest* stage. In the second phase both parties search for contact. The ability of the supplier is exposed and offered to the market. The lacks and needs of the customer give rise to desire and potential demand, which guide a possible search for products or suppli-

Figure 1: Business action theory—A phase model (Goldkuhl, 1998)

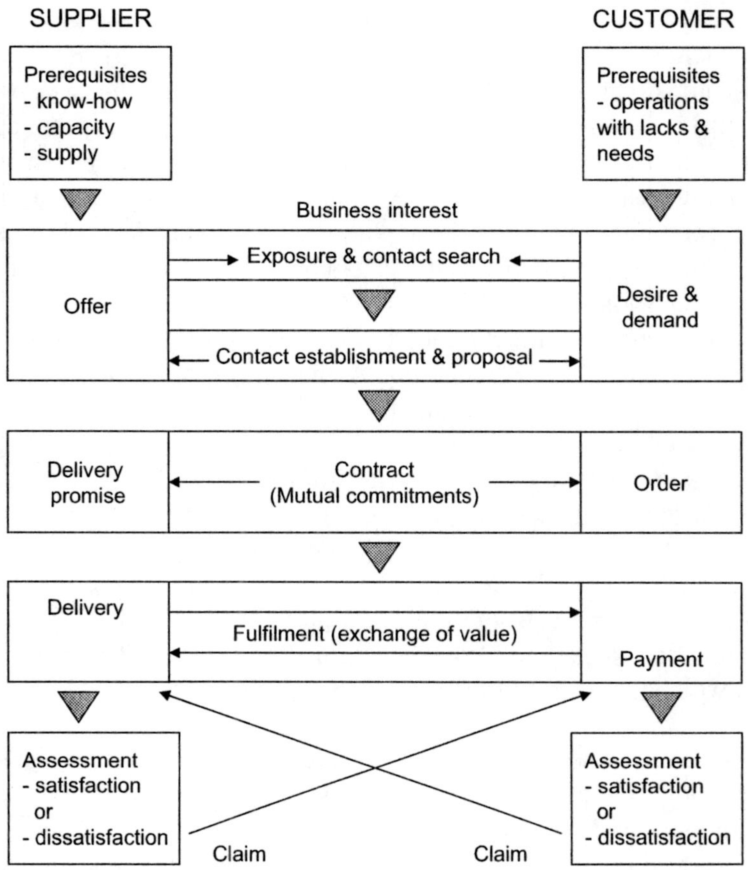

ers. To find each other the supplier and the customer must *expose* their interests to perform business. Advertising can be seen as an example of actions in this phase. In electronic commerce the use of banners is another way of exposing the business interest of the supplier.

When the supplier and the customer have found each other they *establish contact* and perhaps start *negotiating* (phase three). The communication can here be described as *proposal* stating. Bids and counter bids are made. The desire and demand of the customer are expressed. The supplier can make different offers. Of course in many cases there are fixed (and standard) offers, which have to be taken or rejected as such. Proposal is the key notion in this phase. If we analyse proposals from a communicative action perspective, a *dual* character can be seen. A proposal from a supplier (i.e., an offer) can be seen as both an attempt to influence a potential buyer to make a purchase decision and an expression of willingness to sell under certain conditions.

The negotiation in phase three can be transferred into a contractual phase. This is the fourth phase, where the keyword is *agreement*. Customer and supplier come to an agreement concerning the business transaction. The contract is a mutual communicative action expressing the *mutual commitments* made; that is, commitments for future actions. This involves a delivery promise of the supplier. The order of the customer also includes an obligation for future payment. The concept of contract is used in a generic sense. Written contracts are not presumed, but they occur of course in many business transactions. An oral agreement is also seen as a contract. In electronic commerce the contractual phase has been much discussed, since there are many web sites where the customer is unsure when or if he has committed himself to buying a product.

These different commitments must be *fulfilled*; otherwise the contract is broken. The supplier must deliver and the customer must pay (phase five). These material actions can be guided and accompanied by different communicative actions. The supplier can enclose a delivery note together with the delivery. The supplier usually presents an invoice to evoke payment from the customer. The business logic is of course differing regarding deliverance of physical and digital products, which affects organisations conducting electronic commerce.

If not satisfied with the delivery, the customer can make a *claim*. The supplier is requested to make some modification in the delivery. Correspondingly, the supplier can make payment claims towards the customer. This is the sixth and last phase, which involves *assessments* of the fulfillment leading to *satisfaction* or *dissatisfaction*.

This generic business interaction model describes the inherent business logic when customers and suppliers perform business with each other. It describes generic business actions of both communicative and material character performed by supplier and customer. Making business involves with necessity communication; otherwise customer and supplier cannot agree on the business deal. Such communication can be performed through an IOS as well as through other media. Business interaction cannot, however, be reduced to only communication. It must include the material acts of delivering goods and/or services and paying.

The BAT phase model is an interaction and exchange model. It avoids building a theory of one party viewing the other one. This is often done in marketing literature; an active supplier viewing and influencing a passive customer. Such a uni-directional model has been criticised by, for example, Glynn and Lehtinen (1995). Instead, the model gives attention to both parties and the exchange character of making business; that is, the analysis is made from a symmetrical perspective. In the BAT model the two roles have been given equal importance, independently of the relation's state. This is also in accordance with communicative action theories making sender and recipient equally important as a basic theoretical stance; see Habermas (1984, p. 323f). This does not, however, imply that it in some situations cannot be appropriate to put a special emphasis on either part. Within the frame of BAT it is, for example, possible to study the marketing efforts of a supplier as foreground and have the actions of customers as background.

This interaction approach emphasises that exchange is going on in each phase (besides the first phase). Both parties direct actions towards each other. Phase 2, exposure and contact search, includes *exchange of interest*. Seller and buyer signal their possible interest for making business. In phase 3, customer and supplier *exchange proposals*. They communicate bids and counter bids. They express preferences and try to influence each other in order to arrive at an acceptable deal. In the contractual fourth phase the parties *exchange commitments*. They commit themselves to future actions, that is, the proposed exchange of value. This *exchange of value* takes place in the fifth phase, the fulfillment. The assessment phase, the sixth and last phase, can include the *exchange of acceptances or claims*.

BAT acknowledges the *iterative* nature of performing business. There can be iterations within a business transaction between different phases. There is also a *cyclic* nature of performing business, though not graphically described in the BAT phase model. A performed business transaction will be a basis for future business transactions. Thus, from phase 6 there is a return back to phase 1. This is especially relevant in the case of long-term relationships between organisations supported by an IOS, which is discussed further in the next section.

Using BAT as an Analysis Model for Long-Term B2B Interaction

The BAT phase model is a generic model applicable both on short-term and long-term business interaction. A short-term interaction might be a business transaction conducted by a customer and a supplier once and then never repeated again. The actors are labelled as customer and supplier; these roles can be used in both business-to-business and business-to-consumer contexts. In this chapter, long-term business-to-business interaction is one focus, though, since the use of IOS implies an existing relationship between two or more organisations (Senn, 2000). Earlier adoptions of the BAT phase model in this kind of situation have resulted in certain characteristics that have been added to the original model. In this section, based upon Axelsson et al. (2000), the BAT phase model specialised in long-term business-to-business interaction is presented.

In long-term relationships there is recurrent performance of business transactions. Two important aspects might be highlighted as special cases of business interactions: (1) the reduced need to search for new business parties and (2) the existence of long-term agreements.

The first aspect means that phase 2 in the BAT model (see Figure 1) may be understood as short-circuited when there already exists a business relationship. The two parties already possess knowledge about each other and, if they are content with the relationship, they will not be looking for any actual alternatives. There is a mutual trust and loyalty between the parties to continue the business relationship.

Important to notice is the fact that an IOS might be a barrier to change of business partners, even though one part is unsatisfied with the relationship (see e.g., Timmers, 1999, who discusses this risk with EDI-based systems). Large investments in IOS are one example of how relationships can be preserved regardless of how satisfied the business partners are with the existing situation.

The other aspect implies that there are proposals and contracts on two levels. There can be long-term agreements (on a principal level), concerning a business partnership and also plans for delivery of products for a longer period. Based on these long-term agreements there will be a recurrent performance of business transactions. There will of course also be agreements within each business transaction (suborders and confirmations). As stated above, contracts do not necessarily mean written contracts.

In long-term business-to-business interaction, the interaction is therefore divided into three general phases with corresponding sub-phases (Axelsson et al., 2000):

A. *Preparatory phase*
   A1. Initial establishing business prerequisites sub-phase
   A2. Exposure and contact search sub-phase
B. *Relationship management phase*
   B1. Principal proposal sub-phase
   B2. Principal contractual sub-phase
   B3. Adapting business prerequisites sub-phase
C. *Business transaction phase*
   C1. Transaction proposal sub-phase
   C2. Transaction contractual sub-phase
   C3. Fulfillment sub-phase
   C4. Assessment sub-phase

The preparatory phase includes initial stages before the long-term relationship is established (phases 1 and 2 in the general BAT model). Before such a relationship is established the business parties probably "test" each other in repeated business transactions. See for example Ford et al. (1998), who identify four different stages of development in a business relationship; the pre-relationship stage, the exploratory stage, the developing stage, and the stable stage.

In long-term relationships there is a general phase interspersed between the initial preparation and the particular transaction. This is called relationship management since it is concerned with work on the relationship level giving prerequisites for recurrent transactions. In a long-term relationship there can be negotiations not only concerning business transactions. There will be negotiations on a long-term basis forming long-term contracts. The business parties can also suggest other changes concerning the business abilities. A customer can for example suggest that the supplier should make investments in production equipment in order to enhance product quality. Developing and implementing an IOS is an example of such an investment. The detailed content of these three general phases is further illustrated by the empirical example below. An extensive literature review of relationship management is presented by Cousins (2002).

So far, the BAT research has been focused mainly on dyadic business situations consisting of interaction between one customer and one supplier. This does not, however, imply that the BAT phase model is limited to this kind of one-to-one dyad level. In this chapter, the model is applied to illustrate business interactions between several actors. This means that when going through the six phases of a business transaction, different actors act as supplier in different phases. The two roles of customer and supplier, on the other hand, still exist as a pair throughout the entire transaction.

ANALYSING BUSINESS INTERACTION IN NETSHOP

In this section, the BAT phase model is applied to illustrate business interactions taking place between different actors (i.e., different legal units) within an IOS-supported virtual organisation. Before doing this, the concept of virtual organisations is defined.

Virtual Organisations

There are many new patterns of organising facilitated both by IT innovations, such as Internet, and by new ways of looking upon business actors, not only in the light of competition but also from a co-operation perspective. Virtual enterprises and network organisations are examples of concepts surrounding us today. Chaffey (2002, p. 229) defines a virtual organisation as an organisation that uses IT to allow it to operate without clearly defined physical boundaries between different functions. The organisation called Netshop used as an example in this chapter can be characterised as a virtual organisation according to the definitions given by, for example, Hedberg et al. (1997), Mowshowitz (1997) and Kraut et al. (1999).

Hedberg et al. (1997) state that using the term "virtual" or "imaginary" to define this kind of organisation is most of all a matter of taste. They chose to use the word "imaginary" instead of "virtual" in order to avoid focusing too much on the IT connotation of virtual. The concept imaginary also denotes that this kind of organisation is tied together by the imagination of the organiser (i.e., the imaginator). Hedberg et al. (ibid. p. 13) define an imaginary organisation as follows:

> *"The perspective of the imaginary organization refers to a system in which assets, processes, and actors critical to the 'focal' enterprise exist and function both inside and outside the limits of the enterprise's conventional*

'landscape' formed by its legal structure, its accounting, its organigrams, and the language otherwise used to describe the enterprise."

The imaginary organisation is led and designed by an imaginator (an inter-organisational leader) who brings different actors (other legal units) together to establish an organisation that from the outside looks like one single organisation (i.e., bigger than it really is), but actually consists of different organisations interacting with each other in order to produce products or services for a customer. The interacting parties all possess different kinds of core competencies, which together form a competitive entirety. The imaginator identifies all needed core competencies and creates the imaginary organisation out of these. The imaginator might be characterised by leadership notions such as architect or theatrical director. The different business actors involved in the imaginary organisation are all representing independent organisations, but in certain selected respects they have chosen to participate in the game directed by the inter-organisational leader (ibid., p. 195). Goldkuhl and Melin (2001) give for example an empirical example of a network of organisations where one organisation acts as a distinct "director of the game".

Of course there are many other forms of network organisations where there is no such "leading company" as described above, but parties with equal power who play equal roles in setting up and maintaining the network. In this chapter, however, the metaphor of virtual organisation is used since it represents some major characteristics found in the Netshop case described below.

The discussion about the inter-organisational leader above can be related to the notion of organisations as actors (Ahrne, 1994). Organisations cannot act without their human co-workers. The co-workers act on behalf of the organisation; that is, in the name of the organisation (Goldkuhl & Braf, 2002). The imaginator is a human being who performs actions in order to direct the inter-organisational game, but in the same time the actions are performed on behalf of the organisation. The imaginator performs human acts in an organisational role; that is, he or she represents the organisation when acting (ibid.). In the case described below, the imaginator is mentioned in singular form even though there are several human beings acting as imaginators on behalf of the imaginary organisation (i.e., the leader organisation in the virtual organisation).

Kraut et al. (1999) characterise a virtual organisation in the following way:

- Processes transcend the boundaries of a single form and are not controlled by a single organisational hierarchy.
- Production processes are flexible, with different parties involved at different times.
- Parties involved in the production of a single product are often geographically dispersed.

- Given this dispersion, co-ordination is heavily dependent on telecommunications and data networks.

Ticoll et al. (1998, p. 22) take the discussion one step further by stating that virtual corporations only were an important transitional form in the evolution toward a "post-modern" business environment. Instead, they argue that e-business communities are the next organisational form. They define e-business communities as networks of suppliers, distributors, commerce providers, and customers that use the Internet and other electronic media as platforms for collaboration and competition (ibid.). E-business communities are categorised according to their degree of economic control and value integration into four types; open market, alliance, aggregation, and value chain. There are similarities between an alliance e-business community and a virtual (or imaginary) organisation. The hierarchical control is low and, instead, the aim is to achieve high value integration, that is, facilitating the creation and delivery of specific product/service offerings that integrate components from multiple sources. Regardless of this theoretical distinction between different organisational forms, it is in the context of this chapter feasible to use the concept of virtual organisations to characterise the empirical example.

The Netshop Case

In order to illustrate the use of BAT for analysing business interaction, a virtual organisation called Netshop is used as an example. A case study was conducted in this organisation from autumn of 1998 until autumn of 1999 (Axelsson & Segerkvist, 2001; Segerkvist, 2001). The case study aimed at exploring how co-operation between organisations and information systems is conducted in a virtual organisation. In this chapter, however, the Netshop case is only used as an empirical example and the findings from the case study will not be reported here.

The organisation is anonymous in all reporting from the study and has therefore been given the fictive name Netshop. Netshop sells a physical product via the Internet and has no other market channel besides the Internet shops. Netshop was established in 1997 and had, at the time of the case study, Internet shops directed towards the Scandinavian market (one shop for each country). The case study was conducted at the Swedish office with 30 employees. Netshop has 3000 suppliers in Sweden, England, and the USA. These suppliers provide in total 2 millions of products to the customers. Netshop is primarily focused on private customers but does also sell to organisations. Netshop does not possess any own product stock. Instead, Netshop orders the product from the supplier when the customer has ordered this product from Netshop. Thus, Netshop mediates products between customers and product suppliers. Netshop interacts with external actors for logistics, economy, systems development, database design, advertising, graphical design of the web system, suppliers of products, and text writers for the web system.

Netshop has a web-based IOS for the imaginator's order and purchase process. The customers place their orders in this web-based IOS. The external actors; that is, product suppliers, sales ledger, and logistic partner, have their own internal information systems which they use to interact with the web-based IOS, mainly through sending and receiving files by email. If we compare Netshop with Krauts et al.'s (1999) characteristics of a virtual organisation, listed above, this makes Netshop a good example of a virtual organisation.

Empirical Illustrations of Business Interactions in Netshop

In order to illustrate the business interactions within the virtual organisation as well as between Netshop and a customer, the BAT phase model for long-term business-to-business interaction is used, even though the customer might be either a private consumer or a business customer. The reason for using this special case of the BAT phase model is that it gives a richer picture of the actions taking place between Netshop's business actors than the original BAT phase model does.

As stated above, BAT implies a symmetrical perspective on the business interaction analysis, even though there might be an asymmetrical relation between two studied organisations regarding, for example, power balance. The Netshop case is a good example of this, since the imaginator is the most powerful organisational unit within the virtual organisation. Nevertheless, the entire virtual organisation is analysed from a symmetrical perspective where no organisational unit is given more or different attention than the other. The empirical example is presented in six tables following the generic phases of BAT.

Before Netshop could start conducting business transactions, the establishment of business prerequisites took place (see Table 1). In this phase the imaginator had to find partners possessing the core competencies needed to realise the business idea of Netshop. There are both partners immediately necessary for conducting the business transactions, such as the sales ledger, product suppliers, and the logistic partner (these three actors are focused on in this chapter), and partners who make the business process possible through their support activities, such as database and interface designers, text writers, and so on. All these partners initially had to accept their roles in the virtual organisation, that is, to take part in the game directed by the imaginator.

In order to realise Netshop's business idea, a web-based IOS also had to be developed and implemented. The imaginator contracted some of their partners to develop this system. All actors in the virtual organisation also had to adapt to the prerequisites of this IOS to be able to interact with the imaginator. All actors within the virtual organisation had to agree upon routines for how the business interactions were going to be conducted, responsibility distribution between actors, IS interaction, and so on. Adaptation of other business prerequisites can of course take place in the future.

In the exposure and contact search phase (see Table 2), Netshop is exposed to presumptive customers on Internet through advertising in newspapers, by marketing activities directed to special customer groups, and by newsletters. The marketing

Table 1: Establishing business prerequisites phase

BAT subphases	*Customer*	*Netshop – the imaginator*	*Sales ledger*	*Product suppliers*	*Logistic partner*
Initial establishing business pre-requisites		Finding partners with feasible core competencies in order to fulfill the business idea of Netshop	Accepting their roles in the virtual organisation of Netshop		
Adapting business prerequisites		Developing a web-based IOS, including an inter-organizational information systems architecture, to support the business interations, agreeing upon routines and responsibilities related to the business process			

activities are conducted by emails and advertisements on other Internet sites. Future customers are searching for interesting web sites both by using their web browsers and by looking for advertisements in other media. Since there is a long-term relationship between the different business actors there are no exposure and contact search activities taking place between these actors, according to the BAT phase model for long-term business-to-business interaction. This short-circuiting of the exposure and contact search phase on the supplier side was discussed above.

When the customer has found Netshop, contact can be established and Netshop can make the proposals (see Table 3). This phase implies both principal proposals and transactional proposals. Making principal proposals is an activity involving the different actors of the virtual organisation. The imaginator has to compile information about products and delivery services from different product suppliers and the logistic partner. Information about products and prices given by the product suppliers are not a future commitment to selling these products, but only a prognosis of possible product offers (i.e., collected products and price lists from the suppliers). This information serves as an important input for the imaginator when the products are offered on Netshop's Internet site. The offers are, however, only fictive in this phase since there are no promises that Netshop will be able to sell these products.

Table 2: Exposure and contact search phase

BAT sub-phase	*Customer*	*Netshop – the imaginator*	*Sales ledger*	*Product suppliers*	*Logistic partner*
Exposure and contact search	Searching for interesting web sites on Internet	Exposing and advertising in order to marketing Netshop's Internet site			

Table 3: Contact establishment and proposal phase

BAT sub-phases	*Customer*	*Netshop – the imaginator*	*Sales ledger*	*Product suppliers*	*Logistic partner*
Principal proposal		Compiling information about products and services possible to offer to customers		Informing the imaginator of products and prices	Informing the imaginator of delivery times and prices
Transaction proposal	Looking for interesting products in Netshop's offers	Offering products on Netshop's Internet site			

Table 4: Contractual phase

BAT sub-phases	*Customer*	*Netshop – the imaginator*	*Sales ledger*	*Product suppliers*	*Logistic partner*
Principal contractual		Agreeing upon principal contracts concerning how to conduct business transactions			
Transaction contractual	Ordering a product from Netshop's Internet site	Transferring the order to the product supplier by facsimile or telephone		Receiving the order from the imaginator	
		Receiving order confirmation from the product supplier		Confirming the received order to the imaginator by fax or telephone	
	Receiving order confirmation from the imaginator	Confirming the customer's order by mail or email			
		Sending order file to the logistic partner by email			Receiving order file from the imaginator

The product suppliers have only exposed their possible offers, not their existing product stocks. The customer considers the offers made on Netshops Internet site.

The contractual phase is also divided into a principal and a transactional level (see Table 4). At the principal contractual level the imaginator and the other business actors have to make principal contracts concerning how to conduct the business transactions. These contracts might be valid for a decided period or until a new negotiation starts.

The transaction contractual phase starts when a customer uses the web-based IOS to order a product from Netshop. The customer order is received by the imaginator, who transfers the order to a product supplier that has the particular product in its assortment, according to the product lists. If the product supplier is able to sell the particular product, the received order is confirmed to the imaginator by fax or telephone. The imaginator is then able to confirm or reject the customer order by mail or email. This action makes the fictive offer become real if the product supplier has given a positive answer. Then the imaginator sends an order file to the logistic partner by email, in order to inform the logistic partner of its future assignment of delivering the ordered product to the customer.

The next phase in the business transaction is the fulfillment phase (see Table 5). This phase starts by the product supplier sending the ordered product and a delivery note to the logistic partner by mail or UPS. The logistic partner can control this delivery by comparing it to the order file earlier received from the imaginator. The product supplier also sends an invoice for this product to the imaginator, who pays it according to agreed terms. The logistic partner sends the product and a customer invoice to the customer by mail. If the customer has ordered several products that are supplied from different product suppliers, the logistic partner waits until the total order is fulfilled before delivering it to the customer. The logistic partner sends each delivery note to the imaginator by mail or fax as well as a delivery information file to the imaginator's web-based IOS by email. This file is sent once every 24 hours. The logistic partner sends customer invoice information to the sales ledger and the customer pays the invoice, received from the logistic partner, to the sales ledger. If necessary, the sales ledger sends an invoice reminder to the customer before receiving the payment. Finally, the sales ledger transfers money and sends invoice information to the imaginator.

The sixth and last phase is the assessment phase (see Table 6). In this phase the satisfaction or dissatisfaction of both the customer and Netshop is assessed. The customer might send a reclaim to Netshop if he or she is not pleased with any part of the business transaction. The imaginator handles customer reclaims and tries to solve the problems together with the business partners affected by the reclaim. Netshop might, on the other hand, have remaining payment claims on the customer, if the customer has not yet paid its invoice.

Table 5: Fulfillment phase

BAT sub-phases	*Customer*	*Netshop – the imaginator*	*Sales ledger*	*Product suppliers*	*Logistic partner*
Fulfillment				Sending product and delivery note to the logistic partner by mail or UPS	Receiving product and delivery note from the product supplier
		Receiving invoice from the product supplier		Sending invoice to the imaginator	
		Paying the product supplier		Receiving payment from the imaginator	
	Receiving product and invoice from the logistic partner				Sending product and invoice to the customer by mail
		Receiving delivery information file from the logistic partner Receiving the delivery notes from the logistic partner			Sending delivery information file to the imaginator's IOS by email every 24 hours Sending each delivery note to the imaginator by mail or fax
			Receiving invoice information from the logistic partner		Sending invoice information to the sales ledger
	Receiving invoice reminder from the sales ledger if necessary Paying the invoice to the sales ledger		Sending out invoice reminders to the customer if necessary Receiving payment from the customer		
		Receiving money transfer information and money from the sales ledger	Sending money transfer information and transferring money to the imaginator		

Table 6: Assessment phase

BAT sub-phase	*Customer*	*Netshop – the imaginator*	*Sales ledger*	*Product suppliers*	*Logistic partner*
Assessment	Sending a reclaim to the imaginator if not satisfied with the product	Handling the customer reclaim, contacting possibly affected partners Taking care of remaining payment claims			

DISCUSSION

The previous section showed how the generic phases of BAT could be used in order to visualise and analyse business interactions performed by different business actors within a virtual organisation as well as between the virtual organisation as an entirety and its customer. By illustrating business interactions in the Netshop case in this structured way, several interesting findings are revealed. First of all, when all the conducted business actions in a business transaction are described in sequence, it is obvious that the business process of Netshop is complex. It is possible to assume that this is the case in many virtual organisations. Improving a complex business process might involve simplification of business interaction, but this is only possible if the complexity can be visualised and analysed properly. Thus, it seems that the BAT phase model helps us to structure business actions both on a horizontal level between the involved business actors and the customer and on a vertical level, distinguishing between business actions conducted in different phases of the business transaction. The BAT phase model makes the analysis focus upon both exchange of information (i.e., business communication) and exchange of value, that is, exchange of products (goods/services) versus money. This can be related to Tang et al. (2001), who state that co-ordinated and integrated flows of information and materials both inside the organisation and between organisations are vital for effective use of IOS for electronic commerce.

Kumar and van Dissel (1996) have, amongst many other authors, discussed potential risks associated with the use of IOS. If we return to the Netshop example, it is obvious that the imaginator takes a severe risk when offering products to the customer without being sure that the suppliers are able to sell the products. If the customer receives a negative answer instead of an order confirmation in the contractual phase, it is possible that the customer becomes disappointed and, thus, never returns to Netshop (especially if this happens several times). This potential misunderstanding, that the offer given in the contact establishment and proposal phase is a real offer and not a fictive one based on a prognosis, is caused by the design of the business process and by the design of the web-based IOS. The imaginator does not have access to enough information about what products are possible to order from the suppliers; that is, there seems to be an information asymmetry between the imaginator and the suppliers. The web-based IOS does not clarify the status of the offer in enough distinctiveness; thus, the communicative actions remain unclear to the customer.

A business interaction analysis based on the BAT phase model makes it possible to distinguish in which phases the imaginator is most dependent on the other business actors within the virtual organisation. This is important when designing a business process for a virtual organisation since different solutions result in different power structures, according to what core competencies of the virtual organisation have been placed outside the imaginator's business unit. In the Netshop case the other business actors are most active in the fulfillment phase, which is obvious in Table 5. This fact implies that the imaginator is most dependent on its business partners in the most critical phase of the business transaction; that is, when the agreement of the customer's and the supplier's mutual commitments is going to be fulfilled. The BAT phase model offers consciousness about these issues and, thus, makes it possible both to test different solutions before establishing the virtual organisation and to identify problems in existing solutions.

Based on the illustration of the business interaction in the Netshop case it is possible to question whether the IOS developed for Netshop could be improved. The web-based IOS is used for handling customer orders (the purchase process at the imaginator's), but much of the business communication between the business actors are made by sending files and documents via email, fax, or mail. Many ineffective, manual or semi-manual ways of communicating business information could be the result of an emerging business interaction rather than a designed interaction based on proper analysis. The illustration of the Netshop case implies that an extended IOS, developed for the entire virtual organisation, would possibly simplify matters and make business communication more effective and reliable. Analysing business interaction with the BAT phase model could generate results useful both for design and redesign of IOS and business processes. This can be compared to Debreceny et al. (2002), who see that the increasing complexity in decision-making surrounding IOS development demands simultaneous focus on intra- and inter-organisational systems as well as on design of new business models and redesign of existing ones.

Even though this chapter argues that understanding of business interaction is vital, it is only one part of the IOS complexity. The BAT phase model does not provide a total solution for how to make IOS development, implementation, and use less complex and demanding. Instead, it focuses on a specific problem within this complexity; that is, the importance of understanding business interaction when business actions are to be translated into an IOS. Beside this, the IOS complexity makes it necessary to focus on, for example, non-transactional issues, social dimensions of business relationships, and management issues, that are not explicitly addressed by the BAT phase model.

CONCLUSION

While using BAT for business interaction analysis between a customer and a virtual organisation, several important issues are focused.

1) The phase division including generic business actions and their corresponding exchanges of communication and value gives structure to complex business transactions. This results in an opportunity to discuss business interaction in a concrete way since it is visualised by actual business actions. Business interaction might otherwise be a confusing concept that is hard to really capture and understand. A concrete example following business action theory terminology increases the possibility to see what business interaction takes place in a specific business relationship. This is important since it is only then business interaction can be designed or redesigned in a controlled and conscious way. Developing and implementing IOS do to a great extent imply business interaction design. The BAT phase model could give theoretical help in visualising the complexity in inter-organisational contexts regarding business interaction.
2) The distinctiveness in business communication, inherited from speech act theory, implies that, for example, promises, requests, commands, and declarations are focused. Such illocutionary acts are important to analyse during IOS development, since communicative actions will be conducted by the IOS. While performing a business interaction analysis using the BAT phase model, the illocutionary acts are possible to question and discuss. When does, for example, the supplier commit himself to sell the offered product and until when is the offer only to be considered as "fictive" or as a prognosis? What has the customer promised to do when she clicks on the "order" button? If these and other communicative actions are not properly analysed during IOS development, there are probably less possibilities that the IOS will be clear on these issues.
3) The division of the seller role into several co-operating actors simplifies the picture of the business transaction compared to only viewing the virtual organisation as an entirety. The division also makes roles and responsibilities easier to identify and discuss. This can be compared to Cousins' (2002) statement that relationships should not be viewed as an entity but as an intra- and inter-organisational process. On the other hand, the virtual organisation has to be viewed as a systemic entirety as well, if it should not be losing its network properties. Thus, a virtual organisation must both be analysed and viewed as an entirety with a common goal and as different business units acting together with partly differing objectives for their co-operation. The BAT phase model can be used for both these analysis levels since the supplier role in the phase model can be treated as a "black box" or be divided into several actors taking the supplier role in different phases of the business transaction, as shown in this chapter.

4) In this chapter the BAT phase model has been expanded into a new context. Earlier adoptions of the model have been focused on analysis of the dyadic relation between one customer and one supplier (e.g., Melin & Goldkuhl, 1999; Axelsson et al., 2000). The model has, however, proved to be useful also when analysing business interaction between several co-operating business actors, as is the case in a virtual organisation. This expansion of application area for the model is, thus, a contribution to the on-going development of business action theory.

Future Research

In this chapter a suggestion of how to gain deeper understanding of business interaction in complex inter-organisational contexts has been proposed. There is of course much research left to be done within this area. In order to follow up the findings in this chapter, several virtual organisations need to be studied. It would be interesting to analyse virtual organisations experiencing different kinds of problems in their business relationships, and also to distinguish between organisations using an existing IOS from organisations that are about to enter an IOS development and implementation process, just to mention a few issues for future research.

REFERENCES

Ahrne, G. (1994). *Social organizations. Interaction inside, outside and between organization.* London: Sage Publications.

Allen, D.K., Colligan, D., Finnie, A., & Kern, T. (2000). Trust, power and interorganizational information systems: The case of the electronic trading community TransLease. *Information Systems Journal, 10,* 21-40.

Ash, C.G., & Burn, J.M. (2003). A strategic framework for the management of ERP enabled e-business change. *European Journal of Operational Research, 146,* 374-387.

Austin, J.L. (1962). *How to do things with words.* Oxford University Press.

Axelsson, K. (2003). Analysing business interaction in a virtual organisation – Using business action theory to study complex inter-organisational vontexts. *Journal of Electronic Commerce in Organizations, 1*(3), 1-27.

Axelsson, K., & Avdic, A. (2001). IT management during acquisition of ERP-systems - Experiences from goal dialogs at two companies. In D. Remenyi& A. Brown (Eds.), *Proceedings of the 8th European Conference on IT Evaluation* (pp. 293-301). Oriel College, Oxford, United Kingdom, (September 17-18).

Axelsson, K., Goldkuhl, G., & Melin, U. (2000, August). *Using business action theory for dyadic analysis.* Presented at The 10th Workshop on Interorganizational Research, Norweigan University of Science and Technology, Trondheim, Norway.

Axelsson, K., Melin, U., & Goldkuhl, G. (2002). Understanding B2B interaction – A model to accentuate inter-organisational systems design issues. In S. Wrycza(Ed.), *Proceedings of the 10th European Conference on Information Systems (ECIS'2002)* Gdansk, Poland (pp. 541-550, June 6-8).

Axelsson, K., & Segerkvist, P.-A. (2001). Interaction between actors and information systems in web-based imaginary organisations – Experiences from two case studies. In C. Ihlström, B.-M. Svensson & Svensson, J. (Eds.), *Proceeding of 1st Nordic Workshop on Electronic Commerce 2001* (pp. 7-18).

Cavaye, A.L.M., & Cragg, P.B. (1995). Factors contributing to the success of customer oriented interorganizational systems. *Journal of Strategic Information Systems, 4*(1), 13-30.

Chaffey, D. (2002). *E-business and e-commerce management.* Harlow: Pearson Education Limited.

Chan, C., & Swatman, P.M.C. (2002, January). Management and business issues for B2B e-commerce implementation. *Proceeding of the 35th Hawaii International Conference on System Sciences (HICSS'35)*, Hawaii.

Cousins, P.D. (2002). A conceptual model for managing long-term inter-organisational relationships. *European Journal of Purchasing & Supply Management, 8,* 71-82.

Cunningham, C., & Tynan, C. (1993). Electronic trading, interorganizational systems and the nature of buyer-seller relationships: The need for a network perspective. *International Journal of Information Management, 13*(1), 3-28.

Dahlqvist, J. (1998). *Knowledge use in business exchange – Acting and thinking business actors.* Doctoral thesis no. 74, Department of Business Studies, Uppsala University.

Davenport, T.H. (1993). *Process innovation. Reengineering work through Information Technology.* Boston, MA: Harvard Business School Press.

Debreceny, R., Putterill, M., Tung, L., & Gilbert, A.L. (2002). New tools for the determination of e-commerce inhibitors. *Decision Support Systems, 34*(2), 177-195.

Ford, D., Gadde, L., Håkansson, H., Lundgren, A., Snehota, I., Turnbull, P., & Wilson, D. (1998). *Managing business relationships*. John Wiley & Sons.

Glynn, W.J., & Lehtinen, U. (1995). The concept of exchange: Interactive approaches in service marketing. In W.J. Glynn& J.G. Barnes (Eds.), *Understanding service management* (pp. 89-118). Chichester: John Wiley & Sons.

Goldkuhl, G. (1996, July). *Generic business frameworks and action modelling*. Presented at The First International Workshop on the Language-Action Perspective on Communication Modelling (LAP1996), Tilburg, The Netherlands.

Goldkuhl, G. (1998). *The six phases of business processes – Business communication and the exchange of value*. Presented at The 12th Biennial ITS Conference (ITS '98), Stockholm.

Goldkuhl, G., & Braf, E. (2002). Organisational ability – Constituents and congruencies. In E. Coakes, D. Willis & S. Clarke (Eds.), *Knowledge management in the sociotechnical world* (pp. 30-42). London: Springer.

Goldkuhl, G., & Melin, U. (2001). Relationship management vs. business transaction: Business interaction as design of business interaction. *Proceeding of the 10th International Annual IPSERA Conference* (pp. 431-443). Jönköping International Business School.

Grönroos, C. (1994). Quo vadis, marketing? Toward a relationship marketing paradigm. *Journal of Marketing Management, 10,* 347-360.

Gummesson, E. (1999). *Total relationship marketing – Rethinking marketing management: From 4Ps to 30 Rs*. Oxford: Butterworth Heinemann.

Habermas, J. (1984). *The theory of communicative action. Reason and the Rationalization of Society* (Vol. 1). Beacon Press.

Hedberg, B., Dahlgren, G., Hansson, J., & Olve, N.-G. (1997). *Virtual organizations and beyond: Discover imaginary systems*. Chichester, UK: John Wiley & Sons.

Håkansson, H., & Snehota, I. (1989). No business is an island: The network concept of business strategy. *Scandinavian Journal of Management, 5*(3),187-200.

Håkansson, H., & Snehota, I. (eds.). (1995). *Developing relationships in business networks*. London: Thomson.

Keen, P., Balance, C., Chan, S., & Schrump, S. (2000). *Electronic commerce relationships – Trust by design*. NJ: Prentice Hall.

Kim, K., & Prabhakar, B. (2000). Initial trust, perceived risk, and the adoption of Internet banking. In S. Ang, H. Krcmar, W.J. Orlikowski, P. Weill

& J.I. DeGross (Eds.), *Proceedings of the Twenty-First International Conference on Information Systems,* Brisbane, Australia (December, pp. 537-543).

Kinder, T. (2003). Go with the flow – A conceptual framework for supply relations in the era of the extended enterprise. *Research Policy, 32,* 503-523.

Konsynski, B.R. (1992). Issues in design of interorganizational systems. In W.W. Cotterman & J.A. Senn (Eds.), *Challenges and strategies for research in systems development* (pp. 43-63). John Wiley & Sons.

Kraut, R., Steinfield, C., Chan, A., Butler, B., & Hoag, A. (1999). Coordination and virtualisation: The role of electronic networks and personal relationships. *Organization Science, 10*(6), 722-740.

Kumar, K., & van Dissel, H.G. (1996). Sustainable collaboration: Managing conflict and cooperation in interorganizational systems. *MIS Quarterly, 20*(3), 279-300.

Kumar, K., van Dissel, H.G., & Bielli, P. (1998). The merchant of Prato – revisited: Toward a third rationality of information systems. *MIS Quarterly*, (June), 199-226.

Kurnia, S., & Johnston, R.B. (2000). The need for a processual view of inter-organizational systems adoption. *Journal of Strategic Information Systems, 9*(4), 295-319.

Lientz, B.P., & Rea, K.P. (2001). *Transform your business into e – Going beyond the dot com disasters*. Academic Press.

Lind, M., & Goldkuhl, G. (2001). Generic layered patterns for business modelling. In M. Schoop & K. Taylor (Eds.), *Proceedings of the Sixth International Workshop on the Language-Action Perspective on Communication Modelling (LAP2001)* (pp. 109-128). Aachen University of Technology.

Melin, U., & Goldkuhl, G. (1999). Information systems and process orientation – Evaluation and change using business action theory. In W. Wojtkowski, W.G. Wojtkowski, S. Wrycza & J. Zupancic (Eds.), *Systems development methods for databases, enterprise modelling, and workflow management* (pp. 233-244). New York: Kluwer Academic/Plenum Publishers.

Mowshowitz, A. (1997). Virtual organization. *Communication of the ACM, 40*(9), 30-37.

Nygaard-Andersen, S., & Bjørn-Andersen, N. (1994). To join or not to join: A framework for evaluating electronic data interchange systems. *Journal of Strategic Information Systems*, *3*(3), 191-210.

Rayport, J.F., & Jaworski B.J. (2001). *E-commerce*. McGraw-Hill/Irwin.

Reich, B.H., & Benbasat, I. (1990). An empirical investigation of factors influencing the success of customer oriented information systems. *Information Systems Research, 1*(3), 325-347.

Searle, J.R. (1969). *Speech acts. An essay in the philosophy of language*. London: Cambridge University Press.

Segerkvist, P.-A. (2001). *Co-operation in web-based imaginary organisations – IS architecture and actors as conditions for business processes*. Licentiate thesis no. 47, Department of Computer and Information Science, Linköping University. [in Swedish]

Senn, J.A. (2000). Business-to-business e-commerce. *Information Systems Management, 17*(2), 23-32.

Streng, R.J., & Sol, H.G. (1992). A dynamic modelling approach to analyse chain dynamics on the inter-organizational level. In H.G. Sol (Ed.), *Proceedings of the Third International Working Conference on Dynamic Modelling of Information Systems*. Technical University Delft.

Swatman, P.M.C., Swatman, P.A., & Fowler, D.C. (1994). A model of EDI integration and strategic business reengineering. *Journal of Strategic Information Systems, 3*(1), 41-60.

Tang, J.E., Shee, D.Y., & Tang, T.-I. (2001). A conceptual model for interactive buyer-supplier relationship in electronic commerce. *International Journal of Information Management, 21,* 49-68.

Tapscott, D., Lowy, A., & Ticoll, D. (eds.). (1998). *Blueprint to the digital economy: Creating wealth in the era of e-business*. New York: McGraw-Hill.

Ticol, D., Lowy, A., & Kalakota, R. (1998). Joined at the bit. In D. Tapscott, A. Lowy, & D. Ticoll (Eds.), *Blueprint to the digital economy: Creating wealth in the era of e-business* (pp. 19-33). New York: McGraw-Hill.

Timmers, P. (1999). *Electronic commerce – Strategies and models for business-to-business trading*. Chichester, UK: John Wiley & Sons.

Tomkins, C. (2001). Interdependencies, trust and information in relationships, alliances and networks. *Accounting, Organizations and Society, 26,* 161-191.

Turban, E., Lee, J., King, D., & Chung, H.M. (2000). *Electronic commerce – A managerial perspective*. Upper Saddle River, NJ: Prentice Hall.

Turban, E., King, D., Lee, J., Warkentin, M., & Chung, H.M. (2002). *Electronic commerce 2002 – A managerial perspective* (2nd ed.). Upper Saddle River, NJ: Prentice Hall.

Webster, J. (1993). Networks of collaboration or conflict? The development of EDI. In J. Gricar, V. Kilner & J. Novak (Eds.), *Proceedings of the Sixth International EDI Conference,* Bled, Slovenia (June 7-9, pp. 149-169).

Previously published in the Journal of Electronic Commerce in Organizations, 1(3), 1-27, July/Sept, 2003.

Chapter VIII

Issues and Perceptions of Unsolicited Commercial Electronic Mail

Jack T. Marchewka, Northern Illinois University, USA

Chang Liu, Northern Illinois University, USA

Charles G. Petersen, Northern Illinois University, USA

ABSTRACT

The proliferation of unsolicited commercial electronic mail (UCE) or spam is becoming a global concern for many organizations. This chapter explores issues of unsolicited email, the cost and loss of productivity, the impact of UCE and computer viruses, privacy concerns, electronic mail filters, attempts to control spam, and legislative action. A strengths, weaknesses, opportunities, and threats (SWOT) analysis was also applied in this study. The results of a survey concerning the perceptions of UCE are presented. The results clearly show that while the respondents find spam annoying, they spend very little time in dealing with it. Although the respondents express the need to control spam, they do not believe that governmental control is the solution, but rather that Internet Service Providers and organizations should take the responsibility for controlling unsolicited email. Lastly, the respondents are very unlikely to open, let alone read and respond to unsolicited email. The results of this study will be useful for guiding organizational, university, and public policies.

INTRODUCTION

The term "spam" is often used to refer to unsolicited electronic mail (email) and originated from a comedy skit performed on a British television show called Monty Python's Flying Circus (i.e., "Spam, spam, spam. I'm sick of spam!"). The term spam has since evolved and is defined as unsolicited commercial email (UCE) from a sender that the receiver does not know or cannot identify (Fallows, 2003). Just about everyone who has an email account has received UCE from Internet marketers or other organizations that attempt to sell or advertise products or services or solicit monetary contributions that are not expressly requested. Direct Internet marketers, who flood the Internet with many copies of the same message and target individual email accounts, are often called spammers. These messages often include commercial advertisements for questionable products or services, get-rich-quick schemes, or pornography. According to Solomon (2002a), spam or junk email can be categorized as unsolicited bulk email, unsolicited commercial email, chain letters, duplicate postings, pop-up ads, virus warnings, banner ads, jokes, or Internet service provider (ISP) information.

Spam has proliferated over the years because it is a relatively inexpensive medium for reaching a large, growing audience. For example, the cost of an email campaign is only about $1,000, compared to about $20,000 for doing the same campaign using direct mail (Disabatino, 2000). Moreover, the effectiveness of an email campaign becomes a numbers game. Depending on what product or service a direct marketer sells, a response rate of about 2% is typical (Mangalindan, 2002). To be effective, therefore, a direct marketer must send out 5,000 emails in order to receive 100 responses. According to Greenspan (2003c), the payoff for spammers comes from the 7% of the recipients of unsolicited email who order a product or service.

Moreover, the cost of sending out bulk emails is so low there is very little need to target the emails directly to individuals. Subsequently, adults and children often receive unsolicited email that is either inappropriate or offensive. In fact, a recent survey of 1,000 Internet users by Symantec reports that 47% of email users between the ages of seven and 18 have received emails with links to pornographic web sites (Greenspan, 2003a).

It is estimated that the number of worldwide email messages sent annually will increase from 230 billion in 1996 to 9.15 trillion by 2006. Of the 9.15 trillion email messages to be sent in 2006, 2.92 trillion will be spam (Solomon, 2002b). In fact, two of the largest ISPs, America Online (AOL) and Microsoft Network (MSN), report that they block 2.4 billion emails each day, while AOL says that 80% of all its incoming email is spam. Moreover, in August of 2003, Yahoo conducted an internal survey of its email service and found that, given a choice, 77% of the respondents would rather clean toilets than delete spam from their email boxes (Perez, 2003).

The amount of UCE individuals receive also threatens to saturate or create "in box-burnout" whereby consumers become less responsive to legitimate email campaigns as too much unwanted email competes for consumers' attention (Saunders, 2003b). A study of more than 1,200 email users conducted by Executive Summary Consulting, Inc. and Quris suggests that UCE makes up the largest share of most users' emailboxes. Seventy percent (70%) of the respondents also stated that they believed that they received more emails than last year, with 74% saying that an increase in UCE is the major factor (Saunders, 2003a).

Aside from the amount of spam and the issue of offensive and inappropriate content contained in spam, the Federal Trade Commission (FTC) conducted a study of 1,000 random UCEs sent to them by consumers. Interestingly, 66% of the UCE contained false or misleading information in the sender line, subject line, or message content (Fallows, 2003). Moreover, a report by MessageLabs suggests that 70% of spam is sent by hijacked computers (Fallows, 2003).

The proliferation of UCE has brought about a number of concerns and important issues that many individuals and organizations worldwide feel must be addressed. In a U.S. congressional hearing, Orson Swindle, commissioner of the FTC, stated that "spam is about to kill the 'killer app' of the Internet." Email is considered the "killer application" since 93% or 117 million of adult Americans use email, and this is about twice the number of users who engage in any other online activity (Fallows, 2003). Some believe that the business benefits of email are in a potential irreversible decline because of the contaminating by-products of spam (Johnson, 2003).

However, email marketing campaigns can still produce more dramatic return on investment (ROI) for organizations selling products and services than any other direct marketing technique (Parker, 2003). The Direct Marketing Association (DMA) recently released the results of a study at its annual conference that calculated an ROI by considering revenue per contact, cost per customer, and response rate for over 1,500 direct and indirect marketing campaigns that were conducted in the first quarter of 2003. Using an index where a 2 represents profitability, email received an ROI of 14.2, while the next closest direct marketing medium, direct response TV, received an ROI of 8.4. The most significant factor in email's stellar ROI was its low cost, which was only an average of $0.09 per contact, while direct mail, with an ROI of 7.2, cost on average $0.55 per contact (Parker, 2003).

Although the Internet can provide a cost-effective and important medium for organizations to sell products and services, a number of issues associated with UCE must be addressed. This chapter discusses a number of issues and focuses on the cost of personal and organizational productivity, computer viruses and worms, privacy concerns, email filters, various attempts to control spam, and the call for legislative action to control and limit the flow of unsolicited email. The results of a web-based survey conducted by the authors are also summarized later in the chapter. The issues discussed in this chapter and results of this study may provide a basis for guiding organizational and public policies, as well as guiding practices for marketers to make their efforts more effective.

ISSUES

Cost and Loss of Productivity of Unsolicited Commercial Electronic Mail

Unfortunately, the cost of UCE usually comes at the expense of the Internet user, especially anyone who has a measured Internet service—that is, where an individual pays for their connection while he or she reads or sends their email. Often ISPs must bear the cost to store and transmit these messages to their subscribers, but these costs are ultimately passed on to their customers. It is estimated that Internet subscribers are unknowingly paying an estimated euro 10 billion a year in connection costs just to receive unsolicited electronic mail (The European Commission, 2002).

The proliferation of UCE is becoming a global concern for many organizations. One issue in particular focuses on the cost of personal productivity when employees must wade through a daily plethora of spam in addition to important email. According to a recent study reported by *Network World*, a typical company with about 1000 employees may well lose productivity of about $6 million per year when each employee receives 100 or more email messages with a significant percentage of spam (Gibbs, 2003). Another study conducted by Ferris Research, a market research firm located in San Francisco, estimates that unwanted spam cost U.S. organizations almost $9 billion in 2002 (Morrissey, 2003).

The annoyance of spam is a global concern. Figure 1 summarizes the projected impact unsolicited emails may have on organizations worldwide. It is estimated that spam will create a global productivity drain of $198.3 billion by the year 2007 (Greenspan, 2003a).

Figure 1: Source—Radicati Group (Greenspan, 2003a)

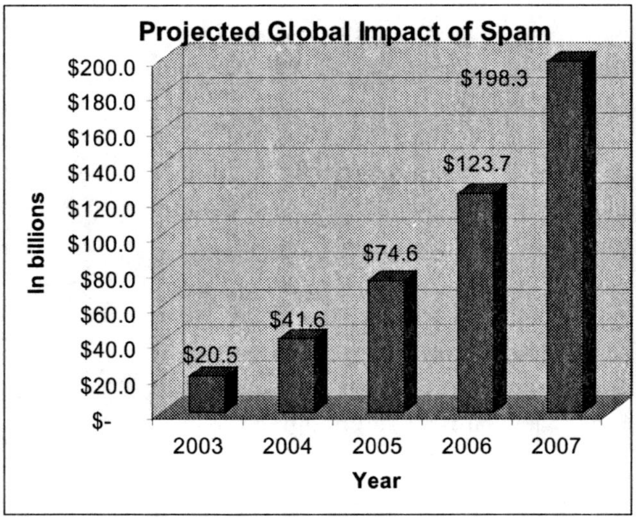

Other studies report that employees spend anywhere from one minute to 90 minutes each day managing UCE, with an average of 6.5 minutes per day (Campbell & Wettemann, 2003). Moreover, the average annual cost of spam per employee has been estimated to be $874. Spam is therefore moving up the chain of command in many organizations as it becomes less of an Information Technology (IT) problem and more of an organizational issue (Morrissey, 2003).

Moreover, some studies have found that spam can range from 30% to 50% of all email received by many organizations each day (Blackman, 2003). In addition, Blackman points out that fighting spam is the top email priority for 84% of small businesses. Jason Catlett, president of Junkbusters Corp., a privacy-rights lobbyist and consultant, states, "An email address like sales@momandpop.com probably gets as many unsolicited emails as sales@ibm.com, but there are fewer people to deal with them." It appears that the burden of unsolicited email often falls disproportionately on small businesses.

However, individuals tend to receive more spam-type emails in their personal emailbox than their work email box (Fallows, 2003). First, a personal email account with a large ISP is a popular target for spam list builders. Second, organizations tend to use filters or other protective measure more frequently than individuals. Regardless, an individual is more likely to find their personal or work-related email address on a spammer's list if he or she is imprudent in giving out their email address.

Although an individual may elect to use the delete key when dealing with unsolicited emails, over time he or she may find that they use this key more and more frequently and inadvertently delete legitimate email. Therefore, it is highly likely that employees will miss critical messages from customers when they are fighting to rid themselves of spam.

Spam and Computer Viruses

Since 1996, the increase in email viruses has led to a growing concern that is now closely related to spam. For example, in 1996 about 74% of computer viruses were spread from diskettes, while 9% came from email. By 2001, only 1% of the viruses were transmitted by diskette, while email accounted for over 83% (Disabatino, 2002a). A study conducted by ICSA Labs in Mechanicsburg, Pennsylvania, reported that the estimated cost of a virus infection ranges from $100 to $1 million, while a study conducted by Ferris Research in San Francisco estimates that viruses cost organizations at least $6 billion a year (Disabatino, 2003a).

The annoyance caused by spam is becoming complicated by the spreading of viruses through email. This issue has gained global attention by the recent SoBig.F virus which turned many computers worldwide into virus-propagating spam machines (Abreu, 2003). The email subject lines included such headers as "Details", "Wicked Screen Saver", "Thank You", or "Approved" that enticed the receiver to open an attachment that contained the SoBig.F virus. Once opened, the infected computer used the receiver's email address book to send infected emails with similar subject headings to others.

This has made detecting the source of the virus difficult. The Internet service provider AOL has estimated that it blocked more than 11 million emails that contained the SoBig.F virus. In addition, the SoBig virus accounted for almost $3 billion in economic damages worldwide (CyberAtlas, 2003). Approximately 30% of China's computers fell victim to the SoBig virus, and according to a survey conducted by the public information network security supervision bureau of the Ministry of Public Security, 85% of the computers in China were infected by viruses in 2003 (Greenspan, 2003d).

More recently, an antivirus software maker, Trend Micro, Inc. reported that thousands of its corporate users in France and Germany have been infected with a virus called Minmail.C that carries the subject message line "our private photos ???" (Reuters, 2003a). Once the email is opened, the virus is triggered and installs a Simple Mail Transfer Protocol (SMTP) program that turns the infected computer in to an email server that sends out thousands of spoofed email messages as if sent from a friend or co-worker. Spoofing is an online trick where one sender forges or fakes the address of another sender (Evers, 2003). Although the virus itself is not believed to be particularly damaging to the computers it infects, it does, however, have the potential to flood and bog down corporate networks.

This represents a new and growing trend where virus writers are using techniques that spammers employ to send bulk spam messages. Conversely, spammers are starting to use methods incorporated by virus writers to send their messages and avoid detection. Today, viruses are easily written to change their signatures and bypass antivirus software, and they are often included as attachments that tempt users who trustingly open email attachments from trusted sources or people they know (Radcliff, 2000).

Privacy Concerns

Many individuals believe unsolicited electronic mail is an invasion of privacy. In fact, almost 90% of online consumers want to have the right to control how their personal information is used after it has been collected (Pastore, 2003a). For example, although most unsolicited emails allow individuals to opt-out or to be removed from a direct marketer's database, the argument is that one should not have to do anything to get off a list you never intended to join. Moreover, some unscrupulous direct marketers use these requests as a way to confirm that an email address is valid and active, and an individual may receive even more unsolicited emails.

Subsequently, many direct Internet marketers place a great deal of value on the email lists that they create. Moreover, the 4% of the recipients of unsolicited email who provide personal information have made this data as valuable as currency on the Internet (Greenspan, 2003b). These lists are often created by scanning Usenet postings, buying other Internet mailing lists, or searching the web for email addresses. Direct marketers can also purchase a "spambot" for $39.95 that searches message boards and can provide a list of up to 100,000 email addresses in an hour (Solomon, 2002b).

In addition, many Internet marketers sell their email lists to others. Once on this list, it becomes difficult to have your email address removed. As a result, adults and children may receive all kinds of unsolicited emails for questionable or inappropriate products and services. A research study conducted by Forrester found that most online shoppers worry that the information they share online will result in unsolicited email or telemarketing calls. Subsequently, 80% of the Internet users surveyed support a policy that prohibits the sale of data to third parties (Pastore, 2003b).

Electronic Mail Filters

Using filters to control spam is a hot issue that is being widely debated (Johnson, 2003). Many individuals and companies have attempted to block unsolicited email using filters that identify spam based on specific or key words contained within the subject heading or content of the email message. These types of filters have not been very effective (Graham & Catlett, 2003). For example, a filter set to an "aggressive" setting may create too many false positive situations where legitimate emails are mistakenly identified as spam. False positives can lead to lost business, angry customers and business partners, as well as frustrated friends and family members. New and improved filters, such as Bayesian and SpamBayes, may offer a practical solution to limit spam. These new filters incorporate an artificial intelligence component that allows the filter to learn what emails a *user* considers to be spam.

However, there are still arguments that cast doubt on whether spam filters can be truly effective. For example, Campbell and Wettermann (2003) report that even with spam filters, individuals still spend an average of 12.5 minutes a day screening and managing their email, at an annualized cost of $1,625. It appears that filtering spam makes it more manageable, but does not eliminate it (Fallows, 2003). Spammers are becoming more and more sophisticated as they attempt to slip messages through the filter defenses (Machlis, 2003). Text can be altered to outmaneuver the filter but still be easily recognized by a human. For example, an unsolicited email may use "SeXXX" instead of "sex", which could be easily filtered. Moreover, another easy way to get around an email filter is to send an email message that contains only an image that includes the content of the solicitation since filters can only search on the text contained in the email. Some spammers have even included a Java script program that changes the content of anemail once it is opened.

Although many companies have attempted to block unsolicited email, the process has not been easy or inexpensive. For example, Xerox set up a firewall in the summer of 2001 and was blocking 150,000 spam emails each month. By the fall, it increased to more than 60,000 messages a day (Solomon, 2002b). Some organizations have gone as far as instituting a policy where employees are not allowed to give out their email address (Disabatino, 2002b). This unfortunately limits contact with important stakeholders such as customers and vendors. An *Information Week* study reports that 58% of the 550 Information Technology professionals surveyed said that they plan on spending 5-20% more on spam-fighting tools in 2003 than they did in 2002, while only 39% said they would expect to spend the same as last year (Greenspan, 2003d).

While many companies may have spam filters in place, chances are they may not have a consistent corporate strategy or training programs in place for educating users. Therefore, spam filters are not a silver bullet technology. Even sophisticated filtering technology will only limit spam as spam volume and spammers' sophistication grows (Campbell & Wettemann, 2003).

Attempts to Control Spam

Many ISPs and other organizations are fighting spam. For example, Microsoft announced that it would incorporate spam filter technologies in its free MSN Hotmail email service that serves over 110 million worldwide users (Pruitt, 2002). In addition, Sprint has also announced that it would provide a new service called Sprint E-mail Protection Services that will filter spam and cleanse incoming email messages of viruses before they enter an organization's network (Weiss, 2002).

More recently, we have witnessed the emergence of new organizations such as Remove.org and Gloabalremoval.org that propose to stop unsolicited emails. Based upon the popularity of the U.S. Federal government's "do not call" list for telemarketers, a person can have his or her email address posted on a similar "do-not-spam" list for as low as $10 a year. Although this may be an inexpensive and novel way to reduce spam, direct Internet marketing firms are under no obligation to comply. However, customer-savvy direct Internet marketers could use this list to scrub their own customer list so that inappropriate emails are not sent to children or to others who may find such content offensive. Many believe that such lists have a low probability of succeeding without government support (Sullivan, 2003). However, there appears to be support for a "do not spam" registry. A survey conducted by InsightExpress indicated that 75% of the respondents are in favor of a national "do not spam" list.

Another attempt to block unwanted UCEs is the use of a blacklist that blocks the network addresses of known spammers. The effectiveness of a spam blacklist is questionable. For example, Gilhooly (2003) describes the experiences of Tivoli Software when they made use of a blacklist called the Open Relay Blocking System (ORBS) to combat spam. Unfortunately, many of the organizations whose network addresses added to the list were innocent of wrongdoing. Tivoli encountered a number of problems using the list when customers tried to contact them for support but kept getting blocked.

On the other hand, Weiss (2003) reports the experiences of a small, independent software company that created a blacklist and then came under attack by spammers who conducted a distributed denial of service (DDoS). In addition, the company's email was spoofed where about 1 million pornographic images and sex-related messages were sent in retaliation for being placed on the blacklist. As a result of the attack in the summer of 2003, a spokesperson for the software company that created the blacklist said that they had had enough and were done fighting spammers. Without a connection to the Internet, the cyber-attackers had virtually cut off the company's lifeline. Although the company reported the DDoS attacks to the local police and the FBI, the response from these agencies was perceived as lukewarm.

Aside from the aggressive counter-attacks by spammers, several other issues make a spam blacklist ineffective (Gilhooly, 2003). For example, a network address usually gets on a blacklist when the blacklist owners test and discover an open-relay mail server that is configured to relay mail on the behalf of any sender. An innocent organization may have one server that is misconfigured and then have its entire domain blocked. This can be a problem as well if the blacklist is poorly managed or if someone is being malicious. Network vigilanteeism can arise because anyone can report anyone else. In addition, a domain can get added to the blacklist even just after a few reports of abuse. There may be no process for domains to prove that being on the list is a mistake or that an organization corrected what got them on the blacklist in the first place. As a result, it can be very difficult for an organization to have itself removed from the blacklist.

Another attempt to control spam is a recent campaign to make consumers aware that buying goods and services from spammers only helps to feed the problem (Pruitt, 2003). This "don't buy and don't reply" approach probably will have limited effectiveness in curbing the deluge of UCE.

Legislative Action

Many countries have begun to take steps to limit or at least control the flow of unsolicited email. For example, Austria's Parliament unanimously voted to make unsolicited "junk" email illegal, while Germany and the Netherlands have taken equally hard positions (D'Amico, 1999). Under a new British law, an organization convicted in a magistrate court of spamming can face a fine of $8,057, while a fine from a jury trial could be unlimited (Reuters, 2003b). Moreover, South Korea established a new law that prohibits the automatic generation of email addresses. If convicted, a person would face criminal charges and fines of up to $8,585 (Williams, 2003).

Although sending spam is still legal in the United States, the Federal Trade Commission has begun an initiative to control and monitor deceptive or fraudulent spam and Internet scams (Rosencrance, 2002). However, the Senate Commerce Committee is considering two bills that will limit spam by requiring email marketers to include a valid return address, prohibit the use of phony or misleading subject headers, and require recipients to opt-in before companies can send unsolicited email to them.

There are two important issues associated with trying to outlaw spam: one is the legitimate direct marketing lobby and the second is the difficulty of enforcement (Graham & Catlett, 2003). Direct marketers want to ensure that spam laws still allow them to contact their customers; however, there are still legal loopholes so big that any laws become meaningless. For example, a company that purchases email addresses from another company can claim that they are an "affiliate". Subsequently, the affiliate can claim that anyone on the purchased list is its customer, too. Enforcement is another issue as well. Although many people are against spam and may have been inspired by the recent FTC do-not-call list, attempts to create a similar program may be quite disappointing to consumers because spammers can easily cloak their identities or operate overseas in order to escape detection and punishment.

However, many organizations are willing to fight back by taking spammers to the courtroom. For example, in August 2003, Amazon.com filed 11 lawsuits against online marketers in the U.S. and Canada for allegedly spoofing Amazon's name when sending email advertisements for such things as home appliances, penis enlargement pills, and car warranties (Evers, 2003). This is especially a problem for companies with trusted domain names and that use email as a primary tool for communicating with customers (Evers, 2003).

Spam's Strengths, Weaknesses, Opportunities, and Threats (SWOT) Analysis

Using a SWOT analysis, Table 1 summarizes the strengths, weaknesses, opportunities, and threats associated with UCE or spam. UCE has several strengths: It is easy to use, it has a very low cost, it can be sent to a wide audience, and the personal information can be sold to other businesses. However, spam also has

Table 1: SWOT analysis of spam

Strengths	**Weaknesses**
• Low-cost	• Annoying
• Large audience	• Burnout leads to loss of message
• Easy to use	• Inappropriate messages
• Personal information can be sold	
Opportunities	**Threats**
• Reach new customers	• Legislation
• Increasing sales	• Filter technologies
• Target specific customers (customizable)	• Blacklists and "Do not call" lists
• Global reach	

several weaknesses. It is annoying to most users, there is so much spam that some email users are suffering from burnout, and people can be offended by the sometime inappropriate messages. Spam, however, does offer opportunities to businesses. It can enable firms to reach new customers, it can increase sales, it is customizable so that it can be targeted to specific customers, and it has a global reach. There are also several threats to spam. There is increasing legislation to limit and curtail spam at the state and federal level in the U.S., but also in other countries, filter technologies have advanced to point where a great percentage of spam is filtered out before reaching its intended destination, and blacklists and "Do not call" lists are starting to gain public momentum.

PERCEPTIONS OF UNSOLICITED EMAIL

Although many people believe that spam is annoying and counterproductive, most cannot agree on a common definition of spam. For example, is one's perception of spam influenced by the frequency of receiving unsolicited electronic mail? Does it depend on the subject matter or message contained in the email? Or is the timing of a particular product or service important?

Depending upon an individual's definition of what spam is or is not, will this person believe unsolicited email is an invasion of their privacy or a drain on their personal productivity? Subsequently, the individual may believe that spam should be controlled. And if so, should it be controlled by Internet marketers (i.e., self-control), ISPs, organizations, or the government? Finally, it is important to understand how individuals deal with unsolicited electronic mail in order to realize its effectiveness. Insight into these questions can provide a basis for public and organizational policies regarding unsolicited email.

A web-based survey was conducted by the authors in November, 2002. The research subjects were undergraduate and graduate business school students at a large Midwest university in the United States. More than 200 students participated in the survey.

Of the 204 responses to the survey, 68% were male and 32% were female. Approximately 92% of the respondents were between the ages of 20 to 29. In addition, 42% indicated that they have two email accounts, while 51% said they have three or more accounts. Table 2 provides a summary of email usage. As can be seen, 78% of the respondents check their email at least twice a day. Moreover, it can be seen by the percentage of emails sent and received that the respondents are considerable users of electronic mail, making them ideal for this study.

In addition, Figure 2 provides a summary of the respondents' self reports of their email that is unsolicited. As can be seen, 4% of the respondents reported that less than 10 % of their email was UCE, 18% of the respondents reported that 10-25% of their email was unsolicited, 26% of the respondents reported that between

Table 2: Summary of email usage

How many e-mail accounts do you have?	
1	7%
2	42%
3 or more	51%
How often do you check your e-mail?	
Less than once a week	1%
Once a week	0%
Twice a week	1%
Every other day	5%
Once a day	15%
Twice a day	20%
More than twice a day	58%
On average, how many e-mails do you receive a day?	
<=5	15%
6-10	31%
11-20	23%
>20	31%
On average, how many e-mails do you send in a day?	
<=5	55%
6-10	37%
11-20	4%
>20	4%
I am very dependent on e-mail for communicating with others.	5.78 *

** Based on 7-point Likert scale ranging from "1" for strongly disagree to "7" for strongly agree.*

26-50% of their email was unsolicited, 34% of the respondents reported that between 51-75% of their email was unsolicited, and 18% of the respondents reported that more than 75% of their email was unsolicited.

Privacy Concerns

Table 3 provides a summary of the respondents' perceptions of privacy. A seven point Likert scale has a median of four and thus provides a benchmark for neutrality. As can be seen in Table 3, the respondents tend to believe that unsolicited email is an invasion of their privacy and is annoying. However, they are somewhat neutral about being offended by the contents or subject headings of unsolicited email and asking to be taken off the senders' lists. It also appears that the respondents are not likely to complain about receiving unsolicited email.

Figure 2: Percentage of unsolicited email received each day

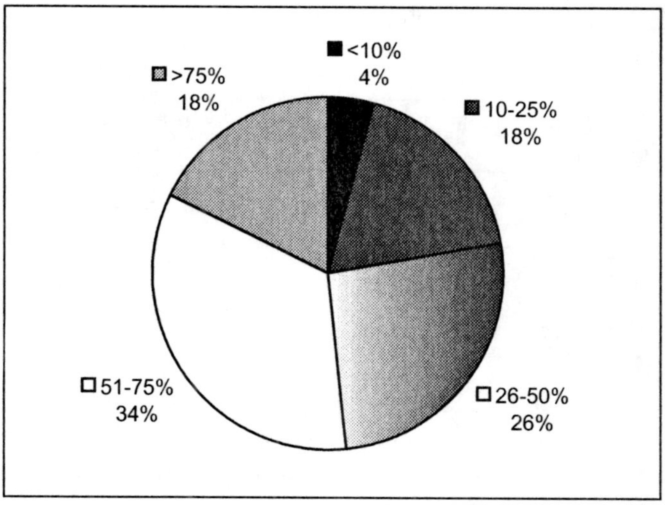

Table 3: Summary of respondents—privacy concerns

Question	Mean	Std Dev
I consider unsolicited e-mail to be an invasion of my privacy.	5.23	1.58
I do not like getting a lot of unsolicited e-mails from a single person or organization.	6.16	1.58
In general, receiving unsolicited e-mail does not bother me.	2.47	1.67
In general, I become annoyed when I get unsolicited e-mail.	5.57	1.65
I am often offended by the subject headings or contents of unsolicited.	4.31	1.93
I am very likely to ask the sender of unsolicited e-mail to take me off their e-mail list.	4.61	2.09
I am very likely to complain to a third party about a sender of unsolicited e-mail.	3.42	1.82

Note: Based on 7-point Likert scale ranging from "1" for strongly disagree to "7" for strongly agree.

Table 4: Summary of respondents—Productivity

Question	Mean	Std Dev
Dealing with unsolicited e-mail has little impact my personal productivity.	4.00	1.83
I am most likely to delete unsolicited email because I do not have the time to read it.	5.33	1.80

Note: Based on 7-point Likert scale ranging from "1" for strongly disagree to "7" for strongly agree.

Productivity

On average, 61% of the respondents said that they spend less than five minutes a day dealing with unsolicited e-mail, while only 15% said that they spend more than 10 minutes a day. Table 4 provides a summary of the respondents' perceptions concerning their personal productivity. It appears that the respondents are neutral in their belief that unsolicited email impacts their personal productivity. However, they are likely to delete these emails because they do not have time to read them.

Control

Table 5 provides a summary of the questions that relate to the respondents' perceptions regarding the control of unsolicited email. It appears that there is a strong belief that unsolicited email should be controlled. However, it appears that the respondents lean towards control by ISPs or the organization itself and to a lesser extent by the government and self-regulation of the direct Internet marketers.

Effectiveness

Effectiveness is defined as whether users are likely to open unsolicited email, read, or even respond to them. Table 6 lists detailed items surveyed in the study to measure the effectiveness of unsolicited email. It appears that the respondents are not likely to open or respond to unsolicited email. In fact, it appears that they are very likely to delete unsolicited email without even opening it. Interestingly, however, they do prefer unsolicited email to unsolicited phone calls.

CONCLUSION

As the Internet continues to grow, Internet marketers will continue to reach millions of potential customers through unsolicited commercial email. Although this marketing channel provides ample opportunities for sellers, many countries, organizations, and individuals have taken steps to limit or control the flow of

Table 5: Summary of respondents—control

Question	Mean	Std Dev
In general, I believe that unsolicited e-mail should be controlled.	6.20	1.35
Unsolicited e-mail should be controlled by the government.	4.39	1.90
Unsolicited e-mail should be controlled by my Internet Service Provider.	5.57	1.52
Unsolicited e-mail should be controlled by my company or the organization that provides me with my e-mail address.	5.58	1.52
Unsolicited e-mail should be self-controlled by the senders themselves.	4.89	2.05

Note: Based on 7-point Likert scale ranging from "1" for strongly disagree to "7" for strongly agree.

unsolicited electronic mail. However, unsolicited electronic mail that may be annoying or considered "spam" by one individual may be welcome and valuable to another. Although some people may consider spam an invasion of privacy, others feel that limiting or controlling the free flow of information is a violation of their civil liberties.

It appears that many organizations may be caught in the middle. An increase in UCE will degrade network performance and take up precious disk space on servers. In addition, harmful viruses attached to emails can lead to lost data and productivity, as well as major disruption. Email filters, virus protection software, firewalls, and the implementation of security policies and procedures consume organizational resources. Although an organization must ensure that protective measures are taken, strict controls and security measures can limit employee contact with key stakeholders such as customers and vendors.

Moreover, security policies and procedures meant to protect the organization and its employees raise several issues. For example, what types of electronic mail will be filtered? Electronic mail filters tend to restrict email based on keywords. Certain words may have different connotations and could result in restricting legitimate email, while allowing offensive or undesirable email to get through.

Another concern is ownership. Does an organization own the email address or does the employee or student? Many people use their email address for both personal and professional purposes so they may feel that an email address belongs to them. On the other hand, if one believes that the organization owns the email address, does that give the organization the right to read and limit the types of emails that an employee or student sends and receives?

This chapter also explores individuals' perceptions of unsolicited electronic mail in terms of its impact on personal productivity and its effectiveness. A sample of students provided a homogeneous sample of frequent users of electronic mail.

Table 6: Summary of respondents—effectiveness

Question	Mean	Std Dev
I am likely to open unsolicited e-mail if I am interested in the topic or subject heading.	2.99	1.88
I am likely to open unsolicited e-mail if the topic or subject heading is timely to my needs.	3.00	1.86
I am likely to open unsolicited e-mail if the address is from someone or an organization with a good reputation.	3.66	1.94
When I receive unsolicited e-mail, I am very likely to open and read the e-mail.	1.83	1.37
When I receive unsolicited e-mail, I am very likely to delete the e-mail.	6.45	1.23
When I open and read unsolicited e-mail, I am very likely to respond.	1.56	1.32
When I open and read unsolicited e-mail, I am very likely to delete it without responding.	6.38	1.41
I am most likely to delete unsolicited e-mail because I am not interested in the subject heading or topic.	5.94	1.56
I am most likely to delete unsolicited e-mail without opening it because I am concerned that it may contain a harmful computer virus.	5.61	1.70
I prefer unsolicited e-mail more than unsolicited telephone calls.	5.64	1.79

Note: Based on 7-point Likert scale ranging from "1" for strongly disagree to "7" for strongly agree.

The results suggest that although the respondents receive a large number of unsolicited emails that they find annoying, they tend to spend little time dealing with it. More importantly, the respondents are very unlikely to open, let alone read and respond to unsolicited electronic mail. This brings an important question as to whether unsolicited email is an effective medium for selling products and services over the Internet. Future research should focus on the effectiveness of email when the consumer opts in to receive solicited email. Interestingly, however, the respondents to this survey overwhelming prefer unsolicited electronic mail to unsolicited telephone calls by telemarketers.

Although the respondents believe that unsolicited email should be controlled, it is not quite clear as to who should control it. However, it appears that control by the government is the least preferred choice. Unfortunately, control by ISPs and organizations results in a myriad of different policies and procedures, with many being ineffective, illegal, or immoral.

More research is needed to further explore these issues. The web-based survey conducted by the authors provides a first step, but is limited to a small section of the population of Internet users. Future research should focus on cross-sections that include different demographics, as well as other private and public organizations. Of particular interest would be the study of people's perceptions in an organization with respect to the policy and procedures the organization under study has in place.

Although the results of the web-based survey suggest that most respondents prefer a non-governmental or private sector solution, the issue concerning the cost of such a solution was not addressed. No doubt there will be a substantial cost to the host organization or the ISP who will be responsible for controlling unsolicited electronic mail. Therefore, it would be interesting to gauge email users' preferences and attitudes towards an increase in costs for service or a reduction in access or service if the electronic mail address is hosted by an individual's employer.

REFERENCES

Abreu, E.M. (2003). SoBig worm aims to turn PCs into spam machines.*Computerworld.* Available online: *www.computerworld.com/securitytopics/security/story/0,10801,84214.html.*

Blackman, A. (2003). Spam's easy target. *The Wall Street Journal*, August 19, B1, B4.

Campbell, I., & Wettemann, R. (2003). The silent ROI killer. *Computerworld*, October 20. Available online: *www.computerworld.com/printthis/2003/0,4814,86145,00.html.*

CyberAtlas Staff. (2003). Virus damage worst on record for August 2003. *CyberAtlas.* Available online: *cyberatlas.internet.com/big_picture/applications/print/0,,1301_3071131,00.html.*

D'Amico, M.L. (1999). Austria bans spam. *Computerworld*, July 16. Available online: *www.computerworld.com/printthis/1999/0,4814,28444,00.html.*

Disabatino, J. (2000). Online marketers stung by spam label. *Computerworld,* November 2. Available online: *MACROBUTTON HtmlResAnchor www.computerworld.com/printthis/2000/0,4814,543480,00.html.*

Disabatino, J. (2002a). Spam taking a toll on business systems. *Computerworld*, February 18. Available online: *www.computerworld.com/printthis/2002/0,4814,68439,00.html.*

Disabatino, J. (2002b).Bottom line hit hard by need to fend off spam and viruses. *Computerworld*, June 17. Available online: *MACROBUTTON HtmlResAnchor www.computerworld.com/printthis/2002/0,4814,72041,00.html.*

European Commission, The. (2002). Commission study: 'Junk' e-mail costs Internet users euro 10 billion a year worldwide. February 2. Available online: *europa.eu.int/comm/internal_market/en/dataprot/studies/spam.htm.*

Evers, J. (2003). Amazon sues to stop alleged e-mail forgeries. *Computerworld,* August 27. Available online: *www.computerworld.com/printthis/2003/0,4814,84433,00.html.*

Fallows, D. (2003). Spam: How it is hurting email and degrading life on the Internet. *Internet & American Life.* Available online: *www.pewinternet.org.*

Gibbs, M. (2003). Solving the spam equation. *Network World, 20*(31), 61.

Gilhooly, K. (2003). Sidebar: The dark side of blacklisting. *Computerworld,* July 28. Available online: *www.computerworld.com/printthis/2003/0,4814,83384,00.html.*

Graham, P., & Catlett. J. (2003). Face off: Are filters more effective than laws in stopping spam? *Network World, 20*(21), 57.

Greenspan, R. (2003a). Spam threatens revenue, kids. *Cyberatlas.* Available online: *cyberatlas.internet.com/big_picture/application/print/0,,1301_2219211,00.html.*

Greenspan, R. (2003b). Spam: Always annoying, often offensive. *CyberAtlas.* Available online: *cyberatlas.internet.com/big_picture/applications/print/0,,1301_30975351,00.html.*

Greenspan, R. (2003c). Spam expected to outnumber non-spam. *CyberAtlas.* Available online: *cyberatlas.internet.com/big_picture/applications/print/0,,1301_3097351,00.html.*

Greenspan, R. (2003d). The deadly duo: Spam and virtues. *CyberAtlas.* Available online: *cyberatlas.internet.com/big_picture/applications/print/0,,1301_3087891,00.html.*

Johnson, M. (2003). Skirmishing with spam. *Computerworld.* Available online: *www.computerworld.com/softwaretopics/software/groupware/story/0.10801,84684.html.*

Machlis, S. (2003). Uh-oh: Spam's getting more sophisticated. *Computerworld.* Available online: *www.computerworld.com/softwaretopics/software/groupware/story/0.10801,77704.html.*

Mangalindan, M. (2002). For bulk e-mailer, pestering millions offers path to profit. *The Wall Street Journal*, CCXL:98, November 13.

Morrissey, B. (2003). Spam cost corporate America $9B in 2002. *CyberAtlas.* Available online: *cyberatlas.internet.com/big_picture/applications/print/0,,1301_1565721,00.html.*

Parker, P. (2003). House lists generate best e-mail ROI. *CyberAtlas.* Available online: *cyberatlas.internet.com/markets/advertising/print/0,,5941_3092381,00.html.*

Pastore, M. (2003a). Consumers fear for their online privacy. *CyberAtlas.* Available online: *http://cyberatlas.internet.com/markets/retailing/print/0,,6061_228341,00.html.*

Pastore, M. (2003b). ISPs blamed for spam problem. *CyberAtlas.* Available online: *cyberatlas.internet.com/big_picture/traffic_patterns/print/0,,5931_15213,00.html*

Perez, J.C. (2003). Yahoo! adds e-mail features to flush out spam. *Computerworld*, October 21. Available online: *www.computerworld.com/printthis/2003/0,4814,85174,00.html.*

Pruitt, S. (2002). Hotmail aims to cut spam off at the pass. *Computerworld*, September 19. Available online: *MACROBUTTON HtmlResAnchor www.computerworld.com/printthis/2002/0,4814,74361,00.html.*

Pruitt, S. (2003). Stop buying from spammers, Net industry says. *Computerworld*, September 26. Available online: *www.computerworld.com/printthis/2003/0,4814,85425,00.html.*

Radcliff, D. (2000). Virus vigilance. *Computerworld*, December 11. Available online: *www.computerworld.com/printthis/2000/0,4814,54943,00.html.*

Reuters. (2003a). E-mail virus turns pcs into spam machines. *Computerworld*, October 31. Available online: *www.computerworld.com/printthis/2003/0,4814,86737,00.html.*

Reuters (2003b). The U.K. cracks down on spammers with new privacy law. *Computerworld*, September 18. Available online: *www.computerworld.com/printthis/2003/0,4814,85174,00.html.*

Rosencrance, L. (2002). FTC targets deceptive spam. *Computerworld*, November 14. Available online: *www.computerworld.com/printthis/2002/0,4814,75880,00.html.*

Saunders, C. (2003a). Spam, saturation plague e-mail marketing. *CyberAtlas*. Available online: *cyberatlas.internet.com/markets/advertising/print/0,,5941_1135831,00.html.*

Saunders, C. (2003b). Consumers don't mistake mail for spam. *CyberAtlas*. Available online: *cyberatlas.internet.com/markets/advertising/print/0,,5941_1467141,00.html.*

Solomon, M. (2002a). What is spam? *Computerworld*, November 11. Available online: *MACROBUTTON HtmlResAnchor www.computerworld.com/news/2002/story/0,11280,75735,00.html.*

Solomon, M. (2002b). Spam wars. *Computerworld*, November 11. Available online: *www.computerworld.com/softwaretopics/software/groupware/story/0,10801,75737,00.html.*

Sulivan, A. (2003). Do-not-spam lists find customers, skeptics. *Computerworld.* Available online: *www.computerworld.com/securitytopics/security/privacy/story/0,10801,83710,00.html.*

Weiss, T.R. (2002). Sprint rolls out antispam, antivirus services to businesses. *Computerworld*, November 12. Available online: *MACROBUTTON HtmlResAnchor www.computerworld.com/securitytopics/security/story/0,10801,75820,00.html.*

Weiss, T.R. (2003). Antispam 'blacklist' providers hit by online attacks. *Computerworld*, September 26. Available online: *www.computerworld.com/securitytopics/security/story/0,10801,85439,00.html.*

William, M. (2003). Spam falls after South Korea strengthens e-mail law. *Computerworld*, September 15. Available online: *www.computerworld.com/printthis/2003/0,4814,84963,00.html.*

Chapter IX

Impact of E-Learning During SARS Outbreak in Hong Kong

Eric T. T. Wong, The Hong Kong Polytechnic University, Hong Kong

ABSTRACT

The potential benefits of e-commerce have been reported widely in the literature, and e-learning has been gradually accepted as a social tool for e-commerce at tertiary institutions (Parker, 2003). In this chapter the impact of e-commerce on the local community during a Severe Acute Respiratory Syndrome (SARS) outbreak in Hong Kong will be briefly described, with an emphasis on the use of E-learning technology as a contingency measure in tertiary institutions. At the height of the SARS epidemic in April 2003, Hong Kong had 60 to 80 new cases of the disease each day. Hundreds of thousands of residents wore surgical masks in an attempt to avoid catching the virus. All schools and universities were ordered closed and governments invoked quarantine laws not used for decades to isolate those who might be carriers. Explained Hong Kong's Chief Executive Tung Chee-hwa in announcing tougher measures to curb the spread of the disease: "Hong Kong is currently facing its most serious contagious disease threat in 50 years." As a contingency measure e-learning technology was employed in the local higher education. This chapter aims to identify some of the practical difficulties involved in an evaluation of the academic performance of two groups of engineering students taking an introductory course - one group studied via e-learning and the other studied through the traditional classroom approach. Preliminary findings showed that with limited time available for the course design and delivery, the examination result of the e-learning class was slightly better than the traditional class. With positive student feedback on the e-learning approach, this would imply that e-learning shows a potential for substituting some of the traditional course elements, especially for topics relating to higher-order thinking skills. To generalize these findings more studies with properly controlled experimental design would need to be carried out. Directions for future work are also suggested.

SEVERE ACUTE RESPIRATORY SYNDROME

Severe Acute Respiratory Syndrome (SARS) has killed more than 800 people worldwide - most of them in Asia - since the disease first appeared in southern China last November. In Hong Kong, 296 people died of the disease and 1,755 became ill. SARS is a pneumonia-like illness and the main symptoms are high fever, dry cough, and shortness of breath or breathing difficulties. While some medicines have been tried, no drug can at this time be recommended for prophylaxis or treatment. Based on currently available evidence, close contact with an infected person will cause the infective agent to be spread from one person to another. According to the World Health Organization (WHO), contact with aerosolized (exhaled) droplets and bodily secretions from an infected person appears to be important.

At the height of the SARS epidemic in early April 2003, Hong Kong had 60 to 80 new cases of the disease each day. Hundreds of thousands of residents wore surgical masks, and stayed away from public places in an attempt to avoid catching the virus.

IMPACT OF E-COMMERCE

During this period, with thousands of Hong Kong residents undergoing voluntary isolation, Internet use surged in the territory. Business people prevented from traveling and home-bound youths playing online games contributed to a 30 percent rise in residential broadband Internet traffic at a fixed-line phone company in Hong Kong. According to the second largest long-distance carrier company, international telephone calls had risen by more than twenty percent.

Providers of virtual services such as online games and video conferencing were benefiting as the city's 7 million residents chose to shy away from face-to-face contact for fear of catching SARS. Software companies have rolled out their video conferencing equipments and software since the outbreak of SARS. The stock price of these companies also climbed in May 2003 by this factor.

Since the outbreak of the SARS epidemic, many companies in Hong Kong have cancelled the meeting and traveling events to the Asia Pacific region, especially those to China and Taiwan. The video conferencing system combined with video and audio equipment has been therefore adopted as an alternative of overseas traveling.

People had more time on their hands after the government shut schools and quarantined residents exposed to the virus. One million children spent several weeks more at home after a city-wide school closure was extended.

According to a Yahoo! business manager in Hong Kong, the company's games web site, which features pool, chess and other interactive games, recorded an over 70 percent surge in viewership in April 2003 compared with a month earlier. Besides spurning movie theaters for online entertainment, people were also using the Internet and emails to keep abreast of developments on the disease. Another local company, which connects customers to its local language news web portal, said peak-hour usage had tripled to 12 hours a day.

During the SARS period, most higher education institutions in Hong Kong had no alternative but to allow their students to stay at home to learn through the Internet and to prepare for their final examinations in May or June. Since e-learning has been widely accepted as a social tool for e-commerce at tertiary institutions, the following study addressed the contingency e-learning measures carried out by a local university staff with the aim of evaluating the impact of e-learning on student learning in higher education.

THE INTERNET IN HIGHER EDUCATION

Computers are appearing everywhere in today's university campuses. From notebook computers to online library catalogues and full-text access of journal articles to course web sites, the infusion of e-commerce has undoubtedly altered the nature of higher education (Green, 2000). A recent campus survey shows that IT has had a major impact on tertiary education in the Special Administrative Region (ACCS, 2002). For example, almost all of the respondents believed that IT had done much to improve instruction on their campuses and nine of the campuses had an IT requirement in place for undergraduate students. In terms of IT resources, Hong Kong tertiary institutions appeared to be adequately equipped and most were providing staff and students with access to computers and the network.

The incorporation of Internet technology was aimed to enhance learning, especially when coupled with more learner-centered instruction (Zhu & Kaplan, 2002). It possesses a "convenience" feature where learning and communication with the instructor can take place asynchronously at the student's own pace or on an as-needed basis (Palloff et al., 2001). It has been suggested that easy access to the lecturer and library resources gradually changes the teaching strategy in higher education to the discovering of information rather than the traditional didactic approach (MacDonald et al., 2001).

When technology is integrated with pedagogy, a new form of learning or "e-learning" may emerge. Smith and Hardaker (2000) listed six basic components of an e-learning framework: lectures, tutorials, textbooks/journals, e-library, web-based learning material, and e-discussion groups. Despite the electronic form of delivery, it was assumed that lectures, tutorials, textbooks, and journals remain the essential components of instruction and that each retains its traditional characteristics. In this view, e-libraries containing full-text journal articles and electronic books facilitate student access but otherwise differ little from the usual "brick-and-mortar" library.

In contrast to these other electronic resources, electronic bulletin boards are widely available and are often included in course software packages or textbook web sites. Also known as e-discussion groups, chat rooms, or online discussion areas, these bulletin boards provide an electronic forum that allows the user to post a message for others to read and to which others can respond (i.e., threaded discussions). These messages remain visible until deleted by the instructor. Bulletin boards are asynchronous, facilitating communication among diverse people who can access the web site at different times. Bulletin boards, therefore, differ from synchronous discussions (whether electronic "chat rooms" or traditional office hours and study groups) that require coordinated, real-time access among students and instructor.

In comparison to more traditional group discussions in a classroom setting, electronic bulletin boards separate the content of the communication from the personal characteristics of the student (e.g., appearance, accent, age). It was suggested that this medium would encourage greater participation by shy students (Reber, 1996). By encouraging students to engage in discussions with a more diverse population, bulletin boards would "enrich and expand students' educational experience beyond the classroom" (Karayan & Crowe, 1997). Because bulletin boards are asynchronous, Smith and Hardaker (2000) suggested that students are able to reflect on course material and provide more thoughtful commentary and questions outside of the class meeting time, direct office interaction with instructors, or peer study groups. In view of the above, the adoption of e-learning seems to be a future trend in higher education. Prior to its evaluation as a contingency measure, a brief account of the e-commerce situation in Hong Kong is given below.

E-LEARNING AS A CONTINGENCY MEASURE

According to a global e-commerce survey conducted in 2002 (TNS Interactive—Global eCommerce Report—2002), the percentage of Internet users in Hong Kong rose from 42 percent in 2000 to half of the total population in 2002. In another study of e-learning perceptions among managers in Hong Kong, compared with their counterparts in Singapore, Straits Knowledge found that: (a) Hong Kong managers were less aware and less confident about e-learning than their Singapore counterparts, (b) awareness of e-learning was directly linked to implementations and investment, (c) implementations were fragmentary, and there were few widely visible lead adopters, and (d) the catalyst and advocacy role played by the Singapore government is lacking in Hong Kong, and probably accounts for the slower adoption rate (Straits Knowledge: Elearning in Hong Kong Organizations, April

2002). In view of the large number of Internet users and number of students in the higher education (68,825 full-time equivalent students taking both undergraduate and postgraduate programmes sponsored by the local government in 2002/2003), it is obvious that there is plenty of scope for improvement in the adoption of e-learning in Hong Kong.

During the SARS outbreak period, as all students were advised to stay at home, the Educational Development Centre of the University suggested to all academic staff the following measures on how to better support students during the period when classes were cancelled:

1. *Reinforce the exchange of information and student work:*
   - Continue posting updated lecture materials to the departmental portal (e.g., www.me.polyu.edu.hk) for students to review/study —
   In accordance with ME past practice, the contents would include word documents, PowerPoint files, and links to existing web pages. Staff were encouraged to provide (1) short directions to students on how to use the material and a question or task to focus their attention, and (2) a web site forum topic in which students could exchange views and discuss the topic or task the lecturer had set.
   - Take advantage of existing web resources —
   As there are thousands of excellent web sites already available, staff were encouraged to construct activities that make appropriate use of an existing web site to help their students accomplish the objectives of individual courses. Students could post what they learn to a forum topic.
   - Use the web to submit work —
   Allow students to submit assignments staff might have already set via email, the course web site, or by post.
   - Use the web to return work —
   As they were approaching examination time, students might be anxiously awaiting feedback from staff on work they had already handed in. Staff were requested to consider responding to students via email or post on their work.
2. *Encourage students to communicate with us and each other:*
   Staff were requested to email students with updated notes and tutorial works on their courses. Individual staff would suggest how students could study on their own so they could continue to make progress. Staff were also told to give some indication of the adjustments they were planning in the course to ease student concerns. Measures suggested include:
   - Start a forum topic devoted to project/assignments—
   Staff were advised to send an email alerting students in their course to the new forum topic and students were reminded that the forum would be checked daily. Staff were also asked to indicate clearly in their notes that students were

welcome to answer each other's questions and that the replies submitted would be looked into from time to time.

- Offer online chat times—

Staff were encouraged to let students know that he or she would be available to online "chat" at prearranged times. As it was noted that this technology worked best with only a few people chatting at once and on topics that were easily addressed in a sentence or two, staff were advised to keep the chat sessions short, like half-hour periods.

- Facilitate small group discussion among students—

Staff were told to encourage student discussion through meeting in chat rooms at prearranged times. Another possibility was for staff to set up "private" small group discussion groups in the forum for students to discuss asynchronously.

AUTHORING TOOL

In view of the limited time available for the e-learning course design, the author chose the WebCT as the authoring tool to create an online learning environment. The reason for adopting the WebCT is that it provides the capability for synchronous and asynchronous discussions, email, file sharing, student grading, student presentations, student assessment, student access to course content and tracking of students' work, and external links to references and that it is multimedia capable (Fredrickson, 1999; Nada, 2000).

Access to WebCT (version 3.8) was through a logon password feature that takes the user to the WebCT homepage. PolyU WebCT administrator has already designed a standard page for all PolyU staff that provides access to the online courses that the staff taught. Additionally, the homepage provides information on mail that had been received since the last access, contains a number of bookmarks to assist both the staff and student, and provides general information that the administrator deems important. The homepage also has bookmarks to a student guide, online help, the PolyU library, online WebCT support, participation in an e-learning community, a link for staff to ready-made content for an online course, and other related links.

The author's homepage has four icons that facilitate access to the course content and related materials, communication tools, study and evaluation tools. A typical course menu is shown in Figure 1. For the author's course, this document was created in Microsoft Word and imported to WebCT. Two icons provide access to course schedules. One provided a detailed description of deadlines for materials, a week-by-week schedule in a table format, and information about written assignments and PowerPoint presentations. This was also created using Microsoft Word and imported to WebCT. The second schedule provided a template for a weekly calendar. Information entered in this calendar was programmed to remind students of materials that were due within the week. This information was summarized by

Figure 1: A WebCT course menu

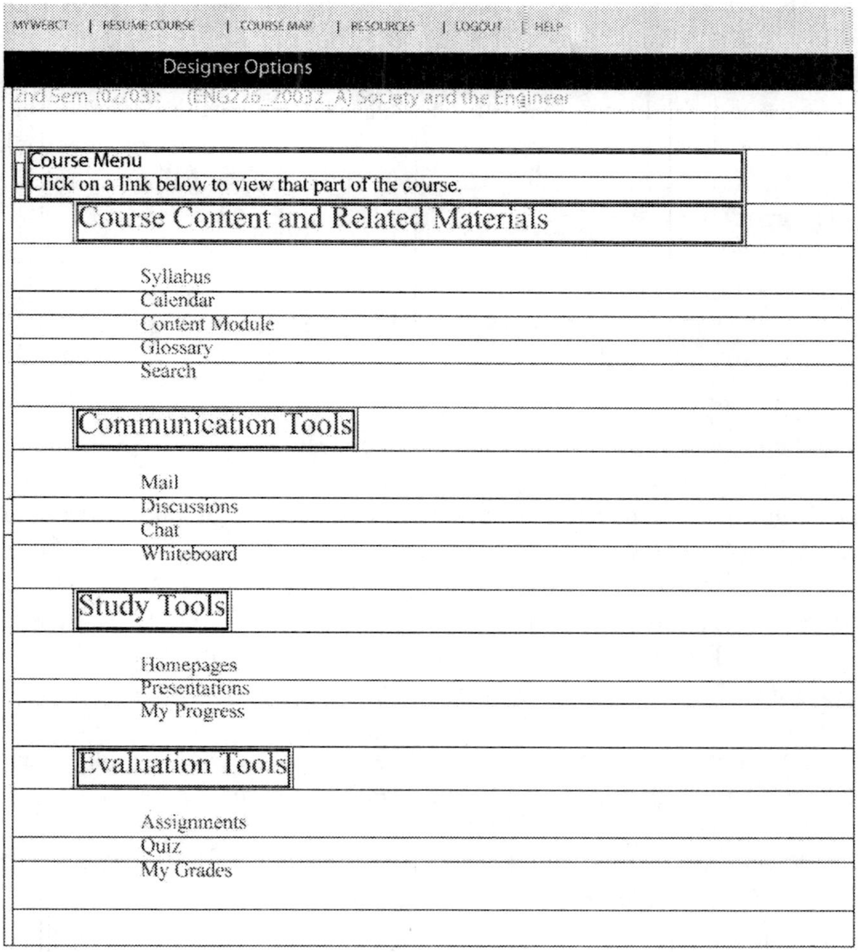

the software on the WebCT homepage and was provided to the student when the student logged on for a session. When the student completed an assignment, or after the date passed, this information no longer appeared. The instructor could easily add or delete from the calendar to provide updated information to the student.

"Chat", a communication tool, allows the author and his students to have real-time conversations. There are four general-purpose chat rooms and one general forum for the course. There is also a general chat room for all courses, which is a room shared by everybody from all courses on the same server. Conversations in the four general-purpose rooms are recorded. The instructor is the only person in the course who can see the records.

Another useful feature of WebCT is the creation of the multiple-choice quiz.

WebCT "Quiz", a study tool, provides the capability for the instructor to build a quiz that is managed by the WebCT software. After the student completes a quiz, the software's grading component scores the quiz and provides feedback that includes the final score, the correct response for each question, and any additional feedback that the instructor builds into the test. The instructor allows the student to see his or her score upon completion of the quiz session and allows additional feedback after everyone in the class has completed the quiz. The instructor can set a time limit for completion of the quiz.

E-LEARNING IN PRACTICE

To illustrate the e-learning activity carried out by the author, a faculty-wide subject, "Society and the Engineer", was used as a platform for experimentation to evaluate the difference in learning outcomes associated with e-learning and traditional courses. A post-only experimental design (i.e., no baseline measure) was adopted since the author had reason to believe the first year students had no prior knowledge of the subject matter and it would not make sense to pretest them if it was expected they would all get a failing score.

This subject is an introductory course for all the engineering programs within the Faculty of Engineering. The subject is taught each fall and spring semester. During the SARS period the total enrollment for the full-time programs was 226 students. A brief description of the subject objective and syllabus was given below, followed by a comparison of the learning outcome achieved by students who had undergone traditional classroom teaching and the e-learning approach.

1. *Subjects:* Students taking this compulsory subject were first year full-time students of the following degree programs:

- BEng (Hons)/MEng in Electrical Engineering
- BEng (Hons)/MEng in Electronic & Information Engineering
- BEng (Hons)/MEng in Mechanical Engineering
- BEng (Hons)/MEng in Industrial & Systems Engineering

2. *Learning Objectives:* The subject was aimed to enable the students to:

- appreciate the historical context of modern technology and the nature of the process whereby technology develops;
- understand the social, political, economic responsibility and accountability of a profession in engineering and the organizational activities of professional engineering institutions;
- appreciate the relationship between technology and environment and the implied social costs and benefits;

- be aware of the short-term and long-term effects on the use of technology relating to safety, health and welfare aspects;
- observe the professional conduct, the legal and moral constraints relating to various engineering aspects.

3. *Sample:* The subject was offered so as to be in line with the University's strategic objective of enhancing the all-around development of students, particularly in the areas of global outlook, critical and creative thinking, social and national responsibility, cultural appreciation, life-long learning, biliteracy and trilingualism, entrepreneurship and leadership.
   To ensure that all students would receive an equal exposure to various fields of engineering within the Faculty, besides the mixing of students from different departments into four classes, all classes would be taught in turn by same staff from the Departments of Electrical Engineering, Electronic and Information Engineering, Industrial and Systems Engineering, and Mechanical Engineering for the same duration, that is, four sessions of three hours each. Additionally, four compulsory seminars with invited speakers from the industry were arranged for the students in January and February 2003.
   The author was responsible for the topics of: (1) education and training of professional engineers and (2) the impact of Chinese development on local industry and supporting organizations in HK. Because of the SARS outbreak in late March, all staff concerned had taught three classes and for each class there were four sessions outstanding. The author carried out his teaching of the outstanding class via the WebCT.
4. *Teaching Strategy:* The learning outcome oriented approach was adopted for both classes to help students to build up their capabilities to learn independently and to be able to use different ways of learning. The main objectives of such an approach are to provide situations in which students can integrate information from different areas of engineering into a meaningful construct for use in solving future problems. Another objective of the learning-outcome approach is to develop effective self-study skills by putting the task of determining what is to be learned and how it is to be learned directly on the students' shoulders. For the traditional class the major components used for the syllabus topics in question would include exploration, small group discussion, information handling and group presentation in class.
5. *Lectures and Assessments:* Students were asked to group themselves into teams comprising four to six students with at least one from each engineering discipline. The lecture notes received by students in both e-learning and traditional classes were identical. Besides using the facility offered by WebCT, all students were sent via email the lecture notes and recommended references (Appendix I). Based on the lecture notes (in the form of PowerPoint files) emailed to them, students had to plan how they would prepare their work for review, and online consultation with the author was encouraged. Oral presentation was cancelled

because of the SARS outbreak. Students were, however, allowed to use the digital video, if appropriate, as a tool for their assignment presentations. Assessment is an indispensable part of teaching and learning since it reinforces the learning style a student adopts. It has been suggested that if a student were tested on lower-order thinking skills, he/she would probably be encouraged to practice the undesirable surface approach to learning (Govindasamy, 2002). Hence, to encourage students to adopt a deep holistic approach to learning, two written assignments aiming to test the students on higher-order thinking skills were used by the author. Both classes of students were asked to explore the assignment topics, to collect information from multiple sources such as the library (where students would be provided surgical masks on entry) and the World Wide Web, and to discuss their views on the given assignments via the WebCT. The main difference is that each group of the traditional course students had to present their assignments orally in class, followed by a question and answer session.

EVALUATION OF LEARNING OUTCOME

1. *Coursework Scores:* At the end of the semester, the academic performance of this class on the two assignments and relevant section (i.e., Section D) of the final examination (Appendix II) was compared with one of the traditional classes having approximately equal mix of students. As there was no oral presentation of the assignments, only the marks of the two written assignments were considered in the calculation of the coursework scores; that is, presentation skills scores of the traditional course students were ignored. The total number of students in the traditional and the e-learning classes were 59 and 56 respectively. As there were three students in the traditional class who did not attempt any question in Section D, only students who attempted Section D were taken into consideration. Hence a sample size of 56 was chosen for the current study, and the coursework scores for the e-learning and the traditional classes were shown in Figure 1. It can be seen that the overall coursework performance of the e-learning class is slightly below that of the traditional class. Also, the e-learning score distribution has a narrower range (C to A) compared with the traditional class (C to A+).
2. *Examination Scores:* In the final examination, there were four sections of two questions each. Each engineering department was responsible for setting two questions in the assigned section. Normally students were asked to attempt at least one question from each section, that is, four questions in total. In view of the cancellation of the last session during the SARS outbreak, students were asked to attempt only three questions out of the four sections and the examination paper was revised accordingly (Appendix III).

   An analysis of the questions attempted shows that for the e-learning class,

Figure 2: Assignment score comparison

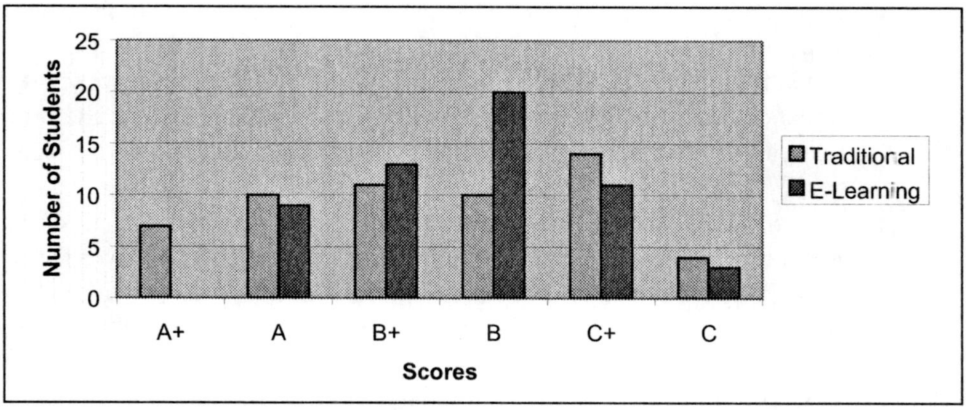

Figure 3: Examination score comparison

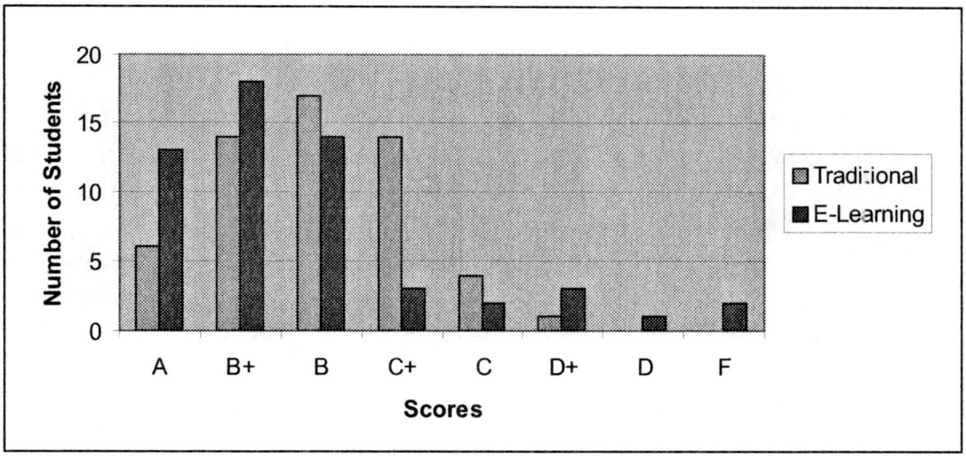

there were 47 and nine students who attempted Question 7 and Question 8 respectively, and for the traditional class there were 51 and 5 students who attempted Question 7 and Question 8 respectively. A comparison of the examination achievement is shown in Figure 3. It can be seen that the examination outcome of the e-learning students seems to be slightly better. However, it is noted that contrary to the coursework scores, the distribution of the examination scores for the e-learning class shows a wider spread than the traditional class.

3. *Analysis of Variance:* In order to study simultaneously the effects of the methods of teaching and assessment, a factorial experiment of the two factors was carried out. There were two kinds of teaching methods (traditional vs. e-learning) and two kinds of assessment methods (formative vs. summative). There were 56 replicates of the experiment and each replicate contained all four treatment combinations, namely traditional-formative, traditional_summative, e-learning_formative and e-learning_summative. The analysis of variance is summarized in Figure 4. Since $F_{0.05,1,224} = 3.84$, it can be concluded that the main effects of assessment methods affect student performance. However, since 0.832 and 0.146 < $F_{0.05,1,224}$, it is clear that the main effect of teaching method does not affect student performance and there is no indication of interaction between these two factors.

QUESTIONNAIRE SURVEY

After the examination, a short questionnaire was sent to 20 students of the e-learning class and there were sixteen feedbacks. Subjects were asked to express agreement or disagreement on a five-point Likert scale. A summary of the survey questionnaire and results is shown in Table 1. It appears that students taking the subject in an e-learning environment found chat to be a more convenient and easy way of having a discussion than the face-to-face instruction that they received prior to the SARS period. This might be explained by the fact that, in a face-to-face ses-

Figure 4: Analysis of variance for methods of teaching and assessment

Source of Variation	Sum of Squares	Degrees of Freedom	Mean Square	F_o
Assessment Method	0.603	1	0.603	23.406
Teaching Method	0.021	1	0.021	0.832
Interaction	0.004	1	0.004	0.146
Error	5.671	220	0.026	
Total	111.596	223		

sion (e.g., lectures or tutorials) other opportunities to communicate synchronously are abundant and chat may face competition from in-class interactions. On the other hand, in the e-learning class keyboard-based chat may appear more desirable because it is one of a few available forms of synchronous communication and most Chinese students were shy in class.

LIMITATIONS OF STUDY

A major limitation of the above e-learning study was that proper experimental design was not carried out because of the time and student number constraints. Otherwise a more formal structured research design with random assignment would have been developed in an attempt to establish covariation, temporal precedence and eliminate alternative explanation results (Cook & Campbell, 1970).

Another limitation is on instructional design. In the ad hoc study the author was designing from a behaviorist/cognitivist stance; he analyzed the situation associated with a syllabus topic and set the learning outcome to be achieved. Individual tasks were broken down and learning objectives were developed. Evaluation consisted of determining whether the criteria for the objectives had been met. In this approach the author decides what is important for the students to know and attempts to transfer that knowledge to the students. The learning package is somewhat of a closed system, since although it may allow for some branching and remediation, the students are still confined to the author's selected design. To help in developing better problem solving skills in real life situations, it is imperative that a product that is much more facilitative in nature than prescriptive should be designed, that is, adoption of a constructivist approach. In other words, the content should not be

Table 1: Results of survey questionnaire

	Points given (maximum 5 points)
WebCT easy to use	4
Lecture notes and assignments easy to download	4.38
Facilitate course material discussion with other students	4
Facilitate coursework discussion with lecturer	4.1
Allows team and shared work	4.3
Possibility of substituting some lecture sessions	3.9
Achievement of educational objectives	3.36
Sense of community with classmates	4
Communicated with team members more	4.2
Found communication with other students to be easier	4.3

pre-specified; direction is to be determined by the student and assessment would be much more subjective because it does not depend on specific quantitative criteria, but rather on the process and self-evaluation of the learner. The standard written tests of mastery learning will be replaced by presentations, discussion notes, seminar reports, and so forth.

The third limitation is that the evaluation of impact on student learning was conducted through test scores and end-of-project survey. The use of performance on end-of-semester examination as an indicator of learning is problematic for several reasons (Oliver, 2000). In the case shown it was assumed that what had been learnt could be performed; that there is a direct correlation between learning and assessment. This is evidently not the case. As suggested by Vygotsky (1962), children may be able to demonstrate more of their learning when working with a more able child than working alone; the same effects have been demonstrated for students in higher education in a number of contexts (see, e.g., Crook, 1991). This suggests that the use of a direct relationship between assessment and learning is inappropriate. In addition, it is important to recognise that there is much at stake in formal assessment. In order to do well, students will present the best image of themselves as measured by the assessment scheme; they will not present an unbiased, comprehensive illustration of their strengths and weaknesses, because it is not in their best interests to do so. Instead, they will emphasize their strengths and avoid showing weaknesses wherever possible. Moreover, students may find themselves unable to demonstrate that they have learnt something under particular assessment conditions – they may not understand the instructions, feel too pressured, or simply have a 'bad day'. Equally, markers may read more into students' responses than is actually there, and marks will be awarded for correct guesses just as they would for the successful demonstration of learning. Thus assessment is neither comprehensive, unbiased, fair in terms of opportunity or even easy to interpret as an indicating tool for learning (Oliver & Harvey, 2002).

With regard to the attitude survey, one must recognize that attitudes expressed are likely to be inconsistent and context dependent, as some social psychologists have demonstrated (Potter & Wetherell, 1987; Jones et al., 2000). It was suggested that expressed attitudes are not things that people possess, they are things that people do. Thus the expression of a particular attitude cannot be interpreted as a simple reflection of some inner state, but must instead be understood as a method by which the students present a particular image of themselves. Such expressed opinions are intimately tied up with the participant's sense of identity.

SUGGESTIONS FOR FUTURE WORK

The results of the ad hoc study should be taken with caution. The performance differences are too small to conclude that e-learning is better than traditional face-to-face teaching in higher education. More work would need to be done and research in the following two areas are suggested:

- *Development of E-Learning Theory:* It was found that the vast bulk of literature in e-learning is practice-based and is typically presented in a descriptive format. The majority of relevant publications consist of a 'here's what we did and here's the evaluation' format which does little for transferability to other institutions or even other courses (Nichols, 2003). In addition, the body of literature appears fragmented and there are few common terms used consistently. It is unlikely that e-learning practice will continue to evolve unless the theoretical underpinnings of e-learning are explored and debated. There are few examples of academic literature specifically concerned with e-learning theory and unfortunately the use of technology in education has tended to be technology-led rather than theory-led (Ravenscroft, 2001). It is well stated by Watson (2001) that "the cart has been placed before the horse".
- *Effects of Computer-Mediated Interactions on Student Learning:* Research in text-based, computer-mediated collaborative learning has shown that collaborative technologies can enhance learning performance and increase the affective experience in the context of group learning over more traditional face-to-face groups by eliminating common time and space constraints that are found in traditional classroom settings (Brandon & Hollingshead, 1999). Text-based computer-mediated instruction can also reduce evaluation anxiety of the participants by allowing for more anonymous communication if the identity of the communicators is hidden. This often produces more creative and open discussions. On the other hand, computer-mediated interactions have been found to reduce the richness of communication that is observed in face-to-face instruction, which lessens the quality of information exchanged. This reduction in the communication contents sometimes has a negative effect on learning.
- *Impact of Culture on Academic Learning:* It was found that the general culture outside the classroom frequently affects academic learning significantly. Watkins and Biggs, in their work on the Chinese learner (1996) and the Chinese teacher (2001) describe in detail these cultural impacts and how Chinese teachers are able to work with these cultural characteristics to design a learning environment within which students can achieve deep levels of understanding. A full understanding of the cultural factors will facilitate the implementation of e-learning in the higher education sector.

CONCLUSION

The rise of e-commerce as an education media raises interesting questions about the future viability of traditional classroom lectures. The occurrence of SARS in Hong Kong offers a unique opportunity for the author to conduct e-learning for the first year engineering students of the PolyU. The effectiveness of the e-learning approach was evaluated through direct experimentation and surveys with students taking the subject. Although the findings agreed with the widely accepted view that the media used to present lectures makes no difference in educational outcomes, students on the whole showed a positive attitude towards e-learning. In view of the limitations of the study, more research would need to be carried out to confirm the future role of e-learning in higher education. It is suggested that further work should be done on the development of e-learning theories and evaluation of the effects of computer-mediated interactions on learning.

REFERENCES

The Asian Campus Computing Survey Project. (2002). Available online: http://www.accsonline.net/research/hku/hku.htm. Retrieved August 31, 2003.

Brandon, D. P., & Hollingshead, A. B. (1999). Collaborative learning and computer-supported groups. *Communication Education, 48,* 109-126.

Coppola, N., Hiltz, S., & Rotter, N. (2002). Becoming a virtual professor: Pedagogical roles and asynchronous learning networks. *Journal of Management Information Systems*, *18*(4), 169-189.

Crook, C. (1991). The zone of proximal development: Implications for evaluation. *Computers and Education*, *17*(1), 81-91.

Fredrickson, S. (1999). Untangling a tangled web: An overview of web-based instruction programs. *T.H.E. Journal, 26*(11), 67-77.

Govindasamy, T. (2002). Successful implementation of e-learning pedagogical considerations. *Internet and Higher Education, 4,* 287-299.

Green, K.C. (2000). *Technology and instruction: Compelling, competing, and complementary visions for the instructional role of technology in higher education.* Available online: http://www.campuscomputing.net. Retrieved December 18, 2000.

Karayan, S.S., & Crowe, J.A. (1997). Student perspectives of electronic discussion groups. *T.H.E. Journal, 24,* 69-71.

MacDonald, C.J., Stodel, E.J., Farres, L.G., Breithaupt, K., & Gabriel, M.A. (2001). The demand-driven learning model: A framework for web-based learning. *Internet and Higher Education, 4,* 9-30.

Nada, H. (2000). The challenges of interfacing between face-to-face and online instruction. *Technical Trends, 44*(6), 37-42.

Nichols, M. (2003). A theory for elearning. *Educational Technology & Society, 6*(2), 1-10.

Oliver, M. (2000). An introduction to the evaluation of learning technology. *Educational Technology & Society*, *3*(4), 20-30.

Oliver, M., & Harvey, J. (2002). What does "impact" mean in the evaluation of learning technology? *Educational Technology & Society*, *5*(3), 18-26.

Palloff, R.M., & Pratt, K. (2001). *Lessons from the cyberspace classroom: The realities of online teaching.* San Francisco, CA: Jossey-Bass.

Parker, M. (2003). E-learning is a social tool for e-commerce at tertiary institutions. In S. Lubbe (Ed.), *The economic and social impact of e-commerce* (pp. 154-183). Hershey, PA: Idea Group Publishing.

Ravenscroft, A. (2001). Designing e-learning interactions in the 21st Century: Revisiting and rethinking the role of theory. *European Journal of Education*, *36*(2), 133-156.

Reber, T.C. (1996). Giving voice to the silent ones: Electronic discussion in a college literature course. *Journal of Staff, Program, and Organizational Development, 13,* 147-153.

Smith, D., & Hardaker, G. (2000). E-learning innovation through the implementation of an Internet supported learning environment. *Educational Technology and Society, 3,* 1-16.

Straits Knowledge. *E-learning adoption factors in Asia Pacific.* Available online: www.straitknowledge.com. Retrieved November 8, 2003.

TNS Interactive. (2002). *Global eCommerce Report - June*. Available online: http://www.tnsofres.com/ger2002/keycountry/hongkong.cfm. Retrieved November 8, 2003.

Vygotsky, L.S. (1962). *Thought and language*. Cambridge, MA: MIT Press.

Watkins, D.A., & Biggs, J.B. (eds.). (1996). *The Chinese learner: Cultural, psychological and contextual influences.* Hong Kong: Comparative Education Research Centre: Australian Council for Educational Research.

Watkins, D.A., & Biggs, J.B. (eds.). (2001). *Teaching the Chinese learner: Psychological and pedagogical perspectives.* Hong Kong: Comparative Education Research Centre.

Watson, D. (2001). Pedagogy before technology: Re-thinking the relationship between ICT and teaching. *Education and Information Technologies*, *6*(4), 251-266.

Zhu, E., & Kaplan, M. (2002). Technology and teaching. In W.J. McKeachie (Ed.), *McKeachie's teaching tips: Strategies, research, and theory for college and university teachers* (pp. 204-224). Boston, MA: Houghton Mifflin.

APPENDIX I

Recommended Textbooks

1. Mitcham, C. (2000). *Engineering ethics*. Prentice-Hall.
2. Johnston, S.F., Gostelow, J.P., & King, W.J. (2000). *Engineering & society*. Prentice-Hall.

Recommended References

1. Asia Engineer - The Journal of the Hong Kong Institution of Engineers.
2. Professional Engineering - The Magazine for the Engineering Profession (IMechE).
3. IEE Review.
4. IEEE Journals and Periodicals.

Recommended Websites

1. Training of Engineers (Local & Foreign Professional Institutions). Online: *www.hkengineer.org.hk/program/home/index.php.*
2. HKSAR Policy on local industries. Online: http://www.policyaddress.gov.hk/pa03/eng/index.htm.
3. Development of China Markets. Online: http://english.peopledaily.com.cn/200301/08/eng20030108_109771.shtml.
4. Education System in HK. Online: www.emb.gov.hk/eng.
5. Guide to British Education System. Onine: http://news.bbc.co.uk/1/hi/education/default.stm.
6. Guide to American Education System. Online: http://www.collegeview.com/college/niche/international/.

APPENDIX II

Written Assignment 1

Select one of the following professional organisations and compare the education, training and experience requirements for corporate membership with the relevant discipline(s) of the HK Institution of Engineers:

The British Computer Society, UK (BCS)
The Chartered Institution of Building Services Engineers, UK (CIBSE)
The American Society of Mechanical Engineers (ASME)
The Chinese Mechanical Engineering Society
The Chinese Society of Electrical Engineering
The Institution of Mechanical Engineers, UK (IMechE-UK)
The Institution of Professional Engineers of New Zealand (IPENZ)
The Institution of Engineers, Australia (IEAust)
The Institution of Engineers of Ireland (IEI)
The Institute of Electrical and Electronic Engineers, Inc. (IEEE-USA)
The Institution of Electrical Engineers, UK (IEE-UK)

[Note - Power Point presentation files are required; Each group has to submit a hard copy of the PPT slides indicating the contribution of each student, e.g. slide 1 to 5 is the work of Student A, slides 6 to 10 were carried out by Student B, etc.]

Written Assignment 2

China's market liberalisation following its accession to the World Trade Organization (WTO) will be a defining moment in the structural transformation of the Hong Kong economy. No longer will the mainland be used primarily as a production base to export to the world; the mainland itself will become a major market for Hong Kong manufacturers. Hong Kong's services companies will also find ample business opportunities in the mainland, following the wide range of market liberalisation measures to be implemented after accession.

As the project engineer in a consumer (or capital) goods manufacturing company with the Headquarters based in Hong Kong, outline and explain the factors that your project team have to consider for a joint venture in a selected province (or city) in China. Please include references (e.g. web-sites) on your work.

[Note: This assignment is to be submitted two weeks after Assignment 1. Maximum number of words allowed – 1600 (excluding references and figures). Contribution of each team member should be clearly indicated on the submission].

APPENDIX III

The Hong Kong Polytechnic University (Faculty of Engineering)

Programmes: Beng (Hons)/MEng in Electrical Engineering
Beng (Hons)/MEng in Electronic & Information Engineering
Beng (Hons)/MEng in Mechanical Engineering
Beng (Hons) in Mechanical Engineering
Beng (Hons)/MEng in Industrial & Systems Engineering
Programme Codes: 41070, 41078, 42070, 43078, 43088, 43091, 45085
Subject Title: Society and the Engineer
Subject Code: ENG226
Session: Semester 2, 2002/2003
Date: 09 May 2003
Time: 18:30-21:30
Time Allowed: 3 hours

Subject Examiner(s): Dr. T.T. Wong (ME)
Dr. H.W. Ngan (EE)
Prof. D. Sutanto (EE)
Dr. Y.M. Lai (EIE)
Dr. Andy Leung (EIE)

Dr. K.C. Lo (EIE)
Dr. W.K. Chan (ISE)

This question paper has a total of _____4____ pages (attachments included).

Instructions to Candidates:

This is an Open Book Examination. Candidates are permitted to bring in hard-print references. Dictionaries or electronic dictionaries, but **not** portable personal computer (PC), may be consulted.

This question paper contains **EIGHT** questions in **FOUR** sections. Attempt **THREE** questions with **not more than one** from each section. All questions carry equal marks.

DO NOT TURN OVER THE PAGE UNTIL YOU ARE TOLD TO DO SO.

Page 1
Section A
Question 1

(a) Intellectual property: what it means to you. Briefly describe the four basic forms of intellectual property. (15 marks)

(b) Comment on the likely impacts of a wider public awareness of the concept of intellectual property on education, business, technology development, life style and other societal activities. (18 marks)

Question 2

(a) Explain why it is important for engineers to study engineering ethics. (10 marks)

(b) Explain what it means by whistle-blowing. What is the difference between internal and external whistle-blowing? Under what conditions should whistle-blowing be attempted? (10 marks)

(c) In the following case, identify the moral obligations that cause the moral dilemma for John. Suggest possible courses of action and recommend what John should do. Explain your answer.

John works as an engineer at a local manufacturer of electric kettles. During a routine check, John accidentally discovers that one of their best-selling models is fitted with a faulty fuse, which means that the kettles may easily cause a fire in case of short-circuit. John immediately reports this to his manager, but his manager says that recalling all the kettles that have been sold will badly damage the public image of the company and cost an enormous amount of money. John is ordered to remain silent over the issue and is offered a salary increase in return. (13 marks)

Section B
Question 3

The accession of China to the World Trade Organization (WTO) in 2001 has generated great business opportunities for Hong Kong Special Administrative Region (HKSAR). It is recognized that the future of HKSAR lies in closer ties and economic integration with mainland China. Many Hong Kong enterprises are gearing themselves for ventures into China. This does not only mean that more external trade activities will be established, but also more technology transfer activities will be anticipated.

Suppose that you are one of the staff members of ABC Company that seeks to establish a major presence in China. Your company is now formulating strategies targeted at the adoption of an "anytime/anywhere" software system to its China's operations that link with the Hong Kong Headquarters and distribution centers in European Union. You are asked by the Managing Director to identify, with explanations, EIGHT major factors in this multi-phased technology adoption process. Write a report in this regard and quote any facts that can support your views. (33 marks)

Question 4

Technology is the combination of knowledge, skill and resources. It sustains economic development and the private corporation as well. For example, genuine technology exchange among the world's leading electronic theatres of endeavour is essential to bring the people in different countries together and that also benefits everyone. However, technological advance can bring significant dangers to mankind.

(a) Select a particular current or future technological project and then describe its benefits and dangers. (12 marks)

(b) How would you suggest the project, quoted in 4(a), be promoted and controlled towards desirable ends? (13 marks)

(c) From your comments on this particular project, say how you extend your views about the responsibilities of professional engineers to be involved in the technological developments in general. (8 marks)

Section C

Question 5

(a) The safety culture of an organisation is a product of individual and group values, attitudes, competencies and patterns of behaviour that determine commitment to an organisation's health and safety programmes. Although immediate causes of accidents are often identified as human error or technical failure, they relate to wider considerations of the organisation as a whole. Also, by and large, professional engineers are particularly held responsible for the safety, health and welfare of the public in the performance of their professional duties.

By considering the following hints, or otherwise, explain your views on the above statements:

i) Clarify safety culture, individual and group values, health and safety programmes as mentioned in the statements;
ii) Quote an engineering accident as example, discuss its immediate causes and effects, and how it relates to the wider consideration of the organization;
iii) Justify why professional engineers are held particularly responsible for the safety and health issues; and
iv) Suggest engineering contribution for improving health and safety in your quoted example. (16 marks)

(b) Insofar as environmental issues have a clear relation to human safety and health, the engineering profession has committed itself to concern for environmental protection and improvement. However, there are environmental impacts which are non-human by nature.
Give an example of the environmental impact which is non-human by nature. State its causes, effects and discuss whether it should be regarded as an engineering concern. (9 marks)

(c) Contemporary technological advances have made massive changes in the environment and that avoidance of its deterioration of the environment can only be achieved if human apply limits to the growth of our society.
Explain the possible effects of the above massive environmental changes. Discuss if contrary to the above statement can be made by making economical growth sustainable with continuing technological advances. (8 marks)

Question 6

(a) Take one of the environmental problems in Hong Kong that we have discussed in the class and describe at least four different engineering technologies that can be used to resolve the problems. Describe how the technologies can be introduced in Hong Kong. (14 marks)

(b) What are usually the factors involved in industrial disasters? For a particular incident that you have studied, identify the hazardous conditions that may have caused the incident. Describe briefly the ethical issues associated with the incident. What system safety methodology should be used to ensure that such incident will not be repeated. (19 marks)

Section D

Question 7

In the first Policy Address of his second term as Chief Executive of the Hong Kong Special Administrative Region, Mr. Tung Chee Hwa, has highlighted the following measures to revitalise the economy:

- Promoting economic restructuring
- Forging closer economic co-operation with the Mainland
- Eliminating the fiscal deficit

(a) As a consequence, some industries have been identified as the main pillars of our economy, what are they? (4 marks)
(b) Suggest the steps which the HKSAR Government could take to enhance these core industries. (18 marks)

The Chief Executive, Mr. Tung, also said, "The knowledge and wisdom of Hong Kong people, their innovative entrepreneurial spirit and agility combine to form a sound foundation for the development of creative industries."

(c) Explain what is meant by creative industries. (8 marks)
(d) Outline the HKSAR Government's plan to encourage diversified development of local industries. (3 marks)

Question 8

(a) Engineering offers a rewarding and lucrative career—one in which you can use your mind to find creative solutions to the challenges facing our society. List and explain *eight* benefits for becoming a professional engineer. (16 marks)
(b) In order to become a Corporate Member of the Hong Kong Institution of Engineers (HKIE), one has to satisfy specific academic, training and experience requirements. In the case of a consulting engineer at his early 40s with responsibilities equivalent to those of the "Engineer" Grade in the Civil Service for approximately 18 years but with only a Higher Diploma in Engineering, do you think he stands a chance of becoming a Corporate Member of the HKIE? Explain. (7marks)
(c) During engineering training it is expected that trainees will make a personal commitment to get the most out of the training opportunities made available

to them by their company. Explain what do you think would be the responsibilities of a trainee during the training period. (10 marks)

--- End of Questions---

Chapter X

Building Competitive Advantage through E-CRM Analytics and Data Integration

Hamid R. Nemati, The University of North Carolina, USA

Christopher D. Barko, The University of North Carolina, USA

Ashfaaq Moosa, The University of North Carolina, USA

ABSTRACT

Electronic Customer Relationship Management (e-CRM) Analytics is the process of analyzing and reporting online customer/visitor behavior patterns with the objective of acquiring and retaining customers through stronger customer relationships. To better understand the role of data integration in achieving the goals of e-CRM, the authors conducted a study by means of a survey. The results of this study propose that although online, offline and external data integration have their complexities, the value added is significant. This survey of CRM professionals is composed of two parts. The first part investigated the nature of the data integrated and the data architecture deployed. The second part analyzed the technological and organizational value added with respect to the e-CRM initiative. The findings suggest that organizations who integrate data from various customer touch-points enjoy a competitive advantage through significantly higher benefits, user satisfaction and return on their investment (ROI) than those who do not. Additional insights are also presented exploring the role of data integration in e-CRM projects at both business to business (B2B) and business to consumer (B2C) firms. For organizations implementing e-CRM, this study reveals that data integration is worth their time, money and efforts in creating a competitive advantage.

INTRODUCTION

With the proliferation of the World Wide Web (web) and electronic commerce (e-commerce), there has been a dramatic change in market dynamics such that customers, both end users and businesses, can check prices and buy from suppliers around the globe, regardless of time and distance (Stephens, 1999). Due to this surge in purchasing power, companies must view their data in a more strategic light. In addition, there is a growing trend of organizations leveraging their data resources by developing and deploying data mining technologies to enhance their decision-making capabilities (Eckerson & Watson, 2001). To address this need, organizations are implementing Organizational Data Mining (ODM) technologies, which are defined as technologies that leverage data mining tools to enhance the decision-making process by transforming data into valuable and actionable knowledge to gain a competitive advantage (Nemati & Barko, 2001). ODM spans a wide array of technologies, including but not limited to e-business intelligence, data analysis, CRM, EIS, digital dashboards, information portals, etc.

As a result of these marketplace trends, organizations must begin implementing customer-centric metrics as opposed to solely adopting product-centric metrics (Cutler & Sterne, 2001). This scenario has triggered increased interest in the implementation and use of customer-oriented ODM technologies such as Customer Relationship Management (CRM) systems. CRM can be defined as the adoption, through the use of enabling technology, of customer-focused sales, marketing, and service processes (Forsyth, 2001). CRM is the process that manages the interaction between a company and its customers. The goal of CRM is to create a long-term, profitable relationship with all of an organization's customers. It is more than just a software package—it is a business process enabled by technology. CRM vendors label these packages as CRM systems because their main goal is to analyze customer behavior and identify actionable patterns. This information is then used to improve goods and services offered to customers while increasing profitability through better relationships. CRM software provides the functionality that enables a firm to make the customer the focal point of all organizational decisions. CRM technologies incorporate some of the best-in-class processes for features such as customer service, product configuration, field service, and customer analysis.

CRM has become a key process in the strengthening of customer loyalty and in helping businesses obtain greater profit from low-value customers. The manner in which companies interact with their customers has changed tremendously over the past few years. Customers no longer guarantee their loyal patronage, and this has resulted in organizations attempting to better understand them, predict their future needs, and decrease response times in fulfilling their demands. Customer retention is now widely viewed by organizations as a significant marketing strategy in creating a competitive advantage, and rightly so. Research suggests that as little as a 5% increase in retention can mean as much as a 95% boost in profit, and repeat customers generate over twice as much gross income as new customers (Winer, 2001). In addition, many business executives today have replaced their cost-effective and cost-competitive strategies with a customer retention strategy—it costs approximately five to ten times more to acquire new customers than to retain established customers (Pan & Lee, 2003).

Most companies are now realizing and understanding the value of collecting customer data but are faced with the challenges of using this knowledge to create intelligent pathways back to the customer. Most data mining technologies and techniques for recognizing patterns within data help businesses sift through the meaningless data and allow them to anticipate customers' requirements and expectations by unlocking the mysteries of customer behavior. These technologies also enable companies to maintain customer privacy and confidentiality while gaining the benefits of profiling, calculating the economic value of the CRM tool, and discovering the key factors that would make or break the CRM project. By integrating these data mining tools with CRM software, organizations are able to analyze very large databases to extract new customer insights. These findings can be used to increase revenue, reduce expenses and identify new business opportunities, offering new competitive advantages through stronger and more profitable customer relationships. Data mining by itself is not a business solution; it is just an enabling technology. However, by assimilating data mining technology with CRM, organizational data can be transformed into valuable knowledge to enhance business decisions that optimize customer interactions. Many organizations now believe one of the fundamental instruments for creating competitive advantage in this environment is to deploy Information Technology that supports and fosters one-to-one relationships with customers (Shoemaker, 2001). For example, consider a catalog retailer that wants to determine to whom they should send current information about new products. The information integrated into the data mining and CRM process is contained in a historical database containing prior customer transactions along with their demographic and lifestyle attributes. This information is collected each time there is any type of interaction with the customer, whether it be through sales, calls, or complaints (Teerlink, 1999). By assimilating these two technologies, this retailer is in a better position to optimize each customer interaction by predicting the characteristics of prospects and/or existing customers who would be most likely to make a purchase.

Similarly, e-CRM can be defined as the process of acquiring a thorough understanding of an organization's online visitors/customers in order to offer them the right product at the right price. E-CRM analytics is the process of analyzing and reporting online customer/visitor behavior patterns with the objective of acquiring and retaining customers through stronger customer relationships. Prior research has found that in order to understand online customers, a company must integrate its data from both online and offline sources (Mena, 2001). In similar fashion, our study also demonstrates that a company cannot thoroughly understand its customers if it neglects integrating its customers' behavioral data from both the online and offline channels. In order to have this complete customer viewpoint, it is imperative that organizations integrate data from each customer touch-point. Our paper elaborates on this critical issue of integrating data from multiple sources and its enabling role in facilitating successful and valuable e-CRM analytics.

In exploring these issues, we first conduct a literature review and provide a foundation for our research. Then we present our research framework and associated propositions. Next we detail the research methodology utilized in our study, and lastly we present and discuss our findings and their organizational implications.

RESEARCH FOUNDATIONS & FRAMEWORK

Several studies (Brancheau, Janz & Wetherbe, 1996; Neiderman, Brancheau & Wetherbe, 1991) show that data have been ranked as one of the top priorities for IS Executives. With the emergence of web technologies, the collection and storage of data, both internal and external to an organization, has increased dramatically. Internal data refers to data generated from systems within an organization, such as legacy and online transactional processing (OLTP) systems. External data refers to data that are not generated by systems within an organization, such as government census data, industry benchmark data, consumer psychographic data and economic data. For instance, consumer demographic and psychographic data are available for each of the 200+ million adults in the United States, and product-based data are available for the 18 million businesses in the United States. If this data is collected, integrated, and formatted properly, it can prove to be immensely beneficial to a firm in better understanding its customers (Rendlemen, 2001). External data should be leveraged in a CRM system to the extent that it adds additional value to the already existing internal organizational data.

Companies approach consumers through various marketing channels. Traditionally, each channel or functional area has been managed separately, and all data pertaining to a channel are housed in their own system in a proprietary format (Eckerson & Watson, 2001; SAS Institute, 2001). Technically, data integration can be defined as the standardization of data definitions and structures through the use of a common conceptual schema across a collection of data sources (Litwin, Mark & Roussopoulos, 1990). This implies that data is accessible across functional areas, making data in different corporate databases available and consistent. For example, if a traditional 'bricks and mortar' company deploys a web site and decides to integrate the web data with its legacy systems, it has to consider various technological and design issues such as data requirements, data quality, data inconsistencies, synchronization, security, and so forth. Once these issues are addressed, an organization must present the data in a way that is consistent and conducive to viewing across heterogeneous enterprise departments (Johnson, 2000). In a B2C company, an example of data integration might be creating an integrated customer database to enable the sales and manufacturing departments to access a single source of customer information even though they each require their own view of the customer.

The volume of data in an organization is estimated to double every 18 to 24 months (Experian Corporation, 2002). Issues arise when determining which piece of information about a particular customer is accurate, up-to-date and relevant. In deciding which parts of the data should be used for analysis, the issues of incompatible data formats, metadata inconsistencies and conflicting levels of data granularity must be resolved. This is a complex and continuous procedure that requires a significant amount of resources.

Even though data integration is such a complex task, organizations successfully tackling this issue have derived immense benefits from it. For example, Staples Inc. integrated all customer and sales data from their store, catalog and online efforts into a common database (SAS Institute, 2001). Integrating all this information allows Staples' marketers to monitor and predict how customers migrate from one channel to another or how they utilize the channels to get what they need. Staples can identify what products are purchased at a store versus their Staples Direct catalog or through their online store. This valuable information gives Staples an edge over its competition and allows marketers to (1) target specific products to customers through preferred channels, and (2) give them the ability to perform cross- and up-selling to customers across multiple channels.

A recent survey from Forrester Research (Baudisch, 2000) suggests that marketing professionals spend 44% of their web site promotion budgets on offline media. This finding raises a number of allocation questions. How do organizations determine (1) which marketing media to use, (2) where their customers spend most of their time, and (3) what their customers' lifestyles are? To better answer these questions, it is essential for online marketers to get a 360-degree (holistic) view of their customers (Experian Corporation, 2002). This holistic view requires organizations to integrate their data to track every customer transaction (customer purchases, returns and complaints) in all customer touch-points (email, phone, online, and direct mail).

A survey by Jupiter Media Metrix (Collins, 2001) revealed that 70% of online customers would not shop at the offline store if they received poor service at the web site. Further, the survey found that only 18% of the clicks 'n bricks retailers (those with both online and traditional operations) offered customers the convenience of integrating their online and offline accounts, as well as the ability to buy online and pick up or return merchandise at the company's local store. Since customer service via email is poor in the case of most retailers, customers want to voice their concerns offline (Collins, 2001).

In another study (Mena, 2001), online retailers spend an average of $100 to $250 to acquire a new customer. On average, this customer will spend about $24 with the retailer, and then more than likely never return as a patron. It was found that only 35% of buyers make a second purchase at a site they initially purchase from. These grim figures suggest that if you want to survive in today's competitive online marketplace and be profitable, you need to go beyond cookies and meta tags—you need to learn what your online customers are like offline (Mena, 2001).

Case studies have shown (Doll & Torkzadeh, 1988) that data integration is useful and cost justifiable under two circumstances: (1) when the interdependence between functional units increases, and (2) when the tasks and environment under which these sub-units operate is more or less fixed; that is, when there will not be short-term changes to the functional information systems to address changing needs. In today's dynamic economy and rampant increase in the number of customer attritions, organizations must be cognizant of customer preferences and demands to optimally manage their delicate yet vital relationship with them. This leads us to our first two propositions.

Proposition 1: The more data sources a company integrates, the better the customer insight, thus creating more value for the company.

Proposition 2: Integrating online data with data from the firms' offline operations will lead to better customer insight, thus creating more value for the company.

Timeliness of data is an important component of user satisfaction (Doll & Torkzadeh, 1988; Ballou, Wang, Pazer & Tayi, 1998; Adams & Song, 1989). Users need to have up-to-date information about customers' needs and preferences (Swift, 2002) to thoroughly understand and satisfy those needs. Traditional measures of customer-centric metrics such as recency, frequency and monetary statistics need to be incorporated into the analysis. Without integrated data (from online and offline sources), these statistics will not be accurate. Traditionally, it was acceptable for organizations to update their customer database on a monthly or quarterly basis. But in today's fast-paced electronic economy where critical decisions are made daily, companies strive for more current information, requiring systems to update their databases much more frequently (daily, hourly, or in real time). This leads us to our next proposition.

Proposition 3: Data that is more frequently refreshed will lead to better customer insight, thus creating more value for the company.

Past experiences or product quality are not the only reasons why customers make purchases. There are factors external to an organization such as new marketplace competitors, economic factors and competitor promotions that alter our buying preferences. In his book "Web Farming", Richard Hackathorn (1998) advocates that organizations must integrate external data into their data warehouse to gain a complete picture of their business.

Researchers have also concluded that without data about why a product was purchased, it is difficult to make accurate inferences about future customer needs. Organizations that have a myopic view of the customer risk experiencing an inference gap—they lack a multi-brand, external view of the customer that captures historical data about customer behavior and preferences across multiple organizations in an industry. Making incorrect inferences about a customer can lead to faulty marketing decisions and lost revenues. However, organizations that achieve an accurate multi-brand view of the customer by integrating external data will be more effective at inferring future needs and better able to service customers due to an enhanced customer understanding (Brohman, Watson, Piccoli & Parasuraman, 2003). Sources of external data include government databases, customer demographic and lifestyle data, credit history data, census data, zip codes, and weather data. This leads us to our next proposition.

Proposition 4: Integrating external data with internal data will lead to better customer insight, thus creating more value for the company.

In many instances, companies focus their limited resources on their core competencies and outsource all remaining business units, sometimes retaining the services of an application service provider (ASP) to manage and host their web site (Eckerson & Watson, 2001). Whether an organization's business processes are performed in-house or outsourced, the collaboration and integration of systems and data from multiple functional areas is complex and difficult. A recent Data Warehousing Institute Industry Report (Eckerson & Watson, 2001) found that organizations are challenged when integrating web technologies into their existing legacy and IT systems. Some of the reasons behind this challenge are scalability issues, managing large clickstream databases, immaturity of technology, lack of experience, and the complexity of modeling web data for analysis. But despite the integration challenges, the benefits to be realized are enormous.

In a recent survey of 800 Information Technology executives by the Meta Group, four out of five companies did not have a 360-degree view of their customers even though 92% of the firms surveyed ranked increasing customer knowledge as a top priority (Cooke, 2000). This study goes on to report that although business and Information Technology managers in these companies are interested in obtaining customer knowledge, a number of serious obstacles prevent them from doing so, that is, building the right data architecture and obtaining useful analytical tools to integrate and use this data effectively. To be truly effective, an e-CRM infrastructure must provide organizations with a single view of the customer, regardless of how they are interacting with the company (Pan & Lee, 2003). Similar research has also found that one of the fundamental requirements for a successful e-CRM solution is the consolidation of all customer-related information into a single view (Storey, Straub, Stewart & Welke, 2000).

For successful CRM analytics, an enterprise-wide, customer-centric data repository should be utilized rather than a channel specific data repository (Beck & Summer, 2001; Swift, 2002; Johnson, 2000). Vasset (2001) suggests that an enterprise-wide, customer-centric data warehouse should be the foundation of any CRM initiative. This leads us to our last proposition.

Proposition 5: Deploying an enterprise-wide data warehouse as the CRM backbone will lead to better customer insight, thus creating more value for the company.

Research in CRM is growing as it is gaining greater acceptance within organizations. However, findings from recent research suggest that organizations generally fail to support their CRM efforts with complete data (Brohman, Watson, Piccoli & Parasuraman, 2003). As a result, considerable attention from researchers in many diverse disciplines is currently focused on CRM. Although there is a growing pool of literature that addresses many aspects of the application of CRM for business solutions, there are few scholarly publications that focus on the study of CRM from an e-commerce perspective. Given the complexity of the issues involved in data integration, the enormous benefits that e-CRM can offer, and the role data integra-

Figure 1: e-CRM value framework

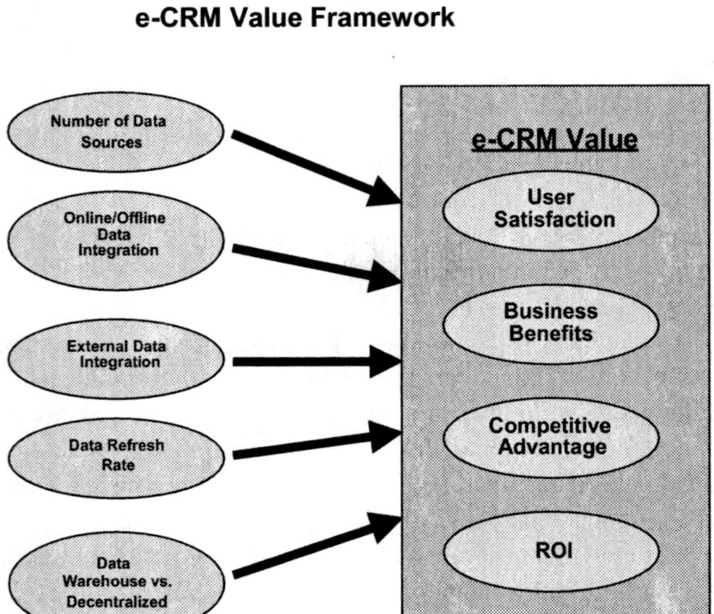

tion plays in achieving e-CRM's goals, we developed an e-CRM Value Framework (see Figure 1) to study data integration issues and their impact on the overall value attained from e-CRM projects. Through this framework, we empirically test our five propositions to determine the impact each factor has on creating e-CRM value for an organization. The results of our analysis reveal that four of the five factors support this new framework and have a significant influence on creating value and building a competitive advantage for an organization.

RESEARCH METHODOLOGY

Our study was comprised of two parts. The first part was a literature review where we looked at the results of previous studies on data integration and its inherent complexity. Based on this literature review, we designed a questionnaire to explore organizational data sources, how these data sources are integrated, the data architectures utilized for this integration, and the key integration issues facing organizations. The second part of the survey addressed e-CRM topics such as specific benefits realized, ROI expectations, user satisfaction levels, and the creation or absence of a new competitive advantage. Demographic information was also collected on respondents and their organizations.

An initial survey instrument containing 17 questions was reviewed by three industry professionals to ensure appropriate and unambiguous content. The objective of this survey was to gain an insight into the various data sources organizations integrate and to reveal that data collection and integration for e-CRM, despite its complexity, can create value for an organization. Respondents were asked to identify benefits they had achieved or expected to achieve from their e-CRM project. Specifically, we probed responders on specific data integration procedures in their organization such as number of data sources integrated, integration of online and offline sources, integration of external data, data refresh rates and whether these data sources were centralized (data warehouse) or decentralized.

Additional survey questions solicited information regarding ROI, user satisfaction levels, competitive advantages, and both the quantity and types of data sources integrated in respondents' e-CRM projects. These questions utilized a Likert scale to allow users to rate the success of their e-CRM initiative based on four equally weighted factors—ROI, competitive advantage, business benefits attained and user satisfaction.

Next we transformed the responses from the questions about ROI, user satisfaction, competitive advantage, and benefits realized into a derived measure representing Total Value to an organization. We defined Total Value as being a combination of ROI, competitive advantage, business benefits attained and user satisfaction. The equally weighted scores obtained from these questions were added together and used as a measure of overall value generated by the e-CRM initiative. This Total Value figure was calculated as follows: Total Value = total benefits + user satisfaction +

competitive advantage + ROI. The total benefits figure was calculated by summing the total number of benefits reported. This value ranged from 0 to 12. Some of the benefits reported were the increased ability to cross-sell/upsell to customers, enhanced product/service customization, increased customer retention, and better customer service and inventory management. User satisfaction of the new e-CRM system ranged from 1 (not satisfied) to 7 (very satisfied). Measuring competitive advantage was calculated as the likelihood (1 = very low, 7 = almost certain) that the e-CRM project enabled the company to achieve a sustainable competitive advantage. And measuring ROI was calculated as the likelihood (1 = very low, 7 = almost certain) that the e-CRM initiative generated the expected ROI.

In measuring each organization's Total Value, we argue that a larger number represents more total value to the organization than a smaller number. For example, an organization with an e-CRM system that delivered eight benefits (8), created very satisfied users (7), enabled a competitive advantage (7), and delivered close to expected ROI (6) (for a Total Value = 28) would be much more valuable to an organization than a system which delivered three benefits (3), unhappy users (1), an unlikely competitive advantage (1), and unsatisfactory ROI (1) (for a Total Value = 6). Using this basis for Total Value, we conducted statistical analyses using ANOVA to determine the correlation between our framework's five e-CRM factors (propositions) and the Total Value the project created for the organization.

A web site was developed for the survey and hosted at the Department of Information Systems and Operations Management at The University of North Carolina at Greensboro. A request to complete the survey was distributed to about 340 entities in the Information Systems and Operations Management Department database of organizations. This database contains data about organizations, consultants, and professionals specializing in CRM technologies. A total of 115 useable responses were received and analyzed from both U.S. and international organizations, providing a 34% response rate.

RESULTS AND DISCUSSIONS

Demographics

Figure 2 reveals demographic information from the survey respondents. Respondents work in a wide variety of industries, with the majority (49%) from CRM/Technology firms and 25% from the transportation, healthcare, advertising and financial industries. Job categories for respondents range from executive management to business managers with the majority employed as CRM professionals (54%), followed by analysts (17%). Organizational revenues represent a fair mix of both small and large companies. Forty-four percent reported sales of less than $100 million while 37% reported sales of greater than $500 million. In regards to CRM project statuses, the majority of respondents (39%) had begun their CRM initiative over a year ago while 24% had started their CRM initiative less than

Figure 2: Respondent demographics (N = 115)

Industry	% Responders
Technology - Software/Services	49%
Financial	12%
Transportation	5%
HealthCare	4%
Advertising	4%
Utilities	3%
Publishing	2%
Other	21%

Position	% Responders
CRM Professional/Consultant	54%
Analyst	17%
C-level Executive	9%
DBA	7%
Business Manager	5%
Other	8%

Revenue	% Responders
<100 million	44%
101 - 500 million	19%
501 - 1 billion	11%
>1 billion	26%

Website Type	
B2B	45%
B2C	35%
C2C	1%
Other	19%

three months ago. The majority of respondents (65%) were also clicks 'n bricks (web and store) companies while 23% were purely web retailers. In addition, 45% of respondents worked for organizations whose primary web operations were B2B (business to business) while 35% worked for organizations classified as B2C (business to consumer).

B2B VS. B2C

Next we conducted a cross-tabular analysis to gain better insights into B2B and B2C organizations. As previously noted, 45% worked for B2B companies and 35% were from B2C companies. There was one C2C (consumer to consumer) firm, while the remainder comprised the "other" category, which we presume were information-based companies such as news agencies and magazines whose revenue is primarily supported through advertising.

The survey data were analyzed across nine categories (see Figure 3). The only category that showed a significant difference between the two types of firms was the data refresh rate. Forty-two percent of B2B companies refreshed their data at least once a day while 58% of B2C companies did the same. The other categories revealed very similar results when comparing the two types of firms.

Next we looked at the sources of data integrated by B2B and B2C firms (see Figure 4). Figure 4 reveals that, in general, B2B firms integrate more data than B2C firms. The top four sources of data collected were customer demographics, online sales, offline sales and customer communication data such as call center data, email data, and so forth.

Figure 3: B2B vs. B2C analysis (N = 115)

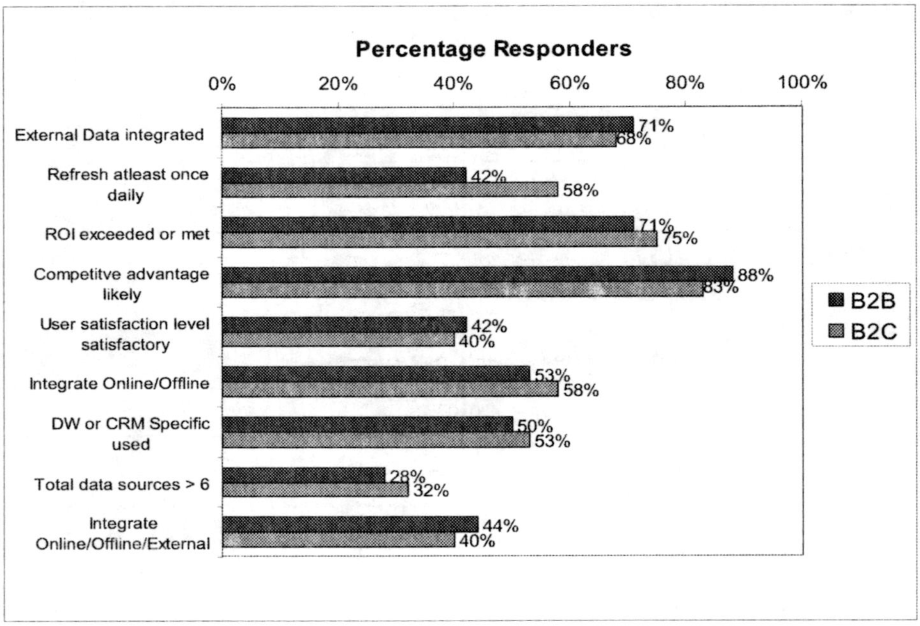

Next we compared the challenges and problems encountered between the firms (see Figure 5). What we observed was that the top three problems faced by B2C firms were lack of planning, change management and organizational politics. The top three problems B2B firms faced were change management, organizational politics and lack of user buy-in. It is interesting to note that all of the top three problems of both B2B and B2C firms are organizational problems, not technical. As far as technical problems, 24% of B2B firms versus 40% of B2C firms identified data quality as a problem. In addition, 29% of B2B firms lack user training while only 15% of B2C firms reported the same problem.

Figure 6 displays the benefits attained between the two types of firms. In general, more B2B firms benefit from their CRM implementations than B2C firms. One interesting findings is that 51% of B2B firms reported customer service benefits while only 45% of B2C firms reported the same benefits. Apparently B2B organizations are more effective at servicing their customers than B2C companies, which might be due to less complexity in servicing the relatively lower volumes of business customers in comparison to the much larger numbers of consumer customers. We previously reported that one of the biggest problems with B2C firms' CRM projects was lack of planning. This problem may be a key reason behind the overall lower benefits realized in B2C firms. Although Figure 5 shows that 35% of B2B firms reported users not buying into the project, Figure 6 implies that in general, B2B firms achieve more benefits from their CRM projects.

Figure 4: B2B vs. B2C Data Sources (N = 115)

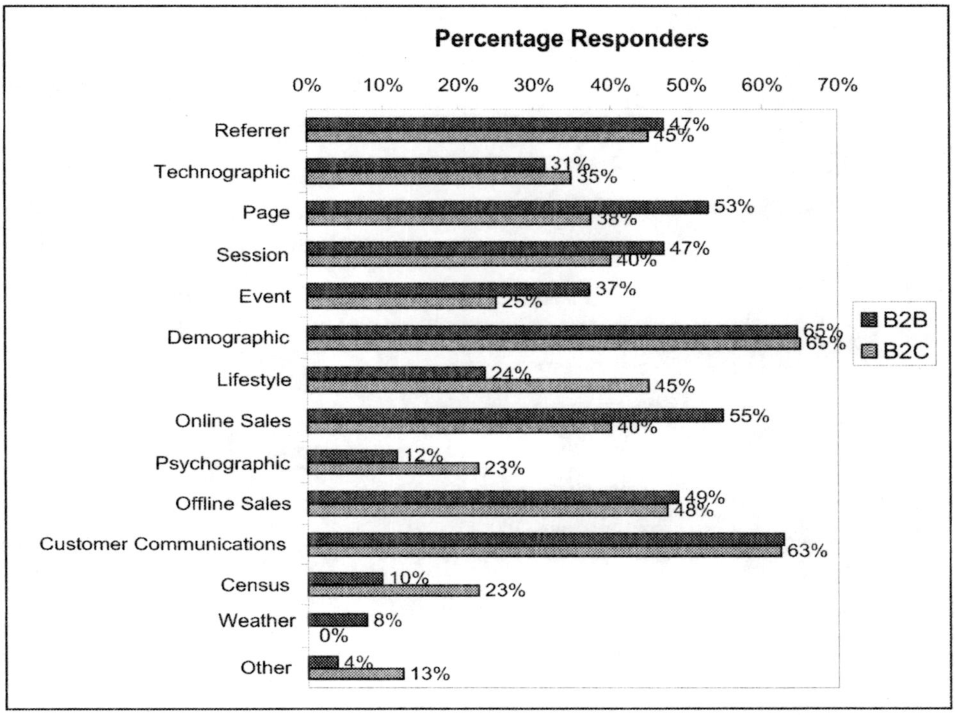

Figure 5: B2B vs. B2C Problems (N = 115)

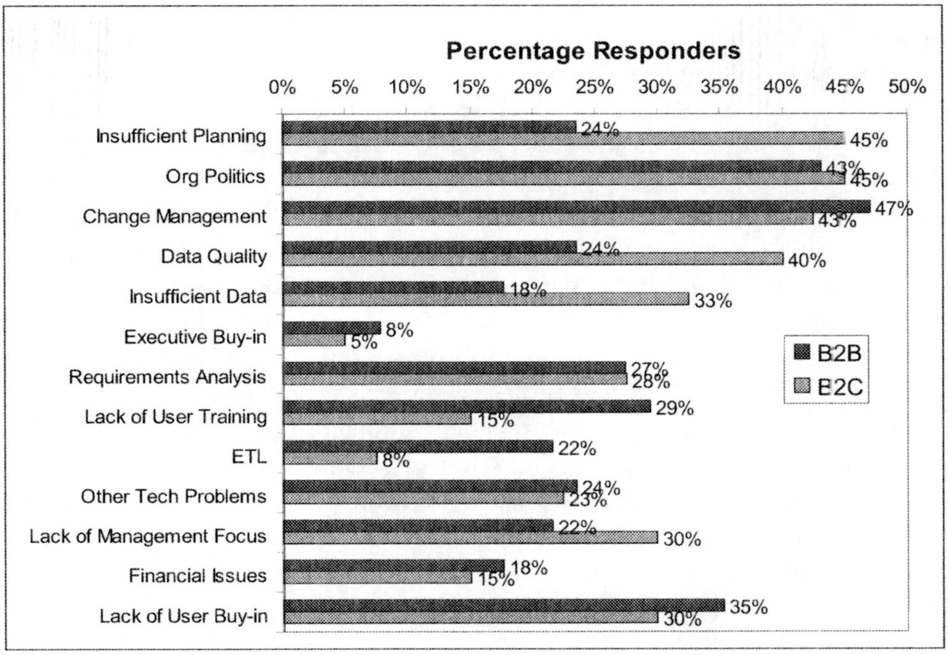

Figure 6: B2B vs. B2C benefits (N = 115)

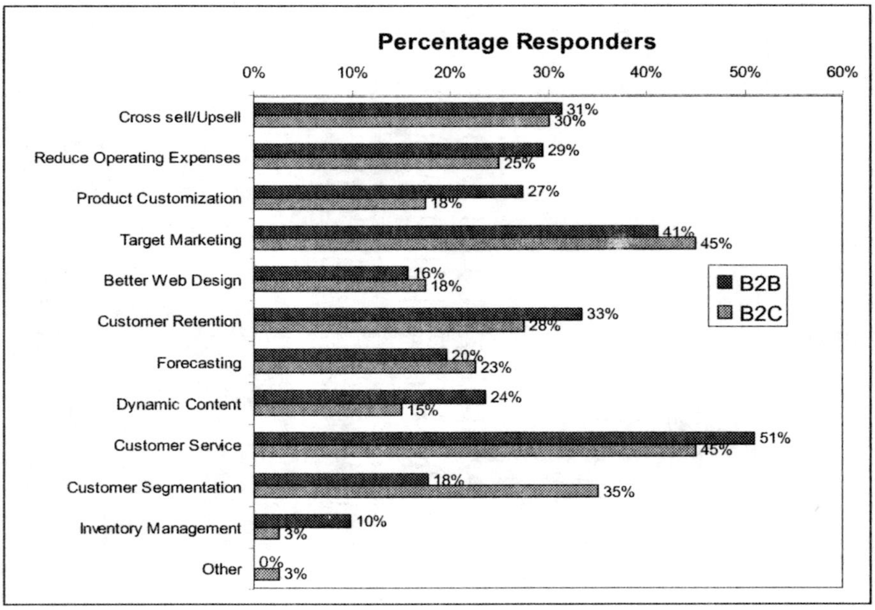

Proposition Testing

See Table 1 for ANOVA results and proposition findings. All propositions were found to be significant (p <= 0.05) in their relationship to Total Value except for proposition 3, which proposes more Total Value if data is refreshed daily. A more detailed explanation and analysis of each proposition follows.

For proposition 1, respondents were asked to specify the number of data sources they integrated into the data repository for the purposes of their e-CRM project. The total number of data sources integrated was calculated. Using ANOVA, we determined the relationship between the total number of data sources integrated and the Total Value was significant (p = 0.008). This finding suggests that Total Value increases as organizations integrate more data sources in their e-CRM projects.

An interesting insight was that only 22% of respondents integrated all four dimensions of clickstream data, as described by Ralph Kimball and Richard Merz (2000), namely session, page, event, and referrer. The session data type is a high-level diagnosis of the complete web session. Examples of segmenting web sessions by customer behavior include "Product Ordered", "Quick Hit and Gone", "Unhappy Visitor" or "Recent, Frequent and Intense Return Shopper" (Kimball, 2000). Referrer data identifies how the web site visitor arrived at the web site. A simple descriptive analysis of the percentages of different ways a visitor arrived at a web site provides valuable information about how to better allocate an organization's advertising budget. The page dimension stores data about the various attributes of each web

Table 1: ANOVA results (N = 115) — Correlation of Measure vs. Total Value

Measure	DF	Sum of Squares	Mean Square	F Ratio	Prob > F	Significant (p <= 0.05)
(1) Number of Sources	13	924.13	71.09	2.376	0.008	Yes
(2) Integrate Data	1	189.90	189.90	5.713	0.019	Yes
(3) Daily Refresh	1	35.03	35.03	1.012	0.317	No
(4) External Data	1	132.26	132.26	3.919	0.050	Yes
(5) DW or CRM database	1	219.10	219.10	6.643	0.011	Yes

page visited. For example, some attributes would be the page name (Product X Description, Payment Page, etc.), when it was visited, how long the user stayed on that page and where the user went from that page.

For proposition 2, respondents were asked whether or not they integrated offline data with their online data. Sixty-two percent said they integrated these data sources while thirty percent did not. The remaining 8% were unsure. Using ANOVA, we determined the relationship between those who integrated offline and online data and Total Value was significant (p = 0.019). Therefore, we propose that organizations that integrate both online and offline data in their e-CRM projects have significantly more benefits than organizations that do not integrate their data.

For proposition 3, respondents were asked how often they updated/refreshed the data in their data repositories. We segmented all responses into two groups—those who refreshed their data at least once a day and those who did not. Using ANOVA, we determined the relationship between frequently refreshed data (at least daily) and Total Value was not significant (p = 0.317). Therefore, we propose that organizations that refresh their data at least once a day do not have a significantly higher value than organizations that refresh their data less frequently. This proposition was rejected.

For proposition 4, respondents were asked whether or not they integrated external data into their data warehouse. Seventy-four percent integrated external data in some form while twenty-six percent did not. Of those who did integrate, sixty-two percent said that external data comprised less than 20% of the total data used for analysis. Using ANOVA, we determined the relationship between integrating external data and Total Value was significant (p = 0.050). Therefore, we propose that organizations that integrate external data in their e-CRM projects enjoy significantly more benefits than organizations that do not integrate external data.

For proposition 5, respondents were asked to identify the data repository used for their e-CRM systems. Fifty-one percent of companies implemented legacy databases, operational data stores (ODS) or data marts as their data repositories, while forty-nine percent implemented CRM specific databases or data warehouses as their data repositories. Using ANOVA, we determined the relationship between the Total Values derived by these two segments was significant ($p = 0.011$). We discovered the total value derived by the group using a data repository other than a data warehouse or a CRM specific database was significantly lower than the group who used a data warehouse or CRM specific database. Therefore, we propose that organizations that implement a data warehouse or CRM specific database as their e-CRM data repository enjoy significantly more benefits than organizations that do not implement these types of data repositories.

In summary, the above propositions show that data integration is essential in accurately assessing customer needs and thus allowing the firm to achieve greater CRM and organizational value. Therefore, we propose that our e-CRM Value Framework (minus proposition 3—daily data refresh) is a model for generating greater total benefits and a competitive advantage for organizations engaging in e-CRM projects. To achieve the greatest amount of benefits, we suggest organizations use a data warehouse as their e-CRM data repository. This data warehouse should contain a healthy number of data sources and house all integrated data including online, offline and external data. With this architecture in place, companies are able to achieve greater profitability by obtaining a better understanding of their customers and their relationships with them.

CONCLUSION

We have presented a new e-CRM Value Framework to better examine the significance of integrating data from all customer touch-points with the goal of improving customer relationships and creating additional value for the firm, ultimately leading to a competitive advantage. Various issues such as number of data sources, integrating offline, online and external data, and data architectures are discussed. We also compared and contrasted the CRM efforts of B2B versus B2C organizations and revealed some of the challenges and opportunities each faces. Our findings suggest that despite the cost and complexity, data integration for e-CRM projects contributes to a better understanding of the customer and leads to higher ROI, greater number of benefits, improved user satisfaction and a higher chance of attaining a competitive advantage. Thus, when all else is equal, a company's Total Value increases when a company integrates data from online, offline and external sources.

We hope that our empirical research and findings can assist practitioners and managers in identifying more efficient and effective ways of creating CRM value through data integration. It should be noted that we have only discussed the data-related issues of integration. Future research on this topic should investigate and identify managerial, financial, environmental, and strategic issues that affect organizational value. In addition, other technical issues to explore include the impact of data quality and the integration role of Web Services.

REFERENCES

Adams, C. R., & Song, J.H. (1989). Integrating decision technologies. *MIS Quarterly,* (June), 199-209.

Ballou, D., Wang, R., Pazer, H., & Tayi, G. K. (1998, April). Modeling information manufacturing systems to determine information product quality. *Management Science, 44*(4), 462-484.

Baudisch, P. (2000). Getting to e-yes: Building customer relationships online. Available online: www.entreworld.org.

Beck, B., & Summer, J. (2001). Data warehousing horizons: CRM: Not just operational and collaborative. *DMReview,* (September).

Brancheau, J.C., Janz, B.D., & Wetherbe, J.C. (1996). Key issues in information systems management: 1994-95 SIM Delphi results. *MIS Quarterly, 20*(2), 225-242.

Brohman, M. K., Watson, R. T., Piccoli, G., & Parasuraman, A. (2003, June). Data completeness: A key to effective net-based customer service systems. *Communications of the ACM, 46*(6), 47-51.

Collins, A. (2001). Customer service counts. *Business 2.0,* March 21.

Cooke, B. (2000). Companies in the dark about customers. Information Week, May 1.

Cutler, M., & Sterne, J. (2001). *E-metrics: Business metrics for the new economy.* NetGenesis Corp. Available online: www.netgent.com/emetrics.

Eckerson, W., & Watson, H. (2001). Harnessing customer information for strategic advantage: Technical challenges and business solutions. *Industry Study 2000,* Executive Summary, The Data Warehousing Institute.

Experian Corporation. (2002). CRM Whitepaper. Available online: www.uk.experian.com/assets/crm_whitepaper1.pdf.

Doll, W. J., & Torkzadeh, G. (1988). The measurement of end-user computing satisfaction. *MIS Quarterly,* (June), 259-274.

Forsyth, R. (2001). *Successful CRM: Global trends*, (June 22). Available online: http://www.crm-forum.com/library/conf/con-031.

Hackathorn, R. (1998). *Web farming for the data warehouse.* San Francisco: Morgan Kaufmann Publishers.

Johnson, B. (2000). *Fault lines in CRM: New e-commerce business models and channel integration challenges: Vol. 1.* CRM Project, (January 1).

Kimball, R. (2000). The special dimensions of the clickstream. *Intelligent Enterprise, 3*(2), January 20.

Kimball, R., & Merz, R. (2000). *The data webhouse toolkit: Building the web-enabled data warehouse.* NJ: John Wiley & Sons.

Litwin, W., Mark, L., & Roussopoulos, N. (1990, September). Interoperability of multiple autonomous databases. *ACM Computing Surveys, 22*(3), 267-293.

Mena, J. (2001). Beyond the shopping cart. *Intelligent Enterprise,* March 8.

Neiderman, F., Brancheau, J.C., & Wetherbe, J.C. (1991). Information systems management issues for the 1990's. *MIS Quarterly, 15,* 474-500.

Nemati, H. R., & Barko, C. D. (2001, Winter). Issues in organizational data mining: A survey of current practices. *Journal of Data Warehousing, 6*(1), 25-36.

Pan, S. L., & Lee, J.-N. (2003, April). Using E-CRM for a unified view of the customer. *Communications of the ACM, 46*(4), 95-99.

SAS Institute. (2001). Staples: Loyal customers and killer marketing. *SAS COM Magazine,* September/October. Available online: www.sas.com.

Shoemaker, M.E. (2001). A framework for examining IT-enabled market relationships. *J. Personal Selling & Sales Management, 21*(2), 177-186.

Stephens, D. (1999, July). The globalization of Information Technology in multinational corporations. *Information Management Journal, 33*(3), 66.

Storey, V.C., Straub, D.W., Stewart, K.A., & Welke, R.J. (2000, July). A conceptual investigation of the e-commerce industry. *Communications of the ACM, 43*(7).

Swift, R. (2002). Analytical CRM powers profitable relationships: Creating success by letting customers guide you. *DMReview*, (February).

Teerlink, M. (1999). *Beyond consumerism: Know your customers' needs, before they do!,* July 26, available oniline: http://www.crm-forum.com/library/art/art-022/brandframe.html.

Vasset, D. (2001). *Using the data warehouse to drive your CRM effort.* February 23, available online: www.CIO.com.

Winer, R.S. (2001). A framework for Customer Relationship Management. *California Management Review, 43*(4), 89-106.

Previously published in the Journal of Electronic Commerce in Organizations, 1(3), 73-89, July/Sept, 2003.

Chapter XI

E-Government Scottish Style: Recent Developments and Some Emerging Issues

Feng Li, University of Newcastle upon Tyne, UK

ABSTRACT

This chapter discusses issues involved in the development of e-government, using recent empirical evidence gathered in Scotland. The research suggests that public sector organisations in Scotland recognise the importance of e-government, but there is a gap between the rhetoric about the potential of e-government and the reality on the ground. In particular, most public sector organisations appear to be more sceptical about the ability of information and communications technologies (ICTs) to break down barriers within and between organisations than those who advocate e-government as a solution to this problem. The current development and some emerging issues will be explored in the Scottish context, and some generic lessons will be highlighted. Finally, a number of themes for future research will be highlighted.

INTRODUCTION

The current UK Government has set out an ambitious agenda for modernising public services. The '*Modernising Government*' strategy can be seen as a continuation of efforts to reform government that have been ongoing since the 1970s, but the development of 'information age government' and the delivery of integrated services across organisational boundaries are now at the heart of the strategy for modernising public services (Cabinet Office, 1999; UK Online, 2002). In particular, as part of a much wider effort to make UK 'the best place for E-Commerce in the world', the UK government has undertaken to make all government services available electronically by 2005 with key services achieving high levels of use.

The result so far has been moderately encouraging despite a range of emerging issues. The Booz Allen Hamilton (2002) report commissioned by the British Government's Office of the E-Envoy and the Department of Trade and Industry concluded that the UK now has the second best environment for e-commerce among the benchmark group of nine countries (the G7 countries plus Australia and Sweden). The UK has several environmental strengths, although these have yet to be translated into high levels of uptake and use of the Internet. The UK's relative strengths are in its market and political environments, business and government readiness for e-commerce. Its relative weaknesses are in citizen uptake, government uptake, and to a lesser extent in infrastructure. This chapter explores issues involved in the government uptake of the Internet and related technologies, and highlights key issues that need to be addressed if e-government is to achieve its full potential.

The devolution of power to Scotland, Wales and Northern Ireland is a central element of the UK government's modernisation agenda. As a result of devolution the Scottish Executive is responsible for the delivery of a wide range of public services in Scotland, and it has generally endorsed the UK government's modernisation agenda. Scotland is an interesting example, a small country of 5 million people within the UK. It embodies many characteristics that need to be addressed in the development of e-government in many other countries. For example, it has a high concentration of population in the central belt with big cities such as Glasgow and Edinburgh. It also has vast rural areas with low population density in the highlands and islands of Scotland. The geographical differentiation both within regions and cities and between different regions within Scotland is also a significant social and political issue; and so are its complex relationships with other countries within the UK and with other European countries. This chapter will use the development of e-government in Scotland as an example to illustrate the current situation and some emerging issues in the development of e-government. The lessons will not only be relevant to other countries in the UK, but also to many other countries throughout the world.

The chapter is largely explorative, combining a detailed literature review with comprehensive empirical research of the public sector in Scotland. The rhetoric of the UK government's modernisation and electronic government strategies is based on the implicit belief that information and communications technologies (ICTs) can be used to transform the public sector; but this research suggests that the reality on the ground is quite different in many aspects.

The next section examines the efforts to reform the public sector that have been going on since the early 1970s, and describes the move from the traditional public administrative perspective to a more managerial or business orientated approach in public administration. Previous research on the role of ICTs in transforming organisations in general and in the development of e-government in particular will be reviewed. Following that the chapter outlines the methodology and techniques used in undertaking this research. Then the chapter presents the findings of an evaluation of the web sites of Scottish public sector organisations, which seeks to evaluate the extent to which web sites currently reflect the objectives and priorities of the UK government's modernisation agenda. The findings of a survey of Chief Executives in Scottish public sector organisations will also be presented, and it describes how they perceive the importance of the Internet now and in the future; the arrangements that their organisations have put in place for managing the implementation of e-government; and their views about the key drivers of and barriers to the development of e-government. Many issues highlighted in the web evaluation and survey will be explored further through in-depth interviews. Finally, some lessons emerged from the study will be discussed and a number of themes for future research will be outlined.

MODERNISING GOVERNMENT: THE SEARCH FOR THE 'THIRD WAY'

Traditionally the public sector was seen as profoundly different from the private sector. The origins of this can be traced back to the first half of the 20th century when the scope and scale of the public sector grew dramatically, as government increasingly intervened in social and economic matters which had previously been left to market forces (Greenwood & Wilson, 1984). The growth of government during this period is closely associated with the development of bureaucracy.

The bureaucratic form of organisation was seen as being particularly suitable to public sector organisations for much of the 20th century because it was based on rational principles and provided a 'countervailing force to corruption and the arbitrary use of power' (Mintzberg, 1996). The theory was attractive to advocates of the classical school of public administration as it supports values such as impartiality, political neutrality, accountability and equality that were regarded as essential in government and public administration (Brown & Steel, 1979). Although bureaucracies produce unintended consequences such as inflexibility, lack of responsiveness and insensitivity, the advantages tended to outweigh disadvantages. Therefore, for much of the 20th century the bureaucratic system was seen as an unavoidable feature of government (Greenwood & Wilson, 1984).

Hood (1991) identified four global 'mega-trends' in public administration during the 1970s and 1980s, including a slow-down or reversal of government growth, privatisation or quasi privatisation, technology and automation, and a more international agenda. These trends have produced a shift away from the traditional public administration perspective towards a more business-orientated approach to management in the public sector, known as 'New Public Management' (NPM). To a large extent, NPM is the result of a marriage between two different ideological streams—public choice theory, which places an emphasis on competition and consumerism, and managerialism, which advocates that there are universal rules of management, which are 'portable and paramount over technical expertise'. In the UK managerialism was more dominant, producing a 'more pragmatic and less intellectually elegant strand of NPM'.

One of the central tenets of NPM was consumerism and the claim that public services needed to be more responsive to the needs of those who use them. However, consumerism in its undiluted private sector form, cannot be superimposed on the public sector, particularly when it is considered that many public services are provided for the benefit of society as a whole and individuals as citizens rather than customers. Public sector organisations need to be concerned with the needs of individual customers but they often need to balance these needs with wider concerns. This has resulted in a search for models that combine the best features of the traditional public administration perspective with modern business theory and practice.

Today, the simplistic notion that government should become more like business is increasingly rejected (Mintzberg, 1996). The public sector is significantly different from the private sector but there are also ways in which management is generic with scope for mutual learning across the sectoral divide. Some practices and methods can be carried over from the private to public sector, but there are many more cases where 'intelligent adaptation' will need to precede adoption (Gunn, 1988). This was often referred to as the 'third way' in public management to distinguish it from both the bureaucratic model of management and the business management perspective.

In 1999, the UK government set out an ambitious programme for 'modernising government' in a White Paper. Its central aim is to 'achieve better government, better policy making, better responsiveness to what people want and better public services' by reforming the machinery of government in the UK, particularly through the use of ICTs (Cabinet Office, 1999). The White Paper acknowledges that some parts of the public sector are as 'efficient, dynamic and effective as anything in the private sector' but there are also some significant weaknesses. Institutions are often organised around the structure of the providers rather than the needs of users, and there is a general lack of responsiveness to the views of the public. The focus is often on inputs rather than outcomes, and there is a culture of risk aversion in which the rewards for success are limited and the penalties for failure severe. Two central themes that run throughout the White Paper are the need for 'joined up' government through greater horizontal and vertical integrations between different service departments and agencies to address issues that cut across traditional organisational boundaries; and the need for more 'citizen-centred' government so that services are integrated at the point of delivery rather than customers and citizens having to navigate their way around a bureaucratic maze. To a large extent the UK government's modernisation programme can be seen as a synthesis of previous ideas and reform proposals, and a pragmatic expression of the 'third way'. The development of e-government needs to be understood in this context.

THE DEVELOPMENT OF E-GOVERNMENT: PREVIOUS STUDIES

E-government is generally taken to encompass three areas of activities through the use of ICTs (POST, 1998): improve the efficiency and effectiveness of the executive functions of government including the delivery of public services; make governments more transparent by giving citizens better access to a greater range of information; and enable fundamental changes in the relationships between citizens and public sector organisations with implications for the democratic process and structures of government.

The trend towards e-government represents a continuation of previous public sector reforms but with a substantially increased role for ICTs. Heeks (1999) describes three distinctive ways in which ICTs can be used to support reforms within the public sector: supplant by automating existing human executed processes; support by assisting existing human executed processes; and innovate by creating new ICTs-executed processes. In the past ICTs were used primarily to supplant and support existing processes and produce efficiency gains. However, at the heart of current efforts to develop e-government is the drive to use ICTs to support innovation by creating new processes and increase effectiveness in terms of better services. ICTs allow government programmes to be designed around the needs of citizens rather than just the structure of bureaucracies or the convenience of civil servants; and internetworking can provide a vehicle for radically transforming the way government programmes are delivered and changing the very nature of governance while at the same time driving down costs (Tapscott, 1996). In the UK the Internet is used to join up service provision across departmental boundaries, to break down silo based delivery networks and allow citizens to interact with government whenever they choose (Cabinet Office, 2000a). The electronic delivery of government services could result in greater convenience, responsiveness and more personalised services than is possible using existing delivery channels.

Using ICTs to support reform and modernisation in the public sector is often based on the assumption that they can enable better information flows within and between organisations. Bellamy and Taylor (1998) argued that many contemporary ideas for reinventing government are based on the feasibility of introducing and managing 'boundary challenging' information flows that are made possible by modern ICTs. They identified four main trends in technologically enabled reform in the public sector: the relocation of intelligence and knowledge to the point of contact with customers; the lateral integration of customer records across organisational structures so that customers become 'whole persons'; a trend towards 'presumption', that is, the integration of customers into the production process to create products that are tailored to their specific requirements; and new kinds of interactive flows of information within and between organisations. Similarly, an OECD (1998) study of the use of ICTs as an instrument of public sector reform in five countries identified a number of generic trends. Models of horizontal (across governmental agencies) and vertical (across levels of government) integration were being employed to provide one-stop-shop to consumers of government services. Service integration included both point of delivery integration and 'back office' integration. Service delivery arrangements were being reconfigured to follow and integrate with 'life events'. Finally, the availability of technology was a driver as well as an enabler of change by making certain government applications possible and creating new public expectations. Some of these trends are clearly reflected in the current e-government initiatives in the UK.

E-Government in the UK

The UK government has made information age government one of the five key commitments in its modernising government strategy, and ICTs are used to 'achieve joined up working between different parts of government and provide new efficient and convenient ways for citizens and businesses to communicate with government' (Cabinet Office, 1999). The key elements of the government's vision for ICTs-driven modernisation include making it easier for business and individuals to deal with government; enabling government to offer services and information through new media (e.g., the Internet and interactive TV); and improving communications between different parts of government so that people do not have to be asked repeatedly for the same information by different service providers. It also gives staff in call centres and other offices better access to information so that they can deal with members of the public more efficiently and more helpfully, making it much easier for different parts of government to work in partnership with each other and with third parties. To achieve these objectives, it is necessary that services and processes be developed around clusters of related functions aligned to the needs of citizens and businesses. More services will be available 24-7; user feedback will be used to improve the design and organisation of services and other processes; and government web sites will be used as single gateways, often structured around 'life episodes', to a whole range of related government services or functions.

The government has followed up the *Modernising Government* White Paper with an IT strategy (Cabinet Office 2000). A central element of the strategy is to use new delivery channels, including the Internet, to improve relations with customers, suppliers and partners. For citizens, it means wider choice of delivery channels, convenience, lower transaction costs, more personal service, greater awareness of services and policies, greater openness and democratic participation. For business, this will lead to quicker interactions, reduced transaction costs and reduced regulatory burdens. For suppliers, it means reduced transaction costs, better inventory management, and shared data environments. For other public bodies, it means greater accuracy and efficiency, reduced transaction costs, better use of knowledge base, and more flexible working arrangements. In Scotland the responsibility for the development of e-government resides with the devolved Scottish Executive. The Scottish Executive developed a complementary strategy for devolved services in Scotland, and the target of making 100% services available electronically by 2005 applies to all public services in Scotland.

E-Government in the Wider Context

Several comparative studies of e-government in different countries have been conducted in recent years (Deloitte Research, 2000; Oakley, 1999; Anderson Consulting, 2000; CITU, 2000a). These studies found that while some countries have examples of innovative use of ICTs in transforming government services, most are at early stages of developing their e-government strategy. Some governments are more advanced than others in developing transactional systems, particularly in areas like taxation and routine form filling. However, there are relatively few examples of integrated transactional services that allow citizens to access more than one part of government at once. The main barriers to the implementation of e-government are not technical but cultural and social. A clear vision, strong leadership and a rigorous implementation process are seen as key conditions for driving forward e-government. Successful e-government depends on the delivery of integrated services, but integrating government services is difficult because of institutional conservatism and technical incompatibilities. There is a need for a whole government approach that includes all levels of government, and more cross-departmental and inter-agency initiatives to ensure that services are structured around the needs of citizens rather than existing organisational structures. While the UK government is making good progress in putting the technology in place to support joined up working there are many difficulties in using such tools effectively. The difficulties are not primarily technical but rather the result of the human and organisational issues connected with the implications of new technology (Cabinet Office, 2000). There is a strong need for the development of e-government to be integrated with the wider modernisation agenda in order to address the change management issues.

Several barriers to the consumer uptake of e-government services have been identified by previous studies, including the perceived lack of 'warmth' or personal interaction and the cost of accessing the Internet, both in terms of the hardware and ISP and telephone charges (British Telecom, 2000). Some people believe existing channels are as convenient as electronic channels; and people often feel more in control using traditional channels when they have confidence that 'something is happening'. Moreover, different people will prefer different channels at different times and for different types of transactions. One lesson from the development of e-government internationally is that it is difficult to seek the views of customers on services that they are not yet aware of (CITU, 2000). Public sector organisations may need to develop services first and then stimulate demand via awareness programmes, marketing campaigns and the provision of incentives. This implies that implementing e-government often requires a staged approach.

Deloitte Consulting developed a six-staged approach from information publishing and dissemination; via basic transactions; multi-purpose portals; portal personalisation; reconfiguration of services to finally full transformation. Similarly, the Australian National Audit Office outlined a four-staged model to provide both a criteria for public sector organisations to use in determining which services should be delivered electronically and a mechanism for evaluating existing initiatives. These models indicated that the development of e-government should be seen as an evolutionary process with organisations going through a number of stages before they can fully realise the predicted benefits. One of the advantages of adopting a staged approach is that it will allow organisations to build up trust and confidence amongst customers as well as tackle the organisational and cultural changes required. As organisations move through the various stages, the issues involved become more complex and involve an increased need to address organisational and cultural changes.

THE RESEARCH DESIGN

The research combines a literature review with a series of carefully constructed empirical research, including an evaluation of the web sites of public sector organisations in Scotland; a postal questionnaire survey of Chief Executives of these organisations; and semi-structured interviews with a small group of stakeholders. The results from these three elements enable the chapter to paint a general picture about recent developments of e-government in Scotland and highlight several emerging issues.

Web Evaluation

As web sites become more complex, the factors that determine their effectiveness have become multi-dimensional. Combining the key features of previous studies on web evaluation (e.g., Simeon, 1999; Misic & Johnson, 1999; Deconti, 1998; NAO, 1998; SOCITM, 2002), the first part of the research evaluates the web sites of various public sector organisations in Scotland in terms of their structure, accessibility, information content, interaction and integration. The structure dimension looks at the extent to which it is either inward or outward looking and is designed to reflect the needs of customers and citizens. Accessibility examines the ease of navigating the site to find information and the accessibility of the site in terms of the needs of users, including those who have special needs. The content dimension examines the extent to which the site includes certain core information that is likely to be of use to customers and citizens. Interaction evaluates the extent to which a site allows for two-way communications, including online transactions between customers/citizens and the organisation. Integration looks at the extent to which a site promotes 'joined up' government by providing signposts or links to the web sites of other organisations. Due to various constraints of the research, issues related to the technical performance of the web sites, such as loading time, presence of broken links, the date of last update, and so forth were not examined in this study.

Postal Survey of Chief Executives of Public Sector Organisations in Scotland

A postal questionnaire survey of Chief Executives of various public sector organisations in Scotland was also conducted. The questionnaire includes a mixture of open-ended and closed questions. The objective was to identify any significant differences in the attitudes of Chief Executives in different parts of the public sector on a range of issues.

Interviews with Key Stakeholders

The final element of the research involved semi-structured interviews with a small group of key stakeholders. These interviews allow issues to be explored in greater depth than was possible in the postal survey. They also provide a national perspective to the research, which complements the organisational focus of the postal survey and web site evaluations. A total of five interviews were conducted, including a senior civil servant in the Scottish Executive; the Chief Executive of a local government; a senior manager in Scottish Enterprise; a local authority IT manager; and a former Chief Executive of a Health Trust. The interviews were semi-structured, which allowed a degree of flexibility while ensuring that the interviews remained focused on the key issues. A short outline was used to provide structure to the interviews and this was sent to interviewees in advance to give them an insight into the issues that would be discussed. Each interview lasted for at least an hour, with some lasting considerably longer. Follow up e-mails and phone conversations were used to clarify particular issues.

E-GOVERNMENT DEVELOPMENT IN SCOTLAND: RESULTS OF WEB EVALUATION

The web sites of 98 public sector organisations in Scotland are assessed. The objective was not to rank individual web sites, but rather to identify overall trends within the public sector as a whole and highlight any significant differences between different sections.

Structure

The overall structure of the site was classified as highly structured, semi-structured, or unstructured. This was designed to determine whether the site was logically structured and integrated as a whole as opposed to being a collection of unrelated information with little or no thought being given to the site's overall structure. Over 70% of the web sites that were evaluated were highly structured. A further 25% were semi-structured, which meant that there was a clear overall structure, but some sections of the site appeared to have been 'bolted on' to this structure in an incremental way rather than integrated into the overall structure. Only 5% of sites were classified as unstructured, meaning that they were clearly a loose collection of unrelated information that had been brought together with little or no thought given to the overall structure of the site. Government departments, agencies and Non Departmental Public Bodies (NDPBs) and local enterprise trusts were more likely to have highly structured web sites than organisations from the health and local government sectors.

Accessibility

The web sites were also evaluated in terms of the ease of navigation around the site for all users; and accessibility to those with special needs, particularly those who are either visually impaired or whose first language is not English. Overall, the web sites rated highly in terms of general ease of navigation factors, with 88% having clear links back to the main menu from throughout the site and 80% having most of the key information within a single 'click' from the main menu. The sites generally rated less well in terms of offering navigational aids, with only 43% having a search facility, 19% a site map, 16% an A-Z index and 4% a separate help section. Some sites offered more than one of these facilities, but overall a quarter of sites offered no navigational aids at all. The vast majority of sites performed poorly in terms of the wider access issues: only 5% of sites offered a text only version of the site and only 4% had been approved by the Royal National Institute for the Blind or similar organisation. None of the web sites evaluated offered facilities for those whose first language was not English.

Information Content

Given the diversity of public sector organisations and the wide range of functions they are responsible for, the information content of their web sites vary considerably. There is, however, certain generic information that best practice guidance suggests should be included in all organisations' sites. This study looked at two main types of information. Firstly, basic content information that the Cabinet Office's guidelines recommend should be on the home page of every public sector organisation's web site. Secondly, core generic information that various best practice guidelines suggest should be included in 'information rich' web sites.

All of the web sites evaluated included the organisation's name on the Home Page and almost all (94%) also included the organisation's logo. However, other basic contact information was far less prevalent. Only half of the sites featured the organisations' postal address on the sites' home page, and only 44% displayed a contact telephone number, 38% a fax number and 27% an e-mail address for general enquiries about the organisation (as opposed to an e-mail address for enquiries about the web site). There were significant variations between the sectors in terms of the provision of basic contact information.

Interaction

If web sites are to move beyond being more than 'brouchureware' then they need to offer opportunities for individuals to interact with organisations, including opportunities to transact business with them. This study evaluated web sites' interactive qualities by looking at a series of factors, which represent progressively higher levels of interaction. A majority of sites included information that would allow customers to interact with the organisation by another medium, for example, contact names (86%), contact telephone numbers (69%) and information about complaints procedures (51%). However, far fewer sites included features that would allow customers to complete transactions online. While 35% of sites included 'clickable' e-mail addresses for named individuals, only 8% included a facility for responding online to consultation exercises and less than 5% included forms that could either be downloaded or completed online. Only two sites out of the total sample of 98 offered a facility for making payments online.

Integration

The study also examined the extent to which web sites facilitate integration between different organisations in the public sector. The guidance published by the Cabinet Office (CITU, 2000) states that the Internet is an important means of delivering 'joined up' government and in demonstrating relationships between different areas of policy and service delivery. This research examined the extent to which web sites contain links to related information on other organisations' web sites.

Over half all the web sites contained a separate links section, with 56% of these organising the links on the basis of organisational names and the remaining 44% categorising them by subject matter. Far less use was made of hypertext links within web sites, with only 14% of web sites making either limited or extensive use of such linkages. Only 8% of the web sites evaluated contained clickable links on the home page acting as a gateway or portal to other related sites. Surprisingly, given the emphasis the government has placed on 'joined up' working, more than a third of all of the web sites that were evaluated did not have any links to other public sector organisations' sites.

Discussion

Despite the subjective nature of some parts of this evaluation, the research clearly indicated that the web sites of public sector organisations were rated highly in terms of the structure and information content but less well in interaction and integration. Given that the latter aspects are most clearly identified with the government's modernisation and information age government agendas, it suggests that public sector organisations in Scotland are currently at an early stage in utilising the Internet to help in achieving these objectives. More specifically, local authority web sites were rated best overall and also rated above average for all of the individual dimensions of performance except interaction. Health sector web sites were rated poorest overall and also performed poorest in terms of each of the individual dimensions. Government departments, agencies and NDPBs web sites were rated best in the interaction and integration dimensions. Enterprise network web sites were rated best in the structure dimension and above average for all other dimensions except interaction.

SURVEY OF CHIEF EXECUTIVES

This research also carried out a questionnaire survey of Chief Executives of public sector organisations in Scotland. The survey was sent to the Chief Executives or their equivalent in 129 public sector organisations in Scotland, including local authorities, health boards, health trusts and local enterprise companies, as well as Scottish Executive departments, agencies and NDPBs. Seventy completed returns were received, representing an overall response rate of 54% (Table 1).

Use of PCs by Chief Executives and their Understanding of ICTS

Respondents were asked about their own use of personal computers at work. They were also asked to rank their general awareness and understanding of current developments in ICTs. Almost 90% of all respondents said that they used a PC at work every day, with a further 9% saying they used one at least two or three times a week. The responses were fairly uniform across all four sub-sectors, although the number of Chief Executives who said they used a PC every day was slightly lower than average in the health sector. Only one respondent said that they did not use a PC at work. The most popular tasks according to the amount of time they spend on the PCs are 'reading e-mails' and 'sending e-mails', highlighted by 94% and 83% respondents. Other applications were used far less, with the next highest being 'working on written documents' (23%) and 'accessing the organisation's internal network or Intranet' (13%). Many respondents said that they only used their PCs for sending and reading e-mails.

Table 1: Responses to the postal survey by chief executives of public sector organisations in Scotland

Sector	Number of Valid Returns	Response Rate within the Sector	Response Rate of the Sector as % of Total
Local Authorities	19	59%	27%
Health Boards and Trusts	21	49%	30%
Scottish Executive Departments, Agencies and NDPBs	14	41%	20%
Enterprise Network	16	67%	23%
TOTAL	70	54%	100%

Seventy percent of respondents claimed to be either very or fairly proficient in using a PC, although this figure needs to be interpreted carefully, given that most of them only used their PCs for a limited number of applications. The remaining 30% of respondents said that they were not very proficient or had no expertise in using a PC. The highest levels of claimed proficiency were in the enterprise network, with 88% saying that they were very or fairly proficient, and the lowest was in local government (48%).

Overall, 68% of respondents said they had a very good or good understanding of current developments in ICTs, compared to 32% who said they had only a basic or very little understanding. The levels of awareness and understanding varied significantly across the four sub-sectors. The highest level of awareness was in the enterprise network sector, followed by local government, with the lowest level being amongst respondents from government departments, agencies and NDPBs, where 80% of respondents said that they had only a basic or very limited understanding of ICTs.

How do Chief Executives Rate their own Organisation's Web Sites?

Forty-four percent of all respondents said that they viewed their organisation's web site at least once a week. The percentage was highest in local government and the enterprise network (50%), and lowest amongst respondents from government departments, agencies and NDPBs, where only 23% of respondents viewed their organisation's web site at least once a week.

Respondents were asked to rank their organisation's own web site against a range of factors. The only factors that a majority of respondents rated as either very good or good were overall design and appearance (71%) and the quality of information provided (68%). Respondents rated their organisation's web site far lower for other factors. Allowing the public to interact with the organisation and promoting 'joined up' government were the lowest rated factors, with only 14% saying their organisation's web site was either good or very good in terms of these factors.

How Important is the Internet to Organisations?

Respondents clearly saw the Internet as being important to their organisations, with 60% saying it was very important and 33% saying it was fairly important. However, they also believed it would be more important in the future, with 90% saying it would be very important to their organisations in the future. Respondents said that they used their Intranets for communicating a wide range of information internally within their own organisations. However, in most cases the Intranet appeared to be used as a parallel system to existing paper-based systems.

Respondents anticipated major changes in the way that their organisations communicate with customers, suppliers and other organisations. The main changes that were anticipated were a substantial decrease in written communications and telephone calls and corresponding increases in communications by e-mail or through the Internet. Only 7% of respondents said that either e-mail or the Internet was currently the most important means of communicating with customers; however, 49% said they would be the most important in the future. The corresponding figures for communicating with suppliers were 8% and 74%, and for communicating with other organisations were 9% and 67%.

Managing the Development of E-Government

Only 15% of respondents said their organisation had a separate strategy for developing e-government, although a further 24% said they were in the process of preparing one. Of the remaining organisations, 19% said e-government was part of a wider corporate strategy, while another 29% said that it was part of their organisation's existing IT/IS strategy. 12% of respondents said that their organisation had no strategy for dealing with the issues raised by e-government.

Sixty-seven percent of respondents said that their organisation had appointed a senior manager to take overall responsibility for the development and implementation of their e-government strategy. However, only 75% of these managers were members of their organisation's senior management team. This means that in practice only 50% of organisations had someone on their senior management team with overall responsibility for the development of e-government.

Implement E-Government through Partnership

Forty-three percent of respondents said it was essential to work with other organisations in the public and private sector in developing e-government initiatives, and another 30% said it was very important. In terms of current partnership arrangements, respondents were most likely to be working with other public sector organisations, either in their own geographical area (78%) or in their own sector (81%). Other partnerships were mentioned less frequently, including joint working between local organisations and central government departments (43%), partnerships with consultants (30%) and other private sector organisations (29%).

Overall, 81% of respondents were aware of the government's targets for electronic service delivery. Twenty-three percent of all respondents said it would be very difficult for their organisation to obtain the target of 25% of services being deliverable electronically by 2002, while 42% said it would be very difficult to achieve the 2005 target of 100% of services being deliverable electronically.

Drivers and Barriers of E-Government

Respondents were asked to rank a number of factors that could be driving or enabling the development of e-government in terms of their importance to their own organisation. The factor that was ranked very important by the highest proportion of respondents was the prospect of improving the accessibility of services (78%). Other factors that were ranked as being very important by a majority of respondents included the prospect of improving the quality of services (70%) and initiatives from the Scottish Executive (59%). Interestingly, a substantially higher proportion of respondents said that initiatives from the Scottish Executive (59%) were very important than said that initiatives from the UK government were very important (35%). The factors that were rated lowest in terms of their overall importance were expectations of suppliers and the public about the ability to conduct transactions electronically (19% and 23% respectively rated these factors as very important drivers) and a concern to match standards of service in the private sector (25%).

Respondents were asked to rank a number of potential barriers to the development of e-government. Lack of access to a PC or the Internet by a large proportion of the population was regarded as being a very important barrier by 54% of respondents. This was substantially more than the next few factors - a lack of common IT systems within and between organisations (cited as being very important by 28% of respondents), a lack of financial resources (26%) and concerns about security and privacy (26%).

INTERVIEWS WITH KEY STAKEHOLDERS

This research also included semi-structured interviews with five key stakeholders in Scotland, which provided significant insights on various issues in the area of e-government highlighted in the survey and in the literature research.

Opportunities Offered by E-Government

All the stakeholders said that the main opportunity offered by e-government in the short to medium term was the potential to improve the efficiency and effectiveness of services and to make financial savings by delivering routine transactions with customers and suppliers electronically. For some this was seen as necessary in order to reallocate resources to other services as a result of financial pressures, and for others it was seen as an opportunity to release resources that could be directed towards the development of new services or the delivery of existing services to a larger number of customers.

The second most important opportunity identified by the key stakeholders was the ability to improve existing services by making them more convenient and responsive to the needs of individuals. This was seen as a major driver of e-government. They believed that demand for electronic service delivery would increase as people became more accustomed to dealing with private businesses electronically and therefore expected the same degree of convenience when dealing with public sector organisations.

Some of the stakeholders recognised the opportunities that e-government could offer in terms of developing services that were tailored to the needs of individuals. However, they also acknowledged that this raised concerns about the sharing of data within and between organisations. There was a general assumption that the public is suspicious of government organisations sharing information, as it raised images of 'big brother'.

All of the stakeholders accepted that in theory the development of e-government should make it easier to provide joined up services. Internet-based technology was seen as offering the possibility of breaking down barriers within and between organisations. Within organisations e-government was seen as supporting the development of 'one stop shops', either in physical offices or call centres, by providing front-line staff with access to more comprehensive information about individual customers. Some stakeholders also said that Internet technology should make it easier to provide 'joined up' services that cut across organisational boundaries but there were major organisational and cultural barriers that needed to be overcome. As one stakeholder put it, 'previously incompatible IT systems was the problem, now the technology is the easy bit, changing attitudes and organisational cultures will be much harder.'

Barriers to E-Government

The lack of access to the Internet amongst certain sections of the population was seen as being the most important barrier to the development of e-government by all of the stakeholders. This was seen as being a particular problem for public sector organisations, as they can't choose their customers. Indeed, many public services are provided specifically for vulnerable or low-income groups who are least likely to have access to the technology. The main consequence of this is that public sector organisations will have to continue to provide services through multiple channels at least in the short term to prevent excluding those who do not have access to the Internet.

The lack of finance for capital investment in new technology was seen as a major barrier, particularly by stakeholders from the local government sector. This was partly explained by the fact that investment in IT was often not seen as a priority when competing for scarce resources against other claims for capital investment, for example, for new schools, roads, and so forth.

All of the stakeholders said that one of the key barriers to maximising the potential offered by e-government was the need to change individual attitudes and organisational culture. There was a clear recognition amongst the stakeholders that e-government was not a technical issue but an organisational change issue. However, many of them felt that this was not universally recognised at senior levels within public sector organisations.

Stakeholders felt that there was currently a perceived problem with security and authentication that prevented the development of electronic transaction services. This was seen as a particular problem for public sector organisations, as the public generally saw them as being in a position of trust. This was seen as a major asset that should not be jeopardised by seeking to develop electronic services before issues of security and authentication have been properly worked out.

Issues Particular to the Public Sector

Most stakeholders said the issues involved in developing e-government were similar to those faced by private sector organisations developing e-commerce. However, the main difference was that public sector bodies did not face the same competitive pressures; therefore the motivations and drivers of change were generally different. Some respondents said that while public sector organisations did not face competition for most of their core services they did face competition for certain functions, for example, the provision of information, and that there was already evidence that private sector companies were looking to provide these services electronically. One respondent also said that the public increasingly compared the standard of service between public and private sector organisations and suggested that this could be seen as a form of 'competition for customer's hearts and minds'.

The stakeholders acknowledged that public sector organisations were generally more risk adverse than private sector organisations. However, they claimed that there were legitimate reasons for this, including the need for public accountability and financial probity in the stewardship of public funds. They also felt that bad experiences of major IT projects that had failed to deliver their promised benefits in the past had made senior managers more risk averse. The public sector is generally more unionised and has more rigid salary scales and conditions of service than the private sector. Stakeholders said this had a number of consequences for the development of e-government. It meant that it was often more difficult and time consuming to achieve changes in working practices because of the need for these changes to be agreed upon through negotiation and collective bargaining. Salary scales were also seen as a problem in terms of recruiting and retaining skilled IT staff, as the remuneration offered in the public sector was generally lower than in the private sector.

Managing the Implementation of E-Government

All of the stakeholders strongly emphasised the need to take an incremental rather than a 'big bang' approach to the development and implementation of e-government. They made a distinction between the need to develop an overall strategic vision that looked at the 'big picture' and the need to implement projects on an incremental or modular basis. This was seen as important in order to develop organisational learning and build up confidence through a series of 'quick wins'. Some of the stakeholders said that this approach needed more sophisticated methods and techniques for prioritising projects and making judgements about relative opportunities and risks. Others said that more use should be made of 'off the shelf' solutions and adaptation of systems developed in the private sector rather than the traditional approach of developing bespoke systems.

The second key issue raised by the stakeholders about implementing e-government was the need to see e-government as a change management issue rather than an IT implementation issue. All of the stakeholders suggested that the main challenges that needed to be faced related to human resources, organisational culture and managing stakeholder expectations. A number of stakeholders said that this meant that communication, training and management development strategies had to be developed and that this had to be budgeted for in making investment decisions.

Stakeholders felt that the government's targets for electronic service delivery were valuable in emphasising the 'political imperative' of developing strategies for e-government. They provided an incentive and motivation for organisations to consider how Internet-based technology could be applied to their own business processes. However, they were seen as 'blunt instruments' when it came to developing e-government strategies within individual organisations. Stakeholders felt that organisations needed to develop their own targets that were tailored to their own needs and circumstances rather than simply accepting the government's targets.

KEY ISSUES EMERGED FROM THIS RESEARCH

The triangulation of the three elements of the empirical work highlighted a number of important issues, including several areas of discrepancies between the intentions of the central government and what actually happened on the ground. The present UK Government's modernisation programme can be seen as a pragmatic attempt to find a 'third way' between the traditional public administration perspective and business management theory. The government has placed an increased emphasis on the effectiveness of public services as well as ensuring they are delivered in an economic and efficient manner. This is clearly reflected in government's strategy for 'joined-up' government and for a more citizen-centred approach to the delivery of public services. This will require the breakdown of traditional barriers within and between organisations. The potential of ICTs to enable the establishment of 'boundary challenging' information flows and the integration within and between public sector organisations is seen as being of central importance in efforts to reform and modernise the public sector. The problem is, however, that some organisations are tempted to adopt simplistic approaches to the use of ICTs to achieve organisational transformation. They see ICTs as providing simple answers to what are complex organisational and social problems. Using technology to break down organisational barriers is likely to challenge traditional working practices and attitudes towards the management of information. It will also redefine the power structure of these organisations both internally and in their relations with one another. If e-government is to be successful in enabling the level of organisational change required to achieve the objectives of the government's modernisation agenda it will need strong leadership from the top rather than being left to functional specialists in IT/IS departments.

Does E-Government Development in Scotland Reflect the Rhetoric of the E-Government Strategy in the UK?

The evaluation of web sites shows that a large majority of these web sites are well structured and provide detailed information about the organisation and its activities. The evidence from the survey and interviews also indicated that public sector organisations in Scotland have recognised the potential importance of the Internet and have made a start in utilising the technology. The fact that 89% of organisations surveyed had their own web site compares favourably with previous surveys of government agencies in England and Wales and large private sector companies in Scotland, which both showed lower proportions of organisations who had developed their own web sites.

However, the web evaluation also clearly indicated that most sites were rated poorly in their accessibility, interaction and integration dimensions, which reflects the gap between what is actually happening in Scotland, and the rhetoric of the e-government strategy in developing joined up government and providing integrated, citizen-centric services. In other words, e-government developments in Scotland currently do not reflect the full intention of the government strategy. This point was further reinforced by the survey finding that 'allowing the public to interact with the organisation' and 'promoting joined-up government' were the lowest rated factors, with only 14% of the Chief Executives saying their organisation's web site was either good or very good in terms of these factors. This is far lower than other factors such as 'design and appearance' (71%) and 'the quality of information provided' (68%). Some stakeholders interviewed recognised that in theory the development of e-government should make it easier to provide joined up services that cut across organisational boundaries, but in order to do so major organisational and cultural barriers need to be overcome. Many of these barriers cannot be resolved with technology alone. In fact, it was felt that the need to change individual attitude and organisational culture was not even universally recognised at the senior management level within the public sector organisations. This was reflected in the fact that less than 40% of organisations have a senior member of the management team other than the IT/IS manager with overall responsibility for the development of e-government related initiatives.

An important lesson from this is that even though the UK government has developed a visionary e-government strategy and strong political imperative in achieving various targets, major attention and effort should also be paid to the implementation process. Simple targets, such as making 100% government services online by 2005, may force various government agencies to focus resources on meeting targets, rather than exploiting the full potential of the Internet and related technologies by transforming the way they do things and ensuring that services that are made available online are of high quality with long-term benefits to both the providers and the users. For example, some public sector organisations may be tempted to build simple web pages in order to achieve government online target, rather than using ICTs to support radical changes in the way services are provided. The links between the e-government strategy and the wider modernisation agenda should be more explicitly highlighted; and more guidance should also be provided to various public sector organisations on different ways that ICTs can be used to transform organisations. The implementation needs to be managed as a learning process so that good practice as well as lessons learnt can be identified and spread quickly.

Drivers and Barriers to E-Government Development

Closely linked to the last point, the research also highlighted some subtle discrepancies in what drives the development of e-government, and what the major barriers are. The objectives of the central government as revealed in the e-government strategy are to use ICTs to facilitate the development of joined-up government and provide citizen-centred, integrated services. The government itself can then be made more efficient and effective, and services be provided more effectively at lower cost. However, the survey shows that what drives the development in Scotland are 'the prospects of improving accessibility of services', 'improving the quality of services' and 'Initiatives' from the Scottish Executive (59%) and the UK central government (35%). The people interviewed believed e-government offers the prospect to improve the efficiency and effectiveness of services and make financial savings by delivering routine transactions with customers and suppliers electronically. The money saved can then be reallocated to other services, or be re-directed towards the development of new services or delivering existing services to more people. Existing services can be made more convenient and responsive to the need of individuals; and some new services can be tailored to the needs of individuals. To some extent such discrepancies perhaps can explain the gap between rhetoric and reality in the development of e-government in Scotland.

The government set a target to make all services online by 2005. The 'political imperative' is useful in providing incentives and motivations for organisations in the public sector to consider how ICTs can be applied to their own processes. This is clearly reflected in the high level of awareness of this target in most parts of the public sector, and the enormous challenges involved in achieving the targets. However, the need to meet the target has also to some extent distracted some organisations from making realistic assessments of their own needs and circumstances, finding innovative ways of doing things, and clearly identifying what businesses and citizens need so they will make high levels of use of such electronic services once they are developed. Some organisations are torn between achieving government online target and using ICTs to facilitate collaboration and joined up working around customer need and providing high quality online services in key areas.

There are also some discrepancies between the barriers highlighted in the survey and those raised during the interviews. The survey rated the following three factors as the biggest barriers to the development of e-government: the lack of access to a PC by a large proportion of the population; lack of common IT systems within and between organisations; and lack of financial resources. The people interviewed recognise the importance of these barriers, but they also emphasised that the biggest barriers are the needs to change people's attitude and organisational culture. Currently the government is structured in departments and silos, but most problems tend to cut across the boundaries between them. To achieve the objectives of the e-government strategy, '[w]e need cultural change within government. It will be a long haul. We have to look at the government framework and have budgets linked up together. It will not be a technical fix—you have to fix government first.' This is clearly not happening, because less than 40% of organisations have a senior manager with overall responsibility for e-government initiatives. In fact, in many cases, the senior managers seem to be observing what is happening in their organisations rather than actively shaping and leading the development.

E-Government, Organisational Transformation and Other Government Agendas

The success of e-government initiatives depends critically on the support of all key stake holders The development of joined up government and the provision of integrated services that cut across organisational boundaries require the sharing of information across organisational boundaries, which redefines the power structures and relationships of these organisations at all levels. Therefore, strong resistance can be expected from those whose positions may be negatively affected. Without strong leadership and political imperative, this may even question the practical feasibility of achieving joined up government in the short to medium term.

As a result, a closer and more explicit alignment between e-government and the wider modernisation agenda in the public sector is absolutely essential. Although at the theoretical and policy levels there is a convergence between these two agendas, there is also a huge gap between the rhetoric of the visionaries and the reality of implementing the changes on the ground. This can partly be explained by the 'time lag' involved in introducing any fundamental changes, but without radical changes in the basic model of government itself, the potential of e-government cannot be fully realised.

Although the need for cultural and organisational changes are recognised by some of the stakeholders interviewed, this was not regarded as one of the main barriers in the survey. Douglas Alexander, the minister responsible for e-transformation, said the government is working to get better services online, but noted the challenge is also to get people using the services. 'It is not just about pipes any more,' he said. 'It is increasingly about content. But it is no longer enough to have all our services online by 2005. We must drive up the number of people using e-services.' What he did not emphasize, however, is that the central government needs to work with public sector organizations as well as researchers and consultants to come up with more innovative ways of doing things. Without radical changes in the way the government itself is structured and managed, the full potential of e-government cannot be realized.

E-Government and Other Competing Strategic Objectives

For the central government, one of the main drivers of e-government is to achieve efficiency gains, which can be translated into cost savings and reduced employment in certain sections of the public sector. In fact, the E-Envoy of the UK central government, Mr. Andrew Pinder, believed that one in five civil service jobs could be cut over the next ten years as part of the drive to create e-government and put government services online in the UK. This means 800,000 public sector workers in total. Although front line staff, such as doctors, nurses, and teachers will not be cut, who make up 50% of the four million public sector employees in the UK, civil servants doing routine tasks can be cut by up to 40% if high level take-up of electronic services can be achieved. Although the cost savings from reduced government salaries could then be re-invested into public services such as health and education, which may create new employment opportunities, the overall impact on employment can be substantial, which clashes with other strategic objectives of the government such as full employment—an issue that will need to be carefully addressed given that the public sectors are the biggest employers in many regions in the UK, including Scotland.

This issue was touched upon during some of the interviews but was not contemplated by Chief Executives in the survey and it did not even feature in the main drivers for e-government. The public sector is generally more unionised and has more rigid salary scales and conditions of service than the private sector. It was often more difficult and time consuming to achieve changes in working practices because of the need for these changes to be agreed upon through negotiation and collective bargaining. However, failing to achieve such cost savings may significantly undermine the overall benefits that can be derived from the e-government initiatives.

Other Emerging Issues

Many other issues were also highlighted in the study. Amongst those issues are privacy and security in the development of e-government. Public sector organisations need to be more cautious than private companies because the information about individuals they deal with is both more extensive and more sensitive. The public generally trusts public sector organisations with this information and a failure to deal adequately with issues relating to the security and confidentiality of information transferred electronically is likely to erode this trust. 'Digital divide' and the lack of access by certain fractions of society—indeed, the lack of demand amongst people without adequate digital access to public services are also of concerns. However, such issues are not perceived to be prohibitive to the development of e-government as revealed in the survey and the interviews.

FUTURE RESEARCH

The main conclusion to be drawn from this research is that ICTs in general and the Internet in particular can offer tremendous potential for improving and modernising the way that public sector organisations deliver services to customers and citizens and manage themselves and their relationships with other organisations. However, the development of e-government is a complex process and the key to its success is managing the process of organisational and cultural change alongside issues relating to technology.

There is no blueprint for the development of e-government across the whole of the public sector, and individual organisations will have to develop a strategy that suits their own needs and circumstances. The transition to e-government will require strong leadership to drive forward the organisational and cultural changes that will be necessary to translate the rhetoric of e-government into reality, but in the Scottish context this is not yet happening. Many senior managers seem to be observing rather than leading the changes. In fact, one frustrated IT manager of a local authority illustrated his job as being asked to 'build a road without a clear destination' and his senior managers in the council are prepared to go wherever he can lead them to.

Clearly a lot remains to be done to understand e-government related issues. Three types of research are particularly needed. First, continuous effort is needed to identify innovative e-government applications in the global context. This is important, because both the technical capacity of ICTs and our understanding of ICTs in organisational contexts have been improving rapidly. New applications that can bring about radical and rapid improvements in the efficiency, effectiveness and flexibility of public sector organisations are continuously being developed. It is important to identify and conceptualise such innovations as soon as they are developed, because many of them can be applied in other relevant areas. Senior managers need to understand the potential benefits and pitfalls of these innovations before introducing them. So the interest in such studies is enormous. Such research can also inform policy makers at various levels of the government when formulating policies and strategies.

In addition to success cases, it is also important to study failed projects in the e-government area so lessons can be learnt and similar mistakes are avoided elsewhere in future projects. Organisational and project failures are usually difficult to study because information is difficult to obtained. However, considerable information about e-government projects are in the public domain and valuable lessons can be learnt from such failures.

Second, in parallel to the first type of studies, it is also important to identify general tendencies in different sub-sectors and regions. Such studies allow researchers, policy makers and practitioners to understand the general picture of current transformation in specific contexts. The findings can also be used to reveal whether new tendencies identified in leading organisations are being taken up in the wider context.

Third, many valuable lessons can be learnt from the private sector in the development of e-commerce and e-business, even though some of them cannot be directly implemented in the public sector. Therefore, comparative studies between the private and public sectors are needed, and lessons from the private sector need to be considered in the public sector context. These studies together can help us understand organisational transformation in the context of the networked economy and information society.

REFERENCES

Bellamy, C., & Taylor, J. (1998). *Governing in the Information Age.* Buckingham: Open University Press.

Booz Allan Hamilton (2002). *International e-economy benchmarking: The world's most effective policies for the e-economy* (Report for the British Government's Office of the E-Envoy and the Dept. of Trad and Industry), London. Online: http://www.e-envoy.gov.uk/oee/oee.nsf/sections/esummit-benchmarking/$file/indexpage.htm.

British Telecommunications. (2000). *eGovernment: Ready or not?* London: British Telecommunications.

Brown, R., & Steel, D. (1979). *The administrative process in Britain.* London: Methtuen.

Cabinet Office. (1999). *Modernising government,* Cmnd 4310. London: The Stationary Office.

Cabinet Office. (2000). *E-governmnent- A strategic framework for public services in the Information Age.* London: HMSO

Cabinet Office. (2000a). Performance and innovation unit report, e-gov. *Electronic government services for the 21st Century.* London: HMSO

CITU. (2000). *Framework for Information Age government web sites.* London: Stationary Office.

CITU. (2000a). *Information Age government: Benchmarking electronic service delivery.* Online: www.citu.gsi.gov.uk.

Deloitte Research. (2000). *At the dawn of e-government.* New York: Deloitte Consulting.

Greenwood, J., & Wilson, D. (1984). *Public administration in Britain.* London: Unwin Hyman Ltd.

Gunn, L. (1988). Public management: A third approach. *Public Money and Management, 8*(1).

Heeks, R. (Ed). (1999). *Reinventing government in the Information Age: International practice in IT enabled public sector reform.* London: Routledge

Hood, C. (1995). Contemporary public management: A new global paradigm? *Public Policy and Administration, 10*(2), 104-227

Mintzberg, H (1996). Managing government, governing management. *Harvard Business Review,* (May/June).

Misic, M., & Johnson, K. (1999). Benchmarking: A tool for web site evaluation and improvement. *Internet Research: Electronic Networking Applications and Policy, 9*(5), 383-392.

National Audit Office (NAO). (1999). *Government on the web.* London: the Stationary Office.

Oakley, K. (1999). *E-government an international study of online government.* Commissioned by Cable and Wireless Communications.

OECD. (1998). *Information Technology as an instrument of public management reform: A study of five OECD Countries* (OECD Working Paper No 99). Paris: OECD.

POST. (1998). *Electronic government: Information Technology and the citizen.* London: Parliamentary Office for Science and Technology. Available: www.parliament.uk/post/egov.htm.

Simeon, R. (1999). Evaluating domestic and international web site strategies. *Internet Research: Electronic Networking Applications and Policy, 9*(4), 297-308.

SOCITM. (2002). *Better connected 2002.* Northampton: SOCITM.

Tapscott, D. (1996). *The digital economy: Promise and peril in the age of networked intelligence.* New York: McGraw Hill.

UK Online. (2002). *UK online annual report 2002.* Online: http://www.e-envoy.gov.uk/oee/oee.nsf/sections/esummit-ukoannrep/$file/indexpage.htm.

Previously published in the Journal of Electronic Commerce in Organizations, 1(2), 44-65, Apr/June, 2003.

Chapter XII

The Impact of the Role of the Government of Egypt on Electronic Commerce Development and Growth

Sherif Kamel, The American University in Cairo, Egypt

Ahmed Ghoneim, Cairo University, Egypt

Sherine Ghoneim, Cairo University, Egypt

ABSTRACT

Information and communication technology with a focus on the digital economy and the implications of the development of electronic commerce is increasingly playing an active role in the development and growth of the global economy. The implications are wide and diversified. This includes the facilitation of trade transactions and acceleration of movement of capital through the new rules of the digital economy with the removal of time and distance barriers. The impacts are varying in density and effectiveness between developed and developing nations. Electronic commerce could be beneficial to business and socioeconomic development in the north (developed world) as well as in the south (developing nations). Small and medium-sized enterprises stand a unique opportunity worldwide to optimally leverage their capacities and excel from the diversified communication channels the digital economy presents. However, one challenge remains critical and that is the growing digital divide emerging between developed and developing nations as well as within developing nations themselves, which could deepen income and wealth inequalities.

In that respect, the government role in developing nations in preventing the widening of the digital divide is becoming increasingly vital with implications that vary and affect business, culture and the society at large. During the past two decades, electronic commerce has had a diversified variety of impacts on organizations of all types and sizes. Such impacts differed from one country to another and from one environment to another, depending on the local conditions and the adaptation of the society. Implications related to the management and leadership of the organizations, their vision, mission and strategies, policies, governance, the organizational learning, ethics and culture among other elements.

This chapter demonstrates the role of the government of Egypt in introducing, diffusing and institutionalizing electronic commerce. Electronic commerce represents a tremendous challenge and at the same time a great opportunity for growth and development, and hence it needs an institutional role to regulate it. Electronic commerce promises great potentials for developing nations giving poor nations and their populations additional access to markets, information, and other resources that would have otherwise been inaccessible. However, there has been a great fear of a digital divide emerging between developed and developing nations. Hence, the governments' involvement of developing nations, such as Egypt, in preventing the appearance or the widening of the digital divide is of paramount importance. With respect to electronic commerce, the role of the government is highly different from its traditional role in other conventional areas that have been subject to extensive research, such as infrastructure and social services amongst others. It is different because electronic commerce is a newly ventured domain for government involvement that requires substantial thinking and structuring of the role it should play; it is more or less a comprehensive new role with aspects related to setting the rules for market operations as well as developing control measures to handle the risk factor associated with electronic commerce-related investments. Electronic commerce represents both a challenge and an opportunity for a developing nation such as Egypt with potentials for growth and development. This chapter introduces electronic commerce in Egypt with a focus on the prevailing status and the institutional role of the government to regulate electronic commerce and develop the electronic trading industry.

INTRODUCTION

The information and communication technology infrastructure and the development of electronic commerce are both playing an increasingly active role in changing and growing the global economy in a digital way. The implications are wide and diversified, including the facilitation of trade transactions and acceleration of movement of capital through innovative rules irrespective of time and distance differences. Electronic commerce could be beneficial to business and socioeconomic development in the north (developed world) as well as in the south (developing nations), but the impacts could vary in density and in effectiveness due to one critical challenge, and that is the growing digital divide emerging between developed and developing nations as well as within developing nations, which could deepen income and wealth inequalities.

Therefore, the government role in developing nations in preventing the widening of the digital divide is becoming increasingly vital with implications that vary and affect business, culture and the society at large. During the past two decades, electronic commerce had diversified impacts on organizations of all types and sizes. Such impacts differed from one country to another and from one environment to another depending on the local conditions and the adaptation of the society. The implications related to the management style and leadership of organizations, their vision, mission and strategies, policies, governance, the organizational learning, ethics and culture among other elements. This chapter demonstrates the role of the government of Egypt in introducing, diffusing and institutionalizing electronic commerce, which represents a challenge and an opportunity for development and hence needs an institutionalized role to regulate it. This chapter introduces electronic commerce in Egypt with a focus on the prevailing status and the institutional role of the government to regulate electronic commerce and develop the electronic trading industry.

A THEORETICAL FRAMEWORK

There are a number of issues that need to be highlighted when addressing the theoretical framework of the role of the government in electronic commerce development and growth, and that includes (a) the importance of institutions in developing healthy market economies; (b) the sequence of institutional building and reform; and (c) the NIE approach in explaining how institutions are formed.

(a) *The importance of institutions in developing healthy market economies:* There is an overall consensus that institutions are needed to support market function properly. According to the World Bank Development Report, institutions support markets by helping to manage risks from market exchange, increasing efficiency and raising returns; hence reducing the transaction costs arising from inadequate information, incomplete definition and enforcement of property rights. Institutions that fit the developed economies are different from the ones that fit economic environments of developing countries (World Bank, 2001; World Bank & OECD, 1998). Hence, it can be safely argued that developing countries experiencing transition to market economies are in need of new forms of institutions that are not necessarily adopted by industrialized countries and that are needed to ensure the functioning of their infant market economies.

(b) *Sequence of institutional building:* The ultimate goal of institutional building in developing countries is to create a market-friendly environment, with supportive government services that ensure its functioning. But agreement on this ultimate goal does not resolve the crucial issue of how to get there, which is ideally through a series of sequential steps that could be defined as follows: (a) to recognize inadequate institutions; (b) to focus on functions that need to be improved, mainly related to smoothing information asymmetries, defining and enforcing property rights and contracts, and regulating competition (Islam, 2002); and (c) to concentrate on relevant institutional design or structure that fits with the overall institutional environment prevailing in the economy. It is important to note that the heterogeneity of the three steps across different countries led NIE theorists to conclude that there is no blueprint for institutional development across all countries and there is no one specific sequence for it (Islam, 2002; Clague, 1997). Respectively, each country should follow a series of steps according to its own priorities, taking into consideration the differences in constitutional orders, cultural endowments, and inherited institutional arrangements. The NIE approach underlines the need for incentives to undertake reform. It emphasizes that what is required are reform strategies based on a careful understanding of the incentives facing actors in the current situation and on an examination of different alternatives to change the institutional equilibrium (Clague, 1997).

(c) *An NIE model of building institutions:* With respect to reform, there is always a need to investigate demand and supply. Demand usually varies from one organization to the other. Demand for institutional change is normally made either by agents who expect that new arrangements will provide them with better opportunities of capturing gains that are lost under existing arrangements (greater efficiency), or by actors dissatisfied by the current distribution of income or wealth. Important factors motivating the demand for institutional change are relative product and factor prices, the law making process, level of technology, and the size of the market (Zaki, 1999). With respect to supply, institutions are created by principals (political rulers or the owners of resources) to govern their relationship with other principals and with their agents (citizens, bureaucrats and employees), and principals are motivated to create institutions that maximize their individual utility. However, an important element that needs to be put into consideration is the cost required for the physical and human infrastructure needed for the design and implementation of new institutional reforms. Moreover, some laws usually need to be changed and here there is an associated cost of alternative choices (of institutional arrangements) available in the social, political and economic domains (Zaki, 1999).

Integrating the demand and supply sides together implies that the pressure of a competitive market as suggested by North (1990) is the most viable mechanism for selecting the most efficient economic institutions. The market's competitive pressure will select socially beneficial forms of economic organization, regardless of the intentions of the actors. If, instead, the creation of institutions is left in the hands of any dominant actor— such as the state, or a cohesive self dominant class— the product will be institutional rules that will give that actor a strategic advantage with respect to other actors, regardless of how socially sub-optimal the outcome of these institutions may be.

BACKGROUND

Electronic commerce promises great potentials for developing nations providing additional access to markets, information, and other resources that would have otherwise been inaccessible. However, the growing challenge of the digital divide and the need to develop measures to prevent it is of paramount importance to governments in developing nations such as Egypt. With respect to electronic commerce, the role of the government is different as opposed to other conventional domains requiring extensive research and substantial restructuring of the role it should play, including setting new rules for market operations and developing control measures to handle the risk associated with electronic commerce-related investments.

The role of the government in the functioning of the economy has experienced continuous change with an objective to pave the way for increased private sector participation. With respect to electronic commerce, the role of the government is different; it is not conventional in the sense of retreating or reducing its engagement, but rather it is a comprehensive new role that encompasses (a) setting the rules for market operations and (b) controlling the risks associated with investments. The role expected to be played by the government should focus on removing deterrents of electronic commerce such as lack of Internet connectivity. Despite rapid growth of the Internet, its access and penetration in developing nations is far below that in developed countries, as shown in Table 1, which demonstrates the growth rate of the Internet. It is important to note that in recent years many developing nations have experienced much more rapid diffusion of the Internet for the given availability of telephone lines than in some developed nations.

In developing nations, the collaborative role of the government and the private sector will be crucial in the diffusion of innovation and in the use of the Internet across the society at large, especially in remote and rural areas. This will be important to maintain the gaps created that lead to the digital divide and can also help reduce it. For example, the average OECD country has 70 times the number of telephone mainlines in developing nations than in sub-Saharan Africa, excluding South Africa. Wilson and Rodriguez (2000) found that an index of country inequality with respect

Table 1: Internet users by region

Region	Users (000)				Users/1,000 People			
	1995	1998	2000	2005	1995	1998	2000	2005
Worldwide	39,479	150,887	318,650	717,083	6.94	25.44	52.45	110.52
North America	26,217	82,989	148,730	229,780	89.4	275.7	479.1	715.4
Western Europe	8,528	34,741	86,577	202,201	21.67	87.54	217.5	501.4
Eastern Europe	369	2,983	9,487	43,767	1.26	10.2	32.7	151.8
Asia-Pacific	3,628	24,559	57,607	171,098	1.11	7.24	16.57	45.90
South/Central America	293	2,722	10,766	43,529	0.62	5.48	21.1	78.6
Middle East/ Africa	444	2,893	7,482	26,708	0.48	2.89	7.22	23.6

Source: Computer Industry Almanac, 2003

to access to communications including personal computers, Internet hosts, facsimile, mobile phone and televisions deteriorated substantially during the 1990s.

Electronic commerce can generate productivity gains by reducing transaction costs, even if the effects so far have proven to be small and limited (Oliner & Sichel, 2000). However, it is projected that within the United States electronic commerce could reach around 6 trillion US dollars by 2004 (Bermudez et al., 2000; Economist, 1999). At the global level, electronic commerce may account for around 25%

of world trade by 2005 (United Nations Conference on Trade and Development, 1999). But the distribution of Internet access among nations worldwide is extremely unequal and despite the rapid growth in Internet access in developing nations, developed nations still account for the majority of Internet subscribers (Suttle, 2000). However, recently, there is a growing share of Internet users in developing nations and in 2001, developing nations accounted for 33% of new Internet users worldwide (United Nations Conference on Trade and Development, 2002). Moreover, electronic commerce is also growing in developing nations but more slowly than the number of Internet users. In developing nations, the proportion of Internet users who are at the same time electronic commerce practitioners is lower than average owing to lower per capita income in addition to other factors such as low credit card usage, lack of relevant and needed products and services and poor logistics and fulfillment services (United Nations Conference on Trade and Development, 2002). In that respect, the gap between developed and developing nations in terms of access to and use of the Internet is smaller than the one in terms of electronic volumes (www.ecom.or.jp).

It is important to note that business-to-business predominates over business-to-consumer but remains small in developing nations. Table 2 shows that while the shares of developing nations in both business-to-business and business-to-consumer

Table 2: Forecast of total electronic commerce (B2B and B2C) in billions of U.S. dollars

Region	2002	%	2006	%	CAGR % 2002-2006
Developing Asia and Pacific	87.6	3.8	660.3	5.1	65.7
Latin America	7.6	0.3	100.1	0.8	90.5
Transition Economies	9.2	0.4	90.2	0.7	77.0
Africa	0.5	0.0	6.9	0.1	91.1
Total Developing Nations	**104.9**	**4.6**	**857.5**	**6.7**	**69.1**
North America	1677.3	73.1	7 469.0	58.2	45.3
Developed Europe	246.3	10.7	2 458.6	19.2	77.7
Developed Asia and Pacific	264.8	11.5	2 052.1	16.0	66.8
Total Developed Nations	**2188.4**	**95.4**	**11 979.7**	**93.3**	**53.0**
World Total	**2293.5**		**12 837.3**		

Source: Forrester Research, 2001

global electronic commerce are expected to remain small in the medium term, business-to-business could remain much weaker, with the proportion between business-to-business and business-to-consumer being 2.5 times smaller in developing nations than in North America (United Nations Conference on Trade and Development, 2002). It is important to note that as long as business-to-business does not take off in developing nations, electronic commerce volumes will remain negligible. Therefore, major efforts need to be put together to improve the infrastructure in developing nations, because business-to-business represents a unique developmental opportunity for developing nations since it can help enterprises and firms generate efficiency gains at all stages of their production and distribution processes. Such gains are vital for development since they effectively affect the competitiveness level, lead to increasing levels of productivity and respectively improve income levels for the economy at large.

IMPACT OF INTERNET GROWTH ON ELECTRONIC COMMERCE

The phenomenal growth of the Internet has certainly been one of the driving forces for the introduction and diffusion of electronic commerce worldwide. The Internet with its massive innovative capacities will no doubt boost efficiency and enhance market integration domestically and globally, especially in developing nations that are most disadvantaged by poor access to information. However, it is important to note that it can also have negative implications for nations that will not have access to information. The Internet, as an output of the information and communication technology evolution, is the largest network of computers in the world, providing a wealth of information and knowledge that reaches over 655 million users worldwide (www.nua.ie). Table 3 shows the current and projected global Internet population.

Electronic commerce is one of the most important topics in today's global business environment. Consequently, understanding the degree to which the Internet will change business and society is a vital research topic. The global society is currently witnessing a phase of transition from an Information Age that was physical to an Information Age that is digital (Lynch & Lundquist, 1996). This transition

Table 3: Global online population

Worldwide Internet Population 2002	Projection for 2004
580 million (Nielsen//Net Ratings) 655 million (International Telecommunications Union)	709.1 million (www.eMarketer.com) 945 million (Computer Industry Almanac)

Source: cyberatlas.internet.com (23 June 2003)

promises to cut costs, save time, increase revenue and provide a general digital sense of the world as one global digital village where people can communicate anytime and anywhere, and where time and distance barriers are reduced and in many ways removed (Kamel, 1995). Today, it costs only a small amount to use the Internet and the cost is going down by the day. In the near future, it will cost virtually nothing (Tapscott, 1996). While the underlying costs of telecommunications are collapsing, the Internet usage is experiencing an unprecedented exponential growth (Kalakota &Whinston, 1996). At the policy level, national and regional plans are being formulated as part of a global consensus to deregulate national networks, to open up nations and territories to competition, to forge alliances between former competitors and to wire up the three-quarters of the world that is still unconnected, in order to minimize the growing digital divide between developed and developing nations that is being perceived as an integral part of the global information society (European Union, 1997).

ELECTRONIC COMMERCE IN EGYPT

The government of Egypt has been instrumental in establishing the nation's information and communications infrastructure to support its developmental plans. The decision made at the highest level of policy making in 1985 was to build a national information infrastructure to become the platform for development of all sectors and industries through better allocation of resources and rationalization of the decision making process by using timely, relevant and accurate information. Since 1985, a public-private sector partnership for development had a remarkable impact on the build-up of Egypt's information infrastructure (Kamel 1995b). It included a large number of projects with effective implications on the different building blocks of the infrastructure including hardware, software, information, interconnectivity and human resources. Today, the information and communication technology sector is one of the largest in the Arab region (International Telecommunications Union, 2001). The Internet was introduced to Egypt in 1993 (Kamel, 1998a). Its use developed from being used solely by the government and academic institutions to becoming more of a standardized search and communication tool used by everyone in the society. The Internet use is constantly being encouraged by the government and by private investors who establish their own Internet service providers.

The Internet was first introduced to Egypt by the Egyptian Universities Network of the Supreme Council of Egyptian Universities. In 1994, as an attempt to diffuse the Internet usage among the society, the Cabinet of Egypt Information and Decision Support Center (IDSC) and the Regional Information Technology and Software Engineering Center (RITSEC) provided free Internet access on a trail basis to the public, private, government and non-government organizations to entice the users to venture into the new technology. This was done with the financial support of the government to aid in the exposure of the local market and to pave the way for the commercialization of the Internet services. The free access formula was accredited for contributing to the boost in the rate of growth of Internet users, especially within small and medium sized enterprises and industry and sector professionals (Kamel, 1998b). In 1996, the government replaced its free Internet access policy with an open access policy and Internet services for the commercial domain were privatized, and 12 Internet service providers started their operation. Today, there are around 50 ISPs serving over 2.2 million Internet users (Fahmi, 2003). Most of the Internet usage in Egypt is for business information gathering (Loch, Straub & Kamel, 2003). Egypt tops the index of bandwidth in the region with a score of 2.11 (American Chamber of Commerce in Egypt Report, 2002). In January 2002, the government of Egypt launched an initiative through its ministry of communications and Information Technology providing free nationwide access to the Internet to all citizens of the country, creating a larger demand for connectivity coupled with the establishment of over 3,000 Internet cyber-cafes in Metropolitan Cairo as well as other locations, and demonstrating the tangible intention of the government to diffuse the use of the Internet among the society.

The Internet evolution in Egypt demonstrates the active role played by the government. With the privatization of the Internet in 1996, the role of the government did not come to an end. The government still provides strong support for different Internet service providers in the form of upgrading the infrastructure to enable them to offer better connection speeds to their users as well as providing them with technical support. Additionally, the government is helping in training software developers in collaboration with local vendors and leading multinationals in the field. In terms of information as web content, the government is trying to magnify the outcome with an objective to make the Internet more relevant and appealing to the community (www.idsc.gov.eg). The efforts exerted by the government include the development of awareness and utilization of the Internet. There are also efforts done by non-government organizations such as the dissemination of economic information and applications developed by the private sector as information providers to encourage business transactions over the Internet. Some of these efforts are taking the form of portals, which are diversified between Arabic search engines, content sites for specific industries, online shopping sites, career services and special sites promoting trade and investment in Egypt (American Chamber of Commerce in Egypt, 2002). The development of portals and web sites in Arabic is one of the major challenges that hinder the growth of the Internet use in Egypt. A booster took place in 2001 with the launch of MSN Arabia; the portal is a product of a partnership between Microsoft Corporation and LinkdotNet, the largest private Internet service provider in Egypt. Other successful examples of Arabic content portals include gn4me.com, arabia.com, masrawy.com and moheet.com.

Moreover, the government has invested time and effort in making national economic information available on the Internet. For example, Egypt's State Information Service (SIS) (www.sis.gov.eg) includes information on investing in Egypt, its economic growth, foreign trade, agriculture and irrigation, industry, energy, transportation and tourism, among others. Additionally, the Information and Decision Support Center (IDSC) publishes its monthly economic bulletin online (www.economic.idsc.gov.eg). The bulletin includes key economic indicators reflecting the performance of the economy. The Egyptian Center for Economic Studies (ECES), an independent organization, publishes online series of articles to contribute to the discussion of ideas and policy options for enhancing economic development in Egypt. The Economic Research Forum (ERF) (www.erf.org.og) is a non-governmental organization whose mission is to provide an institutional mechanism to initiate and fund policy-relevant research, to disseminate research results, and to function as a resource base for researchers. The forum's web site has searchable databases with working papers, conference proceedings, and other publications. Moreover, the Egyptian International Trade Point (EITP) (www.tpegypt.gov.eg) was established in 1993 under the ministry of foreign trade to create international trade efficiency using the Internet, and it represents Egypt's electronic link to UNCTAD's Global Trade Point Network (GTPN). The web site targets listing of trade opportunities for Egyptian businesses, providing information on international customs, banks and packaging requirements, and establishing a database for Egyptian exporters and importers. Relating this to the theoretical model mentioned above, it is observed that the supply side was highly active.

Egypt is viewing electronic commerce as a venue to support business and socioeconomic development plans, where it provides opportunities for increasing trade, promoting investment, facilitating business transactions, providing a larger and more varied market and supplying an unparalleled marketing tool. Electronic commerce as a medium for foreign trade is a catalyst for export, implying a potential increase in Egypt's exports and a better formula for its balance of trade that will eventually have positive impacts on its economy. It can also enable the country to experience a more open economy and increase its comparative advantage worldwide. Many sectors could benefit from electronic commerce besides trading; this includes financial services (insurance, banking, trading); tourism; entertainment; music; advertising and marketing; information services, education and training; the media (electronic books, newspapers, journals, news services) as well as other services such as medicine and real estate. Moreover, it can create job opportunities where Egyptians will have the opportunity to venture and establish small and medium enterprises with global market access. For examples, software developers will be baled to work for international customers. The government of Egypt has formulated a national plan demonstrating its vision to prepare itself for a more competitive and global market environment that is enabled by the Information Age. The plan attempts to capitalize on the cutting-edge information and communication technology that could help rationalize the decision-making process and optimize the allocation of resources within the context of developing nations with all local conditions that relate to culture, norms and values (Kamel, 2000). The objective of formulating and implementing electronic commerce technologies has a strategic objective in leveraging the nation's business development and socioeconomic status. However, it is believed that in order to realize such a long-term objective, the following needs to be realized: (a) to formulate a framework for electronic commerce coherent with the national political, social and legislative environment and compatible with the global environment; (b) to develop the national information infrastructure required for electronic commerce; (c) to promote the use of electronic commerce through pilot projects; (d) to improve awareness and stimulate cooperation among all concerned parties including the government, the industry, the private sector and the general public and (e) to develop the human resources required for successfully enabling electronic commerce. Estimates for electronic commerce in Egypt are only available with respect to business-to-consumer commerce, indicating that only 6% of Internet users make purchases online based on a sample survey of 452 Internet users (American Chamber of Commerce in Egypt, 2002).

INSTITUTIONAL ROLE OF THE GOVERNMENT OF EGYPT

Egypt is in the early stages of adopting electronic commerce; the regulatory framework that defines the environment in which firms conduct business has evolved over decades and centuries. However, it has been adjusted to the needs of the old economy. No wonder then that the Internet economy, characterized by no frontiers, intangibility and to a certain degree, anonymity, requires adaptation of existing laws, rules and regulations. Because of the speed of electronic commerce development, the adaptation process in many cases lags behind, resulting in legal uncertainty (ECATT Report). As electronic commerce stretches over the borders the need for regulation at a national and international level prevails as a requirement. In principle, the institutional role of the government is based on the classical definition of Douglas North, where he identified institutions, or at least the formal institutions which we are concerned with, as the rules and regulations and their enforcement (North, 1990). Since institutions, using such definition, are wide, we will concentrate on the main issues that are of vital importance for electronic commerce, namely security issues which incorporate issues related to encryption and authentication in specific as well as telecommunications, taxation and banking at large. Unsecured transmission on the Internet is often cited as the main deterrent for a rapid growth of electronic commerce. Although much progress is being made in terms of security, the Net is still considered to pose a risk for commercial transactions. Although such lack of security stems from the fundamental design of the basic protocol suite, security measures can be implemented at various levels of Internet communications which are heavily affected by the institutional framework that governs such transactions. Establishing the required institutional infrastructure for electronic commerce is a challenging task. The difficulties encountered in establishing such infrastructure are embedded in the interrelation between the rules and regulations governing the electronic commerce activity per se and the rules and regulations in other domains, and especially in the telecommunications and financial sectors which highly affect the functioning of any electronic commerce transaction.

Formulation of an Electronic Commerce Law for Egypt (The Institutional Infrastructure)

The government has undertaken a number of initiatives to enhance electronic commerce such as the establishment of the Internet Society in Egypt's electronic commerce committee in October 1997; the issuance of ministerial decree number 2 in 1999 by the ministry of trade and supply to formulate a committee to develop the electronic commerce legislation; and, the formulation of the national telecommunications and information technology plan in January 2000 (Brown, 2000). However, all these initiatives remain short of providing an efficient institutional infrastructure capable of handling the promotion, governance and diffusion of electronic commerce. The main deterrent affecting tailoring a law for electronic commerce is a number of critical issues affecting the economy in general and electronic commerce in specific that do not have a foundation in the legal system in Egypt. This includes the legal enforceability of electronic documents, the lack of verifiable means for identities and transactions, controlling anonymity and providing a balance between privacy of deals and national security (United Nations Conference on Trade and Development, 2000).

It is important to note that nations have two alternatives to deal with the legal and institutional requirements of electronic commerce; either having a comprehensive law that regulates all issues related to electronic commerce, an option which a large number of countries have chosen including India, Malaysia, Canada and Germany, or opting for passing specific legislation as electronic commerce develops, an option chosen by the United States. Based on available documentations, Egypt has chosen the first option with efforts being put together to formulate a comprehensive law dealing with electronic commerce with a separate law for electronic signature (www.un.or.at). The currently drafted Egyptian electronic commerce law is comprehensive, dealing with issues related to electronic documents, electronic signature, authentication, encryption, consumer protection, fraud, privacy, taxes and tariff treatment and dispute settlement. However, the law is not detailed and delegates a large number of issues to the executive decree. Moreover, it gives the responsible minister a large room of discretion. Such two aspects have an advantage of making the law flexible but, on the other hand, it increases the uncertainty aspect by making the rules subject to continuous change and vulnerable to pressures from different interest groups. Another separate law is devoted for the electronic signature issue, which is still a draft as well. Following is a presentation of a number of important aspects related to the institutionalization of the role of the government with respect to electronic commerce and covering privacy, security, banking and taxation.

(a) *Privacy versus Anonymity:* Often the anonymity of the Internet makes it more attractive and increases the level of communications, but the anonymity suitable for political free speech often causes hindrance to commerce. Lack of identity can facilitate fraud and deception and can lead to numerous crimes that may not be possible in physical markets. Similarly, credit card frauds can occur even when merchants ask for proof that only the real owner can provide. A survey undertaken in the some Arab countries in 1998 revealed that only 33% of Internet service providers accept payments through their web sites, and only 20% provide a means for secure transactions (NUA Internet Surveys, 1998). Verification services based on digital signatures are being offered by commercial enterprises but still it is not pervasive and no explicit agreement across governments is enacted. Therefore, no matter what systems are supported in the market, continued international cooperation is imperative to achieve an interoperable encryption system capable to provide identity, confidentiality and non-repudiation. The current law in Egypt is tough on privacy violations. For example a firm cannot monitor employee electronic mails unless there is permission. In the banking sector, information cannot be given out even between banks without the consent of the customer (Brown, 2000). Thus the electronic commerce legislation addressing privacy must be carefully drafted to take into account principles in the local market yet recognizing how these principles may conflict with national security concerns and electronic commerce legislation laws in other countries. The current electronic law drafted preserves privacy.

(b) *Authentication:* The biggest vacuum in the legal framework for electronic commerce is lack of verifiable means for identities and transactions (Whinston, Stahl & Choi, 1997). Authentication refers to the ability to verify the identity of persons involved in transactions, which is vital for electronic commerce and can be addressed through a certificate authority, which is a public or private entity that issues digital certificates to be used by sellers and buyers to authenticate identities and messages or to assert that a deal has occurred. Digital certificates operate to verify identity or right to access information or services online; they can also identify web sites and software that are being sent over the web. In the drafted law there is no mentioning of the authentication issue; however, it is dealt with in the electronic signature drafted law. No certificate authority was identified but it is expected that there will be a number of national certificate authorities.

(C) *Encryption:* To secure confidential and authenticated messages, encryption and digital signature technologies that provide content-level security are already being adopted. Network level security secures the conduit, while encryption secures the content traveling through the conduit. At present the widespread use of encryption technologies is discouraged by the lack of technology to integrate encryption into applications, rather than by any impediments imposed by policy (Whinston, Stahl & Choi, 1997). The drafted law contains a provision on encryption; however it defers all of its details to the executive decree with the exception of identifying explicitly the governmental third party that will be responsible for archiving the encryption keys. Hence, the law preserves the secrecy issue but no assessment of the mechanism of ensuring the encryption process can be provided, as it is contained in the executive decree yet to be issued. The challenge that the government is likely to face arises from the relative lack of human and physical resources that are capable of handling such issues. The review of scrutiny and privacy issues in the law revealed that wording of the law emphasizes their importance; however, it delegates a large number of crucial details to the executive decree.

However, if it is assumed that the executive decree includes the necessary remaining provisions it is important to know whether this ensures the success of having an efficient institutional framework for the promotion of electronic commerce. The answer is contingent on the availability of two crucial determinants: (a) the enforceability of such law and other related laws should be guaranteed; and (b) the laws related to telecommunications, banking and taxes and customs administration should be restructured to include the electronic commerce patterns of conducting business in a market economy. With respect to the first issue, it is important to note that Egypt lacks the needed human resources to ensure the success of the law. Human capacities in the fields of law and Information Technology are inadequate and require extensive training to meet the challenge of implementing the law. Law enforcement officials must be aware of how to gather, preserve, and authenticate electronic evidence. This will not only require substantial training of law enforcement personnel, but also sufficient experience with such evidence by investigators, prosecutors, defense counsel, courts, and others until clear rules and standards are established. The volume of electronic evidence that requires analysis is also increasing substantially. The increasing use of computers and the Internet often means that information or records of communications that were previously never retained or routinely destroyed can be recovered, but such recovery may still require sophisticated computer techniques to handle them. With respect to the second issue, the existing laws related to telecommunications, banking, taxation and customs administration are either not ready to deal with electronic commerce or contain loopholes that can impede its success.

(d) *Telecommunications:* Electronic commerce is dependant upon an infrastructure that delivers high quality and high-speed connections. The telecommunications law determines the deployment of advanced services, the extent of universal service, the awarding of licenses to telecommunications providers and the scheme for the awarding of federal government spectrum. The telecommunications law is therefore essential for the success of electronic commerce and should be given as much attention as any electronic commerce legislation (Brown, 2000). The liberalization of the telecommunications sector is currently taking place by limiting government participation in services provision and confining it to the role of a policymaker. Success has been attained in the liberalization of Internet services and the provision of mobile and payphone services. Law Number 19 and Presidential Decree Number 101, both of 1998, were issued to separate telecommunications services provision (operator and the service provider) from the regulatory functions. The newly created Telecommunications Regulatory Authority (TRA) was assigned the independent regulatory functions and Telecom Egypt (TE) took responsibility only as the sole operator and service provider. In 1999, a new telecommunications law was drafted to further liberalize the telecommunications sector (American Chamber of Commerce in Egypt, 2001). TRA is tasked by the law to establish a number of policies and regulations that will ultimately affect electronic commerce; however, the problem arises from the fact that TRA is not separate from the government, creating a conflict of interest, and does not shield it from political influence, which is most likely to affect the progress of electronic commerce. Therefore, it is crucial that TRA is granted more independence to ensure its efficiency and its separation from the political influence.

(e) *Banking:* Egypt suffers from a divide between traditional local banking and international banking practices. For example, a paper system is still utilized to perform clearinghouse functions even though an electronic system would be more efficient. The current paper-based banking system deters electronic commerce. There is nothing that legally prevents banks from operating over the Internet, but because of security concerns they simply are not comfortable with Internet transactions. Thus, banks do not accept payments or transactions online even though they are not legally refrained from doing so. The general reluctance of banks to facilitate online credit card transactions is partially due to the lack of firm legislation to regulate the process. The Central Bank of Egypt perceives the importance of an electronic commerce law for the banking industry. Moreover, fraud legislation is needed to reduce risk and the criminal law needs to be modified to take into account bank practices. Liability should be clearly defined and privacy must be addressed because customer information cannot be exchanged, even among banks, without the prior permission of the customer (Brown, 2000; Business Monthly, 2001). Nevertheless, some private firms are moving forward and implementing IT services and devices, and hoping that the law will catch up. For example, some financial institutions are implementing a smart card system to encourage customers to engage in electronic transactions, with some of these cards having stored value in a chip and others operating as a debit card, such as Citibank, as well as Bank Misr, which started issuing pre-paid Internet cards, and most recently, the National Bank of Egypt started offering the Ahly Internet Card.

Another deterrent in the banking legislation is the inability to open a current account through an Egyptian bank for dealing directly with credit cards. This is due to the fact that the transaction is to be effected through an online server with the credit card service donor (Visa, MasterCard, etc.) which bankers call—the credit card center. In the case of Egypt, the number of credit card centers does not encourage expanding Internet transactions. Therefore, the web stores have to depend on a third party to deal with credit cards' collection of money, which is likely to increase the transaction costs and affect negatively the progress of electronic commerce in Egypt. Moreover, the credit card community in Egypt did not really boom until 1998, when banks started to include personal finance in the domain of their business activity. Prior to that date, banks followed a stiff regime in the process of credit cards issuance. As it was a must in order to issue a credit card to hold and block a time deposit collateralizing the limit with which the credit card is issued—not only this but also banks set relatively high limits as a minimal for issuance—this was around 3,000 U.S. dollars on average. However, since 1998, the banking system experinced major positive changes where banks started to enroll consumer finance in their business portfolios accompanied by an expansionary activity in issuance of credit cards. The rationale of holding time deposit collateral was evaded as the introduction of international banks to the banking industry pushed clean basis credit cards to existence. Banks currently ask for a proof of residence, personal ID and an official letter from the employer for issuing the credit card. However, the limiting factor is that all banks set a minimal wage limit of at least 250 U.S. dollars—which is the wage level that bank officials see appropriate to lower payback risk.

(f) *Taxation:* The distinction between sales and income tax becomes unclear when business is conducted via electronic commerce. However, most of all the fluidity of online taxable entities makes it difficult to establish at any one time what is being taxed, who should be taxed and who can impose taxes. If there is an attempt to apply tax laws to electronic commerce, the first task should be to determine which digital products are taxable under which tax mechanisms such as sales tax, income tax or royalty tax. In the case of tangible (physical) products sold over the Internet, existing tax laws will apply with less difficulty, but in the case of intangible (digital) products there need to be new definitions. For example, while shrink wrapped software is considered tangible property subject to sales tax, downloaded software from the Internet is considered intangible and may not be subject to sales tax. Even when digital products are defined as tangible properties the nature of the Internet may require tax code revisions or a new approach toward taxing transactions. According to existing worldwide regulations, businesses must collect and pay sales taxes if they maintain a substantial presence in the taxing jurisdiction and the same applies in the case of products that are intangible and related taxation (Whinston, Stahl & Choi, 1997).

The challenge is to design a taxation system that is capable of handling both tangible and intangible products and how to avoid circumvention from one mode of trade to the other to escape taxes and at the same time enhance electronic commerce. Moreover, the proposed regulation should be analyzed through a policy framework that ensures that online conduct is treated in a manner consistent with the offline conduct in a technology-neutral manner. The drafted law mentions explicitly the tax treatment of online vendors and advertisements on the Internet; however it deferred the tax treatment of electronic transactions to the executive decree and was silent about the treatment of products and services traded via the Internet. Moreover, the law mentions that Egypt will respect all the international agreements that are signed, implying the exemption from taxes and other duties on electronic transactions and digital products traded via Internet. The World Trade Organization (WTO) members agreed on temporary moratorium against the imposition of customs duties on electronic transactions per se since 1998 and have extended such moratorium (www.wto.org). Nevertheless, it should be mentioned that the existing estimates of lost tariff revenues related to the digital products are likely to be minimal, in the case of Egypt not exceeding 0.1% of total import duties and 0.01% of the total governmental revenue (Mattoo & Schuknecht, 2000; Schuknecht & Perez-Esteve, 1999). Hence, institutional concerns related to that matter should be left as the last step, as any advancement in that regard is likely to result in more costs than revenues.

ELECTRONIC COMMERCE READINESS

The extent of electronic commerce readiness is governed by the degree of information and communication technology diffusion and the institutionalization of the electronic commerce enabling environment. First, although computer penetration and access to the Internet has been growing steadily over the last years, it will take some time until a critical mass is realized. Second, a legal infrastructure governing business and financial transactions and protecting consumer rights cannot be taken for granted. Within this context, the extent of electronic commerce readiness in Egypt has been fairly limited, with the small number of Internet users (2.2 million) and the relatively prohibitive information and telecommunications costs, if compared in terms of per capita income to those in developed countries (Fahmi, 2003). However, it is readily apparent that the difficulties surrounding electronic commerce in Egypt have more to do with traditional ways of conducting business than with legal barriers. For example, one of the barriers is the fact that Egypt is a cash-based society and paper transactions are the dominant mode of conducting electronic commerce; whereas there are slightly over 600,000 credit card users but cards cannot be used online because most of the banks in Egypt do not authorize their use for transactions over the Internet. When linked to the theoretical framework and the model, the demand side is rather weak due to special concerns of weak institutions in other related fields. Table 4 demonstrates the barriers to electronic commerce in Egypt following the measures adopted by the benchmarking telework and electronic in Europe report (ECATT, 2000).

ROLE OF SOCIETY'S BUILDING BLOCKS IN SETTING UP AN ENABLING ELECTRONIC COMMERCE ENVIRONMENT

In the case of developing a national electronic commerce industry, the role of the government is a prerequisite, particularly in the early stages, and the government is expected to play a regulatory role, establish the ICT infrastructure and coordinate efforts at the top policymaking level as well as set an example to the best practice (Ghoneim, 2000).

However, other building blocks in the society have an integral role in enabling an electronic commerce environment. This includes the roles that could be played by the private sector and non-governmental organizations. Table 5 demonstrates the roles that could be played by the government of Egypt and that relate to (a) national strategy and institutional framework, (b) national information and communication technology infrastructure and (c) community development.

With respect to the private sector, non-governmental organizations and the media, there is also a vital role that can be played and that can help seize the numerous business opportunities made available and arising from adopting electronic commerce, as shown in Table 6.

CONCLUSION

Egypt's social and economic development is to a large extent determined by its most precious resource, "human resources", through its size and quality. The intellectual capital of a developing nation like Egypt represents a critical factor for its development and growth in the 21st century. It is important to note that the success of the economy will be determined by the quality of its human resources as the importance of natural resources steadily diminishes worldwide. Therefore, preparing the society for the Information Age necessitates appropriate investments in developing its human resources. In that respect, there is a growing need to formulate a new comprehensive policy to entice the use of information and communication technology in decision-making through accessing a wide scope of national and international information sources covering different sectors coupled with the development and improvement of knowledge capacities to be able to optimize the use of informa-

Table 4: Barriers to electronic commerce in Egypt

Lack of awareness of added value
There is considerable skepticism with regard to the added value of electronic commerce applications due to lack of interest by firms and users for online presence and shopping, respectively, due to lack of access or for security reservations.

Suitability of products for distribution
Not all products can be sold on the Internet. Statistics indicate that for many online shoppers in the Arab region (Egypt included), in 48% of the cases the main reason for buying online is the lack of product availability in the local market, followed by ease of purchase (45%), convenience of comparing products online (32%), comparing prices (24%) and ease of payment (21%). There is a lack of existence of well-established distribution networks to support remote products distribution. Currently, a hybrid model of traditional and online distribution networks is being deployed.

Costs and performance
The limitations of narrow band access have hampered electronic commerce evolution. Moreover, online shopping is perceived by many as an expensive pastime for Internet users rather than an efficient alternative to traditional shopping. The free Internet model introduced in 2002 might improve the situation.

Data security
Compared to private value added networks, the Internet causes considerable security concerns due to its open architecture, necessitating specific technological measures to make data exchange secured and reliable, such as encryption, which are costly. In the Middle East, users generally prefer sending credit card details by alternative methods such as the phone (27%), fax (31%) or email (15%) (DIT, 1998). There is a need to improve security and there is also an evident need for allowing for alternative payment methods to complement the use of the fairly limited credit card use in the society, such as cash on delivery, which suit the local consumer and allow for building trust and alleviating consumer concerns with regard to exchanging payment details over the Internet.

Consumer protection
In business-to-consumer electronic commerce, building trust requires measures that protect consumers from fraud and entitle them to consumer protection rights when buying from shops and retail outlets. There is a need to enhance buyers' awareness and to engage trust in online shopping. A vital user's concern lies in the collection of personalized data about shoppers in databases that may be used for purposes beyond the consent of the shopper, which needs to be dealt with in an appropriate copyright statement and could take the form of a new law for intellectual property rights relevant to the issues of the software industry.

Lack of critical mass
Online marketplaces work better with more consumers and suppliers involved. In Egypt, the market is still relatively small and in its early stages of development. Respectively, the problem is the lack of buyer demand to make online selling a viable and sustainable option but the situation is gradually improving though diversification in market segments that might have not been accessible through traditional retail outlets.

Table 5: Role of the government in setting up an electronic commerce environment

Role of the Government		
National strategy and institutional framework	*National ICT infrastructure*	*Community development*
• To ensure that the legal framework is favorable to electronic trading, defining the legal and regulatory measures that apply to governing business and inter-firm transactions and collaboration, including contract and commercial law, taxation and measures of arbitration and dispute settlement. • To develop the legislative framework addressing the cost and accessibility of telecommunications, intellectual property, privacy and the free flow of information. • To empower national agencies and encourage the creation of efficient and independent business associations, chambers of commerce and industry associations to coordinate electronic trading. • To foster the promotion and application of electronic trading through its use in public sector organizations. • To develop a strategic and shared vision for electronic commerce.	• To develop the national ICT infrastructure and competitively price to enable electronic trading. • To provide reliable low cost and widespread technological resources. • To improve continental interconnectivity and provide gateways to international telecommunication networks. • To establish national VANs dedicated to the provision of electronic commerce solutions to help set up the foundations of business-to-business environment. • To partner with international donor agencies to fund and develop the electronic trading infrastructure. • To encourage the private sector to support, help establish and use the information infrastructure. • To coordinate activities between industry practitioners and service providers. • To establish a framework ensuring the participation of all key players and beneficiaries in the industry.	• To maintain the flexibility to accommodate changing market and legal requirements. • To maintain state-of-the-art technology by establishing a monitoring mechanism to account for changes in the business requirements and technology developments. • To design, develop and implement national policies and plans adopting information and communication technologies within various sectors. • To promote the use of information and communication technology to improve the government and industry-based effectiveness. • To set an example through the adoption of electronic government applications and utilize electronic commerce trade facilitation applications in streamlining international trade processes with respect to import and export procedures. • To encourage the private sector to play an effective role in preparing the grounds for inter-firm partnerships through raising their awareness of potential electronic commerce trading benefits. • To encourage the private sector, NGOs and the media to play an active role in promoting electronic commerce.

Table 6: Role of the private sector, NGOs and the media in setting up an electronic commerce environment

Role of the Private Sector	Role of NGOs	Role of the Media
• To ensure that the role of the private sector could be reflected through stimulating growth and assuming market leadership in developing national ICT through investment and capitalizing on new business opportunities. • To support managers of small and medium size enterprises in information and communication fields. • To establish an organizational framework that eliminates constraints and supports business development. • To encourage the formulation of information services agencies.	• To identify the needs of rural communities and contribute in developing the capacity of its people to minimize the digital divide. • To assess the public concerns with respect to information and communication technology infrastructure needs. • To promote the concern of the workforce to different employers and the government.	• To spread awareness in rural areas of the importance and benefits of the information and communication technology evolution and its implications on business and societal development. • To promote electronic commerce in different newspapers, radio and television channels to provide an easy, accessible, and cheap means of diffusing information to end users. • To provide broad channels of communication to rural and remote communities.

tion to serve the different developmental efforts. Electronic commerce represents a dynamic model for the information society but neither the people nor the firms in many developed and developing nations are prepared for the new technology. Therefore, there is an invaluable need for more awareness creation and readiness to be provided by governments as well as public and private authorities. From a socioeconomic perspective there is a need for public and widespread participation in the evolving information society and for avoiding the risk of creating classes of information haves and have-nots. Electronic commerce will have a profound impact on businesses, institutions and individuals but there is a need to set up a favorable electronic commerce environment to face the challenge of strong internationalization of markets, globalization of corporate strategies, and the increasing mobility of capital and know-how that characterize the economic process worldwide. Finally, to relate the policy recommendations to the institutional framework, it seems that the institutions on the demand side need to be strengthened as well as institutions related to the indirect supply of electronic commerce, which is needed to reach a conducive environment for electronic commerce to function.

REFERENCES

American Chamber of Commerce in Egypt. (2001, April). *Business monthly.*

American Chamber of Commerce in Egypt. (2001, July). *Telecommunications in Egypt.* Business Studies Series.

American Chamber of Commerce in Egypt. (2002, April). *Information Technology in Egypt.* Business Studies Series.

Brown, M. (2000). *Advancing e-commerce in Egypt: Legal and regulatory recommendations.* Report submitted to the Ministers of Economy and Foreign Trade and Communication and Information Technology.

Chase, L. (1998). *Internet world: Essential business tactics for the Net.* New York: John Wiley and Sons, Inc.

Clague, C. (1997). The new institutional economics and institutional reform. In C. Clague (Ed.), *Institutions and economic development: Growth and governance in less developed and post socialist countries.* The John Hopkins University Press.

Electronic Marketing Bulletin. Available: *www.emarekter.com* (last visited December 10, 2001).

European Commission, Information Society Directorate General. (2000, August). *Benchmarking telework and e-commerce in Europe (ECATT) final report.*

Fahmi, H. (2003). The world of telecommunications. *Al Ahram Newspaper,* 8 June.

Ghoneim, S. (2000). *Developing a national EDI strategy: Opportunities & challenges.* Unpublished Ph.D. Dissertation, The Management School, Imperial College of Science, Technology & Medicine, University of London, UK.

Hammond, R. (1996). *Digital business.* London: Coronet Books.

Hashem, S., & Ismail, M. (1998, November). The evolution of Internet services in Egypt: Towards empowering electronic commerce. *Proceedings of the Global Marketplace for SMEs Conference*, Manchester, UK.

Information and Decision Support Center. Available: www.idsc.gov.eg (last visited: January 10, 2002).

Institute of Development Studies (IDS). (2001). *Policy brief,* Issue 14. University of Sussex.

Internet Society of Egypt. Available: *www.ise.org.eg* (last visited: January 09, 2002).

Internet Surveys. Available: *www.nua.ie* (last visited: October 20, 2001).

Islam, R. (2002). Institutions to support markets. *Finance and Development, 39*(1), March.

Kalakota, R., & Whinston, A. (1996). *Frontiers of electronic commerce.* Addison Wesley.

Kamel, S. (1995, May 21-24). Information superhighways, a potential for socioeconomic and cultural development. *Proceedings of the 6th International IRMA Conference on Managing Information and Communications in a Changing Global Environment,* Atlanta, Georgia, USA.

Kamel, S. (2000). Electronic commerce in Egypt. In M. Khosrow-Pour (Ed.), *Managing web-enabled technologies in organizations: A global perspective.* Hershey, PA: Idea Group Publishing.

Kosiur, D. (1997). *Understanding electronic commerce.* Redmond: Microsoft Press.

Lynch, D.C., & Lundquist, L. (1996). *Digital money: The new era of Internet commerce.* New York: John Wiley and Sons, Inc.Matto, A., & Schuknecht, L. (2000). *Trade policies for electronic commerce* (World Bank Paper, No. 2380).

Merriam-Webster's Collegiate Dictionary. (2000). *10th Edition.*

Ministry of Communication and Information Technology. Available: *www.mcit.gov.eg* (last visited: February 5, 2002)

Mintz, S. (1998). *The Internet as a tool for Egypt's economic growth* (an International Development Professionals Inc. Report).

Noll, R.G. (1997). *The international dimension of regulatory reform: With applications to Egypt* (Series of Distinguished Lectures, No. 8). Cairo: The Egyptian Center for Economic Studies (ECES).

North, D.C. (1990). *Institutions, institutional change and economic performance (political economy of institutions and decision).* Cambridge: Cambridge University Press.

NUA Internet Surveys (1998, April 23). *Electronic commerce in the Arab world - An overview*. Available: (*www.nua.com*).

Rodrik, D. (1997). Trade and the demand for social insurance. *Has globalization gone too far.* Washington, D.C.: Institute for International Economics.

Schuknecht, L., & Perez-Esteve, R. (1999). *A quantitative assessment of electronic commerce* (WTO Staff Working Paper ERAD-99-01).

Silverstein, B. (1999). *Business-to-business Internet marketing.* USA: Gulf Breeze Maximum Press.

Tapscott, D. (1996). *The digital economy promise and peril in the age of networked intelligence.* USA: MacGraw Hill.

Whinston, A.B., Stahl, D.O., & Choi, S. (1997). *The economics of electronic commerce.* IN: Macmillan Technical Publishing.

World Bank. (2001). *Building institutions for markets* (World Bank Development Report). Oxford: Oxford University Press.

World Bank and OECD. (1998). *A framework for the design and implementation of competition law and policy.* Washington, D.C. and Paris.

UNCTAD. (2000). *Building confidence: Electronic commerce and development.* United Nations.

Zaki, M. (1999). *Egyptian business elites: Their visions and investment behavior.* Cairo: Konrad Adenaur Stiftung and the Arab Center for Development and Future Research.

Chapter XIII

Linking Technological Compatibility and Operational Capacity Constraints to Communication Technology Adoption

Elliot Bendoly, Emory University, USA

Frederick Kaefer, Loyola University Chicago, USA

ABSTRACT

Two interacting issues have recently been shown to theoretically impact communication technology adoption: the willingness of business partners to use various communication technologies and a firm's operational capacity to accommodate the product/service demands of these potential partners. This study examines the relationship between these two issues and Electronic Data Interchange (EDI), a long standardized communication technology that has been underutilized by business organizations. Our findings suggest that the technological compatibility concerns of firms considering EDI adoption differ depending on if they are product or service oriented. Capacity limitations are found to significantly moderate these compatibility effects. The implications for managers of electronic commerce technologies are discussed.

INTRODUCTION

Developments in the Internet and new communication technologies for business transactions have been rapid, though widespread adoption has not. Vollmer (2001) writes that one of the most commonly specified reasons for delaying the implementation of such e-business technologies is the lack of standards typically associated with them. At the same time established standards for e-business have been in wide use for over 20 years–those associated with electronic data interchange (EDI). Yet, even though the use of EDI has been shown to have many benefits, only a relatively small percentage of firms have adopted the technology (Turban et al., 2002). This under-utilization of a very beneficial electronic commerce technology indicates that management requires more guidance and support for decision-making when considering whether or not to use EDI technologies to communicate with their business partners.

Recently published research has identified several factors that impact the potential benefits that EDI can have for a given organization (Kaefer & Bendoly, 2000). The conclusion of that research was that the simultaneous consideration of the interacting factors was important to reach the correct decision regarding the adoption of EDI technology. One of the relevant factors to emerge from that study was based on the idea that a variety of fundamentally different EDI and non-EDI options remain available to organizations and their business partners. Another factor stemmed from the belief that operational capacity can directly impact the extent to which modes of communication may effectively be used. That is, the greater the number of business partners the supplier can service, the greater need to accommodate transaction requirements through multiple modes of communication if such requirements vary among these business partners. The purpose of this research is to validate the usefulness of such complex considerations in real-world settings by empirically studying the relationship between technological compatibility constraints and operational capacity constraints on EDI adoption. In doing so, we hope to make a contribution that will support managers faced with these and other technology adoption decisions.

The structure of this paper is as follows. Following a more in depth discussion of related literature, we outline the various hypotheses of interest and the factors critical to their examination. The structure of the empirical study, nature of the data collected and methods used in analysis are provided and the findings of this analysis as it relates to the hypotheses proposed in this research are described. A discussion of implications and suggestions for future work are presented in closing.

BACKGROUND

In a recent survey, distributors and manufacturers reported that they still see EDI as an effective e-commerce tool for sending and receiving transactions, despite the growing popularity of the Internet and other available technologies (Avery 2001).

This survey found the primary motivation for engaging in EDI included the need for more accurate information, decreased labor costs and pressure from customers. Another motivation for using EDI instead of newer communications alternatives is that EDI standards exist and are well understood for purchase order documents and invoices, the most common e-business need in exchanging with trading partners (Vollmer, 2001).

Empirical research into the theorized benefits of EDI began two decades ago. Sufficient academic and trade articles had been published by 1993 to warrant Mukhopadhyay's benchmark review on the state of research in the area (Mukhopadhyay, 1993). Mukhopadhyay proposed the consideration of four primary factors when approaching empirical research into EDI benefits. The first outlined was the consideration of the IT context, specifying the type of systems and transactions involved, as well as the level of IT integration throughout the firm and among its partners. The second factor dealt with operational concerns, specifying the type of industry processes associated with EDI use and the characteristics of operational management policies. Network externality was suggested as a third factor, denoting the implications and characteristics of the supply chain partnerships involved. Exogenous factors such as the mitigating effects of industry and economy-wide characteristics were lastly proposed as relevant for consideration. The 1995 study by Mukhopadhyay et al. of Chrysler and its suppliers, and Lee et al.'s study of the retail industry (1999) would ultimately provide support for the application of this framework.

Building on this theoretical basis, Massetti and Zmud (1996) later outlined a second framework by which to distinguish firms that have adopted and utilized EDI technology. To structure this framework, these authors proposed four dimensions, roughly expanding upon Mukhopadhyay's original IT context and network externality concepts, along which the extent of EDI system use could be measured. These dimensions include the volume and diversity of EDI transactions, as well as the breadth and depth of networked partner relationships. By breadth, Massetti and Zmud were referring to the proportion of all partners utilizing the system, as well as the sheer number of such partners. Depth implied the level of integration between such partners (e.g., the proportion of all transactions performed along EDI modes).

In contrast to these external considerations, a subsequent study by Jones and Beatty (1998) focused on the internal benefits and internal technological compatibility to assess the benefits of EDI from the perspective of an organization. These authors assessed the validity and reliability of the items most commonly used to measure the perceived benefits of EDI and the internal compatibility of EDI with the existing organization. However, through their analysis they were unable to find support for positive effects of internal technological compatibility. The implication suggested by this finding is that benefits cannot be properly evaluated independent of a consideration of the external networks for which EDI use is intended. Subsequently this lends credence to greater focus on external issues.

The recent study by Chwelos et al. (2001) represents a return to these external considerations by presenting a model of EDI adoption that incorporates constructs that comprehensively address three categories of factors: technological, organizational and inter-organizational. These authors conclude that while the benefits of the technology or external pressure may motivate the adoption of EDI, there are a number of necessary conditions that contribute to the ability to adopt EDI. They further state that even motivated firms must have technical ability, available resources and willing trading partners before EDI adoption is possible.

A recently published study by Kaefer and Bendoly (2000) suggested two additional summary metrics that might be useful in describing the constraints faced by firms considering EDI adoption. These metrics are referred to as modal or technological compatibility and operational capacity (also referred to as capacitated allowance). In the original study developed by these researchers, these factors were defined as the ratio of useable (i.e., compatible) to available communication technologies, and the ratio of total operating capacity to total market demand, respectively. Both factors were shown to be strong summary predictors of adoption in the complex multi-attribute modeling scenarios examined. Conveniently, they also closely resemble conceptual factors depicted by Mukhopadhyay (1993), Massetti and Zmud (1996) and Chwelos et al. (2001). Therefore their extension and use within empirical research models was justified from a face validity perspective.

From the standpoint of Mukhopadhyay's framework, the technological compatibility factor incorporates issues of IT context and network externality, and is somewhat analogous to both Massetti and Zmud's concept of diversity and Chwelos et al.'s technological considerations. Since, technological compatibility refers specifically to the diversity of partner requirements, it addresses the notion that firms communicating with business partners that have diverse and conflicting needs may be forced into the adoption of a broader set of communication technologies. At the same time, when diversity is the result of only a limited number of business partners, firms may actively seek out more homogenous subsets of business partners to avoid additional technology setup costs. It is interesting to note that similar strategic concepts have already been well established in the mass customization and niche targeting literature of the operations management and marketing disciplines (Lampel & Mintzberg 1996, Sawhney 1998). However, the impact of this factor on EDI adoption hasn't received considerable empirical examination to date.

The operational capacity factor addresses the reality that in addition to the technological constraints imposed by a firm's market environment, a firm must also consider the impact that it's own operational constraints impose. Such a constraint is supported by the simultaneous consideration of Mukhopadhyay's operational concerns and network externality dimensions, and holds some marginal analogy to Massetti and Zmud's concept of breadth. Since the total volume of transactions faced over the planning horizon may be dependent upon the total physical volume of goods and services provided to contracted business partners, firms necessarily gauge (either directly or indirectly) their adoption decisions by the limitations of their own productivity and the availability of trading partners (Kauffman et al., 2000). In fact, 15.9% of the same firms studied by Aranchulam (1997) emphasized the significance of such availability and the capability to take advantage of it. Although this finding is suggestive, the explicit influence that such a restriction can have on the adoption of technologies has not yet been studied in any depth. One notable exception is the work by Dipak et al. (1991) in which the impact that supply constraints have on innovation diffusion is considered. The example that these authors focus upon, in fact, involves the adoption of telecommunication devices, though limited to the level of analysis of individual consumers.

Recent research supports the pursuit of further investigations into the interactions of these factors. Hart and Saunders (1998) claimed that the adoption decisions made by firms can be somewhat paradoxical when trade volume alone is used as a predictor of EDI suitability. At the same time, Arunchalam's (1997) survey of IS managers revealed that 36.3% of those responding considered non-automation and non-sophistication of customers to be a serious barrier to EDI adoption, though no explicit form to such a barrier was suggested. Still more encouraging has been the 1994 study by Premkumar et al. in which the relationship between cost and compatibility measures is examined with regard to its impact on internal and external EDI diffusion. Specifically, the findings of these authors support the idea that greater internal compatibility is associated with better adaptation to and diffusion of EDI. Inter-firm compatibility, however, was not an issue considered in depth.

RESEARCH FACTORS AND HYPOTHESES

As stated previously, formal definitions of the factors used in this research emanate from the theoretical paper by Kaefer and Bendoly (2000). The first of these factors, operational capacity (denoted OC), relates to a firm's physical capacity to satisfy the demand of a large number of business partners and is defined as follows:

$$OC = \frac{\textit{Total capacity of the supplier of products or services}}{\textit{Total available demand of all potential business partners}} \qquad (1)$$

This measures the number of business partners that a firm's operating capacity allows it to supply products or services. The range of values that OC may take are between 1, where the supplier may simultaneously satisfy the demand of all business partners, and 0, where the supplier may only accommodate a small proportion of the total demand for their products or services. Since the demand of business partners may vary, suppliers of products or services may at times elect to cater to either a relatively small number of large business partners or a relatively large number of small business partners, as permitted by their operating capacity. Communication technologies well aligned with operating capabilities allow firms the freedom to move between niche strategies or take middle-ground stances, selecting business partners not based on size but rather on profitability or other strategic factors. Consideration of this effect has been justified by the suggestions of related studies to date (Mukhopadhyay 1993, Massetti and Zmud 1996). The first hypothesis therefore follows:

H1: Supplier-firms with the capacity to accommodate a greater portion of their downstream buyer-market (OC) will be more likely to adopt EDI.

The evaluation of such a hypothesis requires both an assessment of a firm's current operating capacity for a particular good or service and an assessment of the needs of potential clientele. The availability of demand information on all clientele in a market would be ideal, however given a potentially large number of such business partners, the request for data on each from every supplier in a target survey population would prove impractical. The assessment of average demand per business partner is a much more manageable task in the context of supplier targeted survey work. The product of these average demands and the number of potential buying-firms in the market space serves as an estimate of total market demand.

The second factor, technological compatibility (denoted TC), measures the technological needs of business partners and is defined as follows:

$$TC = \frac{\textit{Average number of communication modes usable with business partners minus 1}}{\textit{Total number of modes of communication available minus 1}} \qquad (2)$$

The values of the technological compatibility measure fall between 0 and 1. A value of 0 is associated with scenarios in which each business partner is compatible with only a single mode of communication. A value of 1 signifies that all business partners may use any of the potential modes of communication considered. To differentiate between modes of communication that utilize EDI, the ratio of usable to available EDI technologies is referred to as EDI technological compatibility (TCE), and the ratio of usable to available non-EDI technologies as non-EDI technological compatibility (TCN). These constructs basically represent higher levels of specification for the technological considerations of recent authors (e.g., Chwelos et al., 2001). The following hypotheses can therefore be posed:

H2E: Supplier-firms facing higher levels of EDI technological compatibility (TCE) among business partners will be more likely to adopt EDI.

H2N: Supplier-firms facing lower levels of non-EDI technological compatibility (TCN) among business partners will be more likely to adopt EDI.

Of special interest are the potential interaction effects that capacity and compatibility issues might have with regards to adoption decisions. Regardless of the capacity to accommodate a relatively large number of business partners and transactions, compatibility can moderate the fraction of those business partners whose transactions can meaningfully be considered in EDI benefit assessments. At an extreme, a lack of compatibility may eliminate any potential for EDI benefit. Secondly, compatibility within a large business partner market might only be effective when a sufficient amount of business partner demand can be adequately accommodated by supplier capacity. With these considerations in mind, and due to the limited investigation of such interaction effects in both past and contemporary research, the following hypotheses are proposed for examination.

H3E: The positive impact of EDI technological compatibility (TCE) on the likelihood of EDI adoption will be greater in magnitude when a firm's capacity can accommodate a greater portion of their downstream buyer-market (operational capacity, OC).

H3N:The negative impact of non-EDI technological compatibility (TCE) on the likelihood of EDI adoption will be greater in magnitude when a firm's capacity can accommodate a larger portion of their downstream buyer-market (operational capacity, OC).

METHODS AND ANALYSIS

In order to obtain the information necessary to evaluate these hypotheses a survey was conducted of the 186 member firms involved in the IT Horizons Project, an on-going joint effort by university researchers and a corporate sponsor to determine the status of B2B, B2C and ERP proliferation in the manufacturing community. The corporate sponsor of the project, ManufacturingNet, is the developer and host of Manufacturing Net.com, one of the most popular on-line forums for manufacturers (Agnew, 2001). To elicit the information required to construct the technological compatibility factor, respondents were asked to provide expectations of the willingness of potential business partners to use various EDI and non-EDI technologies to conduct transactions, as well as the number of alternative technologies available (see Appendix A). For the operational capacity measure, respondents were asked to provide estimates of their total operating capacity, the number of potential buyer-firms in that market and the estimated average demand of each of these potential customers. Out of the 186 firms surveyed, 124 provided sufficiently complete responses to be used in the regression analysis of this work. Based on the descrip-

Table 1: Descriptive statistics of the respondent product and Mfg-service firms

	Product Firms		**Mfg-Service Firms**	
	Average	*(Std Dev)*	*Average*	*(Std Dev)*
Maximum Capacity	21.4M units	(80.5M)	157 jobs	(196)
# of Buyers in Market	264	(309)	203	(516)
Avg Demand/ Buyer	539K units	(1.58M)	17 jobs	(49)
Avg # of Compact EDI techs	0.925	(0.403)	1.433	(0.663)
# of other Non-EDI avail	2.27	(2.02)	5.36	(5.14)
Avg # of Compact Non-EDI techs	2.77	(2.04)	4.60	(3.71)
EDI Technological Compatibility (TC_N)	0.282	(0.137)	0.406	(0.212)
Non-EDI Technological Compatbility (TC_N)	0.372	(0.229)	0.353	(0.235)
Operational Capacity (OC)	0.319	(0.108)	0.503	(0.269)

tions provided by these firms, the sample was split into two separate populations: one consisting of firms whose primary source of income reported was production oriented (64 complete responses) and one consisting of firms whose primary focus was manufacturing-service oriented (60 complete responses).

Of the product manufacturing firms responding, 34.4% were in the electronics industry, 18.8% were industrial equipment manufacturers, 21.9% were instrument fabricators and the remaining 25.0% were predominantly machine tool manufacturers. Of the firms providing services to manufacturers, 28.3% were software or system providers, 16.7% were in the area of logistical control, 21.7% were accounting or finance oriented and the remaining 33.3% involved other forms of consulting services (R&D, HR training, marketing, etc.). Further descriptive statistics for the respondent firms are given in Table 1.

Due to the fact that each of the hypotheses involve a binary outcome (the adoption of EDI), the methodology used in interpreting the data collected was logistic regression. The use of logistic regression also enables the interpretation of the impact of different factors when simultaneously taken into consideration, specifically the potential interactive roles that compatibility and capacity can have in facilitating EDI adoption. This analysis essentially involves the estimation of a standard regression equation, whose unbounded dependent variable is transformed

Table 2: Logistic regression results for EDI adoption in product firms

	Without controls		With controls	
	w/o interactions	*w/ interactions*	*w/o interactions*	*w/ interactions*
Constant	0.221 (0.34)	0.287 (0.39)	0.129 (0.45)	0.17 (0.35)
TC_E	0.362 (0.84)	0.032 (2.14)	0.513 (1.95)	0.033 (2.48)
TC_N	-0.849 (0.31) *	-1.404 (0.70) *	-0.934 (0.62) *	-0.507 (1.07)
OC	0.818 (0.48)	0.832 (0.38)	0.537 (0.55)	0.729 (0.45)
$OC*TC_E$		1.739 (1.94)		2.228 (2.34)
$OC*TC_N$		1.928 (0.77) **		1.56 (0.71) *
% Correct	74.5%	79.4%	71.9%	75.2%
Nagelkerke R^2	0.234	.311	0.109	0.134

*** = Significant at the 0.01 level*
** = Significant at the 0.05 level*

into a variable restricted to the range [0,1]. Because of the nature of the transformation used, discussions of the estimated relationships tend to involve reference to the likelihood or odds that an observation falls within one of the two categories. Logistic regressions utilizing the adoption of EDI as the dependent variable were performed for each subpopulation of the sample. Four separate regressions were examined for each group to provide insights into the existence of the effects hypothesized.

The first two models evaluated considered the impact of the main factors of interest in the absence of additional controls, consisting of total transaction cost estimates and annual profit. The initial exclusion of these controls allowed an analysis of the maximum number of data points available since some of the responses to the size-based controls were incomplete (leading to reduced sample sizes of 32 and 29 for product and service firms respectively). This method also provided a means of testing the robustness of the coefficients on the factors critical to this study. The first model further only considers main effects of the factors central to this research, as does the third with the addition of the controls. The second and fourth models include the consideration of the interaction effects of the factors.

Table 2 provides the coefficient estimates (and standard errors of estimate) derived for the product firms in the sample. Shaded areas in this table show the exclusion of factors in any given model.

The first model, excluding both controls and interactions, provides support for hypothesis H2N, since the coefficient of TCN is both in the anticipated direction and is statistically significant (e.g., at the $p < 0.05$ level for both models). Support was not provided for hypothesis H1 or hypothesis H2E. Inclusion of interaction terms in the second model shows this emphasis shifting towards a moderated effect, OC*TCN. When the interaction of the two factors is considered, support is provided for hypothesis H3N. Support is not provided for hypothesis H3E; however, the signs on the coefficients correspond to those hypothesized. When controls are added, a slight reduction in the percentage of firms correctly classified through parameter estimates of logistic regression is observed. This reduction is essentially an artifact of the loss of observations due to missing control data (as mentioned earlier). Furthermore, the Nagelkerke R2 associated with these regressions showed a marked reduction due to this loss. Fortunately, the coefficients on terms that were statistically significant in the non-control regressions did not noticeably vary when the control was added, hence lending to the robustness of these effects.

As a final check on the appropriateness of operating capacity, the identical analysis was performed utilizing the number of current partners, rather than this factor, which represents the average potential number of partners. Consistently poorer fits were observed in such cases, supporting the earlier contention that the average long-term view might be more meaningful given the extent of such technological investments.

An equivalent line of analysis conducted on data provided by firms categorized as manufacturing service providers is presented in Table 3.

As a general observation, the regressions for service firms provided relatively worse fits than those performed for the product sub-sample. The first model evaluated provided support for both hypothesis H1 and hypothesis H2E. The second furthermore provided support for hypothesis H3E. Signs on these significant coefficients were again in the anticipated directions. Support for hypothesis H2N and hypothesis H3N, however, was not apparent.

As before, the addition of controls contributed to slight reductions in the percentage of firms correctly classified, and relatively large reductions in the Nagelkerke R2 observed. The loss of observations also reduced the statistical significance of specific parameters, such as the coefficients on TCE and that of OC in the presence of

Table 3: Logistic regression results for EDI adoption in Mfg-service firms

	Without controls		With controls	
	w/o interactions	w/ interactions	w/o interactions	w/ interactions
Constant	-0.632 (0.37) **	-0.597 (0.38) *	-0.305 (0.31)	-0.101 (0.30)
TC_E	198 (1.08) **	1.845 (1.12)	1.574 (0.91)	0.136 (1.21)
TC_N	0.403 (0.90)	0.303 (0.94)	0.351 (0.95)	0.245 (1.10)
OC	-0.413 (0.19) *	-0.337 (-0.17) *	-0.356 (0.12)	-0.244 (0.61)
$OC*TC_E$		1.457 (0.82) **		1.279 (0.83)
$OC*TC_N$		-1.095 (121)		-0.697 (0.71)
% Correct	70.3%	72.9%	67.6%	70.5%
Nagelkerke R^2	0.189	.220	0.099	0.107

*** = Significant at the 0.01 level*
** = Significant at the 0.05 level*

interactions, to p-levels above the 0.05 level. Fortunately, the signs and magnitudes of these coefficients appeared to remain stable. Furthermore, the coefficients on OC in the absence of interactions and OC*TCE remained statistically significant, again alluding to the robustness of the theoretical results.

DISCUSSION

The findings suggest that two interacting factors proposed in previous theoretical research find support empirically among both product and manufacturing service oriented firms. The most relevant compatibility considerations differ for product and service firms. Product firms tend to see the potential heterogeneity in the use of non-EDI modes by their business partners as a driving force for EDI adoption, whereas service firms see the willingness of their business partners to use EDI technologies as the primary driver. Operational capacity, as defined here, was shown to both significantly moderate technological compatibility effects and provide significant direct effects on adoption. In general, the greater the capacity for a firm to accommodate the demands of their market, the greater the effects of compatibility on their EDI adoption decisions. This result empirically supports the hypotheses regarding the interaction of the two factors studied. Although this study was limited to the consideration of a handful of factors that limit adoption, and the continuous evolution of EDI and other B2B technologies requires a continuous re-examination of adoption justification, several implications exist for both practitioners and researchers.

Implications for managers of electronic commerce technologies are that they would benefit from simultaneously considering both internal capabilities as well as the variety of business partner capabilities in assessing the benefits of technologies that they are considering adopting. In the specific case of Electronic Data Interchange, managers should attempt to assess the levels of technological compatibility and operational capacity that they currently face in order to support their decision on whether or not to adopt EDI (or other shared B2B technologies). If a firm finds that regardless of a relatively high level of technological compatibility among their potential future business partners, its own long-term operating capacity prevents it from taking advantage of the use of a common technology with a large enough number of partners, then the justification of adoption should be strongly questioned.

As a similar example, regardless of how large a percentage of market players a firm perceives themselves doing business with in the future, if they feel they will not be able to convince these partners to likewise adopt a common high investment technology, then alternate mechanisms for communication should be pursued. This interaction-based approach to communication technology adoption decisions is much more meaningful than the single item considerations supported by more traditional research studies (e.g.. Mukhopadhyay 1993) and is encouraged both by this study's findings and suggestions of more contemporary researchers (Chwelos et al., 2001).

Other implications from the findings reported here relate to the relative power of a firm in a marketplace. Such power in general has been cited in past research to have a important role in the adoption decision of business partners (Iacovou, Benbasat & Dexter 1995, Wang & Seidmann, 1995). Firms with greater relative levels of capacity may therefore also represent those more capable of ensuring adoption by their business partners. The consideration of the linkage of operational capacity to power and the joint effect of these two issues on technology adoption provides an interesting line of research for the future.

On a final note, the present study's ability to successfully extend analytically-driven theoretical results into an empirical realm is encouraging. Though this study focused on the role that these factors played in the adoption of EDI, a natural extension would be an investigation into the extent to which adopting firms realized anticipated benefits. If the logic behind the roles of these factors in the adoption process holds, hypotheses nearly identical to the ones posed here may be postulated and tested. Future work should focus on the evaluation of benefit and adoption decisions for alternate information technologies.

REFERENCES

Agnew, M. (2001). Syndicators spin out more news for Web sites. *InformationWeek,* 826, 90-93.

Arunchalam, V. (1997). Electronic data interchange: Issues in adoption and management. *Information Resources Management Journal*, 10, 22-31.

Avery, S. (2001). E-commerce study: EDI still popular among distributors. *Purchasing*, 130, 96.

Chwelos, P., Benbasat, I., & Dexter, A.S. (2001). Empirical test of an EDI adoption model. *Information Systems Research,* 12, 304-321

Dipak, J., Mahajan V., & Muller E. (1991). Innovation diffusion in the presence of supply restrictions. *Marketing Science*, 10, 83-92.

Hart, P. J., & Saunders C. S. (1998). Emerging electronic partnerships: Antecedents and dimensions of EDI use from the supplier's perspective. *Journal of Management Information Systems,* 14, 87-111.

Iacovou, C. L., Benbasat I., & Dexter A. S. (1995). Electronic data interchange and small organizations. *MIS Quarterly*, 19, 465-485.

Jones, M.C, & Beatty, R.C. (1998). Towards the development of measures of perceived benefits and compatibility of EDI: A comparative assessment of competing first order factor models. *European Journal of Information Systems,* 7, 210-220.

Kaefer, F. & Bendoly E. (2000). The adoption of electronic data interchange: A model and practical tool for managers. *Decision Support Systems,* 30, 23-32.

Kauffman, R. J., McAndrews J., & Wang Y. (2000). Opening the "black box" of network externalities in network adoption. *Information Systems Research*, 11, 61-82.

Lampel, J., & Mintzberg H. (1996). Customizing customization. *Sloan Management Review,* 38.

Lee, H. G., Clark T., & Tam K. Y. (1999). Research Report. Can EDI benefit adopters? *Information Systems Research*, 10, 186-195.

Malone, T.W., Yates J., & Benjamin R. I. (1987). Electronic markets and electronic hierarchies. *Communications of the ACM*, 30, 484-497.

Massetti, B., & Zmud R. W. (1996). Measuring the extent of EDI usage in complex organizations: Strategies and illustrative examples. *MIS Quarterly*, 20, 331-345.

Mukhopadhyay, T. (1993). Assessing the economic impacts of electronic data interchange technology. In R. Banker, R. Kauffman, & M. Mahmood (Eds.), *Strategic Information Technology Management* (pp. 241-264). Hershey, PA: Idea Group Publishing.

Mukhopadhyay, T., Kekre S., & Kalathur S. (1995). Business value of information: A study of electronic data interchange. *MIS Quarterly*, 19, 137-156.

Premkumar, G., Ramamurthy K. & Nilakanta S. (1994). Implementation of Electronic Data Interchange: An Innovation Diffusion Perspective. *Journal of Management Information Systems*, 11, 157-186.

Sawhney, M. S. (1998). Leveraged high-variety strategies: From portfolio thinking to platform thinking. *Journal of the Academy of Marketing Science*, 26, 54-63.

Turban, E., King, D., Lee, J., Warkentin, M. and Chung, H.M. (2002). *Electronic Commerce 2002: A Managerial Perspective*. Upper Saddle River, NJ: Prentice Hall.

Vollmer, K. (2001). The growth of the Internet means business needs more EDI, not less. *Internetweek*, 856, 25.

Wang, E. T. G., & Seidmann A. (1995). Electronic Data Interchange: Competitive externalities and strategic implementation policies. *Management Science*, 41, 401-418.

APPENDIX - QUESTIONNAIRE ITEMS FOR MEASUREMENT

1. Do you currently possess and make use of EDI technology for communicating with your customers? _____
2. What is your maximum operating capacity (in items of units produced) [for service firms, in terms of jobs or services rendered]? _____
3. How many potential buyers are in the market you are currently targeting? _____
4. What is the average demand per each of these buyers (in terms of units produced) [for service firms, in terms of jobs or services rendered]? _____
5. Consider each of the following EDI technologies. What is the likelihood that any one of these options would be technologically compatible for use by both your firm and each of your customers?
   Private EDI _______ [%]
   VAN EDI _______ [%]
   Internet ED _______ [%]
6. Consider each of the following Non-EDI technologies. What is the likelihood that any of these options would be technologically compatible for use by both your firm and each of your customers?
   Telephone _______ [%]
   Fax _______ [%]
   Automated-Fax _______ [%]
7. Aside from those listed, how many additional Non-EDI communication options are available to you? _____
8. What is the likelihood that any of these additional options would be technologically compatible for use by both your firm and each of your customers? _____ [%]

Previously published in the Journal of Electronic Commerce in Organizations, 1(2), 1-13, Apr/June, 2003.

Chapter XIV

Pushing Elusive Alliances into the Light - Discovering the Value of Informal Networks on the Internet

Rian van der Merwe, Curtin University of Technology, Australia

Leyland F. Pitt, Curtin University of Technology, Australia

ABSTRACT

Sociologists have for many years explored the value of social capital, or the resources embedded in social relations and social network structures. In recent years, organizational forms such as strategic alliances and network organizations have been an important new form of entrepreneurial venture, particularly in business markets. An important and often overlooked type of alliance on the Internet is what we call the "elusive alliance". These alliances are not formally acknowledged, they are difficult to identify and can often be unknown, even to the members of the alliance themselves. They consist of informal links and social networks on the Internet—unspoken connections and codes of conduct that are extremely valuable because of the social capital embedded in them. This chapter aims to find ways to formally identify and expand these alliances in entrepreneurial ways that will improve their effectiveness, usefulness and ultimately, their social capital, translated into financial returns. We use Social Network Theory as the framework to study these networks.

INTRODUCTION

Sociologists have for many years explored the value of social capital, or the resources embedded in social relations and social network structures (Lesser, 2000; Lin, 2001a, 2001b). In recent years, organizational forms such as strategic alliances and network organizations have been an important new form of entrepreneurial venture, particularly in business markets (Achrol, 1997; Achrol & Kotler, 1999). As new forms of cooperation, these organizational forms represent attempts by existing firms to exploit strategic opportunities as collaborators, with each bringing particular resources and skills, or both, to the alliance (Lewis, 1990; Lorange, 1990). Typically, there are outcomes for all parties, with positive or negative results being shared, according to some predetermined procedure. Academics have rushed to study these new organizational forms, for apart from simply being interesting, they represent important if ephemeral structures in a global business environment.

An important and often overlooked type of alliance on the Internet is what we call the "elusive alliance". These alliances are not formally acknowledged, they are difficult to identify and can often be unknown, even to the members of the alliance themselves. They consist of informal links and social networks on the Internet—unspoken connections and codes of conduct that are extremely valuable because of the social capital embedded in them. A good example of the elusive alliance is the countless number of web sites dedicated to music artists. Web sites relating to a particular artist may link back and forth between official and unofficial fan sites, and they may even link to e-commerce companies where fans can buy the artist's merchandise—e.g., Amazon.com or CDNow.com. This paper aims to find ways to formally identify and expand these alliances in entrepreneurial ways that will improve their effectiveness, usefulness and ultimately, their social capital, translated into financial returns. The framework we use to study these networks is Social Network Theory.

In general, social network theory explains the mechanisms and structures that individuals use to accumulate power in social settings, leading to the related construct of social capital (Scott, 1991; Wasserman & Faust, 1994). This can be viewed as an asset benefiting the actors who have possession of it and constituting a resource available to an actor defined by its function (Coleman, 1990). Contingent to the theory of social networks is the theory of structural holes (Burt, 1992). Structural hole theory views social capital as entrepreneurial opportunities inherent in structural disconnects. "Structural holes are disconnections or non-equivalencies between players in the arena... Structural holes are entrepreneurial opportunities for information access, timing and control" (Burt, 1992).

This short discussion on "Elusive alliances" and Social Network Theory leads us to the question that serves as the general definition of the research problem:

To what extent can Social Network Theory and its related constructs be used to describe and enhance elusive alliances on the Internet?

This chapter explores this problem by investigating the following specific research questions:

1. Can Social Network Theory and Social Capital Theory be used to describe the formation of elusive alliances on the Internet?
2. Can Social Network Analysis be used to identify key nodes and links in the network?
3. Once the key nodes or links in the network have been identified, can the distinguishing characteristics of these actors be described in managerially useful ways? More specifically:
   (a) Can those nodes that are at the center of successful strategic alliances be used to influence a large network of nodes more effectively?
   (b) Can Structural Hole Theory be used to find entrepreneurial opportunities in these networks?

It is necessary to understand the basics of network theory as well as to have an idea of what this theory may explain, before an in-depth study to answer these questions can be commenced. This chapter starts with a review of Social Network Theory and Structural Hole Theory. It continues to describe how these theories can be applied to networks on the Internet, and elusive alliances in particular. An example of a large elusive alliance network in the service industry is then presented and analyzed. Areas for future research are identified, and in closing some conclusions are drawn about managerial implications and the limitations of the study.

Social Network Theory and the Theory of Structural Holes

Social network theory is based on the network concept, which "emphasizes the fact that each individual has ties to other individuals, each of whom in turn is tied to a few, some or many others, and so on" (Wasserman and Faust, 1994). It is possible to model these relationships between individuals to represent the structure of the network. These models use actors and ties to represent networks. Actors are defined as "discrete, individual, corporate, or collective social units … e.g. people in a group, departments within a corporation, public service agencies in a city, etc." (Wasserman & Faust, 1994). Ties are the relationships between actors. Through network analysis techniques it then becomes possible to "study the impact of the structure on the functioning of the group and/or the influence of this structure on individuals within the group" (Wasserman & Faust, 1994). Social network theory thus provides an alternative to the notion that actors function independently, making their own choices without consideration of the actors around them with which they have ties or relationships. Its strong theoretical and mathematical basis provides a framework for testing hypotheses about social relationships and their influences.

As a natural extension of Social Network Theory, social capital deals with the intrinsic value of network structures. In general terms, social capital "consists of resources embedded in social relations and social structure, which can be mobilized when an actor wished to increase the likelihood of success in a purposive action" (Lin, 2001b). Lin (2001a) points out two important components concerning this definition. First, resources are embedded in social relations rather than in the individual. The properties of the network and an actor's position in that network are more important than the actor himself. Second, access and use of these resources are dependant on an actor being aware of their presence. If an actor is not aware of ties or relationships between him and other actors, he cannot use the resources available to him. Social capital then seems not to exist, and will only come into existence for that actor once he becomes aware of it. The ability to identify networks and key role-players in these networks will therefore make it possible to identify social capital where the relevant actors may be completely unaware of them.

From the definition it is inferred that social capital depends first on an actor's position in the network (is he in the right place to access the resources?), and second it depends on the nature of the resources in the network (are the resources worth accessing?). Adler and Kwon (2000) summarize the many benefits of social capital as follows:

- Social capital provides actors in the network with access to broader sources of information at lower costs.
- Social capital provides actors in the network with extended power and influence.
- Social capital facilitates solidarity between actors, as strong networks encourage compliance with rules and customs without the need for formal controls.

Without elaborating on the mathematics, we will explain social network analysis here briefly by focusing on very simple network structures, namely one-mode directional and nondirectional networks. One-mode networks are made up of a single set of actors, e.g., people or organizations. Directional ties in a network have an origin and a destination, for example person A regards person B as a close friend, which does not necessarily mean that person B regards person A as a close

Figure 1: Directional vs. nondirectional networks

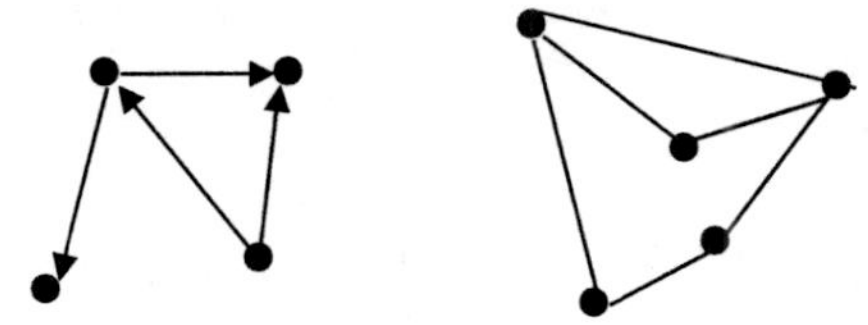

Figure 2: Redundant vs. non-redundant links (taken from Burt, 1992:17)

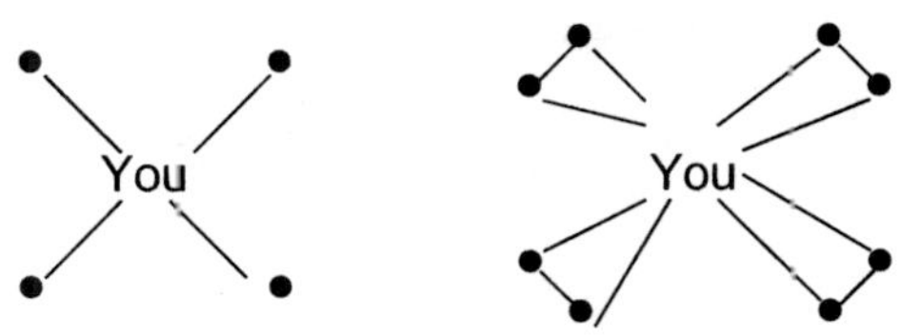

friend as well. Nondirectional ties have no direction, for example if person A lives near person B, it automatically implies that person B lives near person A. We will use graph theoretic notation to represent maps of the social networks. These graphs are also referred to as sociograms (for a more detailed description of graph theory and other theoretical approaches to social networks (see Wasserman & Faust, 1994). The sociogram in Figure 1 shows the different notations for directional and nondirectional ties.

An important concept relevant to our discussion is that of redundancy. Contacts are redundant when they lead to the same people, and therefore to the same information (Burt, 1992). Consider the two networks in Figure 2.

In Figure 2, there are four links with actors in the network on the left. In the network on the right, there are 8 links with other actors. However, some of the actors in the network on the right are connected to each other, and therefore lead to the same contacts and the same information. Each of the four connections between these eight actors consequently results in one redundant link. Both networks in Figure 2 therefore have four non-redundant links. Even though the network on the right has more apparent links than the one on the left, 4 of these links are redundant.

When social networks are constructed and sociograms set up, network analysis techniques can be used to identify key attributes and characteristics of the networks. Table 1 outlines the characteristics and constructs that are used in this study.

Table 1: Outputs of social network analysis (summarized from Wasserman and Faust, 1994)

Characteristic	**Description**
Actor prominence	The ties of the actor make it particularly visible to other actors in the network. These actors are identified using *centrality* measures and *prestige* measures.
Actor centrality	Different measures that investigate the amount of ties an actor is involved in: • *Degree centrality* measures the proportion of actors that are adjacent to a particular actor. • *Closeness centrality* measures how close an actor is to all the other actors in the network. • *Betweenness centrality* identifies actors that are between many actors in their linkages with each other.
Actor prestige	Different measures that investigate which actors are the object of extensive ties, thus focusing solely on the actor as a recipient. • *Degree prestige* measures the relative amount of actors that link to a particular actor. • *Proximity prestige* only measures actors adjacent to a particular actor.
Cohesive subgroups	Subsets of actors among whom there are relatively strong, direct, intense, frequent ties. Also referred to as *cliques*.

Figure 3 : A graphical example of a structural hole

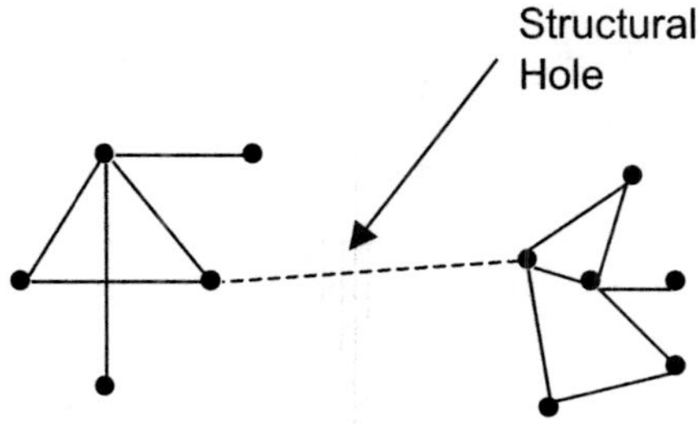

The actor dynamics especially (centrality, prominence and prestige) can be very useful for business networks on the Internet, as this will identify the most influential actors in the network. A relevant expansion of Social Network Theory is Ronald Burt's theory of structural holes, to which we now turn our attention. This theory aims to explain "how competition works when players have established relations with others" (Burt, 1992).

In general networks provide two types of benefits: information benefits and control benefits. Information benefits refer to who knows about relevant information and how fast they find out about it. Actors with strong networks will generally know more about relevant subjects, and they will also know about it faster. According to Burt, "players with a network optimally structured to provide these benefits enjoy higher rates of return to their investments, because such players know about, and have a hand in, more rewarding opportunities" (Burt, 1992, p. 13). Control benefits refer to the advantages of being an important player in a well-connected network. In a large network, central players have more bargaining power than other players, which also means that they can, to a large extent, control many of the information flows within the network.

Burt's theory of structural holes aims to enhance these benefits to their full potential. A structural hole is "a separation between non-redundant contacts" (Burt, 1992). The holes between non-redundant contacts provide entrepreneurial opportunities that can enhance both the control benefits and the information benefits of networks. Figure 3 shows a graphical representation of this definition.

We will now look at how structural holes can facilitate the optimization of information benefits and control benefits.

Structural Holes and Information Benefits

There are several ways to optimize structural holes in a network to ensure maximum information benefits:

- *The size of the network.* The size of a network determines the amount of information that is shared within the network. You have a much better chance to receive timely, relevant information in a big network than in a small one. The size of the network is, however, not dependant merely on the number of actors in the network, but the number of non-redundant actors. The utility of a network with reference to its size can be described by a function known as Metcalfe's Law. Robert Metcalfe, founder of 3COM Corporation and the designer of the robust Ethernet protocol for computer networks, observed that new technologies are valuable only if many people use them. Specifically, the usefulness, or utility of the network equals the square of the number of users (Metcalfe's Law, 1999). The more people use a piece of software, a network, a particular standard, a game, or a book, the more valuable it becomes and the more new users it will attract, increasing both the utility and the speed of its adoption by still more users. Therefore, a large network of non-redundant contacts will provide the biggest information benefits.

- *Efficient networks.* Efficiency in a network is concerned with maximizing the number of non-redundant contacts in a network in order to maximize the number of structural holes per actor in the network. It is possible to eliminate redundant contacts by linking only with a primary actor in each redundant cluster. This saves time and effort that would normally have been spent on maintaining redundant contacts.
- *Effective networks.* Effectiveness in a network is concerned with "distinguishing primary from secondary contacts in order to focus resources on preserving primary contacts" (Burt, 1992, p. 21). Building an effective network means building relationships with actors that lead to the maximum number of other secondary actors, while still being non-redundant.
- *Weak ties.* In his 1973 paper entitled "The strength of weak ties", Mark Granovetter (1973) developed his theory of weak ties. The theory states that because a person with strong ties in a cluster more or less knows what the other people in the cluster know (e.g., in close friendships or a board of directors), the effective spread of information relies on the weak ties between people in separate clusters. "Weak ties are essential to the flow of information that integrates otherwise disconnected social clusters into a broader society" (Burt, 1992). Structural holes describe the same phenomena as weak ties because both emphasize the need for entrepreneurs to fill the gap between different clusters and non-redundant contacts. Structural holes go one step further, though, and stress that what makes the gap important is not the weakness of the tie but the structural hole over which it spans. Building and maintaining weak ties over large structural holes enhances information benefits and creates even more efficient and effective networks.

To achieve networks rich in information benefits it is necessary to build large networks with non-redundant contacts and many weak ties over structural holes. Some of these information benefits are:

- More contacts are included in the network, which implies that you have access to a larger volume of information.

- Non-redundant contacts ensure that this vast amount of information is diverse and independent.
- Linking with the primary actor in a cluster implies a connection with the central player in that cluster. This ensures that you will be one of the first people to be informed when new information becomes available.

Structural Holes and Control Benefits

Once structural holes are defined within a network and the network is optimized to provide maximum information benefits, an important question is how these benefits can be used to capitalize on the opportunities in the network. Control benefits answer this question. Structural holes not only provide information benefits, they also give actors a certain amount of control in negotiating their relationships with other actors. To understand the role of structural holes in this regard, it is necessary to understand the concept of tertius gaudens. Taken from the work of George Simmel, the tertius gaudens is defined as "the third who benefits" (Simmel, 1923). It describes the person who benefits from the disunion of two others. For example, when two people want to buy the same product, the seller can play their bids against one another to get a higher price for the particular product. Structural holes are the setting in which the tertius gaudens operates. An entrepreneur stepping into a structural hole at the right time will have the power and the control to negotiate the relationship between the two actors divided by the hole, most often by playing their demands against one another. A relevant case in point is that of Calyx & Corrola. Established in 1988, this company stepped into the structural hole between flower growers and flower-buying customers by aiming to deliver flowers directly from grower to customer within 12 days of cutting. Normally, growers deliver their flowers to different sellers who then sell the flowers to customers. These flowers are generally one to two weeks old. Owner Ruth Owades said: "I envisioned a table with three legs, and Calyx & Corrola was only one of them. The second was the best flower growers available, and the third was Federal Express, the number one air carrier" (Wylie, 1991). Customers place their orders by mail, phone, fax or the Internet. These orders are transmitted electronically to growers, who then use FedEx to ship the completed order (Watson, Zinkhan & Pitt, 2000). As the tertius gaudens between grower and customer, Calyx & Corolla has control over the relationship between them. By cutting the flower shops out of the equation, they can negotiate price and distribution with a large amount of power because they are connected directly to the customer.

Linking Information and Control Benefits – The Power of Structural Holes

Where structural holes provide a platform for tertius strategies, information is the substance with which the strategy is performed (Burt, 1992). Accurate, timely and relevant information delivered between two non-redundant contacts at the right time creates an immense opportunity to negotiate and control the relationship between these actors. That is the power of structural holes, and that is why the theory is so relevant for business networks on the Internet. The next section will elaborate on this.

The concept of structural autonomy binds the theory together in an attempt to identify the actors in a network that are best positioned for the information and control benefits that a network can provide. An actor's goal is first to have no structural holes at their end of the relationship (as these holes could be used by other actors to develop relationships for their benefit, or even to replace the actor); and second to have as many structural holes at the other end of one's relationships with actors (to optimize the entrepreneurial opportunities available to one). "Players with relationships free of structural holes at their own end and rich in structural holes at the other end are structurally autonomous" (Burt, 1992).

Social Networks and Structural Holes Applied to Elusive Alliances on the Internet

Can Social Network Theory and the Theory of Structural Holes be applied to networks on the Internet, and how would this be useful to practitioners and researchers? That is the issue this paper intends to address. In an attempt to answer this question, the theory is applied to a large elusive alliance on the Internet. We investigate the informal online connections formed by Citigroup Australia (www.citigroup.com.au), an international banking company specializing in personal, corporate and investment banking.

In order to apply the theory on the Internet, it is firstly important to define some of the key concepts. The actors or nodes are distinct web sites, and the relationships or links between them are the hyperlinks provided on one web site to go to one of the other web sites. For each of the web sites in question, it is thus asked does web site X link to web site Y? It is important to note that if X links to Y, it does not necessarily mean that Y links to X. We are therefore constructing a one-mode directional network.

The Citigroup Australia web site was studied to identify all the hyperlinks linking to pages outside the site. Ten external links were found. Each of these 10 web sites was then visited in turn to see (1) whether or not they link back to Citigroup Australia and (2) to which external web sites each of them link in turn. The external web sites identified in this iteration were then visited to check whether or not they link back to the site from which the link originated. The study was thus performed by identifying external links up to the third level away from Citigroup Australia. A sociogram matrix with 47 nodes was then constructed (see Appendix A).

Analysis of the data occurred in three stages:

- Prominence analysis (centrality measures and prestige measures)
- Cohesive subgroups (clique analysis)
- Structural hole analysis

This process is progressive as well as recursive—each stage is important not only to the next stage, but each stage also calls the analyst back to the previous stage. For example, prominence measures largely determine the nodes on which structural hole analysis will be performed, and structural hole analysis is interpreted using both the prominence measures and clique analysis. Each of these stages will now be discussed. Two software packages were used to perform the analysis, namely UCINET V and STRUCTURE (for these and other software packages that can be used for social network analysis, see http://www.heinz.cmu.edu/project/INSNA/soft_inf.html). UCINET V is one of the most popular, comprehensive and user-friendly social network analysis tools. STRUCTURE was written by Ronald Burt specifically to do structural hole analysis.

Prominence Analysis

Three centrality measures were computed, namely degree centrality, closeness and betweenness. Degree centrality calculates a normalized value of the amount of actors adjacent to a particular actor. This is an important measure because it provides "an intuitive notion of how well connected a point is within its local environment… the corresponding agent is central in the sense of being 'well-connected' or 'in the thick of things'" (Scott, 1991). Because this is a directional network, we divided this measure into two parts, namely out-degree and in-degree. Out-degree computes the number of links sent to another actor, while in-degree refers to the number of links received by each actor (Valente, 1995). Results for the top actors in each category are shown in Table 2 and Table 3.

It is interesting to note that Salomon Smith Barney Australia with 35 outgoing links have only two incoming links. It is clear that these measures should therefore

Table 2: Out-degree centrality

Web Site	**Out-Degree**	**Normalized Out-Degree**
Salomon Smith Barney Australia	35	76.087
SSB Access	26	56.522
Citigroup Australia	10	21.739
Axiss Australia	8	17.391
Australian Prudential Regulation Authority	7	15.217
Citigroup Global	6	13.043
Citibank SSB	5	10.870
SSB Global Equities On-line (GEO)	5	10.870
Citibank Global	4	8.696
Diners Club International	4	8.696

Table 3: In-degree centrality

Web Site	In-Degree	Normalized In-Degree
Citibank Global	10	21.739
Australian Bureau of Statistics	5	10.870
Australian Taxation Office	5	10.870
Citibank Australia	5	10.870
Citigroup Australia	5	10.870
Australian Stock Exchange	4	8.696
Bloomberg	4	8.696
Citibank SSB	4	8.696
Citigroup Global	4	8.696
Citigroup Private Bank	4	8.696
Diners Club International (Australia)	4	8.696
Reuters	4	8.696
Salomon Smith Barney Global	4	8.696

be analyzed separately, and in conjunction with the measures to follow, before any conclusions are made about the level of centrality of a particular actor. Also note that Citigroup Australia is present in both tables, as would be expected.

Closeness measures how close an actor is to all the other actors in the network. Wasserman and Faust (1994) elaborate by saying that "an actor is central if it can quickly interact with all others… actors occupying central locations with respect to closeness can be very productive in communicating information to other actors". The measure finds actors with the shortest communication paths to the others. Again, different measures for out-closeness and in-closeness were calculated. The top actors in each category are shown in Table 4 and Table 5.

Table 4: Out-closeness centrality

Web Site	Out-Closeness
Salomon Smith Barney Australia	77.966
Securities Institute of Australia	65.714
Citigroup Australia	56.098
Diners Club International (Australia)	37.705
Australian Indigenous Leadership Centre	36.220
Learning Links	36.220
Diners Club International	28.571

Table 5: In-closeness centrality

Web Site	In-Closeness
Salomon Smith Barney	3.498
Citibank Global	3.415
Citibank Australia	3.410
Citigroup Private Bank	3.410
Citibank SSB	3.407
Citibank e-Business	3.395
Citibank Icard	3.367
Personal Banking for Overseas Employees	3.367
Worldwide Securities Services	3.365

The third and last dimension of centrality that was measured is betweenness. Betweenness identifies actors that are between many actors in their linkages with each other. This measure is important because "a point of relatively low degree [centrality] may play an important 'intermediary' role and so be very central to the network… The betweenness of a point measures the extent to which an agent can play the 'broker' or 'gatekeeper' with a potential for control over others" (Scott, 1991). In this sense it is strongly related to Structural Hole Theory. The actors that scored highest on this measure are shown in Table 6.

As expected, Citigroup Australia, as the originating web site, has the highest betweenness centrality.

Table 6: Betweenness centrality

Web Site	Betweenness
Citigroup Australia	184.400
Salomon Smith Barney Australia	141.683
Citibank	57.583
Citibank SSB	49.533
Diners Club International (Australia)	47.000
Citigroup	25.517
Citibank Australia	19.700
SSB Global Equities On-line (GEO)	6.233
Axiss Australia	4.833
Diners Club International	3.000

Clique Analysis

Cohesive subgroups, or cliques, are subsets of actors among whom there are relatively strong, direct, intense, frequent ties. The method of n-cliques was used to analyze the subgroups in this network. In traditional clique analysis, a clique is defined as "a subset of nodes, all of which are adjacent to each other, and there are no other nodes that are also adjacent to all the members of the clique" (Wasserman & Faust, 1994). n-cliques is different in that it specifies a cutoff value, n, as "the maximum path length at which members of the clique will be regarded as connected" (Scott, 1991). A basic clique analysis of adjacent actors is therefore an n-clique with n = 1. We decided on an often-used value of n = 2. A 2-clique "is one in which the members are connected either directly (at distance 1) or indirectly through a common neighbor (distance 2)" (Scott, 1991).

Of the many different ways to analyze n-cliques in directional relations, we used recursively n-connected cliques. This means that there is a path of length n or less from i to j, and a path of length n or less from j to i, and the path from i to j uses the same nodes and arcs as the path from j to i, in reverse order (Wasserman and Faust, 1994). A UCINET V analysis using n=2 and a minimum set size of three actors identified six 2-cliques, shown in Table 7.

We can see that Citigroup Australia features extensively in these cliques.

Structural Hole Analysis

The final stage of this network analysis is structural hole analysis. Burt's (1992) STRUCTURE software was used for this purpose. The analysis was performed on the Citigroup Australia Web Site, which is the starting point of this network and naturally also one of its most central actors. The analysis calculates several measures, the most important of which are:

- Oi, the lack of holes around the actor itself.
- cij, the constraint of absent primary holes. An actor's (i) entrepreneurial opportunities are constrained to the extent that another of his contacts (q), with whom he has a strong relationship, invested heavily and therefore also has a strong relationship with actor j. To put it another way, "your entrepreneurial opportunities are constrained to the extent that you have invested the bulk of your network time and energy in relationships that lead back to a single contact" (Burt, 1992). cij must therefore be low for structural holes (entrepreneurial holes) to exist.
- pij, the "proportion of i's network time and energy invested in each relationship" (Burt, 1992).

Structural holes occur around a specific actor when he has a large Oi (no or few structural holes around the actor himself); and there is a large pij and a small cij at the other end of a relationship with another actor (large amount of time and energy

Table 7: n-clique analysis

Nr	Actors in 2-clique
1	Citibank Global
	Citibank Australia
	Citibank e-Business
	Citibank SSB
	Citigroup Private Bank
2	Citibank Global
	Citibank Australia
	Citibank I-card
3	Citibank Global
	Citibank SSB
	Worldwide Securities Service
4	Australian Indigenous Leadership
	Center
	Citigroup Australia
	Dinersclub Australia
	Learning LinksSSB Connect
5	**Citigroup Australia**
	Dinersclub
	Dinersclub Australia
6	**Citigroup Australia**
	SSB ConnectSSB Access

invested in the relationship, small constraint on the actor's entrepreneurial opportunities). These conditions give rise to what Burt (1992) calls the hole signature of an actor. This visual representation of the difference between pij and cij provides an easy way to identify the structural holes around a specific actor.

Structural hole analysis for CitigroupAustralia revealed an Oi=1, which means that there are no structural holes around this actor. Further analysis revealed the following values for pij and cij, shown in Table 8.

The signature hole is shown in Figure 4. A large band in the hole signature indicates an opportunity relationship, "relationships in which the player has the greatest room to negotiate, and so control" (Burt, 1992). Narrow bands indicate constraint relationships, where "the player is most out of control" (Burt, 1992). A

Table 8: Structural hole analysis for Citigroup Australia

Web Site		p_{ij}	c_{ij}	$p_{ij} - c_{ij}$
A	Salomon Smith Barney Australia	0.0450	0.1333	0.0883
B	Diners Club International (Australia)	0.0194	0.1333	0.1139
C	Australian Indigenous Leadership Centre	0.0178	0.1333	0.1155
D	Learning Links	0.0178	0.1333	0.1155
E	SSB Access	0.0163	0.0667	0.0504
F	Citigroup Global	0.0070	0.0667	0.0597
G	Citigroup Private Bank	0.0059	0.0667	0.0608
H	Citibank Australia	0.0053	0.0667	0.0614
I	Citigroup Asset Management Australia	0.0053	0.0667	0.0614
J	Australian Institute of Aboriginal and Torres Strait Islander Studies	0.0044	0.0667	0.0623
K	Citibank SSB	0.0044	0.0667	0.0623

third category, residual relationships, is reserved for instances where a small amount of time and energy is invested in a particular actor (small pij). These relationships are usually ignored, as "there is little to protect and little to gain by alleviating constraint" (Burt, 1992). It should be noted, however, that these actors could potentially have value to the main player if the relationship is developed further.

From the table and figure it is clear that the biggest entrepreneurial opportunities exist between Citigroup Australia and Diners Club International (Australia),

Figure 4: Hole signature for Citigroup Australia

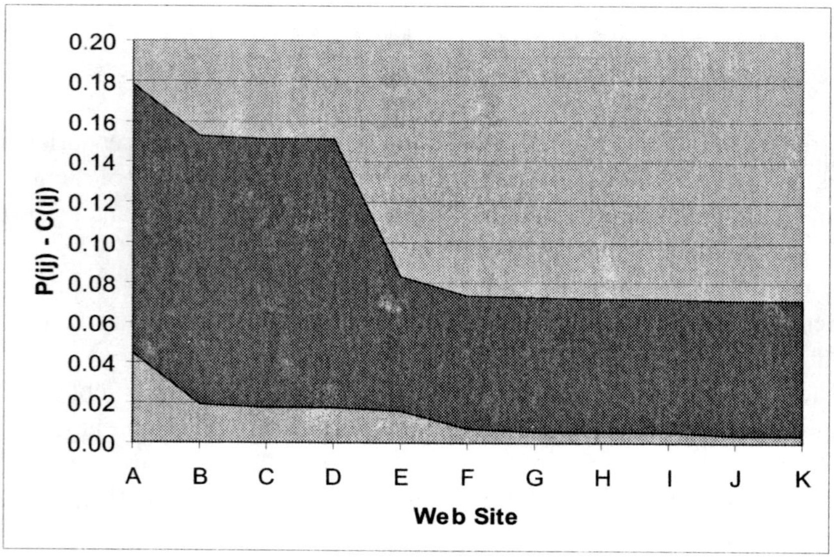

Australian Indigenous Leadership Centre and Learning Links respectively. These are the opportunity relationships in this network.

INTO THE LIGHT (INTERPRETING THE RESULTS)

The two important outcomes from this analysis enable us to answer research questions 3a and 3b posed in the Introduction, namely:

- Can those nodes that are at the center of successful strategic alliances be used to influence a large network of nodes more effectively?
- Can Structural Hole Theory be used to find entrepreneurial opportunities in these networks?

First, the prominence analysis calculated three measures that can be used effectively to identify the most important actors in the network. The specific measure(s) used in the interpretation depends largely on the nature of the network and what the marketer intends to accomplish in the network. For example, if the intention is to introduce information to a network of web sites as fast as possible, in-degree centrality, in-closeness centrality and betweenness would be the best measures to use, as these measures indicate which actors are most likely to be reached when someone visits one of the sites included in the network. Studying these measures for the Citigroup Australia network, the measures will therefore lead us to introduce new information on web sites like Citibank Global, Citigroup Australia, Salomon Smith Barney and Salomon Smith Barney Australia. The 2-clique analysis confirms these results, as most of these sites are part of one or more cliques. Centrality measures are also strongly linked to the diffusion of innovations. Valente (1995) notes "For networks, structural centrality is associated with more rapid diffusion for advantageous innovations and slower diffusion for more risky/uncertain innovations". Centrality is therefore not only an important measure to decide which actors are the most influential in a network, it also directly effects the speed with which new information is disseminated.

Secondly, the structural hole analysis identified three possible entrepreneurial opportunities in the network, namely between Citigroup Australia and Diners Club International (Australia), Australian Indigenous Leadership Centre and Learning Links respectively. These opportunity relationships can now be investigated to see whether or not it is practically possible to find a tertius strategy. In this case, the most interesting opportunity exists between Citigroup Australia and Diners Club Australia. The fact that Diners Club is a subsidiary of Citigroup also raises some interesting questions. If these companies are in business together, why is there a structural hole between them? A typical tertius gaudens strategy in this case will involve a third-party organisation that puts itself between these two organisations and negotiates the relationship between them. An entrepreneurial opportunity for the third-party organisation may be to serve as in intermediary not only between these two organisations, but between Citigroup and its other subsidiaries as well. This new network will free up resources for Citigroup that has previously been tied up in managing relationships between and among subsidiaries. The third-party organisation will then spend most of its resources on managing these complex relationships. Citigroup will have effectively outsourced their network management function, freeing up valuable resources that can be used for core business functions.

Every network will have a different structural hole analysis output, and each network should be analysed and interpreted separately. The Citigroup case shows that although it is impossible to provide a set blueprint for interpreting the results, each network and its analysis will raise enough questions to point the researcher/ manager in the right direction to identify entrepreneurial opportunities.

Conclusions and Managerial Implications

This chapter established an answer to the first question in the research problem stated in the Introduction: Can social network theory and the theory of structural holes be used to describe the formation of strategic alliances in business markets on the Internet? The answer is yes, it can. The paper also scratched the surface of the other two questions in the research problem. It showed how maps or sociograms can be created to represent business networks on the Internet; it showed how Social Network Theory will enable us to identify important actors; and it showed how network theory, combined with the Theory of Structural Holes, can be used by managers to identify entrepreneurial opportunities in their own market and beyond.

One limitation of the research is that only one network was used to illustrate the point, and there may therefore be a limitation to the generalization of the findings. Future research could apply this method to more (and even larger) networks in order to establish whether or not the findings of this paper are accurate. Further research will also expand on these preliminary findings and seek ways to formalize the argument for proper use in any industry.

This research permits the identification of strategic alliances and networks without the disadvantage of intrusive effects that result from survey or case research. Not only does it permit the description of networks and alliances, it also allows the identification and depiction of key nodes within them—links or main players who form the basis of the network structure.

As mentioned in the paper, and as illustrated in the Citigroup Australia case, there are two main uses of this information. First, prominence analysis can be used to identify the most important actors in a network. This information is essential for managers who want to disseminate information into a network as quickly as possible. Prominence measures not only allow managers to identify the actors that will have the most influence on the network, it also shows them which actors to target if they want to distribute the information in the network in the fastest way possible. This observation finds a strong tie-in with and is thoroughly backed up by Diffusion of Innovation theories (see Valente, 1995 and Rogers, 1995). Second, managers can use this information to identify entrepreneurial opportunities in the network, and it will also give them an indication of the opportunities that may exist around themselves—opportunities that can be exploited by third-party organizations.

In a world that is increasingly global, these two important outcomes are a vital contribution to our knowledge of business marketing and strategy.

REFERENCES

Achrol, R. S. (1997). Changes in the theory of interorganizational relations in marketing: toward a network paradigm. *Journal of the Academy of Marketing Science,* 25(1), 56-72.

Achrol, R. S. and P. Kotler (1999). Marketing in the network economy. *Journal of Marketing,* 63, 146-164.

Adler, P. S. and S. W. Kwon (2000). *Social Capital: The Good, the Bad, and the Ugly. Knowledge and Social Capital - Foundations and Applications.* E. L. Lesser. Boston, MA: Butterworth Heinemann.

Burt, R. S. (1992). *Structural Holes: The Social Structure of Competition.* Cambridge, MA: Harvard University Press.

Coleman, J. S. (1990). *Foundations of Social Theory.* Cambridge, MA: Harvard University Press.

Granovetter, M. S. (1973). The Strength of Weak Ties. *American Journal of Sociology,* 78, 1360-1380.

Lesser, E. L. (2000). *Leveraging Social Capital in Organizations. Knowledge and Social Capital - Foundations and Applications.* E. L. Lesser. Boston, MA: Butterworth-Heinemann.

Lewis, J. (1990). *Partnership for Profit - Structuring and Managing Strategic Alliances.* New York: Free Press.

Lin, N. (2001a). *Building a Network Theory of Social Capital. Social Capital - Theory and Research.* In N. Lin, K. Cook and R. S. Burt. New York, Aldine de Gruyter.

Lin, N. (2001b). *Social Capital - A Theory of Social Structure and Action.* Cambridge: Cambridge University Press.

Lorange, P. (1990). Building Successful Strategic Alliances. *Long Range Planning,* (December), 34-46.

Metcalfe's Law (1999). Online: http://searchnetworking.techtarget.com/sDefinition/0,,sid7_gci214115,00.html. Accessed on May 13, 2002. Last updated on Nov 25, 1999.

Rogers, E. M. (1995). *Diffusion of Innovations,* 4th ed. New York: Free Press.

Scott, J. (1991). *Social Network Analysis - A Handbook.* London: Sage Publications.

Simmel, G. (1923). *The Sociology of Georg Simmel.* New York: Free Press.
Valente, T. W. (1995). *Network Models of the Diffusion of Innovations.* NJ: Hampton Press.
Wasserman, S. & K. Faust (1994). *Social Network Analysis - Methods and Applications.* Cambridge: Cambridge University Press.
Watson, R. T., G. M. Zinkhan and L. F. Pitt (2000). *Object-Orientation: A New Perspective on Strategy.* Academia/Industry Working Conference on Research Challenges.
Wylie, D. (1991). Calyx & Corolla, Boston: Harvard Business School.

Previously published in the Journal of Electronic Commerce in Organizations, 1(2), 14-31, Apr/June, 2003.

Chapter XV

Technology Trust in Internet-Based Interorganizational Electronic Commerce

Pauline Ratnasingam, Central Missouri State University, USA

Paul A. Pavlou, University of Southern California, USA

ABSTRACT

Trust in Internet-based Business-to-Business (B2B) e-commerce is an important issue for both practicioners and academicians. Whereas the traditional notion of dyadic interfirm trust primarily focuses on trust in a trading partner firm, trust in e-commerce also implicitly incorporates the notion of trust in the transaction infrastructure and underlying control mechanisms (technology trust), which deals with transaction integrity, authentication, confidentliality, non-repudiation, and best business practices. This researcch explicitely examines this new institutional character of trust in B2B e-commerce, arguing that business value realization is heavily dependent on the dimension of technology trust, captured as perceived benefits and actual organizational performance, even after controlling for the positive effects of partner trust. Given the absense of adequate metrics to capture the notion of technology trust in B2B e-commerce, this research develops and validates a measure for technology trust and tests its effec on benefits and performance. This chapter contributes to theory by bridging the gap between technological solutions (technology trust) from an institutional trust perspective, trading partner trust (relationship trust) and business value (perceived benefits and organizational performance). The proposed theoretical model is tested in organizations actively involved in B2B e-commerce using survey methodology. The findings from 288 firms validated the importance of technology trust for organizational success in B2B e-commerce.

INTRODUCTION

Internet-based information technology has revolutionized the way information is shared among organizations, resulting in radical transformations of organizational practices for procurement, deliveries, and financial transactions. The Internet is also promoting the inception of a major directional change in inter-organizational relationships, which encompasses relational contracting, working partnerships, and trust-based relationships (Dwyer, Schurr & Oh, 1987; Morgan & Hunt 1994, Cannon & Perrault 1999). Previous research suggests that trust in Internet-based business to business (B2B) e-commerce is an important factor for both practitioners and academicians alike (Heil, Bennis & Stephens, 2000; Hoffman, Novak & Peralta 1999, Keen, 2000, Pavlou 2002). In sum, the literature on inter-organizational relationships has shown that trust is a key factor for relationship success. Trust is a key element of social capital (Mayer et al., 1995), and it has been related to desirable outcomes such as supplier performance (Ganesan, 1994) conflict reduction, (Zaheer et al., 1998), satisfaction (Geyskens et al., 1998), and competitive advantage (Barney & Hansen, 1994).

Whereas the traditional notion of trust has predominantly focused on trust in the trading partner, trust in e-business implicitly incorporates the notion of technology trust, which is broadly described as the subjective probability by which organization assess that the underlying technology infrastructure and control mechanisms are capable of facilitating inter-organizational transactions according to their confident expectations (Ratnasingam & Pavlou, 2002). Drawing upon the rich trust literature and recent conceptualizations of the role of trust in business relationships and e-commerce (e.g., Lee & Turban, 2001; Tan & Thoen, 1998), trust is explicitly viewed both from the traditional social (trading partner trust), and also from a technological perspective (technology trust). As described in this article, the technological perspective draws from the notions of institution-based trust (Zucker, 1986), structural assurances and situational normality (McKnight et al., 1998; Pavlou & Ratnasingam, 2003), and impersonal structures (Shapiro, 1987).

The proliferation and hype of the Internet for B2B e-commerce has increased the focus of trust on e-commerce technologies. The confidence that large trading partners had in using EDI via value-added-networks (VANs) in the late 1980s was not an issue because the VANs came with embedded security mechanisms that provided formal acknowledgements and locked the registered trading partners. On the other hand, the Internet enables large and small-medium-enterprises (SMEs) to transact around the clock (24x7) with limited security mechanisms using Internet-based EDI, extranets, and Web services. For example, extranets are mostly implemented by a single organization who permits registered trading partners to visit a private web site protected by a firewall. Moreover, online B2B marketplaces have also become important in e-business (Bakos, 1998; Palmer, Bailey & Faraj, 2000; Pavlou, 2002; Sarkar, Butler & Steinfeld, 1995), and an increasingly large number of inter-organizational transactions occur over their technology platforms. Forrester Research (www.forrester.com) predicts that transactions through these B2B marketplaces will reach $2.7 trillion in 2004 (Blackmon, 2000). However, the spatial and temporal separation between buyers and sellers imposed by the Internet generates an additional uncertainty around online transactions. Therefore, since the Internet is exposed to the public and is inherently known to be an insecure environment for B2B e-commerce, we propose that technology trust is even more critical in these situations and requires explicit conceptualization beyond the traditional view of dyadic trust in specific trading partners.

This study aims to examine the importance of establishing technology trust (via security services and best business practices) that contributes to inter-organizational trust. However, technology trust does not aim to substitute the traditional view of trading partner trust, but it rather aims to complement it as an important means of creating business value. In doing so, this study contributes to the trust and e-commerce literatures by proposing a unique scale of measurement for technology trust derived from the security and institutional trust literatures. The study's practical contribution comes from the measurement scale applied in technology trust for e-commerce practitioners to become aware, measure, develop, and nurture technology trust. We believe that given the increasing importance of B2B e-commerce and the uncertain nature of the Internet environment in the digital economy, understanding the underlying factors that help build technology trust is of fundamental managerial importance.

In this study we examine the new character of trust, aiming to provide theoretical and empirical insights on the following questions: (1) What is the nature and role of trust in B2B e-commerce? (2) What is technology trust and how does it create value in B2B e-commerce? The chapter is organized as follows. In the next section, we examine the literature on technology trust and its relationship to business value leading to the development of the research model and a justification of the research hypotheses. We then describe the research design, sample characteristics, instrumentation and administration of the survey in the research method section. Finally, we present the findings and discuss them in light of managerial and theoretical implications, concluding with suggestions for future research.

LITERATURE REVIEW

Previous research on technology trust mostly focused on security issues. In this study, we introduce technology trust derived from institutional technology infrastructures and protocols embedded as security mechanisms in Internet-based B2B e-commerce applications as governance mechanisms embedded in best business practices. This line of reasoning is consistent with institutional trust initially suggested by Zucker (1986) and extended by McKnight et al. (1998). Institutional trust in the context of B2B e-commerce resembles a network of organizations that are governed by specific structures and policies in the form of institutional mechanisms, assurances and guarantees. For example, in her seminal study, Zucker (1986) suggests that institution-based trust is the most important mode by which trust is created in an impersonal economic environment (without familiarity) and similarity (communality), providing evidence that trust was formed not because people knew each other personally, but because of existing institutional structures such as; licensing, auditing, laws and governmental enforcement bodies. Institutional trust provides favorable conditions conducive to situational success (Pavlou & Gefen, 2002). This suggests that if the Internet provided favorable conditions, such as legal, regulatory, business, and technical environment perceived to support situations, it would be possible to build trust and promote favorable trusting outcomes (McKnight & Chervany, 2002). Thus, they rely on structural assurances and situational normality. We adapt structural assurances that refer to beliefs that protective structures – guarantees, contracts, regulations, promises, legal recourse, processes or procedures as best business practices conducive to situational success (Shapiro, 1987; Zucker, 1986). Situational normality, on the other hand, refers to beliefs that the situation is favorable to situation success (as the existing Internet-based B2B e-commerce applications have embedded security mechanisms that facilitate technology trust) (Pavlou & Ratnasingam, 2003).

McKnight and Chervany (2002) describe institutional-based trust as a critical part of Internet transactions. Based on these arguments, we propose the term "technology trust" to capture a subset of institution-based trust, drawing from the adherence to technical standards, security procedures, and protection mechanisms. Institution-based trust has its origins in the sociological literature, suggesting that beliefs, intentions, and behaviors are generated by situations followed by impersonal assurances that expectations can be fulfilled. Shapiro (1987) describes institution-based trust as the belief that a party has about the security of a situation because of guarantees, safety nets, and other structures. Following McKnight et al. (1998), structural assurances contribute to technology trust in a B2B marketplace as it creates safeguards and beliefs that organizations are bounded to behave in a trustworthy manner. Structural assurances are associated with trust because of cognitive consistency, especially when experience is not a major factor. McKnight and Chervany (2002, p.13) advance this argument to today's B2C e-commerce, arguing that beliefs that the Internet has legal or regulatory protection for consumers (institution-based trust) should influence trust in a particular e-vendor (interpersonal trust). Based on these arguments, we expect institutional structures that contribute to technology trust should positively influence buyers' trusting beliefs (inter-organizational trust). However, this study does not propose inter-organizational trust as a mediating variable, aiming to focus on the direct value-added role of technology trust. Hence, this paper focuses explicitly on technology trust and its direct impact on business value in B2B e-commerce.

CONCEPTUAL DEVELOPMENT

The conceptual framework specifying the proposed research hypotheses is shown in Figure 1.

Novel Character of Trust in B2B E-Commerce

Following the extant definitions of trust (e.g., Doney & Cannon, 1997; Mayer et al., 1995; Rousseau et al., 1998) applied to an e-commerce context, we define inter-organizational trust in B2B e-commerce as "the subjective probability with which organizational members collectively assess that a particular transaction will occur according to their confident expectations" (Ratnasingam & Pavlou, 2002). The focus on a particular transaction suggests that trust in B2B e-commerce cov-

Figure 1: Research model and research hypotheses

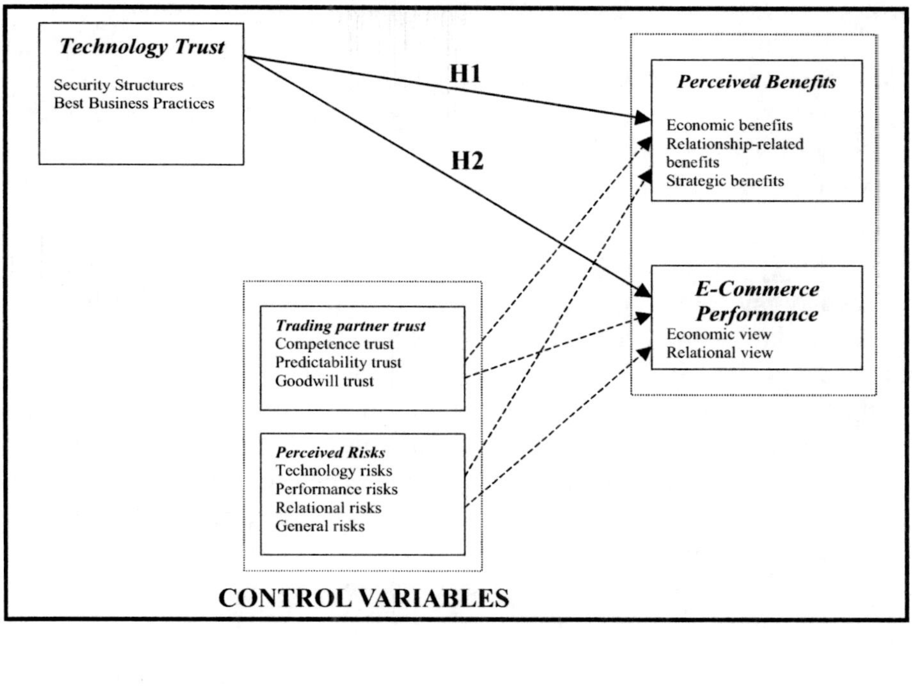

ers two major targets that need to be trusted for a transaction to occur according to an organization's expectations, namely the trading partner and also the underlying technological infrastructure (Tan & Thoen, 2001). Therefore, the novel character of trust focuses also on technology trust, in addition to the traditional trading partner trust.

Technology Trust

Technology trust is based on technical safeguards, protective measures, and control mechanisms that aim to provide reliable transactions from timely, accurate, and complete data transmission (Cassell & Bickmore, 2000). Technology trust encompasses security services such as; digital signatures, encryption mechanisms (public key infrastructure), authorization mechanisms (user IDs and passwords), and best business practices that enforce regular audit, top management commitment, standards, and contingency procedures (Bhimani, 1996; Jamieson, 1996; Marcella et al., 1998; Oppliger, 2002; Parker, 1995). The proposed construct of technology trust in B2B e-commerce is comparable to conceptualizations from other researchers. In addition to institutional based trust applying structural assurances and situation normality by McKnight et al. (1998), Zucker (1986) and Tan and Thoen (1998) used the term "control trust". They adopted the definitions of both Mayer et al. (1995) and Gambetta (1988) to include "the willingness of the party" and the "subjective probability." Control trust refers to embedded protocols, policies, procedures in e-commerce that help to reduce the risk of opportunistic behaviors among consumers and Web retailers. Lee and Turban (2001) also measured trustworthiness of Internet shopping based on consumer evaluations of technical competence and perceived Internet performance levels (such as speed, reliability and availability).

We herein define technology trust as "the subjective probability by which an organization believes that the underlying technology infrastructure and control mechanisms are capable of facilitating inter-organizational transactions according to its confident expectations." Table 1 presents the characteristics of each dimension from various sources, followed by a definition and its purpose in the next section.

Technology Trust Dimensions

Technology trust dimensions in e-commerce (Table 1) include transaction (a) confidentiality, (b) integrity, (c) authentication, (d) non-repudiation, (e) access controls, (f) availability, and (g) best business practices.

First, confidentiality mechanisms aim to protect e-commerce transactions and message content against unauthorized reading, copying, or disclosure using encryption mechanisms. Confidentiality mechanisms are enforced via encryption applying data encryption standard, public keys and private keys that codes and decodes e-commerce transactions in order to protect its privacy. Connection confidentiality services protect the data transmitted in a connection versus a connectionless confidentiality services that only protect single data units.

Table 1: Description of technology trust dimensions

Source	**Confidentiality**	**Integrity**	**Authentication**	**Non repudiation**	**Access Controls**	**Availability**	**Best Business Practices**
Bhimani 1996	Privacy	Accuracy	Genuine	Acknowledgement	Unauthorized access	Allows Authorized Access	Auditing
Jamieson 1996	Protection from unauthorized reading, copying	Completeness	Originality	Non-denial	Protects Transmission Media	Protection from hackers	Standards Written policies Procedures
Marcella et al, 1998	Protection against disclosure	Reliability	Authoritative Valid	Acknowledgment	Protects Manipulation	Authorized access	Risk analysis Contingency Procedures
Parker 1995	Privacy	Not being altered	Being true		Authorized access	Right to use	High quality standards

Second, integrity mechanisms provide transaction accuracy and assurance that e-commerce transactions have not been altered or deleted. Integrity mechanisms apply accounting controls that enforces reference numbers for each e-commerce transaction so that there is accountability. Connection integrity services with recovery provide integrity of data with recovery if lost. Connection integrity services without recovery do the reverse.

Third, authentication mechanisms provide transaction quality of being authoritative, valid, true, genuine, worthy of acceptance or belief by reason of conformity to the fact that reality is present. Authentication mechanisms are enforced by using biometrics, smartcards and digital signatures that reveal the identity of the trading party. Peer authentication services aim to provide the ability to verify that a peer entity of an association is the one it claims to be (i.e., it provides assurance that an entity is not attempting to masquerade or perform an unauthorized replay). Alternatively, data origin authentication services aim to allow the sources of data received to be verified as claimed. Authentication mechanisms are important because they are a prerequisite for proper authorization, access control and accountability.

Fourth, non-repudiation mechanisms protect the originator of e-commerce transactions and uses acknowledgement procedures applying digital signatures. Non-repudiation mechanisms are enforced by maintaining a paper audit trail and regular audit checks so that backups of electronic transactions are kept. Non-repudiation services with proof of origin provide the recipient of message with proof of origin whereas non-repudiation services with proof of delivery provide the sender a message with proof of delivery.

Fifth, access control mechanisms provide authorization mechanisms thereby assuring that transactions are sent and received without interruption. Access control mechanisms monitor network access by means of a firewall so that access is only given to authorized trading parties. Access control mechanisms focus on technology infrastructure by examining the quality and security of network access controls.

Sixth, availability mechanisms protect transactions against weaknesses in the transmission media and protect the sender against internal fraud or manipulation by using authorization mechanisms. Authorized mechanisms focus on the 'human' entity. Availability mechanisms are enforced by monitoring the profile and behavior of authorized parties who are given user IDs and passwords to use the system.

Finally, best business practices focus on policies, procedures, standards, and top management commitment that enforce regular audit, and ensure the smooth functioning of inter-organizational transactions.

Business Value

We broadly describe business value to outcomes that include two components, namely (a) perceived benefits and (b) actual performance.

Perceived Benefits

Perceived e-commerce benefits refer to potential gains received by organizations engaging in inter-organizational e-commerce activities. We identify three types of perceived benefits — perceived economic, relationship-related, and strategic benefits (Doney & Cannon, 1997; Fearson & Phillip, 1998; Ganesan, 1994; Morgan & Hunt, 1994; Riggins & Rhee, 1998; Senn, 2000; Smith & Barclay, 1997). First, perceived economic benefits are derived from the automated processes that contribute to direct savings in costs and time (efficiency). Second, perceived relationship-related benefits refer to positive trading partner trust relationships in the form of open communications, information sharing, cooperation, and commitment. Finally, perceived strategic benefits refer to closer ties between trading partners, satisfaction, improved reputation, business continuity, organizational performance, and the potential for competitive advantage. In the next section we justify the research hypotheses presented in the research model.

Technology Trust and Perceived Benefits

Technology trust draws from e-commerce technologies, third party services, and organizational actors (auditors, security analysts, and top management personnel) who are committed to enforcing best business practices. The relationship also draws from the literature on security services in e-commerce (Jamieson, 1996; Lee & Turban, 2001; Marcella et al., 1998). Most e-commerce technologies are embedded with automated security protocols that enable firms to ensure security services. Implementing encryption mechanisms protect online transactions from being intercepted, manipulated, and deleted, thus contributing to transaction integrity (Marcella et al., 1998; Riggins & Rhee, 1998; Senn, 2000). Transaction integrity leads to economic benefits from savings in time and costs, as timely accurate information are received and acted upon. For example, Mukhopadhyay, Kekre & Kalathur (1995) conducted a study of nine Chrysler assembly centers and found that EDI improved the quality of information sharing and reduced inventory, transportation, and administrative costs.

Authorized login procedures, e-mail acknowledgments, and confirmations provide confidentiality, authentication, and non-repudiation security services. Such functional acknowledgments in the form of email feedback, or other e-commerce protocols provide reliable and timely feedback mechanisms, thus contributing to relationship-related benefits such as quality of customer service, reliability and satisfaction. Organizations who demonstrate skills in producing high-quality goods, products, and services enforce best business practices, and achieve high levels of trustworthiness that contributes to perceived strategic benefits. B2B e-commerce applications enable product and service differentiation, tighter links with trading partners, and overall business value. Therefore we hypothesize that:

H1: Technology trust is positively associated with perceived economic, relationship-related and strategic benefits in B2B e-commerce.

E-Commerce Performance

In this study, e-commerce performance is evaluated in two ways. First, an economic view examines the actual performance as in transaction volume, dollar value, sales, and profit that cumulatively contributes to tangible business value. Furthermore, the speed and automation of e-commerce technologies contributes to cost reductions derived from time and cost savings. Second, a relational view examines the extent of actual organizational satisfaction and commitment in business relationships that result in intangible business value.

Technology Trust and Electronic Commerce Performance

Technology trust contributes to increased e-commerce performance in several ways. Efficiency economic benefits from technology trust concentrate on reducing transaction costs, derived from speed and automation of e-commerce technologies. In addition, these applications provide real-time tracking information technologies where technology trust allows firms to log into the supplier's extranet web site, track shipment details, and estimate arrival dates of the goods they ordered (Riggins & Rhee, 1999). Subsequently, trustworthy firms are able to satisfy their end customers' needs by delivering the goods on time, thus contributing to increased customer satisfaction and relationship-related business value. Increased satisfaction from technology trust, in turn, leads to perceived strategic benefits and actual economic benefits derived from increased volume, diversity, and dollar value of e-commerce transactions (Iacovou et al., 1995; Smith & Barclay, 1997). Tallon et al. (2000) argue that 'management practices' have an important role in the process of IT strategies intent towards a firm's business value, suggesting that best business practices can increase technology trust and ultimately influence B2B e-commerce performance. Therefore we hypothesize that:

H2: Technology trust is positively related to increased economic and relational B2B e-commerce performance.

Control Variables

Trading partner trust refers to the traditional dyadic view of trust. We define trading partner trust or inter-organizational trust as "the subjective probability with which organizations assess that another organization will perform potential dyadic transactions according to their confident expectations." This study identifies three types of trading partner trust, namely competence, predictability and goodwill trust. First, competence trust emphasizes reliance on trading partners' skills, technical knowledge, and ability to fulfill B2B e-commerce contracts. Second, predictability trust emphasizes belief in a trading partner's consistent behavior that provides sufficient knowledge for other trading partners to make predictions on the other organization's reliability and honesty based on past experiences (Lewicki & Bunker, 1996). Finally, goodwill trust emphasizes reliance on trading partners' care, concern, and benevolence that allows a trading partner to make commitments, and further invest in mutual relationships (Mayer et al., 1995).

Perceived risks refer to potential weaknesses, barriers, and losses faced by organizations that have adopted e-commerce. Risks can occur internally or externally, by human or non-human (e.g., technology-related risks), accidental or intentional, and could be caused by disclosure, destruction, modification of e-commerce transactions, and by denial of services attacks from hackers (Das & Teng, 1996; Jamieson, 1996; Marcella et al., 1998). This study identifies three types of perceived risks, namely perceived technology performance-related, relational, and general risks. First, perceived technology performance-related risks refer to misuse of e-commerce technologies, incompatible infrastructure, and uncertainties of e-commerce operations that contribute to failure in e-commerce performance. Second, perceived relational risks refer to trading partner's lack of knowledge, expertise, and a situation of imbalance of power that encourages opportunistic behaviors, conflicting attitudes, and reluctance to change, thus leading to dissatisfaction (Hart & Saunders, 1998). Finally, perceived general risks refer to poor business practices, environmental risks, and lack of standards and policies. In this study, trading partner trust and perceived risks has an effect on perceived benefits and e-commerce performance.

RESEARCH METHODOLOGY

The proposed research model was empirically examined using a survey research method. The survey questionaire was mailed out to 2,500 organizations provided by Greatlists.com (www.greatlists.com). The list of organizations was purchased on the basis that they have been actively using e-commerce technologies, drawing from a sample of 10,000 organizations from Greatlists.com. The associations these firms had with their trading partners included different roles in their exchange relationships (such as buyers, sellers, manufacturers, and suppliers) from a cross-section of industries, such as retail-wholesale trading, manufacturing-distribution, computer-communications, financial services, education, and health. These organizations come from both small-medium enterprises (50-500 employees) and large organizations (more than 500 employees) and their organizational reach is regional, national, and global. In addition, they had to indicate the types of e-commerce technologies and applications implemented in their organization (such as EDI via VANs, Internet-based EDI, extranets, or e-services), and the types of business transactions they exchange (including purchase orders, invoices, advance shipping notices, product information, and payment transactions). Furthermore, we sought how they choose and maintain their trading partners in a long term basis.

Table 2: Characteristics of the respondents

Definition of Characteristics	Value of the characteristics
Age of the participants	35-55 years
Gender of the participants	90% male, 10% female
Number of years in e-commerce experience	10-20 years
Number of years employed in the organization	7-20 years
Job title	E-Commerce coordinators, IT managers Security analysts, senior operations managers, e-commerce specialists
Size of the organization	SMEs (50-500) and large (>500 – 4000) employees
Role of the organization	Buyer, supplier, manufacturer, retailer
Types of e-commerce technologies and applications	EDI/VANs, Internet-based EDI Extranets, outsourcing on the web (Web services)
Number of trading partners	20-500 trading partners

The questionnaire was targeted at top-level management (including IT managers, e-commerce co-ordinators, and senior operations managers) who have wide experience and are best positioned to assess their organization's e-commerce activities, performance, and collective trust perceptions. They were asked to respond based on their perceptions of their relationships with a self-selected trading partner. Table 2 presents the characteristics of the participants that responded to the survey questionnaire.

Survey Instrument

Other than the technology trust construct, all measures were adapted from the literature, even if they had to be modified to reflect the study's specific context. These measures were adapted following standard psychometric scale development procedures (Bagozzi & Phillips, 1982). In cases in which the construct measure required significant deviations, the items were adapted following the conceptual definition. All items were measured on five-point Likert scales anchored at 'strongly disagree' (1), to 'strongly agree' (5) and 'neither agree nor disagree' (3) neutral point. In the next section we describe in detail the items used to measure the constructs in the research model.

Technology Trust (TTRUST)

A three-stage procedure was employed following the recommendations of Straub (1989) for developing and validating new measurement instruments. First, we specified the domain of technology trust by reviewing the extant literature. Following this review and based on the proposed conceptual definitions, a preliminary version of the instrument was generated, which was assessed for content validity. In terms of the dimensionality of technology trust, the literature review revealed that despite its multiple dimension, technology trust has been viewed as a uni-dimensional measurement variable. To test the measurement adequacy of technology trust and the other four constructs, the questionnaire was refined from an earlier case-study research conducted (Ratnasingam & Klein, 2000). Second, we conducted several formal pretests, which assessed the measurement properties of the proposed scales and refined several items. Finally, we proceeded with a confirmatory study that validated the measures for their reliability and convergent and discriminant validity.

Technology trust was measured using twenty items to include different trust and security-based mechanisms drawing upon the descriptions of Jamieson (1996), Marcella et al. (1998), and Parker (1995), and our own conceptualization. Given the newness of this measure, seven dimensions of technology trust were captured following past research on security services. Confidentiality examined privacy and security mechanisms, integrity examined the accuracy of business transactions, authentication examined trading partner's characteristics that uniquely identify transactions, non-repudiation assessed transaction feedback mechanisms, access controls examined network controls to prevent hackers from intruding into the system and provides access to authorized trading partners, availability examined system availability and information for authorized partners, and best business practices examined institutional standards, policies, and top management commitment.

Perceived benefits were measured using seventeen items drawing from the descriptions (Fearson & Phillip, 1998; Nath et al., 1998; Senn 2000) using three different dimensions — perceived economic benefits, relationship-related benefits, and strategic benefits. E-commerce performance (PERF) was measured using 10 items following Doney and Cannon (1997), Morgan and Hunt (1994), and Smith and Barclay (1997) and captured two performance dimensions — monetary value and relational performance. Trading partner trust (PTRUST) was measured using nineteen items following the descriptions of Doney and Cannon (1997), Ring and Van de Ven (1994), Smith and Barclay (1997), and Mayer et al. (1995), and captured competence, predictability, and goodwill trust. Finally, perceived risk (RISK) was measured using 22 items that covered three risk dimensions — technology performance-related risks, relational risks, and general risks.

Survey Administration

The survey instrument went through two phases of extensive pretesting before administration. First, the instrument was reviewed by faculty for comprehensiveness and clearness. Second, a small group of IT managers, e-commerce coordinators, and senior operations managers were asked to complete the questionnaire and provide feedback. Based on these pretests, the survey instrument was revised for coherence, and it was mailed out to the selected 2,500 organizations. The invitees were informed that the goal of the survey was to understand the concept of trust in electronic marketplaces, and they were assured that the results would be reported in an aggregate format in order to guarantee their anonymity. Given the study's need to assess collective organizational perceptions, the key respondents were requested to evaluate the perceptions of the entire group of people responsible for their firm's e-commerce efforts. In order to motivate organizations to respond, the respondents were offered a report that summarized the results of the survey and compared their company against other firms. A second wave of mailing was sent to the non-responding companies three weeks later. Finally, 40 responses were received through telephone interviews conducted by one of the authors. The author supervised a group of senior undergraduate students who conducted telephone interviews with non-respondents and went over the survey questionnaire in an attempt to increase the rate of responses.

Response Rate and Non-Response Bias

Out of the 2,500 participants, 120 letters were undeliverable, and a total of 288 responses (including the 40 responses collected via telephone interviews) were obtained resulting in an effective response rate of 12.1%. Non-response bias was assessed by a comparison of sample statistics to known values for the population between (a) respondents and non-respondents and (b) early and late respondents. Early respondents were identified by selecting those that responded during the first three weeks (53%) against those responding later, including telephone responses (47%). These tests were based on sample characteristics — (a) organization size, (b) annual revenue, and (c) number of employees, (d) e-commerce experience, and (e) the actual scale responses. Both tests showed no significant differences for these three characteristics at the $p<0.1$ level; therefore, the risk of non-response bias to the internal validity of this study's results was restricted.

Measure Validation

The questionnaire items were initially submitted to an exploratory factor analysis and item-to-total examination. All items tapping the same construct had high correlations, whereas items tapping different constructs had significantly lower correlations. Measure validation was initially examined for reliability analysis by computing Cronbach's alpha coefficient for each construct. All measures have extremely high levels of reliability, all above a 0.88 level. Next, a formal three-step sequence for assessing convergent and discriminant validity was employed. First, factor analysis was conducted (with rotations) to detect high loadings on hypothesized factors and low cross-loadings. Second, given the large number of questionnaire items, the factors were set to the expected number of constructs, and the survey items were reduced to their principal constructs. Third, principal components analysis was used as the extraction method for factor analysis with Varimax rotation. All items load significantly on their hypothesized factors, and using the 0.40 rule-of-thumb all cross-loadings are low, explaining 51% of the total variability. In sum, all items load on their hypothesized factors, which provides evidence of convergent and discriminant validity (Bagozzi & Yi, 1982). Hence, the responses to the multi-item measures generated an overall factor for each of the five constructs based on their weighted average. In the next section we present the results of the regression analysis and discuss the findings.

FINDINGS AND DATA ANALYSIS

Tests for the two hypotheses were provided by evaluating these multiple regression equations:

$$\mathbf{BENEF = b_0 + b_1\ TRUST + b_2\ PTRUST + b3\ RISK}$$
$$\mathbf{PERF = b_4 + b_5\ TTRUST + b_6\ PTRUST + b_7\ RISK}$$

Perceived Benefits

Table 3 shows the results of the regression analysis with perceived benefits as the dependent variable (R2 = .36, F = 75.2, $p < .001$). The impact of technology trust on perceived benefits is significant (b1 = .52, t = 10.06, $p < .001$), validating H1. The control effect of trading partner trust was significant (b2 = .15, t = 2.99, $p < .01$), validating previous research, while the effect of risk was positive, yet non-significant. Multicollinearity was not a serious concern since all relevant checks returned a tolerance value above 0.70.

E-Commerce Performance

As shown in Table 3, technology trust (b4 = .43, t = 7.43, $p < .001$) is positively associated with e-commerce performance, rendering strong support for H2. Trading partner trust was a significant control variable on e-commerce performance (b5 = .21, t = 3.78, $p < .001$), supporting the extant literature (Zaheer et al., 1998). The control effect of perceived risk was substantial and partially significant (b6 = 1.89, $p < .1$). Despite a correlation between technology and partner trust, multicollinearity was not a serious concern since all relevant checks returned a tolerance value above .70. Finally, the variance explained by this regression was particularly high (R2 = .53, F= 105.2, $p < .001$), suggesting that the proposed independent factors, and particularly technology trust (31%) largely influence perceived e-commerce performance.

Table 3: Regression analysis results

Variables	Construct	Perceived Benefits	t-value	Performance	t-value
Independent	Technology Trust	0.517	10.06***	0.426	7.43***
Control	Partner Trust	0.150	2.99**	0.213	3.78***
	Perceived Risks	0.06	0.73	0.07	0.83
	R-squared (adjusted)	0.355		0.526	
	F ratio	$F_{3,284} = 75.2$***		$F_{4,283} = 105.2$***	

Note: * $p < 0.05$, ** $p < 0.01$, and *** $p < 0.001$

DISCUSSION

By rendering empirical support to the proposed conceptual model and hypotheses, this study provides several new insights on technology trust in B2B e-commerce. First, an important finding is the value-added role of technology trust that describes confidence in the underlying technological infrastructure and associated control mechanisms. This study gives empirical evidence that technology trust has the potential to improve online transactions. Even if trading partner trust has been proven a source of favorable outcomes in traditional exchange relationships (e.g., Geyskens et al., 1998, Zaheer et al., 1998), this study shows that in the B2B e-commerce environment, technology trust is yet another source ofbusiness value. We posit that trust in e-business transactions implicitly incorporates the notion of technology trust, which is described as the subjective probability by which an organization assesses that the underlying technology infrastructure and control mechanisms are capable of supporting inter-organizational communications, transactions, and collaborations. The value-added component of technology trust also comes from the fact that it enables geographically disperse organizations to communicate and coordinate business activities (Lucas & Baroudi, 1994), allowing organizations across the globe to effectively utilize it without geographical restrictions.

In doing so, this research makes a theoretical contribution to the institution-based trust literature (Zucker, 1986) by theorizing a specific variable that draws from confidence in technology-based impersonal structures (Shapiro, 1987). Rather than focusing on the general concept of security mechanisms as in structural assurances and situational normalities (McKnight et al., 1998), this study extends previous research by operationalizing and validating a comprehensive set of specific technology-driven sub-constructs that cumulatively constitute a specific instance of institution-based trust. In addition, this study also makes a theoretical extension to the work of McKnight and Chervany (2002) from the B2C to a B2B context, stressing the importance of technology trust in inter-organizational relationships.

Drawing upon the emerging trust literature in B2B electronic commerce (e.g., Lee & Turban, 2001; Tan & Thoen, 1998), we explicitly view trust both from the traditional view (trading partner trust), and also from a technological perspective (technology trust). Similarly, the results of our study confirmed the findings of Morris et al.'s (2002) study of employees on the importance of information technology in virtual structures. From an empirical perspective, this study provides empirical support to McKnight et al.'s (1998) theoretical work on trust formation in a B2B e-commerce context. More specifically, the results support the notion that technology trust leads to positive trusting outcomes and increased e-commerce performance. Second, a key finding of this research is the relative strength of the technology and trading partner trust (as in competence, predictability and goodwill trust) on value potential and realization. Even if there are concerns for common-method variance, the fact that technology trust has a stronger effect on the dependent variables (relative to trading partner trust) suggests that it is at least an important independent variable to consider in online inter-organizational relationships.

The behavioral aspect of trading partner trust on a particular transaction may include influencing the underlying infrastructure and supporting control mechanisms. Hence, even if not explicitly hypothesized in this study, a relationship is expected between the two dimensions of inter-organizational trust. Following McKnight and Chervany (2002), this study proposes that technology trust (trust in the situation) is a critical antecedent of trading partner trust. McKnight and Chervany (2002, p.13) argue that in business-to-consumer electronic commerce, "beliefs that the Internet has legal or regulatory protection for consumers (institution-based trust) should influence trust in a particular e-vendor (interpersonal trust)." Based on these arguments we expect that institutional structures that constitute technology trust should positively influence buyers' trust in trading partners. However, it is important to note that trust in a trading partner should also influence technology trust by giving perceptions that the trading partner's benevolence would go the extra mile to assure the reliability of the technology infrastructure and prevent abnormal situations (Pavlou, 2002). Hence, a reciprocal relationship between technology and trading partner trust is expected. These two constructs essentially form the two fundamental dimensions of inter-organizational trust (Pavlou & Ratnasingam, 2003).

At least to this dataset, technology trust is shown to have a much stronger effect compared to trading partner trust, both on perceived benefits and on e-commerce performance, suggesting that it can add value on its own right, not necessarily indirectly as an antecedent of trust. Following Ratnasingam and Pavlou (2002), we expect that technology trust to have both a direct and an indirect (through trading partner trust) on transaction performance and perceived benefits. Such direct and indirect effects of institutional trust on valued outcomes are also proposed by McKnight and Chervany (2002). The relationship also draws from the literature on security services in electronic commerce (Jamieson, 1996; Lee & Turban, 2001; Marcella et al., 1998), thus also influencing perceived risks (as in perceived technology-performance related, relational and general risks) of e-commerce. For example, most electronic commerce technologies are embedded with automated security protocols that enable firms to ensure security services, thus contributing to low technology-performance related risks from connectivity and compatibility problems. Finally, this chapter contributes to the trust literature by proposing a new scale with excellent measurement properties to capture the construct of technology trust, which is an important theoretical construct and a practical value-creator in B2B e-commerce.

Implications for Practicing Managers

Many managers have recognized the importance of trust in developing value for a sustainable competitive advantage in exchange relationships. This research proposes a new trust dimension for a B2B e-commerce context that may help managers and e-commerce practitioners to develop trustworthy exchange relationships. By properly utilizing technology trust, this study paves the way for managers to understand how the adoption of B2B e-commerce could positively affect their exchange relationships and their own technology-related trustworthiness for business value. The efficiencies from e-commerce technologies derived from high-speed automation initially contribute to economic benefits in the form of time and cost savings. Consistent accurate, complete and correct transactions transmitted in a timely manner contribute to a pattern in trading partner's behavior, which in turn leads to predictability trust and relationship-related benefits. Trading partners are more willing to share information, cooperate and collaborate thus leading to goodwill trust where they will further invest in their relationships, thus contributing to improved services and reputation leading to additional perceived strategic benefits. Finally, this study provides a tentative guide for early adopters of e-commerce technologies by improving their levels of awareness for the role and impact of these technologies on instituting and maintaining collaborative exchange relationships.

Corporate executives must also be aware of the importance of technology trust in the competitive global environment of B2B e-commerce. Although governance mechanisms may provide assurances that help mitigate perceived risks of e-commerce, our findings provide evidence that both technology trust and trading partner trust are fundamental to successful B2B e-commerce. Competent and well-trained trading partners tend to exhibit trustworthy ways of implementing e-commerce applications that contribute to timely, correct, and accurate information for trading partners to act upon. This reliable communication in turn leads to improved strategic decision-making, higher satisfaction, commitment, and business continuity, leading to higher levels of trading partner trust. Therefore, this study informs managers of how the new character of trust can be strategically used to realize business value beyond transaction efficiencies and cost reduction.

Implications for Research

This research attempts to make a theoretical contribution to the area of trust in B2B e-commerce by integrating the trust literature with theories from security, privacy, and control to propose a new theoretical construct, which describes the importance of trust in the underlying technology infrastructure. The proposed new construct was theoretically derived and empirically tested, and the findings revealed its significant value added potential in e-business. Hence, rather than assuming that trust in the technology is implicitly embedded in the traditional view of trust, this study explicitly examines and measures this new facet of trust. This study also makes an important empirical contribution by proposing how trust can be strategically used beyond the traditional dyadic level to directly contribute to perceived benefits, organizational performance, and B2B e-commerce success.

In this study, we developed measures for technology trust from previous security, policy and e-commerce literature. Most previous work focused on security issues and risks in e-commerce. We translated these dimensions in addition to a set of new dimensions related to best business practices, control mechanisms, and security safeguards, proposing a new construct, namely, technology trust. In doing so, we do not underscore the importance of explicitly studying security issues that are particularly important in e-commerce. Rather, we make a modest attempt to integrate relevant security issues along with other technological issues into a new construct that cumulatively builds trust in the infrastructure and control mechanisms. This new construct corresponds to the notion of building institutional structures to support business activities.

Given the importance of technology trust in B2B e-commerce, future research should extend this construct and attempt to provide a comprehensive set of antecedents and consequences of technology trust. It is important to note that technology trust, similar to trading partner trust, is a perceptual belief that has its basis on objective realities about the actual credibility of the underlying infrastructure and control mechanisms. Nevertheless, it is important to note that technology trust does not have its basis in interpersonal relationships, even if it may be affected by trading partner trust. Therefore, trust solely focuses on the credibility dimension and cannot be extended to the interpersonal benevolence (goodwill) dimension of trust that is possible in inter-organizational relationships.

Limitations and Suggestions for Future Research

This research conceptually views trust as a collectively held belief by a group of organizational members. However, our empirical study was limited to a single respondent that was asked to evaluate the trust perceptions of the entire group. Future research should attempt to collect responses from several respondents within the organization to assess communal trust. Second, this research examined only a subset of the many possible relationships between technology trust and its antecedents and consequences. Since technology trust has been shown to be associated with favorable outcomes, future research could propose and examine its antecedents and consequences. Third, it is important to note that technological advances are likely to change the nature of technology trust; hence, it is important to note that the proposed operationalization describes the current state of practice. Finally, the results and implications of this research are constrained by the research method employed, and the proposed causal relationships are limited by the cross-sectional nature of the methodological design. Therefore, longitudinal research and alternative statistical methods could complement these empirical findings.

CONCLUSIONS

In this study, we proposed a new trust dimension that may help managers develop trustworthy online exchange relationships. By understanding and properly utilizing technology trust, this study paves the way for managers to understand how the adoption of B2B e-commerce could positively affect their exchange relationships and their own trustworthiness for business value. By proposing how technology trust can create business value, this research opens new avenues for research on facilitating B2B e-commerce success. The results of this study clearly provide evidence that the role of technology trust in B2B e-commerce is important, as it promotes several performance outcomes beyond the traditional role of trading partner trust. Technology trust and trading partner trust can in turn create business value and win-win situations for building successful long-term collaborative relationships. This chapter will hopefully entice researchers and practitioners to further examine how the new character of trust can be employed in e-business to realize value in today's e-business.

REFERENCES

Bagozzi, R. P. & Philips L. W. (1982). Representing and testing organizational theories: A holistic construal. *Administrative Science Quarterly*, 27(3), 459-489.

Bakos, Y. (1998). The emerging role of electronic marketplaces on the Internet. *Communications of the ACM,* August, 41(8), 35-48.

Barney, J.B. & Hansen, M.H. (1994). Trustworthiness as a source of competitive advantage. *Strategic Management Journal*, (15), 175-216.

Bhimani, A. (1996). Securing the commercial Internet. *Communications of the ACM*, 39(6), June, 29-35.

Blackmon, D. A. (2000). Where the Money Is. *The Wall Street Journal,* 30-32.

Cannon, J.P. & Perreault, W.D. (1999). Buyer and Ssller relationships in business markets. *Journal of Marketing Research*, 36, 439-460.

Cassel, J. & Bickmore, T (2000). External manifestations of trustworthiness of the interface. *Communications of the ACM,* 43(12), 50-50.

Das, T.K. & Bing-Sheng Teng. (1996). Risk types and inter-firm alliance structures. *Journal of Management Studies*, 33(1), 827-843.

Doney, P.M. & Cannon, J.P. (1997). An examination of the nature of trust in buyer-seller relationships. *Journal of Marketing*, April, 35-51.

Dwyer, R.F., Schurr, P, H., & Oh, S. (1987). Developing buyer-seller relationships. *Journal of Marketing*, 52(1), 11-27.

Fearson, C. & Phillip, G. (1998). Self-assessment as a means of measuring strategic and operational benefits from EDI: The development of a conceptual framework. *European Journal of Information Systems,* 7(1), 5-16.

Gambetta, D. (1988). *Trust: Making and Breaking Cooperative Relations*. Oxford: Basil Blackwell.

Ganesan, S. (1994). Determinants of long-term orientation in buyer-seller relationships. *Journal of Marketing,* 58, April, 1-19.

Geyskens, I., Steenkamp, J-B., & Kumar, N. (1998). Generalizations about trust in marketing channel relationships using meta-analysis. *International Journal in Marketing,* 15, 223-248.

Hart, P. & Saunders, C. (1998). Emerging electronic partnerships: Antecedents and dimensions of EDI use from suppliers perspective. *Journal of Management Information Systems*, 14(4), 87-111.

Heil, G., Bennis, W., & Stephens, D. (2000). *Douglas McGregor, Revisited: Managing the Human Side of the Enterprise.* John Wiley and Sons.

Hoffman, D.L., Novak, T.P., and Peralta, M. (1999). Association for Computing Machinery. *Communications of the ACM,* 42, 80-85.

Iacovou, C.L., Benbasat, I., & Dexter, A.S. (1995). Electronic data interchange and small organizations: Adoption and impact of technology. *MIS Quarterly,* 19(4), 465-485.

Jamieson, R. (1996). *Auditing and Electronic Commerce.* EDI Forum, Perth, Western Australia.

Keen, P.G.W. (2000). Ensuring e-Trust. *Computerworld,* March 13.

Lee, M.K.O. & Turban, E. (2001). A trust model for consumer Internet shopping. *International Journal of Electronic Commerce*, 6(1), 75-92.

Lewicki, R.J. & Bunker, B.B. (1996). Developing and maintaining trust in work relationships. In Kramer, R.M. & Tyler, T.R. (Eds.), *Trust in Organizations: Frontiers of Theory and Research* (pp. 114-139). Thousand Oaks, CA: Sage.

Marcella, A.J., Stone, L., & Sampias, W.J. (1998). *Electronic commerce: Control issues for securing virtual enterprises.* The Institute of Internal Auditors.

Mayer, R.C., Davis, J.H., & Schoorman, F.D. (1995). An integrative model of organizational trust. *Academy of Management Review,* 20(3), 709-734.

McKnight, H.D., Cummings, L.L., & Chervany, N.L. (1998). Managers as initiators of trust: An exchange relationship framework for understanding managerial trustworthy behaviour. *Academy of Management Review*, 23(3), 513-530.

McKnight, H.D. & Chervany, N.L. (2002). What trust means in e-Commerce customer relationships: An interdisciplinary conceptual typology. *International Journal of Electronic Commerce,* forthcoming.

Morgan, R.M., & Hunt, S.D. (1994). The commitment-trust theory of relationship marketing. *Journal of Marketing*, 58, 20-38.

Mukhopadyay, T., Kekre, S., & Kalathur, S. (1995). Business value of information technology: A study of electronic data interchange. *MIS Quarterly,* 19, 137-156.

Nath, R., Akmanligil, M., Hjelm, K., Sakaguch, T., & Schultz, M. (1998). Electronic commerce and the Internet: Issues, problems and perspectives. *International Journal of Information Management*, 18(2), 91-101.

Palmer, J.W., Bailey, J.P., & Faraj, S. (2000). The role of intermediaries in the development of trust on the WWW: The use and prominence of trusted third parties and privacy statements. *Journal of Computer Mediated Communication,* 5(3), Online.

Parker, D.B. (1995). A new framework for information security to avoid information anarchy. *IFIP*, 155-164.

Pavlou, P.A. (2002). Institution-based trust in inter-organizational exchange relationships: The role of online B2B marketplaces on trust formation. *Journal of Strategic Information Systems* (11:4), forthcoming.

Pavlou, P.A. & Gefen, D. (2002). Building effective online exchange networks with institution-based trust. *Proceedings of the 23rd International Conference in Information Systems (ICIS),* Barcelona, Spain, (December 15-18), forthcoming.

Pavlou, P.A. & Ratnasingam, P. (2003). Technology trust in B2B electronic commerce: Conceptual foundations. In K. Kangas (Ed.), *Business Strategies for Information Technology Management.* Hershey, PA: Idea Group Publishing, forthcoming.

Ratnasingam, P. & Klein, S. (2001). Perceived benefits of inter-organizational-trust in e-Commerce participation–A case study in the telecommunication industry–7th American Conference in Information Systems, (AMCIS) Boston, Massachusetts, Aug 3-5.

Ratnasingam, P. & Pavlou, P. (2002). *Technology trust: The next value creator in B2B electronic commerce.* International Resources Management Association Conference – Washington, Seattle, USA.

Riggins, F.J. & Rhee, H.S. (1998). Toward a unified view of electronic commerce. *Communications of the ACM,* 41(10), 88-95.

Ring, P.S. & Van de Ven, A.H. (1994). Developing processes of cooperative inter-organizational relationships. *Academy of Management Review,*19, 90-118.

Rousseau, D.M., Sitkin, S.B., Burt, R.S., & Camerer, C. (1998). Not so different after all: A cross-discipline view of trust. *The Academy of Management Review,* 23(3), 393-404.

Sarkar, M.B., Butler, B., & Steinfield, C. (1995) Intermediaries and cyber-mediaries: A continuing role for mediating players in the electronic marketplace. *Journal of Computer Mediated Communication,* 1(3).

Senn, J.A. (2000). Business to business e-commerce. *Information Systems Management*, Spring, 23-32.

Shapiro, S.P. (1987). The social control of impersonal trust. *American Journal of Sociology*, 93, 623-658.

Smith, J. B. & Barclay, D.W. (1997). The effects of organizational differences and trust on the effectiveness of selling partner relationships. *Journal of Marketing,* 51, 3-21.

Straub, D. W. (1989). Validating instruments in MIS research. *MIS Quarterly,* 13, 146-169.

Tallon, P.P., Kraemer, K.L & Gurbaxani, V. (2000). Executives perceptions of the business value of information technology: A process-oriented approach. *Journal of Management Information Systems*, 16, 45-173

Tan, Yao-Hua. & Thoen, W. (1998). Towards a generic model of trust for electronic commerce. *International Journal of Electronic Commerce*, 3, 65-81.

Zaheer, A., Mc Evily, B., & Perrone, V. (1998). Does trust matter? Exploring the effects of inter-organizational and interpersonal trust on performance. *Oganization Science,* 9(2), 141-159.

Zucker, L.G. (1986). Production of trust: Institutional sources of economic structure: 1840-1920. In Staw, B. & Cummings, L. (Eds.), *Research in Organizational Behavior*, Greenwich, CT.

APPENDIX—SURVEY INSTRUMENT

Constructs and Sources	Measurement criteria
Technology Trust	1. We implemented a firewall in our e-commerce system
Source: Jamieson (1996)	2. We apply encryption mechanisms
Marcella et al (1998)	3. We undertake regular system integrity tests and audits
Parker (1995)	4. We apply sequence/reference numbers in our e-commerce system
	5. We apply application controls in our e-commerce system
	6. We apply accounting controls in our e-commerce system
	7. We apply Web seal assurances in our e-commerce system
	8. We apply formal logon procedures (user-IDs and Pass words) in our e-commerce system
	9. We use message receipt confirmations and acknowledg ments
	10. We apply digital signatures
	11. We apply network access controls
	12. We apply authorization mechanisms
	13. We apply segregation of duties
	14. We receive top management commitment in our organiza tion
	15. We abide by standards (industry and universal) and poli cies
	16. We abide by a trading partner agreement
	17. We undertake regular audit checks
	18. We undertake regular training and education of staff
	19. We undertake regular risk analysis
	20. We apply contingency procedures in our organization

Perceived Benefits of E-Commerce

Source:Fearson and Phillip (1998)	
	1.Our organization experiences reduced operation, transaction and administrative costs
Nath et al., (1998)	2. Our organization experiences reduced error rates
Senn (2000)	3. Our organization experiences improved accuracy of informa tion exchanged
	4. Our organization experiences faster response to orders and thus reduced lead time
	5. Our organization experiences reduced inventory levels
	6. Our organization experiences optimized supply chain
	7. Our organization experiences improved customer service and product quality
	8. Our organization experiences improved productivity
	9. Our organization experiences improved profitability and increased sales
	10. Our organization gains competitive advantage
	11. Our organization shares risks with our trading partner
	12. Our organization experiences improved communication
	13. Our organization experiences improved cooperation with our trading partners

14. Our trading partner shares information (i.e., accurate, timely, speedy, complete and relevant)
15. Our organization experiences increased level of commit ment with our trading partners
16. Our organization experiences improved organization's im age and reputation
17. Our organization experiences increased long-term invest ments and continued trading partner relationships

E-Commerce Performance

Source:	
Doney and Cannon (1997)	1. Our organization experiences importance of e-commerce system
Morgan and Hunt (1994)	2. Our organization experiences an increase in the volume of transactions derived from e-commerce application
Smith and Barclay (1997)	3. Our organization experiences an increase in profit (monetary value) derived from e-commerce applications
	4. Our trading partner will continue to be a major source of revenue for us
	5. Our organization will increase the number of trading partners
	6. Our organization will engage in long-term business investments with our trading partners
	7. Our organization perceives an increase in the level of open communications in our trading partners
	8. Our organization perceives an increase in the level of cooperation in our trading partners
	9. Our organization perceives an increase in the level of commitment in our trading partners
	10. Our organization's reputation has increased as a result of our trading partners

Control VariablesTrading Partner Trust

Source:	
Doney & Cannon (1997)	1. Our trading partner has the ability, skills and competence to operate business to business e-commerce applications
Ring & Van de Ven (1994)	2. Our trading partner depends on our organization
Smith and Barclay (1997)	3. Our trading partner exhibits consistent behavior in their business interactions
Mayer et al (1995)	4. We can be rely on our trading partners to keep their business promises
	5. Our trading partner adheres to policies, terms of contract, and trading partner agreements
	6. Our trading partner is predictable
	7. Our trading partner is willing to share information, and provide support relating to e-commerce adoption
	8. Our trading partner demonstrates care and concern in important decisions
	9. Our trading partner is committed to business arrangements, and exhibits cooperation
	10. Our trading partner exhibits cooperation

11. Our trading partner has positive feelings towards our organization
12. Our trading partner engages in long term trading relationships
13. Our trading partner is willing to put in more effort and invest in our relationships
14. Our trading partner is honest in providing information (e.g. accuracy of deadlines)
15. Our trading partner in a situation of conflict and handling discrepancies'; feels angry and hostile towards our organization
16. We experience a situation of pressure with our trading partner's imbalance of power
17. Our trading partner considers our organization's security concerns
18. Our trading partner is our driving force for adopting e-commerce
19. Our trading partner has explicit agreements (regarding roles and responsibilities)

Perceived Risks of E-Commerce

Source: Jamieson (1996)	1. Our organization experiences compatibility problems with hardware and software
Marcella et al (1998)	2. Our organization experiences additional infrastructure and initial implementation costs
Parker (1995)	3. Our organization experiences confidentiality concerns due to viruses
	4. Our organization experiences lack of adequate accounting controls
	5. Our organization experiences internal security errors that led to lack of integrity (i.e. delayed and inaccurate messages)
	6. Our organization experiences complexity in operating business transactions
	7. Our organization experiences task and environment uncertainties
	8. Our organization experiences trading partner reluctance to change
	9. Our organization experiences a shortage of training, knowledge, and awareness
	10. Our organization experiences poor reputation of trading partner
	11. Our organization experiences conflicting attitudes from our trading partners
	12. Our organization experiences lack of trust from our trading partners
	13. Our organization experiences opportunistic behaviors from our trading partners
	14. Our organization experiences partnership uncertainties from our trading partners
	15. Our organization experiences lack of security from our trading partner's system
	16. Our organization experiences a difficulty in identifying or quantifying costs and benefits

17. Our organization experiences repudiation problems from our trading partners
18. Our organization experiences authentication difficulties from our trading partners
19. Our organization experiences availability of technology concerns from our trading partners
20. Our organization experiences lack the standard infrastructure (e.g. data and payments concerns) for our payments
21. Our organization experiences lack of government policies
22. Our organization experiences poor business practices from our trading partners

Previously published in the Journal of Electronic Commerce in Organizations, 1(1), 17-41, Jan/Mar, 2003.

About the Authors

Mehdi Khosrow-Pour is currently executive director and president of the Information Resources Management Association (IRMA) and senior technology editor for Idea Group Inc. (Hershey, Pennsylvania, USA). He is also editor in chief of the *Information Resources Management Journal* (IRMJ), *Journal of Electronic Commerce in Organizations* (JECO), *Annals of Cases on Information Technology* (ACIT), *Information Management* (IM), and consulting editor of the *Information Technology Newsletter* (ITN). He is the author/editor of more than 20 books on various topics of information technology utilization and management in organizations, and more than 50 journal articles.

* * * *

Karin Axelsson holds a PhD in Information Systems Development from Linköping University, Sweden. She is currently assistant professor in the Department of Computer and Information Science at Linköping University, where she is responsible for single-subject courses in information systems. Her main research interests are focused on e-commerce, inter-organizational information systems, and development and applications of business action theory. She is a member of the Swedish research network VITS, in which she is responsible for the research area of inter-organizational relations and electronic commerce. This research area includes projects about business relations, inter-organizational business development, business networks and IT, and IOS development.

Christopher D. Barko is an Information Technology professional at Laboratory Corporation of America. His IT industry experience spans many years in various consulting, business intelligence, software engineering and analyst positions for a number of Fortune 500 organizations. He received his BBA in Computer Information Systems from James Madison University and MBA from the University of North Carolina at Greensboro, where he specialized in Decision Support Systems. His current research interests include organizational data mining, business intelligence and customer relationship management, and how these technologies can enhance the organizational decision-making process to optimize resource allocation and improve profitability. His research has been published in several leading journals such as the *Journal of Data Warehousing, Journal of Computer Information Systems*, and others. He is president of Customer Analytics, Inc., a consultancy that leverages advanced analytics to deliver profitable database marketing solutions.

Elliot Bendoly is an assistant professor of Operations Management at Emory University's Goizueta Business School. He received a PhD in the fields of Operations Management and Decision Sciences from Indiana University. His research focuses on organizational behavioral issues in resource allocation decisions and on operational/strategic constraints to the benefits of ERP and transactional IT. He has published work in the *Journal of Applied Psychology*, *European Journal of Operational Research, Decision Support Systems, Information & Management* and *Journal of Economic and Management Strategy*.

Chuan-Feng Chiu received his PhD in Computer Engineering from Tamkang University, Taiwan (2002). He received his MS and BS in the same major in 1999 and 1995, respectively. Since 1999, Dr. Chiu published many refereed papers in international conferences and journals. Dr. Chiu's research interests focus on multimedia database, e-commerce, mobile agents, and multimedia software engineering. Currently, he is working at Panasonic, Taiwan.

Ahmed Farouk Ghoneim is currently an assistant professor in the Faculty of Economic and Political Science at Cairo University. He is the deputy director of the Center for Economic and Financial Research and Studies (CEFRS), Cairo University, and an advisor to the Minister of Industry on foreign trade issues and international agreements. He is a research associate at the Economic Research Forum for Arab Countries, Iran and Turkey (ERF). He works as a consultant to several international organizations including the World Bank and the World Intellectual Property Organization (WIPO). He holds a PhD in Economics and his special interest in research include mainly trade policy, regional trade integration, the multilateral trading system, the World Trade Organization, and the economics of IPR. He held different policy oriented positions, among which was an advisor on foreign trade issues to the Minister of Foreign Trade.

Sherine Ghoneim (BA, Economics, American University in Cairo, 1986; MSc, Management, Boston University, 1990; PhD, Information Management, "Developing a National EDI Strategy: Opportunities and Challenges," The Management School, Imperial College of Science, Technology & Medicine, University of London, 2000) is a staff member and assistant professor with the Faculty of Computers and Information at Cairo University teaching Information

Systems Management and E-Commerce Foundation courses. Ghoneim's research interests are focused on Information Systems management, e-commerce, e-government and health informatics. Ghoneim is published widely in acclaimed journals such as the *European Journal of Information Systems* and *Journal of Strategic Information Systems*. The publications are typically founded on both academic and professional relevance where the author reflects on her 20 years of professional experience in the field of information and knowledge management with leading international organizations such as General Electric Information Services - Egypt and UK, International Network Services - UK, Economic Research Forum-Egypt and Global Development Network - USA.

Yi "Maggie" Guo (BE, Information Engineering, Northern Jiaotong University, Beijing, China; MS, MIS, University of Nebraska at Omaha) is finishing her PhD in the Information and Operations Management Department at Texas A&M University – College Station, USA. Yi's research interests include e-commerce, online shopping experience, flow theory, and agent-based systems in knowledge management. For more information contact: mguo@cgsb.tamu.edu.

Frederick Kaefer is an assistant professor of Information Systems in the School of Business Administration of Loyola University, Chicago (USA). He has a PhD in MIS from the University of Iowa. His research interests include the planning and use of communication systems, neural networks and decision support systems. He has published in journals such as *Decision Support Systems, European Journal of Operational Research* and *Informs Journal on Computing.*

Sherif Kamel is an associate professor of management information systems, the Information Systems Unit head at the Department of Management and the director of the Institute of Management Development of the School of Business, Economics and Mass Communication at The American University in Cairo. Previously, he was the director of the Regional IT Institute (1992-2001) and the training manager at the Cabinet of Egypt Information and Decision Support Center (1988-1991). He designs and delivers executive development programs in information technology management and applications for public and private sector organization in many developing countries. In 1996, he was one of the co-founding members of the Internet Society of Egypt. He has published many articles in IT transfer to developing countries, electronic commerce, human resources development, decision support applications and knowledge management. He serves on the editorial and review boards of a number of information systems and management journals and is the associate editor of the *Annals of Cases on Information Technology Applications and Management in Organizations.* He is currently a member of the executive council of the Information Resources Management Association (IRMA) and acts as its director of communications. He is a graduate of London School of Economics and Political Science (UK) and The American University in Cairo (Egypt).

Feng Li (BSc, MA, PhD) is chair of E-Business Development at the University of Newcastle upon Tyne Business School, UK. Previously he lectured at Strathclyde University Business School, UK. For 15 years he has been investigating the impacts of information and communications technologies on the strategies and business models of organizations. He is the author of two books and numerous journal articles, and he speaks regularly at international conferences and to business executives from both the private and public sectors. Professor Li is a member of several programmes on ICTs, e-commerce/e-business, supply chain/ value chain, and virtual teams. He has worked closely with companies in the banking, telecommunications, manufacturing, retailing, and electronics as well as the public sectors. He is particularly interested in new rules of the networked economy and their implications for strategies, business models and organizational designs. Professor Li is the winner of the Blackwell Prize for E-Business and Technology Management at British Academy of Management 2002 (BAM2002), and his recent work on Internet banking and on the telecommunications industry has been extensively reported in the *Financial Times, Daily Telegraph, Guardian Weekly, Sky News*, and the BBC as well as many other news and professional online and offline media. Professor Li can be contacted at feng.li@ncl.ac.uk.

Chang Liu, DBA, is an associate professor of Management Information Systems at Northern Illinois University, USA. He received his Doctorate of Business Administration from Mississippi State University in 1997. His research works have been published in *Information & Management, International Journal of Electronic Commerce and Business Media, Journal of Global Information Management, Journal of Internet Research, Journal of Computer Information Systems, Mid-American Journal of Business, International Journal of Mobile Communications, Journal of International Technology and Information Management, Journal Informatics Education Research*, and *Communications of the International Information Management Association*. Dr. Liu teaches Database and Electronic Commerce courses and received the Excellence in MIS Graduate Teaching Award in 2002 and 2003.

Jack T. Marchewka, PhD, is an associate professor and the Barsema professor of Management Information Systems in the Department of Operations Management and Information Systems (OMIS) at Northern Illinois University, USA. In addition, he is also the director of the Experiential Learning Center (ELC). His current research interests include IT project management, electronic commerce, and knowledge management. His articles have appeared in the *Information Resources Management Journal, Journal of Global Information Management, Information Technology and People, Journal Informatics Education Research, Communications of the International Information Management Association*, and the *Journal of International Technology and Information Management.*

Ashfaaq Moosa is a data analyst at Upromise, Inc., a firm that helps families save for college. He has worked on various customer-focused data integration and data mining projects for various industries including retail, real estate and financial. He graduated with a Master's of Science in Information Technology and Management from the University of North Carolina at Greensboro. He may be reached at ashfaaq@yahoo.com.

Hamid R. Nemati is an assistant professor of Information Systems at the Information Systems and Operations Management Department of the University of North Carolina at Greensboro, USA. He holds a doctorate degree in Management Sciences and Information Technology from the University of Georgia and a Master's of Business Administration from the University of Massachusetts. He has extensive professional IT experience as an analyst and has consulted with a number of major corporations. Before coming to UNCG, he was on the faculty of J. Mack Robinson College of Business Administration at Georgia State University. His research specialization is in the areas of organizational data mining, decision support systems, data warehousing, and knowledge management. He has presented nationally and internationally on a wide range of topics relating to his research interests. His research has been published in a number of top-tier scholarly journals.

David Paper is an associate professor in the Utah State University Business Information Systems Department, USA. His refereed publications appear in journals such as *Information and Management, Communications of the AIS, Journal of Information Technology Cases and Applications, Information Resources Management Journal, Journal of Managerial Issues, Business Process Management Journal,* and *Journal of Computer Information Systems.* His industry experience includes working and consulting with organizations such as the Space Dynamics Laboratory, Texas Instruments, DLS, Inc., the Utah Department of Transportation, and the Phoenix Small Business Administration. His teaching interests include database management, business process reengineering, worker empowerment, lean principles, and organizational change.

Paul A. Pavlou is a PhD candidate of Information Systems at the Marshall School of Business in the University of Southern California, USA. His research interests focus on IT-enabled collaborative interorganizational relationships, electronic commerce and online consumer behavior, the role of dynamic capabilities in interorganizational new product development teams, institutional trust in online auction marketplaces, and cross-national studies of e-commerce and e-government. Paul has several publications in refereed journals, books, and conference proceedings. His research has appeared (or is scheduled to appear) in *MIS Quarterly, International Journal of Electronic Commerce, Journal of Strategic Information*

Systems, Electronic Markets, Journal of Electronic Commerce Research, Journal of Logistics Information Management, and in conference proceedings.

Eric Pedersen is an associate professor of Visual Technologies and Computer Information Systems at Dixie State College (DSC). He has worked at DSC since 1989. In addition to his faculty work, he has been the Principal Investigator in the DSC Center of Excellence for Computer Graphics since 1991. He has co-founded several e-businesses and is currently conducting research in e-commerce and completing his PhD in Business Information Systems at USU.

Victor Perotti is an assistant professor of Management Information Systems (MIS) in the College of Business of the Rochester Institute of Technology. He teaches MIS and e-business courses at both the graduate and undergraduate levels. Dr. Perotti has recently been honored for both his teaching and research. In March 2000, he was awarded the Richard and Virginia Eisenhart Provost's Award for Excellence in Teaching. Before joining the College of Business, Victor was a research assistant at The Vision Lab at The Ohio State University. At Ohio State, he wrote several publications in the area of visual perception. Since that time, Victor has been doing research on a variety of MIS topics, centered on the theme of understanding business data through visualization.

Charles G. Petersen, PhD, is an associate professor of Operations Management at Northern Illinois University, USA. Dr. Petersen teaches both graduate and undergraduate supply chain management and previously served as the coordinator for the integrated undergraduate business core. He holds a BS in Industrial Engineering from Iowa State University, an MBA from Washington University, and a PhD in Operations Management from Indiana University. Dr. Petersen's primary research interests are in the areas of supply chain management, order fulfillment, and electronic commerce. His scholarly work has been published in *Decision Sciences, Production and Operations Management, International Journal of Production Research, International Journal of Production Economics*, and *International Journal of Operations & Production Management.*

Leyland Pitt has been named to the chair of Electronic Marketing in the School of Marketing, Curtin University of Technology, Perth, Australia. He also holds positions as adjunct professor of Marketing in the Graduate School of Business, Ecole Nationale Ponts et Chaussees in Paris, the University of Vienna, Austria, and the University of Lulea, Sweden. He holds a BCom(Hons), MBA and PhD in Marketing from the University of Pretoria, and the MCom in Management from Rhodes University. Prior to joining Curtin he was professor of Marketing at Cardiff University, UK, and he has also held chairs in marketing at Henley Management College and Brunel University, UK, and the University of Cape Town, South

Africa. In addition, he has taught Marketing and Electronic Commerce in MBA and executive programs at schools such as Warwick Business School, London Business School, the Graduate School of Business at Columbia University, and the Graham School of Continuing Studies at the University of Chicago. The Academy of Marketing Science has recognized him as one of the world's Outstanding Marketing Teachers for 2002. Leyland Pitt's particular areas of interest in research and teaching involve marketing and the new electronic media, the staging of consumer experiences, and marketing strategy. He is the author of more than 100 papers in scholarly journals, and his work has been accepted for publication in journals such as *California Management Review, Sloan Management Review, Information Systems Research, Journal of the Academy of Marketing Science, the Journal of Advertising Research, Communications of the ACM,* and *MIS Quarterly* (for which he also served as associate editor). He is also a winner of the award for the best paper in the *Journal of International Marketing* (2000).

Pauline Ratnasingam is an assistant professor of the Computer Information Systems Department at Central Missouri State University, Missouri (USA). Pauline Ratnasingam received her Bachelors in Computing (Information Systems) and Honors in Information Systems from Monash University, Melbourne, Australia. She received her PhD titled "Inter-organizational Trust in Business to Business Electronic Commerce" from Erasmus University, Rotterdam School of Management, The Netherlands. She lectured on topics such as: Project Management, Management of Information Systems, and Electronic Commerce in Australia, New Zealand, Europe and America. She is an associate member of the Association of Information Systems, and is a member of the Information Resources Management Association and Academy of Management. Her research interests include business risk management, Internet-based business-to-business e-commerce, organizational behavior, inter-organizational relationships and trust. She is the recipient and principal investigator of a National Science Foundation Scholar Awards Grant for $60,000 (Grant Number: 01227550), research project title: *"Inter-Organizational Trust in Business-to-Business Electronic Commerce."* She has published several articles related to this area in national and international conferences and refereed journals.

Martyn Roberts is a principal lecturer in Business Information Systems at the University of Portsmouth. He has worked in both the IS industry and academia and has taught in the UK and in the U.S. His research is based around the strategic use of IS in SMEs and in particular with companies that have experienced high growth rates. His work has been published in a number of journals and conferences. Recently Martyn has pioneered the introduction of eCommerce/eBusiness in the University and has a growing list of publications in the area.

Timothy Shih is a professor and chairman of the Department of Computer Science and Information Engineering at Tamkang University, Taiwan, R.O.C. He is a senior member of IEEE and a member of ACM. His research interests include multimedia computing and networking, distance learning, e-commerce, and content-based multimedia information retrieval. He was on the faculty of the Computer Engineering Department at Tamkang University in 1986. In 1993 and 1994, he was a part-time faculty member of the Computer Engineering Department at Santa Clara University. He was also a visiting professor at the University of Aizu, Japan, in 1999, and a visiting researcher at the Academia Sinica, Taiwan in 2001. Dr. Shih received his BS and MS in Computer Engineering from Tamkang University and California State University, Chico, in 1983 and 1985, respectively. He received his PhD in Computer Engineering from Santa Clara University in 1993. Dr. Shih has edited many books and published more than 270 papers and book chapters, as well as participated in many international academic activities, including the organization of many international conferences and special issues of international journals. He is the founder and co-editor-in-chief of the *International Journal of Distance Education Technologies* (Idea Group Publishing, Hershey, PA). Dr. Shih has received many research awards, including Tamkang University research awards, NSC research awards (National Science Council of Taiwan), and the IIAS research award of Germany. He also received many funded research grants from domestic and international agencies. Dr. Shih has been invited frequently to give keynote speeches, tutorials, panels, and talks at international conferences and overseas research organizations. Dr. Shih can be reached at tshih@cs.tku.edu.tw.

Patricia Sorce is co-director of the RIT Printing Industry Center and associate professor of Marketing, RIT College of Business, where she has served for 21 years. She teaches in the areas of marketing research, buyer behavior and database marketing. She earned a PhD in Cognitive and Experimental Psychology from the University of Massachusetts. Many of her scholarly publications build on a theme of understanding human decision making with a focus on consumer behavior. She has published in referred marketing, management and psychology journals. These publications have spanned a wide range of topics including basic research in psychology (retrieval processes in long-term memory), marketing segmentation analysis (lifestyles of older consumers), and most recently, Internet buying behavior. Before her appointment as co-director of the RIT Printing Industry Center, she served as associate dean of the College of Business from 1996 through 2001.

Rian van der Merwe is research assistant and a student for the Doctor of Philosophy Degree in Marketing at Curtin University of Technology, Australia. He received both his bachelor's and Master of Science Degree in Industrial Engineering with High Distinction at the University of Stellenbosch, South Africa. His research interests focus on Internet marketing, electronic commerce and strategic alliances on the Internet.

Leo R. Vijayasarathy (Leo.Vijayasarathy@mail.biz.colostate.ed) is assistant professor of Computer Information Systems in the College of Business at Colorado State University, USA. He earned his doctorate in 1994 from Florida International University. His research, which examines the adoption, use, and consequences of systems that facilitate electronic commerce, has been published in *Electronic Markets, European Journal of Information Systems, Information & Management, Internet Research, Journal of Management Information Systems,* and *Quarterly Journal of Electronic Commerce.*

Stanley Widrick serves as department chairman of Management, Marketing and International Business in the College of Business at Rochester Institute of Technology. He is an expert in developing international business plans based soundly in the theories of marketing, international business and financial performance. He has also worked as a consultant for a wide variety of industries including: Eastman Kodak Company, General Motors, Bausch & Lomb, Rochester Telephone Company, and numerous other corporations and governmental agencies. His writings on marketing strategies, pricing decisions, and buyer behavior have been published in a variety of journals and conference proceedings including *Business and Society, the Journal of Consumer Marketing, Advances in Consumer Research, the Journal of Retailing, the Journal of Consumer Affairs, the Journal of Product and Brand Management,* and others.

Xianzhong Mark Xu received his PhD in MIS from the UK Open University Business School in 1998, and is currently a senior lecturer at the University of Portsmouth Business School. His research interests are in e-commerce strategy and implementation, executive information systems with a focus on strategic information scanning, information support and executives' information behavior. He has published widely in international journals such as *Information Systems Management, Information & Management*, and *International Journal of Information Management*. He is a regular reviewer for the *Journal of Operational Research Society*.

Index

R

S

T

U

V

W